ADVANCES IN PROJECTIVE
DRAWING INTERPRETATION

ADVANCES IN PROJECTIVE DRAWING INTERPRETATION

By

EMANUEL F. HAMMER, PH.D., F.A.CLIN.P.

Clinical Professor
Institute for Advanced Psychological Studies
Postdoctoral Training Program in Psychoanalysis and Psychotherapy
Adelphi University
Garden City, New York
Director and Cofounder (With John N. Buck & Karen Machover)
American Projective Drawing Institute
New York, New York

CHARLES C THOMAS • PUBLISHER, LTD.
Springfield • Illinois • U.S.A.

Published and Distributed Throughout the World by

CHARLES C THOMAS • PUBLISHER, LTD.
2600 South First Street
Springfield, Illinois 62794-9265

© *1997 by* CHARLES C THOMAS • PUBLISHER, LTD.
ISBN 0-398-06742-2 (cloth)
ISBN 0-398-06743-0 (paper)

Library of Congress Catalog Card Number: 96-47845

Printed in the United States of America
SC-R-3

Library of Congress Cataloging-in-Publication Data

Advances in projective drawing interpretation / [edited] by Emanuel F.
Hammer.
  p.   cm.
  Includes bibliographical references and index.
  ISBN 0-398-06742-2 (cloth). — ISBN 0-398-06743-0 (paper)
  1. Projective techniques.   2. Drawing, Psychology of.
3. Psychodiagnostics.   I. Hammer, Emanuel F. (Emanuel Frederick)
RC473.P7A34   1997
616.89′075—DC21   96-47845
                                                      CIP

CONTRIBUTORS

JOHN N. BUCK, Ph.D., for much of his lifetime career, was Chief Psychologist at the Lynchburg State Colony, Virginia. As the father of the House-Tree-Person projective drawing technique, he literally needs no introduction to the readers of this book.

TODD BURLEY, Ph.D., practices clinical psychology in Pomona, California, and teaches at the California School of Professional Psychology.

DENNIS FINGER, Ed.D., is Assistant Professor in Counseling and School Psychology and Coordinator of the Graduate Program in Psychological Services at Kean College, Union, New Jersey. He is in private practice in Hoboken and Montclair, New Jersey and is on the faculty of the American Projective Drawing Institute, New York City.

CORINNE E. FRANTZ, Ph.D., took her postdoctoral training at the Adelphi University program in Advanced Psychological Studies. She is a neuropsychologist in private practice in Springfield, New Jersey; on the contributing faculty of the Graduate School of Applied and Professional Psychology, Rutgers University; and a Clinical Associate, American Projective Drawing Institute, New York City.

JACQUELYN GILLESPIE, Ph.D., is a clinical psychologist in private practice in Orange, California and an Associate Professor of Psychology at California Graduate Institute, Los Angeles.

LEONARD HANDLER, Ph.D., is Professor of Psychology and Director of the Psychology Clinic at the University of Tennessee where he had become a leading influence in the field of projective drawings and has mobilized a cadre of graduate students to turn their doctoral energies and imagination to challenge after challenge in this field.

KAREN MACHOVER, M.A., spent her professional life as Senior Psychologist at Kings County Psychiatric Hospital in Brooklyn, New York, where she innovated and developed the Draw-A–Person as a projective technique. As the mother of the D–A–P, she, like John Buck, also needs no further introduction.

MICHAEL J. MILLER, Ph.D., is Attending Psychologist, Cabrini Medical Center, New York and Clinical Instructor in Psychiatry, New York Medical College, Valhalla, New York.

ZYGMUND PIOTROWSKI, Ph.D., has spent the major focus of his long and productive career on projective techniques, notably the Rorschach, but he has not neglected the T.A.T. and drawings, where in the latter area he has joined the editor-writer in their joint chapter, on the Personality of the Clinician, in this book.

J. S. VERINIS, E. F. LICHTENBERG, and L. HENRICK, Doctors Verinis, Lichtenberg and Henrick, collaborators on the study relating the varied responses to the request to Draw-A–Person-in-the-Rain to different diagnostic categories, are, respectively, at the West Side Veterans Hospital, the Chicago Medical School, and the Audy Home, all in Chicago, Illinois.

ZEV WANDERER, Ph.D., F.A.Clin.P., after the bulk of his career in this country, now practices in Israel at the Israel Center for Behavior Therapy, Eilat Towers.

YVONNE L. ZAHIR, B.A., is a graduate of Goddard College and a product of both the Basic and Advanced American Projective Drawing Institute Workshops. She is currently at work on a study of artists in mid-life—from which her case study for the present book draws.

To
Lila, Diane Robin and Cary Marc
and to
my students and supervisees from whom,
over the years, I have learned as I
taught (several of whom have become
contributors of chapters to this book)

It is ourselves we seek to see on the canvas, as no one ever saw us, before we lost our courage and our love.
William Carlos Williams (1996)

PREFACE

The art and the craft of projective drawing interpretation, over the close to half century since my earlier book, *The Clinical Application of Projective Drawing*, has advanced in reach and in penetratingness, has grown in experience, in scope, breadth, depth, and quality. The aim of the current book is to take us to this outer edge of the technique's acquired virtuosity, versatility, and usefulness. In addressing the tool's timeliness, we tend to sense, too, something of its profound timelessness.*

When the gifted Czech novelist Milan Kundera turned recently to nonfiction and produced his probing work, *Testament Betrayed: An Essay in Nine Parts* (1995), he was particularly struck with Nietzsche's admonition that we not "corrupt the actual way our thoughts come to us."

Working the same vein, for 50 some years, and culminating in her book *Childhood* (1984), the French author, Nathalie Sarrante, continually underscored the essence of capturing experience as it is felt before it passes through the filter of language.

Images meet these requirements, and projective drawings would please Kundera. And Nietzsche. And Ms. Sarrante. (The Rorschach and Thematic Apperception Test, the verbal projective tools, would not please them as much.)

This book might start with, as it is, over its course, fueled by, Chekhov's insistence that "an artist isn't obliged to solve problems, only to state them correct" (V. S. Prichett in *Chekhov: A Spirit Set Free*). Freud, in good measure, felt similarly about the psychoanalyst's obligation. And so, too, we might in addressing the task of projective techniques. If the

---

*For example, masterly drawn beast and animal-human combinations (ex.: bison standing upright on human legs) discovered recently in a cave in the Ardea, in France, were judged to be over 30,000 years old, making them the world's oldest known paintings, and the birth of art, and at the same time, in the anthropomorphic animal creatures, the birth of projection in drawings.

It was Dashiell Hammett, I recall, who once observed (if I may paraphrase him): There is in man a need to see himself, to have himself expressed. This is the thrust that sent early man to daubing his cave walls with ochered representations of himself in the hunt. No creation can have an older, a deeper, a more authentic basis. This, then, is our art. And its people are us.

portraits are true, solutions naturally generate out of them. (Of course, anything we might—can—actively suggest in the direction of solutions, we are most satisfied to accomplish.)

Congruent with Chekhov's view, deepening it and bringing it closer to projective drawings, the gifted artist Klee wrote that "Art does not reproduce the visible, but makes visible" (Klee, 1961, p. 76).

It is toward these ends that early in my career I went to work with John N. Buck, the father of the House-Tree-Person Technique. Those were exciting times. John Buck and Karen Machover, as so often happens, were simultaneously coming at the same discoveries (the former, the projective possibilities in the drawing of a House, Tree, and Person, and the latter, in the drawing of a Person of each sex) and from different parts of the country, Virginia and New York, respectively. And also, just about then, the Draw-A-Tree came across the waters from Switzerland.

Sprawling offshoots followed. One after another there appeared the Draw-A-Family; the drawing of an Animal which tapped the more biological side of the biosocial coin; the Draw-A–Person-In-The-Rain, which was innovated to assess the self as experienced in conditions of environmental stress; Kinget's Drawing Completion Test; and Harrower's Unpleasant Concept Test ("please draw the most unpleasant thing you can think of") which, after the comparatively more neutral content, suddenly presents the subject with the challenge of addressing a highly intense one.

This was in the 1950s and it was then I wrote *The Clinical Application of Projective Drawings* to draw the sprawling field together into an integration. Since that time my clinical work and my research explorations have kept me at the center of the stream that is projective drawings.* Forty years in clinical science, as Dickens might have put it, is a short time and a long time. Much has evolved and discoveries have been made. One thinks, for example, of the gains made in the use of projective drawings to pick up the presence of organic brain damage (Chapter 2), of the signs for predicting acting-out (suicide, homicide, assault, rape, sexual abuse: Chapter 3), of the experimental work offering sturdy support to the use of chromatic drawings to descend deeper into the hierarchal structure of

---

*Through the extended trajectory of my work I have wrestled with the task of bringing the research and the clinical data into synchronization—a daunting enterprise. The work reported in Chapter 5, for me, comes closest to satisfying this challenge.

personality (Chapter 5), of the demarking of sex differences in the developmental patterns of children's drawings (Chapter 10).

At this point, we may freshen our sense of the history of the development which flowed from the exciting notion that a subject's art work might serve as entry to the mysteries and secrets of that subject's personality— reviving the adventure earlier attendant on the discovery of the analysis of dreams, and of the Rorschach, for this same purpose. In this fertile and creative experience, the titans were, as indicated above, John N. Buck and Karen Machover. Both the H–T–P and the D–A–P grew out of the earlier use of drawings for the assessment of intelligence. Buck had been using the drawings of a House, Tree, and Person as subtests in the Performance Scale (along with Kohs Blocks, Object Assembly, etc. quite similar to the scales Wechsler was developing). But Wechsler beat Buck to publication. And Machover had been using the Goodenough Draw-A–Man test to appraise children's IQ. Both Buck and Machover, along with we others who were using the Goodenough, noticed that an even richer yield in terms of personality projection, was coming through. And so this rich dividend was harvested by the converting of the use of drawings from an IQ test into a projective technique. By combining Buck's House, Tree, and drawing of one Person with Machover's drawing of two Persons, one of each sex, we gain a richer, both broader and deeper, tool.

In the current work, I have assembled the *essential papers* since my earlier book and have added new material as needed and some rather interesting case illustrations, both contributed and my own. The goal is to bring together within one set of covers the most valuable of the scattered contributions of the latter decades so they are more available for convenience and, all the more, for synthesis. For their kind permission to reproduce some of the material, now here revised and expanded, appreciative thanks are extended to the American Psychological Association ("D–A–P: Back Against the Wall?" and Z. Wanderer, "Validity of Clinical Judgements Based on Human Figure Drawings," both from *Consulting & Clinical Psychology*), Western Psychological Services (Case C by Hammer, and Case S. G. by Buck), *Journal of Clinical Psychology* (J. S. Verinis et al., "The Draw-A–Person in the Rain Technique: Its Relationship to Diagnostic Category and other Personality Indicators"), Plenum Press ("Projective Drawings: Two Areas of Differential Diagnostic Challenge" from B. Wolnan, Ed., *Clinical Diagnosis of Mental Disorders*), *Journal of Personality Assessment* (Hammer, "Critique of Swengen's 'Empirical

Evaluation of Human Figure Drawings' "), Grune & Stratton (Machover, "Sex Differences in the Developmental Patterns of Children as Seen in Human Figure Drawings"; Hammer, "The H–T–P Drawings as a Projective Technique with Children" and Hammer, "Acting-Out and Its Prediction by Projective Drawing Assessment"), *The Arts in Psychotherapy,* Elsevier Science (Gillespie, "Object Relations as Observed in Projective Mother-and-Child Drawings").

Invited contributors were chosen for their pertinence and their range and inventiveness, or for their fecundity, all of which allows a spotlight to be thrown upon the cutting edge of our field as we move into the twenty-first century—and the study of our subjects' emotions, personal needs, and humanity, and simultaneously, the study of the most direct of all of the projective tools for illuminating them.

The collection of chapters in this current work mixes the best, the most richly heuristic of that which has appeared since my previous book in 1958 which integrated and defined the sprawling and scattered field of projective drawings, and the new, written freshly for this book.

The signature pieces are (1) the differentiation of two diagnostic challenges, schizophrenic and organic brain damage from neurotic conditions and from each other (Chapter 2); (2) the prediction of imminent acting-out states of dangerousness to others or to self, of homicide, suicide, rape, sexual abuse, assault, violence, exhibitionism, and so on (Chapter 3); (3) the use of the chromatic drawings to descend deeper into the projective technique process to elicit a more hierarchal personality portrait (and the very affirming experimental follow-up—perhaps the most supportive experiment to emerge in all of those performed in our field) (Chapter 5); and (4) the investigation of the personality dimensions which differentiate those interpreters who possess the talent to effectively practice the art of drawing interpretation from those who do not—and thus illuminate an explanation of the extended years of mixed experimental results, both negative and positive, which plague validity studies (Chapter 18).

As to the new and invited contributed chapters, I find them deeply pleasing. Nearly every one is a small monument to clinical virtuosity. (What is such clinical virtuosity? The linking of pure authenticity and utter clarity.)

References

Klee, P. *The Thinking Eve.* London: Lund, Humphries & Co., 1961.

Kundera, M. *Testament Betrayed: An Essay in Nine Parts.* New York: Harper-Collins, 1995.

Prichett, V. S. *Chekhov: A Spirit Set Free.* New York: Grune and Stratton, 1988.

Sarrante, N. *Childhood.* New York: Braziller, 1984.

CONTENTS

CHILDREN'S PROJECTIVE DRAWINGS

RESEARCH STUDIES AND RESEARCH ISSUES

PERSONALITY OF THE CLINICIAN

ADVANCES IN PROJECTIVE DRAWING INTERPRETATION

Chapter 1

THE VIEW FROM A STEP BACK

Images are fast replacing words as our primary language.
Richard Avedon
Darkness and Light (1996)

My experience as I read novels or poetry and attend plays, or as I practice in our field, is of a common tapestry that links both. It has satisfyingly become apparent that it is to our creative cousins, the poets and playwrights and novelists, that we might turn for confirmation of our clinical findings, for insight, and for graceful articulation of our mutually held wisdoms.

The process—its very essence—of projective techniques is keenly brought to life in these words by John Steinbeck:

A man's writing is himself. A kind man writes kindly. A mean man writes meanly. A sick man writes sickly. And a wise man writes wisely.

Samuel Butler has stated it more broadly:

Every man's work, whether it be literature or music or pictures or architecture, or anything else, is always a portrait of himself, and the more he tries to conceal himself, the more clearly will his character appear in spite of him.

Overlapping literature and clinical areas, that is, fictional characters and actual people, we are reminded of Henry Murray's memorable and ingenious classification: "Every man is in certain respects (a) like all other men, (b) like some other men, (c) like no other man."

In therapy, to most neurotic patients, pointing out their issues in category *a* is reassuring; it's the *b*s and *c*s that may be threatening. Psychoanalytic work may focus on the patient's defenses, his or her particular nature and operation, which fall in the area of *b* for the most part (it is hard to think of any that are in *c*) which are more apt to appear, if at all, in fiction—say, for instance, Peter Pan or Dr. Jekyll and Mr. Hyde (although even the latter may be seen as a metaphor in the class "like some other men," i.e., multiple personality). As examples, the

3

defenses of denial or of reaction-formation may respectively be seen in the domain of "like some other men," as are similarly sexual feelings toward one's mother or daughter, or conversely, father or son. In the category of "like all other men" may be placed the natural feelings of ambivalence toward parents.

Whereas novelists, playwrights, and poets deal with all three, a proper projective technique report deals only with *b* and *c.*

When we use projective techniques, we tend to rely upon molecular data from seemingly trivial sources (at least as the patient may view it) from the way the subject draws a house, or tree, or person, or what he may see in ink blots presented to him. As therapists, we tend to base our understanding, however, more upon the client's actions in important, rather than trivial, situations. We regard the personality as revealed in relation to one's mate, one's family members, one's boss or supervisor, one's therapist, and one's friends as a better indicator than the personality revealed while asking for change, speaking to the bus driver, or tying a shoelace. Let us examine some of these molecular, rather than molar, bits of behavior, the seemingly trivial or inconsequential. If a man has just asked his boss for a raise—an assertive sign—having gotten it, he then decides, while out during his lunch hour, to call his wife. He finds that he does not have a quarter for the call and thinks to break a dollar with the proprietor of a newsstand near the phone booth. But he hesitates, feels inhibited about the "imposition" and then searches for something to buy in order to break the dollar. He doesn't particularly want any gum, but elects to buy a pack in order to get the change. Now, which is the more valid data to go by in knowing this man on the assertion dimension?

Well, the answer is actually both, but the point is that the minor action is not to be dismissed as, against the major action (asking for a raise), negligible. Might it be that this is a man who is capable of assertion, when he has to, but at the price of significant *inner tension* and a pushing himself to engage in that which, to him, does not feel natural?

Similarly, let us consider a man who is mild, meek, and deferential in behavior but whose dreams are filled with gore, aggression, and sadistic rage. Are the content of his dreams to be dismissed, for, after all, this is a man who actually is very different than his dreams? Similarly, should the physician whose patient shows no sign of TB dismiss the microscope finding of TB in the man's sputum? There are in psychology latent conditions, as there are in medicine. And again in psychology as in medicine, the challenge is to predict which—and perhaps how imminently— the latent condition may surface and define the overt.

The very heartbeat of this book pulses with the realization that the relatively minor situations, namely, the way in which a person draws, are not to be dismissed as reflectors of personality. In fact, in one's more minor, unguarded casual interactions in life itself, one sometimes is more naturally oneself. Certainly in response to one's supervisor or boss, one's teacher, and one's analyst (at the beginning, at least) one is pouring more energy and defensive maneuvering into making a good impression, rather than being more authentically oneself.

Of course, the reliability, in addition to the validity of data, is to be assessed. In terms of body language, for example, does a person generally sit in a certain characteristic way? Does he or she generally sit on a couch with arms widely outstretched on the back of it, as feet are equally widespread, thus conveying the sense of aggrandizingly taking in all that one can encompass?

Or does one generally, and usually, sit with knees together, elbows in, shoulders a bit hunched, and hands clasped, sending out a picture of nonthreatening, submissive compliance or dutifulness?

Or, are the legs wound around each other with the elbows planted on the crossed legs and the chin nestled into the hands, all in all conveying a narcissistic sense of exquisite self-involvement? And, furthermore, does the subject draw his figure drawing Person in the same posture?

And are the drawings of the first individual, the one with arms and legs splayed widely out, too large, pressing out against the limits, the edges of the page? Is the line quality of the second person, consistent with the dutiful posture, hesitant, faint and timid?

Let us take two hypothetical men through three minor situations together. Working together they decide to have lunch with each other and as they walk along, both their shoelaces, as in such stories such things happen, come undone at the same time. One puts his foot up on the bottom railing of the fence they are walking along in order to tie his shoe, whereas the other brings himself all the way down to the shoe, on the ground, in order to tie it. At lunch they both order soup and one brings the spoon up fully to his mouth, whereas the other ducks his head down toward the spoon to meet it. Stopping off at a library on the way back to work, one picks up a book and tilts it in order to read the title along its spine, whereas the other man instead tilts his head. If the requirements of reliability are met by it being the same man who brings the shoe up to himself, the soup up to his mouth, and accommodates the book rather than his head, and conversely, it is the other man who accommodates himself to all three, the shoe, soup, and title, then we can dignify our little story with some academically sounding concepts, respectively, *autoplastic* and *alloplastic.* Do we not from these little, seemingly unimportant, tidbits of behavior have a means for predicting which one will make the better executive and which one will fit more comfortably and naturally into a job for the post office or the army? We might thus, from apparent minutea of behavior, easily make an astute guess about the subject's assertiveness or compliance, and related qualities of self-esteem and other associated attitudes.

Neither I nor other psychologists were the first to make such observations. Alexander the Great expressed his wisdom with the following: "And the most glorious exploits do not always furnish us with the clearest discoveries of virtue or vice in men; sometimes a matter of less moment, an expression or a jest, informs us better of their characters and inclinations, than the most famous sieges, the greatest armaments, or the bloodiest battles whatsoever."

Coming forward through history, Charles Darwin, arguably the father of modern biology, then later observed, "The movements of expression in the face and body are in themselves of much importance for our welfare . . . they reveal the thoughts and intentions of others more truly than do words, which may be falsified." Here he takes us closer toward the very phenomenon tapped in projective drawings.

Stanislavski, coming from the theater and closer to the present, has said, "Many invisible experiences are reflected in our facial expression, in our eyes, voice, speech, gestures, but even so it is no easy thing to sense another's innermost being."

Freud, bringing us now to our own field, noted, "He that has eyes to see and ears to hear may convince himself that no mortal can keep a secret. If his lips are silent he chatters with his fingertips; betrayal oozes out of him at every pore. And thus the task of making conscious the most hidden recesses of the mind is quite possible to accomplish." And thus, among other modalities, projective drawings were born. Our muscles, or psychomotor expression, we have found, are more eloquent, or at least more reliably authentic, than words.

Within psychoanalysis, it was Wilhelm Reich who developed the concept that the body's posture, motility, distribution of muscular tension, energy, facial expression, gestures and voice, being all intimately linked with the person's character structure, who moved us closest to assessing personality via drawings. Reich's discoveries that one's defenses are not merely "mental" but operate directly in the "muscular armor" is seen again and again in the expressive (as opposed to the content) aspects of drawings, as in line quality for one. The muscular expression is *caught* on paper, there to be studied and understood. And here we address Yeats' large question—"How can we tell the dancer from the dance?" Or for our purpose: the drawer from the drawing?

To come full circle now to the insights of John Steinbeck and of Samuel Butler, Virginia Woolf joins with her observation, "Every secret of a writer's soul, experience of his life, and quality of his mind is written large in his work;" and we might add, is etched large in his drawings.

Moving now to the heart of the present book, it is an American artist, William Baziotes, who has noted about his paintings: "They are my mirrors. They tell me what I am like at the time."

At the same time, it is to the vernacular, to clothing, to dreams, and almost to what not in our world that we might turn for understanding of the communication in projective drawings, for they all employ the same language of symbolism. E.W.L. Smith, in *The Body in Psychotherapy* (1985), points out how the vernacular may serve to decipher the clues in body language. We may ourselves see that the same clues apply equally to the drawings of the Person:

> Holds his head high
> Meets one with open arms
> Looks down his nose
> Stiff upper lip
> Looks others in the eye
> Turns away
> Stiff-necked person
> Heavy handed
> Drags his heels
> Yawns
> Bites his lip
> Leans on others
> Sits on it
> Weak in the knees
> A high stepper
> Leans toward me
> Leans away from me

We may similarly turn to the vernacular for support of the language of symbolism running through the House drawing. The treatment of the roof area, for example, reflects the subject's fantasy life in terms of its emphasis in the drawing, and correspondingly in the personality system. Colloquial overlap with this may be found in expressions like "something wrong upstairs," or "a few shingles loose," or "bats in the belfry." Symbols have that universal validity whereby the presence of a symbol in one modality serves to confirm its meaning when it appears in another.

As to the Tree, we need turn no further than to Joyce Kilmer's well-known poem *Trees* with its metaphoric line, "Lifts its leafy arms to pray." At its other end we have the colloquialism, "well-rooted" to connote firmly "planted" on the ground or on practical reality.

We are also struck with the seemingly psychoanalytic insights of even, say, for example, an uninitiated blue-collar worker who refers to someone as a "tight-assed guy." How in the world does he or she sense the anal-retentive character structure of which the early psychoanalysts spoke? Through our common language runs a deeper wisdom. And colorful speech picks it up for expression.

Using clothing as an example of the common symbols that run through it, and dreams, and the Rorschach and TAT and Projective Drawings, I am reminded of a patient I was working with in analysis. He was a young man in his late twenties who had a dream that he was lying on a couch, as he does for sessions, and an older man, as I am, entered the room and took out a pair of scissors, picked up the patient's tie off his chest and snipped off the lower half. Since patients do not have "tie anxiety," the item of clothing might, by virtue of its structure, being elongated, by virtue of its hanging down from the middle of the patient (that is, midway between the shoulders) and by virtue of its special association with the male attire, do service to receive the feelings, symbolically, that the patient attaches to something more intimate that has these characteristics.

Similarly, we find that the uniform of a profession that takes vows renouncing the sexual use of the penis, namely, priests, perhaps gives evidence to this effect in its clothing. The priest not only takes the tie off his clerical clothing, but in this uniform announces all the more actively that there is no tie. Thus, the white part of the collar, in stark relief to the black uniform, meaningfully dips down into a bigger square of white at the very front of the collar as if to more boldly and starkly advertise NO TIE.

Thus, hovering at the depths within us all floats a large storehouse of symbols from which—consciously or unconsciously—all creative writers, all artists, all poets, all dreamers, all projective technique subjects must draw. Symbolism is a common language, a language of its own, an instrument of expression often from the unconscious. There is nothing arbitrary to it, possessing, like language in general, its own lucidity it also reaches for a universality of meaning. Like all language, it seeks for economy of communication, facility, multilayerness, richness of codeterminedness, and underlying comprehensiveness. It is conceptual, existential, and more than other languages, experiential and laced with, and prone to deal with, passion, rage, and other affect.

We may now move fully into the domain of this book, projective drawings. To start we may consider a little exercise I have devised, Make-A–Mark. This is too simple to be called a projective technique and so the more modest word, exercise. What the subject is asked to do, on a piece of paper and with a pencil, is merely to make a mark. Even with a situation whose challenge is so meager in complexity, subjects distribute themselves across an array of dimensions, fully seven in number:

Content: One person will make a simple dot, another a somewhat more substantial circle, a third a line, and even within the category of line, subjects distribute themselves among the choices of making a horizontal line, a vertical line, or a diagonal line. Some move toward a somewhat more elaborate response, a triangle, or still further in this direction, a square or a hexagon. Some a cube. Subjects might draw a squiggle, others a more sharply angled zig-zag line like the depiction of lightning, and so on.

Placement: Placement might be a bold, middle of the page one, or a sinking toward the bottom denoting a depressive tone, an elation-like rising toward the top of the page, a seeking for security by clinging to the edge of the page, or more acute need for security by tucking the mark into a corner of the page, or even beginning the mark toward one of the edges, or corners, and extending it actually off the page.

Size: Size varies all the way from the miniscule to coming close to filling the entire page.

Pressure: Pressure ranges from the most timid and tentative one where the mark can barely be seen, through a firm assertive application of the pencil to the page on to a brutal aggressive one which savagely cuts through the fiber of the page.

Complexity: While allied to content, complexity is a somewhat separately discernible dimension seen in its simplest with the mere dot response and moving to its higher complexity in the seven-lined mark which had all seven lines with their mid-point crossing at a center, thus representing an elaborate asterisk.

Speed: The amount of time taken for the task.

Initial Reaction Time: The amount of time until the task is begun, ranging from the impulsive to the methodical and on to the lethargically slow.

Now, even casual observation of the responses notes a correlation between the variables suggesting a consistent personality style expressing itself in the various available ways. Thus, a dot is more prone to be offered with this content seeking placement off in a corner of a page and expressed in a faint pressure: showing (a) simplicity, (b) unassertive, hesitant pressure, and (c) retreat into the "safety" of corner placement.

A slash is prone to be offered with paper-attacking pressure, and large size going from, say, upper left to lower right corner. And the same thing with a lightning-like-looking zig-zag.

The passive horizontal line tends to sink depressively toward the bottom of the page, whereas the assertion-connotating vertical line soars toward the top.

Potential for acting-out might reflect itself in the combination of *Shape* and *Size* via a long extension, of *Placement* via its slashing from one corner of the page to its opposite diagonal corner, of *Pressure* via a heavy, rageful attack of the paper, of *Time* via both a quick, impulsive, immediate initial reaction time and brief total time.

Thus, if the impression of what we are is there, and to be read from the simple Make-A–Mark expression, the greater complexity in the tasks addressed in the chapters to follow is rich and often fascinating.

REFERENCES

Avedon, R. *Darkness and Light,* New York: Oxford University Press, 1996.

Kundera, M. *Testaments Betrayed: An Essay in Nine Parts,* New York: Harper Collins, 1995.

Sarrante, N. *Childhood,* New York: George Braziller, 1984.

Smith, E.W.L. *The Body in Psychotherapy,* New York: International Universities Press, 1985.

William, C.W. *Collected Poems,* New York: St. Martin's Press, 1996.

Chapter 2

TWO AREAS OF DIFFERENTIAL DIAGNOSTIC CHALLENGE: SCHIZOPHRENIA AND ORGANICITY*

INTRODUCTION

My experience in conducting the annual American Projective Drawing Institute summer workshops suggests that clinicians and clinical students, using projective drawings for differential diagnostic assessment, experience the most uncertainty in two areas: (1) in the differentiation of the vague and shimmering spectrum from schizoid to borderline and latent schizophrenia onto schizophrenic conditions, and (2) in the differentiation of organic brain damage from the former group. Thus, when a patient is sicker than neurotic, this is not usually too difficult to ascertain. But then we tend to become uncertain and perplexed. Is the individual essentially psychotic or is the pathology one of organicity? It is at this interface that the clinician's difficulty throws him or her, here that he or she becomes lost.

SCHIZOID TO SCHIZOPHRENIC CONTINUUM

Figures 1 to 21 illustrate the continuum from schizoid to schizophrenic on which the clinical psychologist is most often asked to make his diagnostic contribution.

Figures 2-1 and 2-2 represent the drawing of a male and a female by a schizoid patient. The drawn male (Figure 2-1) is more mannequin-like than human and actually suggests a store dummy. Figure 2-2 was described as "She looks like a paper doll." The patient's projections thus are not of flesh-and-blood beings, but of derealized humans who cannot engage in emotional give-and-take. Within the patient, the sap of affect has grown thin. He feels himself to be a synthetic being rather than a full living

*Permission granted to reprint, with expansions and revisions, by Plenum Press, from Wolman, B. (Ed.), *Clinical Diagnosis of Mental Disorders*, 1978.

11

person. This is an individual who does not seem to be buoyed by any connection he feels with the human. He appears to have lost the sensations of spontaneity, play, warmth, autonomy, and even emotional authenticity. The bloodless man and woman drawn suggest feelings of alienation within the subject. A sense of isolation—of distance, aloneness, and separateness from the human environment—appears central to his portrait of himself. He lives beside life more than in it.

Consistent with his drawings, on the TAT he demonstrated a failure to include much about the relationship between the people shown in the stimuli. On the Rorschach, the number of his Movement responses was diminished, and, when they were given, the Forms were static. The humans or animals did not act, but were only about to act or were acted upon. Color was also absent, vitality low, and zest for living muted. Emphasis was almost exclusively on Form as a determinant, again implying minimal feelings of emotional life within.

The implications for therapy are that his sterility and restriction of personality, and his markedly schizoid structure, will limit and define his behavior in the therapeutic situation. A long period of treatment would be necessary to achieve a gradual melting through the wall of his detachment by human warmth and interest, and would have to be extended with care to avoid stimulating further protective withdrawal.

Further along the continuum of feelings of depersonalization, we find the subject who drew Figures 2-3 and 2-4 as her respective achromatic Persons and Figure 2-5 as her chromatic Person (executed in blue). These drawn Persons express, and reiterate the expression of, the patient's feeling that she does not exist at all behind her surface facade.

The subject who offered the drawing of a Person in Figure 2-6 communicates the same existential feeling of nonbeing. Perhaps this is all the more so because his obsessive compulsive defenses cause him to emphasize such rare extremes of detailing as the cufflinks, the clocks in the socks, the shoelaces, and even the shoe soles, against which the expected human details of hand, eyes, nose, mouth, and ears are all the more strikingly absent and meaningfully communicative in their absence. His Rorschach projection of a butterfly "as if pressed in a book in someone's collection" approaches stating the same theme, but nowhere as strikingly.

Along the continuum, the woman who drew Figure 2-7 is situated further into the schizophrenic process. The ghoulish tone, the hollow-eyed quality of an empty, baglike head, the upper and lower parts of the body regressed to mere nonspecific circles, and the arms and legs turned

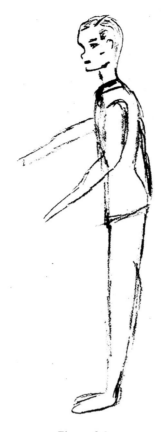

Figure 2-1.

into arrows as a reflection of the raw, primitive, primary-process-like anger which so overrides reality testing as to replace human limbs all show the degree to which inner, archaic processes are overflooding logically based perceptions. Distortive qualities approach the rampant here.

To backtrack, within the borderline span of the continuum, we may next observe Figure 2-8. The patient who drew this person was a well-built, immaculately dressed, 37-year-old black man. He had served in the Navy and received an honorable discharge, having attained officer rank. He then attended college and received his B.A. After this, he was an assistant preacher in a southern church for several years, and then came to the North. He was referred for examination because he had been convicted on three counts of assault, involving two men and a woman. The police officer had found a straight razor, a packing knife, and a

Figure 2-2.

Figure 2-3.

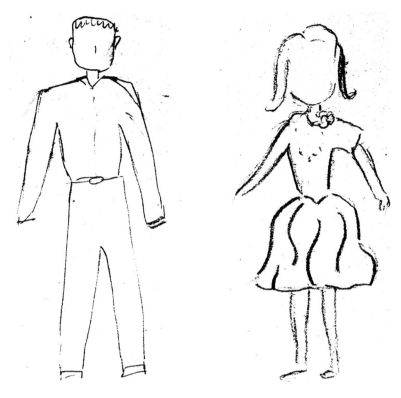

Figure 2-4.   Figure 2-5.

penknife on the defendant's person. The complainants had never seen the defendant before. One man and the woman had been standing near a candy booth when the defendant pushed his way between them, knocking the woman off balance and causing her to fall. The man—according to his story—shouted "Are you crazy or something?" which enraged the defendant, who then struck the man on the side of the head and struck the woman about the mouth. At that point, the second man appeared and came to their assistance, and the defendant pummeled him with his fists.

The defendant's version was that the man who had exclaimed "Are you crazy or something?" had added "you black nut!" Thus the referring probation officer raised some question concerning a racial issue having inflamed the defendant's reaction. The diagnostic query which accompanied the referral for an examination was "Is this man emotionally sick, is

Figure 2-6.

there any presence of significant pathology, and is he capable of peculiar reactivity?"

On the Rorschach, the patient emerged as a borderline schizophrenic individual. Primary thinking processes seeped through to color his perception of the world. His Person drawings were both of nudes, his drawn female a massive, threatening figure and his drawn male (Figure 2-8) a timid figure with hands behind his back, eyes suspiciously and paranoidally alerted, and chin exaggerated in a demonstration of needs to prove himself assertive. What is more important, however, is the reality-testing impairment. He described his drawn male as "standing there and talking . . . talking to a neighbor or someone he sees passing on the street." Here, the strikingly inappropriate description of a nude male standing and talking to a neighbor or passerby on the street conveys the impaired reality testing and dissociative capacities of the subject.

Figure 2-9, an adult male subject's depiction of a woman with a clear implication of a beard on her face, suggests the borderline process his entire projective technique picture conveyed. Reality testing is impaired but not sweepingly so. It tends, rather, to exist in a circumscribed area. In

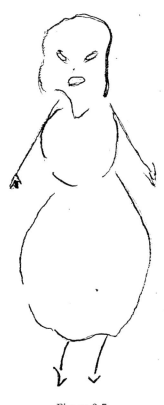

Figure 2-7.

contrast, Figure 2-10, also representing a male subject's perception of women, tends to push further into the schizophrenic area. We find not only the beard-depicting (otherwise ununderstandable) line protruding from the woman's chin but also the transparent arm, the empty eye socket, and the suggestion of the beginning of a penis before the lower page edge interrupts the drawing. Here, of course, the reality-distorting confusion of sexual identity goes considerably further than in the preceding illustration.

Contaminated thinking and fabulized combinations may express themselves in drawings as on the Rorschach. Figure 2-11 shows a contamination of arms and cape, where it appears as if the cape grows out of the shoulders where arms should. This is to be understood in the context of the Egyptian figure offered, a symbol of a long-since-dead person distant in both time and place. Figure 2-12, drawn by a 14-year-old girl, also presents us with a contamination, this time carried a bit further. Arms

Figure 2-8.

become wings, legs become suggestive of tail feathers, and the entire figure appears ready to fly upward into, presumably, autistic realms.

Well into the schizophrenic domain, Figure 2-13 stands as a reflection of frank pathology. The geometric rendition of hands, feet, and ears suggests an arbitrary perceptual tendency (to overabstract and possibly also to rely on magical signs). The robotlike head and neck add to the depersonalized quality, while the absence of a mouth and the pupilless eyes reflect the communication difficulties schizophrenics so agonizingly experience. The ears alerted so conspicuously out from the head convey a strong tendency to ideas of reference, if not actual auditory hallucinations. The line for the ground suddenly comes up in a rather peculiar way as if to add some stability to the figure's footing, no matter how artificially. This patient is an individual who, at the most, has a pseudointegration of personality, with the frail links barely keeping him together. His

Figure 2-9.

illness appears to serve, at best, as a mere expedient for survival amid the contradictions within him. The patient appears to have constructed an unreal world into which he is retiring.

Figure 2-14, drawn by a frankly paranoid schizophrenic man, carries this process much further and expresses the automatonlike experience of being controlled by hallucinatory voices telling him what to do. The compensatory grandiosity, at the same time, is embellished across his chest in the purple band across the green.

Figure 2-15 carries the reflection of the depersonalization process still further. This patient's identification is with a fluid and formless being, a truly tragic conception of personal identity. Ego boundaries fade, and the figure melts away. Haunted by a picture of himself as a creature whose outlines blur, he has eventually given in, and now, a back-ward patient in a mental hospital, he has lost sight of who and what—and if—he is. A search through the hospital folder revealed a Draw-a-Person

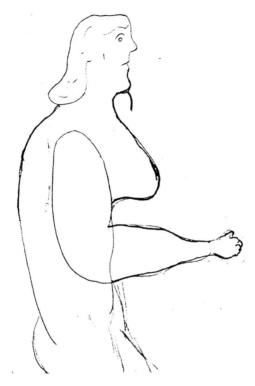

Figure 2-10.

projection done, on admission, many years earlier. His Person was standing rigidly at attention, body and head very stiff, legs pressed closely together, arms straight and held to the body. The kinesthetic emphasis was on the rigid stance and on the tension with which the body was held, keeping the self closed off against the world. The overall impression was of a person frozen into a posture, unable to move over the threshold of exchange or action.

Still further along the continuum to massive deterioration, Figure 2-16 reflects an individual with body image totally shot, with peripheral lines no longer present around the face, and a body wall through which the intestines have spilled.

Figure 2-17 stands as an extreme example of paranoid schizophrenic reaction. The savage mouth expresses the rage-filled projections loosened from within. The emphasized eyes and ears, with the eyes almost emanating magical rays, reflect the visual and auditory hallucinations the patient actually experiences. The snake in the stomach points up his delusional

Figure 2-11.

Figure 2-12.

sensations of a reptile within, eating away and generating venomous evil.

Two other issues of schizophrenic expression in projective drawings deserve mention before closing this section: anthropomorphism and the

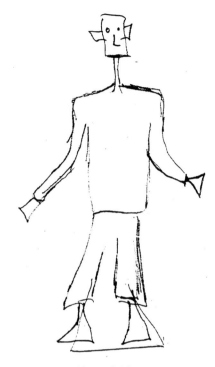

Figure 2-13.

prediction we extend when we offer the diagnostic impression of pre-schizophrenia.

An anthropomorphic version of the House may be seen in that drawn by the subject offering us Figure 2-18. The front of the House conveys a quality of two eye-positioned windows, a circular "nose," and a door which in this context serves as a mouth, all then set off by the "bangs" which hang down like hair from the crown of the house. Anthropomorphism, in drawings, appears to represent the schizophrenic diminishment of reality testing, on the one hand, but all the more the totally projective coloring of the outer world due to insufficient ego boundaries and an inability to sense where the self ends and the outer world begins. (The regression often draws from the infantile stage of the baby in its psychic connection with the mother.) As an illustration of the process, I recall a 6-year-old girl I was treating who in leaving the office after a session one day, kicked the leg of a chair. When I inquired about this, she explained that the chair was going to kick her. Here, the projective mechanism is so much more global than in mere paranoid processes

Figure 2-14.

where projection is onto other people. In the anthropomorphic process, the projection is also indiscriminantly onto inanimate objects.

In Figure 2-19, drawn by an adult, we find a depiction of a Tree which becomes more humanlike than treelike. The branches extend out as exaggerated ears, the foliage becomes bushy hair, and all the more unequivocably a face is put onto the trunk. The full-blown schizophrenia, which is all too evident here, can be more subtly sensed in Figure 2-18.

As to "preschizophrenia": here, as stated, we chance a clear-cut prediction. The diagnosis of borderline schizophrenia implies a reasonably stable condition positioned with partial overlap onto the schizophrenic domain. In preschizophrenia, however, the implication is that the individual, while presently not overtly schizophrenic, will soon, usually within a reasonably short period of time, manifest open pathology. Figure 2-20 may be taken as a reflection of "normality" in almost every regard but one. The figure is intact, the detailing is good, the proportions are accurate, and distortions do not exist. The one thing amiss,

Figure 2-15.

however, and that a most striking one against the appropriateness of all the other factors, is that the figure is toppling over backward. The eyes go blank, and the arms are kept rigidly at the side without any potential flexibility to break the figure's fall. Because the drawing is so well done, the imbalance is all the more meaningful. That the imbalance is one of falling over *backward* renders the figure all the more vulnerable. The imminent loss of personality equilibrium, of psychic balance, is the subjective experience of an individual threatened with an impending schizophrenic break.

Figure 2-21 is even more extreme in this regard. The figure is placed up on the top of a mound as if to use it as a launching pad away from reality. Something I advise students to do in "reading" projective drawings is to put their own bodies in the position of the drawn figure and thus experience kinesthetically, as a supplement to the visual taking in of the data, what the drawing communicates. (This is much like the kinethetic method used in remedial reading, which adds a modality to the visual learning.) If one places oneself in the same position as the drawn Person, one can feel in the upward and sideways tug of the shoulders the pull within the body away from the ground. It is as if the figure, with perhaps a faint suggestion of a nosecone hat and fingers trimmed for trailing behind, is ready to soar up and away. The empty

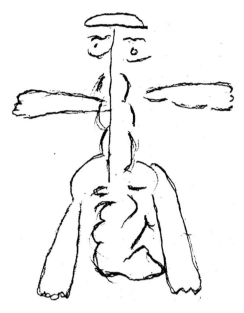

Figure 2-16.

eye sockets add a depersonalized quality to the autism and psychic imbalance. Figure 2-21 is a more extreme expression than is Figure 2-20, in that in Figure 2-20 the loss of emotional balance, while clear, is a statement of losing equilibrium and falling; Figure 2-21 is a statement of abandoning groundedness altogether and going off into one's own idiosyncratic, delusional orbit, leaving reality behind.

ORGANICITY REFLECTED IN PROJECTIVE DRAWINGS

·In practice, much as it may surprise the uninitiated, the responsibility for the assessment of the presence of organic brain damage is often passed along, by both the psychiatrist and the neurologist, to the clinical psychologist. EEG's are generally vague and ambiguous except in the more severe cases, and neurological examination cannot pick up the subtleties which organic damage produces in alterations of the perceptual processes.

The clinical psychologist often finds that his greatest uncertainty in differential diagnosis is in separating the organic from the schizophrenic in their respective expressive-perceptual performances. Goldworth (1950) found that 32 percent of his sample of schizophrenics and 58 percent of

Figure 2-17.

his sample of people with organic brain damage drew heads which were characterized by the judges as "bizarre" or "grotesque." In contrast, none of his sample of 50 normals and only four of his group of 50 neurotics drew heads so characterized. Thus, where the projective technique interpreter quite easily determines that the case before him is "sicker" than normal or neurotic, he's often left with the dilemma "But is it schizophrenic or organic?"

In meeting this assessment challenge, in the projective battery usually the H–T–P (particularly the drawings of House and Tree) is the most determining. The H–T–P, I find, is superior to the Bender-Gestalt for detecting organicity in that with the Bender the patient has something specific and concrete to lean on, to copy from. These Bender figures are relatively simple, and the patient has to be fairly organically impaired before he, with the organic's concrete orientation, cannot merely repro-

Figure 2-18.

duce the elemental figure directly before him. The kinds of performance on the Bender-Gestalt that have established their association with brain dysfunction—problems in spatial organization, difficulty in forming angles, omission of parts in the service of simplification—are more readily picked up in their subtler variety of expression when there is nothing from which to copy. With the House-Tree-Person drawings, the patient has a blank page before him and merely a vague conceptual stimulus— "house," "tree," or "person"—to build from. This is directly parallel to what Landisberg finds comparatively with H–T–P and Rorschach:

> Evidence of organicity is discerned in a more clear-cut fashion with the H–T–P than with the Rorschach, and such evidence may be reflected earlier on the former technique. This is a result of the fact that the H–T–P, comparatively speaking, forces the individual to use his mental resources in a more independent and volitional manner. Blots are blots. The patterns and boundaries may be ill defined, but they do serve as props. And the organic, concrete as he is, has at least a little to build from. But with just a blank sheet of paper in front of him and just a word to conceptualize from, his basic weakness and shakey responses are more prone to come to the fore. (Landisberg, 1973)

In a study comparing the Rorschach, the Bender-Gestalt, and projective drawings, it was found that the drawings exceeded both the Bender and the Rorschach in detecting organicity (*Proceedings,* 1960).

Let us turn now to the task of differentiating organic from schizophrenic conditions, a task all the more complicated in subjects of rela-

Figure 2-19.

tively lower intellectual functioning. Since the emphasis of the responsibility within the projective drawing battery is borne by the subtasks of the drawing of House and Tree, we may keep in mind the relatively representative schizophrenic drawings of lower-IQ subjects (Figures 2-22 and 2-23), which will stand in contrast to those we will later inspect of the organic. The drawing of a House with its obvious anthropomorphic quality of wide-mouthed door, eyelike-placed windows, and curlicue-of-hair chimney, embellished further with tielike pathway, seems to look more like a schematic face than a house. The "classic" split Tree, which is essentially two one-dimensional trees side by side, reflects the shattering or disintegration of self experienced by the schizophrenic. To add another House drawing illustrating anthropomorphism, Figure 2-24 embodies leglike walkways, earlike laterally placed chimneys, and hairlike fence on the roof. The gestalt is more like a walking automaton than a

Figure 2-20.

house. Not all schizophrenics anthropomorphize, or "split" their Tree drawings, but simple organics do not!

General principles which run across the various drawings of the H–T–Ps of organic patients are found to be as follows:

1. There is a preoccupation with symmetry and balance in the drawing. The marked need for the maintenance of symmetry may be shown in the House drawing, for example, by a window drawn on one side calling for the immediate drawing of a window on the other side to maintain exact balance, by a door to the right matched by one to the left, etc. Sometimes a chimney at the top of a House must be balanced by steps, which look exactly like the chimney, at the bottom of the House and positioned exactly beneath it. If the House is turned upside down, the steps then look just as much like a chimney, and the chimney looks just as much like steps. The drawing of each and every branch on the left side of the Tree calls for the exact mirror image branch on the right side of the Tree, and so on.

2. Equally striking is the separation of the parts within the drawing.

Figure 2-21.

This is often reflected in the Tree branches constituting separate units, rather than fluidly interrelating with the trunk. Thus a space appears between each branch and the trunk. If a ground line is drawn, a space usually separates it from contact with Tree trunk. "Segmentalization" designates such rendition of each major detail drawn in and of itself rather than integrated with the rest of the drawing.

3. Oversimplified, unidimensional figures are offered in place of more complex ones. Stark, barren, mere skeletal representation of this Tree and just the outline of the House reflect the concreteness of the organic's thinking. This is most graphic in the drawing of the Tree, where a one-dimensional trunk with an elementary one-dimensional, symmetrically placed branch system (and usually with no secondary or tertiary system) gives the impression of an entity reduced to its most simple representation. This is equivalent to a stick figure for the drawing of a human (although few organics suffer such impairment as to have to do this for the Person drawing on the basis of the still more exaggerated concreteness which would require this). Goldstein and Sheerer (1941) earlier demonstrated that the brain-damaged patients, with their concretistic tendencies, reorganize gestalts in the direction of simplification. Bender (1949) also utilized this principle of simplification in her scoring of the Bender-Gestalt.

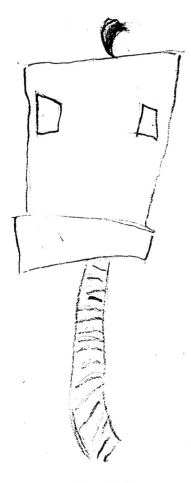

Figure 2-22.

4. As an extension of the tendency toward simplification, we find that organically damaged patients tend to omit one or more of the essential details within the drawing.

5. Perseveration, a well-known sign of organicity, occurs noticeably in the drawings. Thus cross-hatching put into a window, indicating window sashes, is then carried uncritically into the drawing of a chimney, which is left looking like a window protruding off the roof top. On the chromatic drawings, perseveration may be seen in the use of the same single color from one drawing to the next, so the House, Tree, and Person are all drawn in whichever color was chosen for the first one drawn. In the drawing of the Tree, each branch is drawn just like the preceding one, and sometimes the perseveration extends to the roots as well. In Figure

Figure 2-23.

2-25, an entire border of branches and roots around the trunk makes the Tree look more like a centipede.

6. Verbal expressions of impotency are frequent. There is much greater perplexity and "catastrophic" anxiety in the expressions of impotency than we ordinarily get from the neurotic, who may be expressing mere feelings of inferiority relative to the task. Whereas the neurotic will erase and improve his or her drawing, the organic, feeling massively impotent, does not even envision the possibilities of improvement. He rarely will erase no matter how poor the drawing, or cannot achieve any improvement by his erasing and redrawing efforts. Thus, the finished drawing looks just as it did before the erasing and redoing attempts.

7. Excessive pressure is generally employed, and this excessive pressure tends to be accompanied by poor union of the lines (as is also seen in the Bender-Gestalt).

8. An excessive amount of time is generally employed, not in absolute terms, but in relative terms; the organic has labored, as it were, to produce a molehill. Thus, fully 3 min. may be taken for a simplified drawing which a nonorganic subject could readily produce in 15 sec.

Figure 2-24.

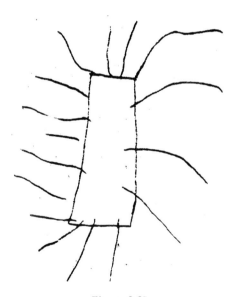

Figure 2-25.

9. Ineptness in terms of the form of the drawing will reflect both the organic's reduced ability to synthesize and his rigidity of approach.

10. Difficulties in abstracting may be seen in response to the questions of the Post Drawing Interrogation. When asked how old the Person

drawn might be, the organic patient will respond literally and concretely, "He's only a few minutes old," meaning that he was drawn only a few minutes ago, or "It's only on a piece of paper."

11. Buck (1970) points out: "Where organicity is far advanced, the quality of the responses on the Post Drawing Interrogation will, of course, be affected as well as the drawings, but where organicity is in the earlier stages, there is often a striking disparity between the quality of the subject's verbalization (which remains high) and the quality of the drawn concepts (which is far lower)."

When we look at the particular drawings, we find the following leads in that of the House:

1. There is usually a sharp contrast between the quality of House and Person drawings, with the House far inferior. This may be because the House represents a more difficult challenge, a more clearly three-dimensional object, with its aspect of greater depth, to be translated by the patient suffering cerebral pathology onto the two-dimensional page.

2. There is, therefore, a strong propensity to present the House in facade, that is, as merely a front without any indications of side walls or depth.

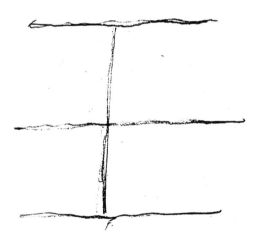

Figure 2-26.

3. A boxlike rendition of the House is frequently offered, sometimes looking, additionally, like a blueprint of the rooms has been superimposed on the front of the House. See Figures 2-26 and 2-28, respectively, for a severe and a somewhat less severe instance of such organic damage.

(Figure 2-27, drawn by the same subject who drew the House in Figure 2-26, represents the "classic" type of organic's Tree with its unidimensional trunk and branches, its segmentalization of at least two of the branches not touching the trunk, its absence of secondary and tertiary branch systems, its total barrenness, and the exact symmetry of each branch on the left balanced by an almost identical branch on the right.)

4. The organic will often write in verbal designations of the various elements within the drawing (see Figure 2-29). Feeling insufficient to convey the required concept in drawing, he retreats to the use of an inappropriate second medium to buttress the graphic. (Figure 2-30 by the same subject, a less classic type of organic's Tree, still serves to convey the exact symmetry of such patients' Tree drawings.)

The characteristics of organics' Tree drawings having been cited and illustrated, we now consider drawings of Persons by this group. As mentioned earlier, the drawing of a Person is less differentiating between organics and nonorganics than are the other drawings.

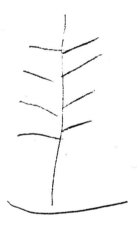

Figure 2-27.

Disproportionately large heads were found by Vernier (1952) to distinguish brain-damaged subjects from other subjects, as he also found head and neck distortions to do.

Machover (1947) found that frontal lobe injury produced a decrement in the quality of the drawing of the human figure. In line with this, Bender (1949) found that postencephalitic patients demonstrate a lower Goodenough mental age (scored on the drawing of a Person) than their

Figure 2-28.

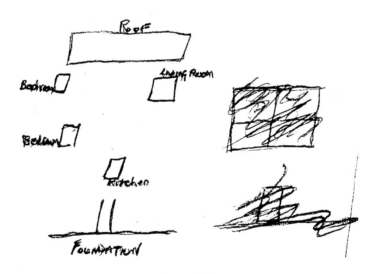

Figure 2-29.

Stanford-Binet mental age. This was also demonstrated by Neal (1942) and by Shaskan, Yarnell, and Alper (1943). Hence the Goodenough scoring of the drawing of a human figure can serve as a "Don't Hold" test item, with the standard IQ test serving as the "Hold" or baseline from which to judge the discrepancy. Thus, to take the broader span of behavior as the configuration, an IQ level which appears to fall increasingly lower as one goes from a standard IQ test to the Goodenough scoring of the figure drawing, and then progressively still lower on the drawing of House and Tree, presents us with a relationship which should always make the examiner suspect the presence of an organic condition.

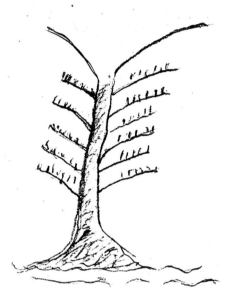

Figure 2-30.

Figure 2-31.

To conclude the examples, we might examine the consistency of the organic indicators we have been discussing by seeing their emergency in a single case across the various drawings of the battery. The subject, an adult male of 38 years, was examined because of an offense of rape and forced oral sodomy. The psychiatric examination ended with "diagnosis deferred" and a request for psychologicals. Following the suggestion of organic brain damage elicited by the drawings, referral for further and extensive medical examination uncovered a traumatic brain damage resulting from a car injury many years before.

The pencil drawing of a House (Figure 2-31) shows the barrenness, simplicity, and elementalness characteristic of the Houses we have been discussing. The exact symmetry of the upper window on the left balanced by the upper window on the right, the lower window on the left balanced by the lower one on the right, and their attachment to the side wall itself are typically organic. Sometimes organics will attach the window to the inside of the side wall and sometimes even to its outside.

Figure 2-32, the achromatic Tree, is almost "classic" in its concrete simplicity, its one-dimensional branches, and its elemental, exact balancing of left and right.

The Person drawing (Figure 2-33) is not necessarily organic (as for the most part the Person drawings of organics are not) except for the characteristically larger head (perhaps reflecting feelings of compensation in the site of experienced impairment) and the specific and rare indicator of a trauma to the head in the damage expressed between the eyes.

What is so typical of organics is that the chromatic House and Tree are so little different from their achromatic counterparts. The chromatic House (Figure 2-34) here makes the same statement of brain damage expressed in the pencil-drawn House, except for the writing-in to label parts of the drawing and for the fact that now the symmetry is extended even further. To left-right symmetry there is now added a top-bottom symmetry, and the chimney above is exactly balanced by a "door" extending below the House. Even the ground is treated in segmentalized, fractionated, concrete fashion in the chromatic drawings where it is introduced. The ground does not run off to each side in a continuous horizon line, as a minimum capacity for abstraction would ordinarily suggest it does.

The chromatic Tree (Figure 2-35) is again just about what its pencil counterpart was. The "buglike" appearance of the Trees of organic subjects, earlier mentioned, is perhaps all the more graphically conveyed here. Ground and Tree are segmentalized rather than joined. The chromatic Person was a repeat of the achromatic one, again as organics tend to do.

The drawings here combine to reflect the patient's impairment of ego functions by the initiating cortical damage. Cerebral incapacity, in turn, serves largely to weaken the coordinating and integrating mechanisms of the ego, to reduce inhibitory powers, and thereby to open the floodgates to the impulses which, in this case, led to rape.

Figure 2-32.

Figure 2-33.

A last point: The more consistency we find in the broad sweep of the H–T–P signs of organicity appearing in the other tests too, the more confidence, of course, we place in our diagnostic impression. Thus, excessive time employed in making the drawings relative to the quality of the drawing produced should make us look for long reaction time on the Rorschach, with meager content offered. Insufficiency of the drawn content should make us look for low form percent on the Rorschach, the verbal writing in of the parts of the drawing ("window" or "door," etc., written over its drawn counterpart) for its related correlate of color naming on the Rorschach, and the expressions of impotence, perplexity, repetitiveness, or perseveration running across the various tests. The "catastrophic" feelings of mental impairment and damage are likely to be countered by a frantic effort, again in all the tests, to cling to the specific, the actual, the static, and the literal—all generically encompassed in the mental set we term "concretistic."

Figure 2-34.

Conversely, the possibility of cerebral damage is contraindicated when the H–T–P and Bender-Gestalt are, respectively, well organized and effectively executed, and their component parts are well integrated with each other; when the drawings show good body-image organization, requiring, in turn, ego controls and adequate eye-hand coordination; when Rorschach, TAT, and H–T–P reflect imagination, reality-testing intactness, and cognizance of the requirements of conventional thinking; and when the projectives and the Wechsler demonstrate the capacity for abstract levels of thought. Cortical intactness is consistent with the ability to perceive and to psychomotorically produce things accurately.

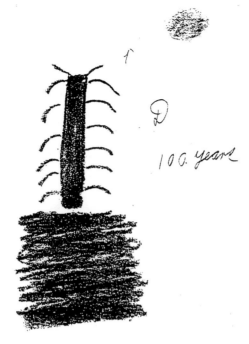

Figure 2-35.

CONCLUSION

Three interrelated areas of relevance to, and within, projective draw-ings have been addressed in this chapter.

1. Directions of promising validation research were focused: (a) com-parative relationship between dimensions or elements within the draw-ings rather than the individual details, (b) introduction of dynamic stimuli, (c) avoidance of the unsubstantiated criterion of psychiatric diagnostic pigeonholes, (d) content and global evaluation, (e) children's drawings, (f) affective associations to the drawings, (g) use of a larger battery of drawings as the sample, and (h) separation of the data of studies for possible sex relatedness.*

2. The complexities of the shifting variables along the continuum where schizoid adaptations shade into the borderline domain and the borderline gives way to schizophrenic processes were discussed and illustrated in their projective drawing expression.

3. Cerebral damage was seen to reflect itself in projective drawings via

---

*Actually, the material referred to in this paragraph appears in Chapter 12 on research.

(a) exaggerated, exacting symmetry; (b) segmentalization; (c) oversimplified, unidimensional presentations; (d) omission of essential details; (e) perseveration; (f) impotency, perplexity, and "catastrophic" feelings; (g) excessive pressure; (h) time employed for the drawing particularly long for the product resulting; (i) ineptness, reduced ability to synthesize, and rigidity; (j) difficulty abstracting on the Post Drawing Interrogation; (k) subject's verbalizations of a strikingly higher quality than that of the drawings; (l) quality of House and Tree drawings noticeably inferior to that of Person drawing; (m) House presented as facade, with no sides evident; (n) boxlike House with blueprint effect superimposed on front; (o) verbal designation of various items of the drawing written in; (p) disproportionately large heads, occasionally with head and neck distortions; (q) lower Goodenough IQ than IQ obtained on a standard intelligence test; and (r) concretistic emphasis.

Some investigators have endorsed the view that impaired perception is the hallmark of the organic (e.g., Niebuhr & Cohen, 1956), while others have minimized the role of perception in favor of the "outgoing" or motor processes (Stoer, Corotto, & Curmutt, 1965). The present writer's experience is that both stand as sensitive radar, catching the subtleties of cerebrally impaired expression on the drawing page.

REFERENCES

1. Abel, T. M. Figure drawings and facial disfigurement. *American Journal of Orthopsychiatry*, 1953, *23*, 253–261.
2. Apfeldorf, M., & Smith, W. J. The representation of the body self in human figure drawings. *Journal of Projective Techniques and Personality Assessment*, 1966, *30*, 283–289.
3. Apfeldorf, M., Walter, C., Kaiman, B., Smith, W., & Arnett, W. A method for the evaluation of affective associations to figure drawings. *Journal of Personality Assessment*, 1974, *38*, 441–449.
4. Bender, L. Psychological principle of the visual motor gestalt test. *Transactions of the New York Academy of Sciences*, 1949, *70*, 167–170.
5. Buck, J. N. Personal communication, 1970.
6. Caligor, L. The detection of paranoid trends by the 8 Card Redrawing Test (8 CRT). *Journal of Clinical Psychology*, 1952, *8*, 397–401.
7. Cauthen, N., Sandman, C., Kilpatrick, D., & Deabler, H. D–A–P correlates of *Sc* scores on the MMPI. *Journal of Projective Techniques*, 1969, *33*, 262–264.
8. Coopersmith, S., Sokol, D., Beardslee, B., & Coopersmith, A. Figure drawing as an expression of self-esteem. *Journal of Personality Assessment*, 1976, *40*, 368–374.

9. Craddick, R. Size of Halloween witch drawings prior to, on, and after Halloween. *Perceptual and Motor Skills*, 1963, *16*, 235–238.

10. Craddick, R., & Leipold, W. Note on the height of Draw-a-Person figures by male alcoholics. *Journal of Projective Techniques*, 1968, *32*, 486.

11. Cramer-Azima, F. J. Personality changes and figure drawings: A case treated with ACTH. *Journal of Clinical Psychology*, 1956, *20*, 143–149.

12. Cutter, F. Sexual differentiation in figure drawings and overt deviation. *Journal of Clinical Psychology*, 1956, *12*, 369–372.

13. Davis, C., & Hoopes, J. Comparison of H–T–P drawings of young deaf and hearing children. *Journal of Personality Assessment*, 1975, *39*, 28–33.

14. Goldstein, H., & Faterson, H. Shading as an index of anxiety in figure drawings. *Journal of Projective Techniques and Personality Assessment*, 1969, *33*, 454–456.

15. Goldstein, K., & Sheerer, N. Abstract and concrete behavior. *Psychological Monograph*, 1941, *43*, 1–151.

16. Goldworth, S. A. A comparative study of the drawings of a man and a woman done by normal, neurotic, schizophrenic, and brain damaged individuals. Doctoral dissertation, University of Pittsburgh, 1950.

17. Gray, D. M., & Pepitone, A. Effect of self-esteem on drawings of the human figure. *Journal of Consulting Psychology*, 1964, *28*, 452–455.

18. Griffith, A., & Peyman, D. Eye-ear emphasis in the DAP Test as indicating ideas of reference. In B.I. Murstein (Ed.), *Handbook of projective techniques.* New York: Basic Books, 1965.

19. Gutman, B. An investigation of the applicability of the human figure drawing in predicting improvement in therapy. Unpublished doctoral thesis, New York University, 1952.

20. Hammer, E. An investigation of sexual symbolism: A study of H–T–P's of eugenically sterilized subjects. *Journal of Projective Techniques*, 1953, *17*, 401–413.

21. Hammer, E. (Ed.). *The clinical application of projective drawings.* Springfield, IL: Thomas, 1958.

22. Hammer, E. Critique of Swensen's "Empirical evaluation of human figure drawings." *Journal of Projective Techniques*, 1959, *23*, 30–32.

23. Irgens-Jensen, O. *Problem drinking and personality: A study based on the Draw-a-Person Test.* Oslo: Universitetsforlaget, 1971.

24. Kamino, D. K. An investigation of the meaning of the human figure drawing. *Journal of Clinical Psychology*, 1960, *16*, 429–430.

25. Klopfer, W. "Will the real Rorschach please stand up?" *Contemporary Psychology*, 1972, *17*, 25–26.

26. Koppitz, E. M. *Psychological evaluation of children's human figure drawings.* New York: Grune & Stratton, 1968.

27. Lakin, M. Formal characteristics of human figure drawings by institutionalized and non-institutionalized aged. *Journal of Gerontology*, 1960, *15*, 76–78.

28. Landisberg, S. Personal communication, 1973.

29. Levy, Minsky, and Lomax. In preparation, 1978.

30. Lord, M. Activity and affect in early memories of adolescent boys. *Journal of Personality Assessment*, 1971, *35*, 418–456.

31. Ludwig, D. Self-perception and the Draw-a-Person Test. *Journal of Projective Techniques*, 1969, *33*, 257–261.

32. Machover, K. A case of frontal lobe injury following attempted suicide. *Rorschach Research Exchange*, 1947, *11*, 9–20.

33. Machover, K. *Personality projection in the drawing of the human figure.* Springfield, IL: Thomas, 1949.

34. Neal, J. *Encephalitis: A clinical study.* New York: Grune & Stratton, 1942.

35. Niebuhr, H., Jr., & Cohen, D. The effect of psychopathology on visual discrimination. *Journal of Abnormal and Social Psychology*, 1956, *53*, 173–177.

36. Phillips, L. *Human adaptation and its failures.* New York: Academic Press, 1968.

37. *Proceedings of the 16th International Congress of Psychology*, Psychological testing in diagnosing cerebral pathology. 1960, 811–812.

38. Roback, R. Depression and size of the drawn human figure. *Journal of Abnormal Psychology*, 1966, *71*, 416.

39. Schmidt, L. D., & McGowan, J. F. The differentiation of human figure drawings. *Journal of Consulting Psychology*, 1965, *23*, 129–133.

40. Shaskan, D., Yarnell, H., & Alper, K. Physical, psychiatric and psychometric studies of post-encephalitic Parkinsonism. *Journal of Nervous and Mental Disorder*, 1943, *96*, 653–662.

41. Stoer, L., Corotto, L., & Cormutt, R. The role of visual perception in the reproduction of Bender-Gestalt designs. *Journal of Projective Techniques and Personality Assessment*, 1965, *29*, 473–478.

42. Swensen, C. H. Empirical evaluations of human figure drawings. *Psychology Bulletin*, 1957, *54*, 431–466.

43. Swensen, C. H., & Sipprelle, C. N. Some relationships among sexual characteristics of human figure drawings. *Journal of Projective Techniques*, 1956, *30*, 224–226.

44. Tolor, A. Teachers' judgments of the popularity of children from their human figure drawings. *Journal of Clinical Psychology*, 1955, *11*, 158–162.

45. Vane, J., & Eisen, V. The Goodenough D–A–P test and signs of maladjustment in kindergarten children. In B. I. Murstein (Ed.), *Handbook of projective techniques.* New York: Basic Books, 1965.

46. Vernier, C. M. *Projective test productions: I. Projective drawings.* New York: Grune & Stratton, 1952.

Chapter 3

THE PREDICTION OF ACTING-OUT ERUPTIONS: ASSAULT, RAPE, SEXUAL ABUSE, HOMICIDE, SUICIDE, EXHIBITIONISM*

In his consideration of the perceptual and graphomotor processes involved in projective drawing assessment, Dr. Emanuel F. Hammer takes the psychodiagnostic clinician on an interesting and rewarding journey that culminates in the latter's deeper appreciation of the many factors that enter into projective drawings. Hammer, who has a special sensitivity for and competence with the interpretation of graphomotor expressions, suggests the intriguing ways in which such projective procedures, with due caution on the part of the clinical psychologist, may make their significant contribution to the assessment of acting out likelihood.

There is little wonder, as one explores Hammer's approach and conclusion, that projective drawings continue to be an important component in the psychodiagnostic test battery that so many clinical psychologists use.

—Lawrence Abt, Ph.D.

Eruptions of violence have not one, but actually two victims: primarily the target, of course, but secondarily also the person acting out. The explosion of the impulses breaks the latter's control system, actually shattering his/her personality integration and it exacts a prison sentence or hospitalization, and often a psychotic or borderline psychotic phase, after which the person's life is, in a major way, disrupted. Witness Chapman, who assassinated John Lennon, and Hinkley, who attempted to kill the president. The initiators' lives are not, and will never be, the same again. This is more or less true for even the milder forms of acting out. With exhibitionism, say, when the perpetrator is arrested, the shame and the possible disruption of the person's job and, more certainly, marriage, are terribly costly.

The prediction of imminent aggressive acts, of assultiveness, homicidal potential, suicidal risk, rape; these are the most practical of all the

---

*Permission granted to reprint, with expansion and revisions, by Thiese Med., from Abt, L. and Weissman, S., *Acting Out,* 1965.

challenges with which the diagnostician is ever confronted. It is here that we face issues of life-and-death, the problems of urgency and immediacy. It is here we wrestle with the most awesome of decisions, one of depriving a person of his or her liberty (and recommending incarceration or hospitalization) or of risking the clinical judgement that he or she will not seriously harm others or self.

Projective drawings are examined in the interest of distilling the principles that may serve to guide us in the assessment of acting-out potentials.

Projective Psychology has, by now, established the concept that every act, expression, or response of an individual — his gestures, perceptions, selections, verbalizations, or motor acts — in some way bears the stamp of his personality.* In projective drawings, the subject's psychomotor activities are caught on paper. The line employed may be firm or timid, uncertain, hesitant or bold, or it may even consist of a savage digging at the paper. The difficulties of capturing and recording the transient qualities of overt movement are thus met by the innovation of graphomotor techniques.

Wolff[30] has made an interesting contribution to the area in his concept of the "rhythmic quotient," based upon careful measurements of drawings made by children, blind persons, epileptics, and even by a sample of African subjects. He has discovered that there are definite proportional ratios in the size of form elements which are characteristic of each individual, which do not vary much with his age, and which appear relatively early in life, thus demonstrating the reliability of expressive movement.

In assessing acting-out potentials, the clinician may use any technique which taps personality via the psychomotor, as opposed to the verbal, modalities and has the distinct advantage of requiring less of an inferential leap in making predictions. Projective drawing, with its infinitely subtle language concerning body image and its motor tendencies, comes closer than do the Rorschach, TAT, and other verbal-

---

*In fact, the pressing forward of facets of self-portraiture in art, the earliest form of "projective drawing," actually has been recognized for hundreds of years. Leonardo Da Vinci, the genius of so many spheres of activity, is credited with one of the early observations of this process of projection. The person who draws or paints, he recognized, "is inclined to lend to the figures he renders his own bodily experience, if he is not protected against this by long study" (Kris, 1952).

expressive tools to *directly* sampling motility phenomena.*

Now, when a subject cooperates consciously and does not resist on a subconscious level, it is generally agreed by clinicians that the Rorschach usually provides a richer personality picture, but when the subject is evasive or guarded—as are those referred for assessment because of getting into acting out difficulties—projective drawings have been found to be the more revealing device.[21]

A particular individual's Rorschach may not yield nearly so much dynamic or structural material as does his projective drawing, or vice versa. The former condition, the writer has found, is more likely to occur in concrete-oriented, more primitive personalities, along with the occurrence of the Performance Scale IQ on the Wechsler exceeding the Verbal Scale IQ. The latter condition, of the Rorschach (or TAT) protocol providing a richer yield than the projective drawings, occurs more frequently in verbal, "intellectual" subjects, with Wechsler Verbal Scale IQ's exceeding Performance Scale IQ's.[13]

The bulk of what the Rorschach yields of the subject's personality comes by way of a relatively indirect route. The subject's Rorschach percepts must, first, be translated into and, second, be communicated in, verbal language. In drawings, on the other hand, the subject expresses himself on a more primitive, concrete, motor level. In addition to the writer, Landisberg[20] has also found that patients exhibiting guardedness seem more likely to reveal their underlying traits and psychodynamics in the drawings. She states, "They are able to exercise more control over their verbal expression, seem to be more intellectually aware of what they might be exposing on the Rorschach. They tend to lose some of this control in their creative, motor expression (employed in drawings)."

An incident was related to the writer by a psychiatrist-colleague who had undergone a psychological examination in being screened for psychoanalytic training. Whereas he was able to withhold Rorschach responses and TAT themes, he felt might be damaging to his chances for admission to the psychoanalytic program, he was not able to manipulate his projective drawing production in a similar manner. While drawing the female person, for example, he tried to place a smile on her face. But she turned

---

*Such motility phenomena include psychomotor tempo, flow of movements, smoothness, and integration versus jerkiness and irascible unpredictability of action, speed of response, naturalness of motion, impulsiveness, rate and intensity of expressive movements, dimensions of constriction versus expansiveness, and dimensions of withdrawal versus charging forward into the environment.

out looking strict and forbidding. Attempting to present his relationships with females in as benign a light as possible, he proceeded to erase and redraw, but each new rendition only gave her face a more formidable and menacing expression than before. In spite of all his efforts, in the end, she wore a stern expression. In his own words, "I just couldn't control the way she turned out."

Another case in point was that of an adolescent boy who was brought before a juvenile court on five charges of breaking, entering, and larceny and three charges of entering and larceny. Clinically, he appeared as a hostile, aggressive lad who, however, in his Rorschach and drawings, attempted to give a benign impression. In the interview following the drawings, he offered the information that he had been "trying to draw a school boy, but the way it came out, it looks like a tough guy that hangs around the river."

These performances underscore the words of Machover[23]: "Stereotyped defenses are less easy to apply to graphomotor than to verbal projections."

The present writer's experience with inmates at Sing Sing Prison[12] further supports this view. Incarcerated subjects, for example, because of their basic mistrust and bitter resentment of authority figures in general, remain suspicious of all personnel employed at the institution, even after years of "public relations" effort on the part of the psychiatric and psychological staff. Loaded down with pervasive fear of revealing themselves to an authority figure even remotely associated with the prison setting, they manifest defensiveness, and the inmates dare not "see" anything off the beaten track. The number of their Rorschach responses, for example, tends to drop to a meager 10 to 12, with the most frequent record consisting of one noncommittal response given to, and thus dismissing, each card. Their TAT themes assume a barren quality, remaining for the most part on a relatively superficial and descriptive level. Expressions become stereotyped, and the inmate sticks to the "safe" response. Attempts at conformity and undeviating acceptability in voiced Rorschach and TAT percepts are the rule. Richness of imagination is stifled, and real feeling is hidden behind an obscuring curtain of constant control. The scanty record thus obtained loses the pitch and the subtle nuances necessary for full or for accurate assessment of the individual type of personality reaction pattern.

In addition, inmates as a group are generally among those subjects who cling, for various reasons, to the concrete. They become anxious and threatened when confronted with the ambiguous stimuli of the Rorschach, and attempt to steer clear of real involvement with this type of projective situation, at least insofar as communicating and explaining verbally what it is that they may see.

To illustrate, sex offenders, for example, who are seen psychotherapeutically after psychological examination often confide to their therapist, once rapport has been cemented in a transference setting, that on the Rorschach they did not reveal everything they saw, e.g., "especially those dirty sex pictures that were there." In responding to the projective drawing task, on the other hand, these patients must reveal something of their sexual adaptation in one of two ways: either in their manner of handling the direct or symbolic sexual areas of the House, Tree, Person figures or else, all the more, by their omitting to draw areas that carry sexual implications, for example, the genital zone or secondary sex characteristics of the drawn Person, the chimney on the House, and the branches on the Tree.[11,12]

Fox,[10] also reports, "drawings, relative to other projective techniques, are . . . difficult to falsify, and in its application there is no barrier to education or language." Bellak's[4] experience is in the same direction: "The verbal expression of aggression may be successfully controlled when its muscular expression is clearly seen . . . in tests probing the subsemantic area."

But if the above demonstrates the *relatively* more appropriate utility of projective drawings to the problem of assessing acting out potentials, such cues on projective techniques, in general, remain a most elusive cluster of data to catch.

First, it should be emphasized that at this time a high degree of accuracy in our generalizations from projective drawings to life situations cannot be expected. It does appear, however, that we can achieve gross accuracy, particularly if we use a battery of tests, but we must always assume that the projective techniques have not revealed all major personality variables and their patterns of interaction. Also, "We must always make the limiting assumptions that fate often tips the scales of external circumstance one way or the other, regardless of the individual's character structure and intentions, and that to a significant extent the prominence of character features and pathological trends depend on external circumstance," observes Schafer.[29]

Murray[25] goes even further by pointing out that, "The patterns of the imagination (as revealed in projective tests) and the patterns of public conduct are more apt to be related by contrast than by conformity."*

There are several examples in which the latent and the manifest levels of behavior are inversely related. Oral dependency needs may, for example, be conspicuously evident in the projective drawings. While such a finding may occur in an alcoholic subject who more or less acts out his oral dependency needs, it may also occur in the projective drawings of a striving business executive who is attempting to deny these needs in himself by proving quite the opposite in his behavior.

It is only by integrating the behavioral picture with the projective technique data that the full personality evaluation can be derived. When we view the frustrated oral needs evident in the drawings alongside of the driving, overstriving behavior in the business executive's overt behavior, it is the viewing of these two levels side-by-side which may allow for the speculative prediction of eventual ulcers, but we can not always predict from the presence of dependency needs on the projective drawings the overt form of these needs.

Homoerotic elements reflected in the drawings may be considered as another example. Whether the homosexual orientation, suggested by these drawings, results in inhibited heterosexuality, compensatory Don Juanism, or overt homosexual activities depends, in part, upon the interaction of the basic potential of the subject with the influences in his environment, the latter factors being generally outside the scope of those tapped by projective techniques.

To mention one more example, if the projective drawings suggest extreme aggressiveness, and the patient behaviorally assumes the role of a meek, docile, self-effacing and submissive individual, a *comparison* of the two levels of data may permit the valuable inference that this subject must suffer from the effects of suppression and/or repression of a significant amount of aggressive impulses. The mild exterior he presents, we may then deduce, is at the expense of creating considerable tensions within him.

Another handicap which interferes with clinicians' attempts to predict overt behavior exists in the fact that manifest behavior of any importance is invariably highly overdetermined, the resultant of numerous interacting factors: identification figures, superego pressures, social and cultural

---

*Thus, on the TAT the correlation between aggressive content (ideational) and overt aggressive behavior is inverse (those who discharge aggression in behavior have less to discharge in fantasy). On drawings, however, since what is tapped is the motoric, the correlation is not inverse, but direct.

settings, type and strength of defenses, traumatic experiences, and possibly constitutional predisposition would all have a great bearing on the ultimate overt pattern.[29] Often, we are able to infer the presence of a powerful trend, kneaded deeply into the personality, but cannot say which of several possible manifest forms it may assume. While it is true that at times the clinician can be impressively successful in predicting overt behavior, he cannot with confidence assume that he can consistently so interrelate the indicated factors as to predict, very specifically, the future behavior. The subject's resources and limitations with respect to adaptive, sublimatory activity, and achievement are often difficult to take into account. These factors tend to depend so much on situational support and threats, and on other external elements over which the subject frequently has little control (and which themselves cannot be predicted).

The broadest common denominator, then, which interferes with prediction of future behavior and postdiction of genetic events is the operation of *multiple determinism*, both internal and external. Projective tests merely elicit feelings (and a small sample of behavior), and any conclusions derived from the projective test data are made predominantly by way of inference. Psychodynamic inference "is not something which is built into the tests, but enters the realm of general personality theory."[17] Inferences from projective drawings, then, are not only bound by the extent of the clinician's knowledge of this clinical tool, but also by the limits of our present-day knowledge of psychodynamic principles.

Nevertheless, in spite of all of the above, in that which follows we will see that *clues* to acting out are at times available in projective drawings, to be picked up, if only tentatively and speculatively, if one is sensitized to such subtleties.

To start, however, with the grosser and less subtle indications brought to eye-level in drawings, let us consider several instances of "acting out" *directly* on the drawing page itself.

DIRECT ACTING OUT ON PAPER

An adolescent boy, referred to the writer because of excessive truancy, the flaunting of rules in school, and generally rebellious behavior, reflected his characteristic role in life in his drawing of a person as presented in Figure 3-1. The drawn male is dressed in a soldier's outfit as a reflection of the subject's need for greater status and recognition as a male than he feels he possesses. The drawn person turns his back on the world, much as the subject himself has done, and *introduces a regulation into the picture merely to break it.* His adding the sign, "No Spitting," just so that the drawn person may disobey (defy, via spitting, even defile) it, clearly parallels the subject's seeking out rules and regulations merely to break them, to prove to himself and others that they do not apply to him, that he is outside the sphere that authority encompasses, that he is bigger and better than the rules and the people who make them.*

The line that should close the front part of the drawn Person's head is strangely, conspicuously, omitted connoting that which should stay in the head—as thoughts, fantasies, etc.—instead, uncontainedly, spill over.

For his drawing of a female, he offers us Figure 3-2, a female whose face is smeared and debased. He describes her as "A young girl, flat as a board, trying out her new nonsmear lipstick, and it smears." Here, again, we note that he directly acts-out his anger on the drawn page, besmirching the figure's face in an aggressive laying on of the crayon. (We note, also, that he amputates one of her hands where it should attach to the arm and what she is holding falls from her unusable hand.)

When we get to the Unpleasant-Concept-Test (the subject is asked to draw the most unpleasant thing he can think of) we note that he once again *acts out,* and this time all the more directly, his need to debase and vent his acute rage (see Figure 3-3). Where subjects popularly offer the concept of war, disease, or death, this subject instead draws a man with a ludicrously elongated nose, a huge penis hanging out of his open pants, and then stabs him with a long sword running through his body. He then adds the tag, *Dad.* Throughout the subject's drawings impulses surge forward in raw, unvarnished and unsublimated form.

In clinical practice, we may generally assume that a subject who acts out this violently and savagely on paper—and particularly when this acting-out reaches such inappropriate extremes—that he would be prone to also act out the same needs to depreciate others, to search out rules and regulations to break, and to release his accumulated anger at the authority figures and the immediate world around him.

Figure 3-4 represents another case of intense and multiple statements of a theme, mounting up to suggest the likelihood of this theme bubbling over into acting out. This figure was drawn by an adolescent boy who happened to be one of a group of subjects studied in an effort to get a normative population from a local high school.

---

*Re. hands tucked under, and pinned by, the belt, see p. 58.

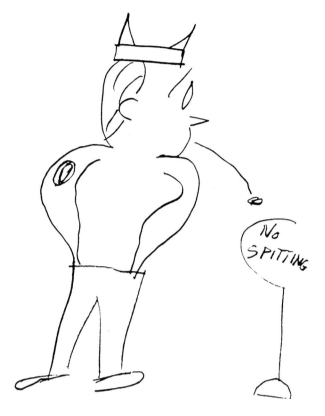

Figure 3-1.

The expansion of the shoulders into exaggerated, sharply-pointed, aggressive corners, the knife in the hand, the gun carried in the belt, the rough clothing and cap, the piercing eye, the sharp nose, and the mustache pulled down into a depiction of walrus tusks more than soft hair all add up to a reflection of an individual who is drastically motivated to prove himself aggressive, dangerous, and prone to violence.* The fact that the feet are particularly out-sized and the shoes taken off, and the emphasis on toe nails, suggest the primitiveness of his impulses, and that the subject appears to have shed considerations of social constraint and more sublimated behavior. When we add to this the fact that the entire figure seems to be pulled off balance by the aggressively pointed shoulder, we get a picture of an individual who suffers from a

---

*To prove himself—to follow the counterpoint also conveyed—not the feminine 'castrate' suggested by the two breast-placed pockets and conspicuously empty or absent crotch. His inadequacy feelings beneath the aggression may be seen in the petal-like fingers and the damaged or broken wrist. It is here that therapy might profitably focus.

Figure 3-2.

feeling of emotional instability which may quite easily be triggered into aggressive behavior.

After seeing so vocal a rendition of a compensatory and hostile theme, the writer consulted the school records and found that this youngster was indeed an acter outer, having gotten into trouble for numerous fights in school, once having thrown a blackboard eraser through a closed school window, and recently having mugged a fellow student for money in the school bathroom.

To turn to an example provided in the drawing of a tree, Figure 3-5 was offered by a 12-year-old boy who had been referred because he had been observed picking up baby pigs with the prongs of a pitchfork, throwing down baby chicks and crushing them under the heel of his shoe, and at one time setting fire to a bale of hay underneath a cow. On top of this, he had recently released a tractor to roll down a hill onto some children. (Fortunately, the children dodged the vehicle in time.)

His drawn tree speaks as eloquently as does his behavior. It is a graphic communication, saying in distinct and unequivocal language: "Keep away from me!" Spear-like branches with thorn-like "leaves" deco-

Figure 3-3.

rate a sharply pointed tree trunk. The branches reach out aggressively in a premise of inflicting significant harm to all those who come within reach. The drawing is steeped in sadism, aggression, and angry resentments.

Similarly, the drawing of a house in the House-Tree-Person (H–T–P) technique may also catch the clues to potential acting out. One 12-year-old boy (see Figure 3-6) heralded his eventual running away from home by drawing a house in which a child was escaping through the top window, and a lower window as depicted slammed down on the mother's neck, pinning her there.* In spite of the family's beginning to involve itself in therapy at that point, four months thereafter the youngster did actually run away from home, and it was not until a couple of days later that he was found asleep in a park.

At times the implications for acting out may be gotten more from the strained efforts at control than from the direct depiction of the impulses

---

*Later therapy with this mother found her both quite intrusive and massively controlling.

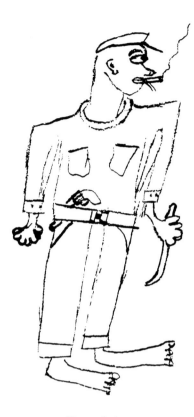

Figure 3-4.

themselves. Figure 3-7 was offered by a 15-year-old youth who was brought to the clinic because, according to his mother, he had threatened to kill her. The initial question which raised itself in our minds was of a differential diagnosis between vocalization on the part of an adolescent who merely wanted to get his mother off his back versus an actual homicidal potential.

The projective drawings administered at the time to the youngster provided rather vivid evidence on the side of the actual possibility of serious capacity for violence pressing forward in him. The strained facial expression, the exaggerated attempts to maintain control over bodily impulses, the head pulling tensely to the side with the eyes reflecting acute inner strain and efforts at control are all brought to focus by the hands presented almost as if to carry the suggestion of being manacled together to provide *external* controls against his lashing out in angry fury. To experience the actual kinesthetic feeling, the reader has only to

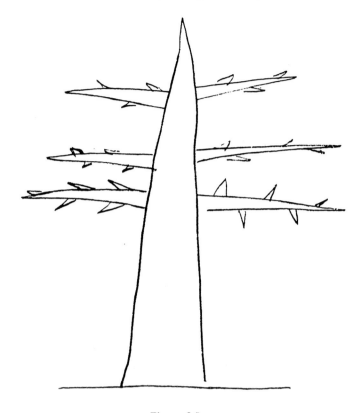

Figure 3-5.

reproduce the entire body position and twisted pull of the head on the neck along with the facial expression to feel in one's own musculature the struggle of control versus intense aggression within. Such a kinesthetic verification of the visual data may also convey a feeling of the almost vivid immediacy to this potential eruption.

The fact that his drawn tree was presented as conspicuously off-balance adds all the more to the personality picture of a youngster whose felt equilibrium was very much in jeopardy and who was shaky in maintaining defenses against his volcanic violence within.

Following the emerging of this tension-flooded picture, the boy was referred to a mental hospital for more detailed observation. The impression of his therapist there later supported the implication that this was indeed a youngster who carried the active seeds of matricide.

The next case adds a second illustration of the principle of *overemphasized control* in the drawings, providing the clues to potential acting out in overt behavior. Figure 3-8 was drawn by an exhibitionist. We see in the

Figure 3-6.

hand drawn as tucked-in under a belt which anchors it—and keeps it from moving to engage in forbidden acts (of exposing himself?)—the strong conflict of impulse versus control. When, however, external controls have to be resorted to (such as, in this instance, and also in Figure 3-1, strapping the hand down), we may presume that internal controls are insufficient and the likelihood of acting out all the more probable. This is supported by the fact that while he draws the Person with hands pinned, at the same time the drawn Person does engage in the exhibitionism of the extremely long, phallic-shaped nose. The impulses circumvent the efforts at control, and while contained below, pop out above.

At times, issues of life-and-death import themselves may be picked up by the projective drawings.* Figure 3-9 was drawn by a man suffering from an involutional depression. He drew the large figure first; then when he saw that he could not complete the entire figure on the page, he

---

*As they were in the case of the youngster who suffered matricidal impulses.

Figure 3-7.

drew the smaller figure. He momentarily paused, looked at both figures, said that the larger figure lacked a collar, picked up the pencil he had laid down, and drew the "collar" by slashing the pencil across the throat of the drawn male. It was almost as if, the writer got the eerie feeling, the patient were committing suicide on paper. Along with this, the patient offered a story to TAT Card 1 which consisted of the boy's picking up and smashing the violin. We recall Bellak's theory of the violin's representing the body image and here find consistency with the suicidal impulses acted out on the drawing page. The witnessing of this man slashing his drawn throat on paper was too vivid a demonstration to take

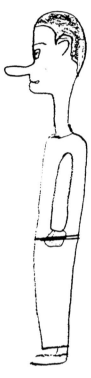

Figure 3-8.

lightly. Conferring with his psychiatrist resulted in the patient's being institutionalized. Some time later the patient actually made a suicidal attempt, but fortunately, owing to the protective surroundings of the institution, this was detected, and the bathrobe belt with which he attempted to hang himself was cut down in time. It was, incidentally, the neck which was prophecized as the site of self-attack.

In summary of this section, then, we may see in the cases presented that *the stronger, the more frank, the more raw and unsublimated the expression of impulses which break through in the projective drawings, the more the defensive and adaptive operations of the ego may be presumed to be insufficient in their assimilative function, and the more the likelihood of acting out may be taken to mount.*

SIZE

Of the variables employed by subjects to express their aggressive patterns, one of the most frequent ones is the handling of space on the paper. The drawing which is too large, which tends to press out against

Figure 3-9.

the page's edges, denotes a similar tendency to act out against the confines of the environment.

Figure 3-10 was drawn by a 28-year-old male. The most conspicuous aspect of the subject's drawing performance is the large size he gives the drawn male, causing it to crowd the drawing page at both top and bottom. Along with this, the firm line pressure, the overextended, broadened shoulders, and the stance (with the feet spread apart and the arms hanging away from the body, ready for action) all reinforce the impression one gets of someone who is trying "to prove himself." The subject cannot prove himself big enough in stature (that is, there is not

Figure 3-10.

room enough on the page to draw the person as large as he would wish it to be), nor generally impressive enough. The zoot-suit treatment, the stern, hard facial expression, and the almost ape-like, long arms that extend too far down the body length all emphasize the subject's attempt to prove himself on paper—to prove himself manly, active, deserving of status, and one not to be taken lightly.

When we learn that the subject was examined because of a rape offense for which he had been convicted, we then see the close parallel of his trying to prove himself more manly than he actually feels, on paper as well as in real life. The absence of belt and the open crotch area* suggest it is impulses below the waist which are acted out.

Precker,[28] too, found that exaggerated size may be considered as evidence of aggressiveness or motor release. Zimmerman and Garfinkle[31] as well found that lack of restraint in the size of drawings correlated with aggressiveness and a tendency toward the release of this aggressiveness into the environment.

SEQUENCE

By analyzing drawing test data in terms of the sequential emergence of drive derivatives, defense, and adaptation, we may witness dynamic and economic shifts which at the same time lay bare structural features of the personality of the subject. By examining samples of ongoing drawing processes, we have an opportunity to study in slow motion, as it were, the structural features of conflict and defense.

In the microcosm of the interaction between a subject and the drawing page, we may, for example, see a subject give tiny shoulders to his drawn person, then erase them, and finally endow the drawn person with compensatory, overly-broad shoulders. Such a subject then looked at his drawing in a perplexing fashion as if some automatic phenomena had taken over, and he couldn't understand how this process got away from him. He commented, "I guess the shoulders expanded a little too much" as if *it* rather than he did it. From this we may postulate that the subject's first reaction to a new situation is one of inferiority feelings which he then quickly attempts to cover-up with a facade of capability and adequacy, which, however, he overdoes to the point of compensatory acting out which breaks away from him.

In a study of sex offenders sent to Sing-Sing prison,[13] lack of ego-strength and inadequate control of impulses have shown up as forming an important factor in the total picture. By this is meant the relative concept of a weak control mechanism for an approximately average amount of impulse strength, or else a control mechanism of about average strength, given the overwhelming task of keeping in check, pressures building up from excessive push. The majority of the sex offenders studied fell into the former category.

---

*It is in contrast to the able drawing of angulation of lines in the lapel that the inability to adequately join the lines of closure at the crotch significantly reveals its story.

In fact, the vast majority of rapists and pedophiles studied had ego pictures of *rigid* control by weak control mechanisms, a control so inflexibly and tightly spread that it manifested a capacity for sporadic breakthrough of impulses. Only the incest group harbored a predominance of individuals in whom consistently *inadequate* control, as a result of a shattered ego, was the basic longstanding situation.

To illustrate the attempts at rigid control of the rapist and pedophile group, punctuated by short erupting interludes, the following excerpt from the psychological report on a rather representative case is cited:

> In reproducing the Bender-Gestalt figures, the subject started out by making them noticeably small, but ended with the last two figures growing excessively large; this would tend to reflect strong needs at constrictive control over emotional impulses which, however, cannot remain successful for a prolonged time without cracking and allowing an impulsive release of uncontrolled affect and/or behavior.

Conversely, defenses gaining dominance over impulses, and hence a contra-indication to acting out are conveyed by the opposite sequence: for example, a male, 38 years of age, first drew a large, threatening female with feet placed in a broad stance and with face wearing a stern expression. She was clothed in a riding habit and carried a large whip in her hand. Following this depiction of a threatening, stern, and punitive female figure, the subject gazed at his drawing for a long time and then hesitantly reached for the next sheet of paper and drew a small, puny male who stood with shoulders drooped dejectedly, head bent, arms behind the back: all-in-all a most submissive, subjugated posture. The subject thus views females as menacing, and then attempts to placate them by assuming a passive, appeasing role.

Sequential analysis of the set of drawings may provide clues to the amount of drive or energy of the subject, and it may also provide data which allow an appraisal of the subject's control over this drive. Does the subject, for instance, break down under the emotionally-tinged associations that are presumably aroused by the different drawing concepts, or is he able to handle himself well in these spheres? Does energy maintain itself, peter out, or erupt? Progressive psychomotor decrease, as he proceeds from one drawing to the next in the set of projective drawings, suggests high fatiguability. Progressive psychomotor increase suggests excessive stimulability and potentials for acting out. A modulated, sustained energy level reflects more healthy personality integration.

Frequently, subjects are somewhat disturbed initially, but soon become calm and work efficiently as they proceed from the first to the last drawing. This is presumably simply "situational anxiety," and is not indicative of anything more serious.

PRESSURE

Pressure of pencil on paper has been found, like size, to be an indication of the subject's energy level.[14,15,28] In regard to reliability, it was found by Hetherington[14] that subjects are rather remarkably constant in their pressure.

Alschuler and Hattwick[1] reported that children who drew with heavy strokes were usually more assertive and/or overtly aggressive than other children.

Consistent with this, Pfister, as reported in Anastasi and Foley,[3] found that psychopaths, one of the most troublesome of the groups who act out, characteristically employ heavy pressure.

One youth, examined by the present writer at a reformatory, drew his house, tree and person with so fierce a digging at the paper that his pencil actually tore through the paper at various points along the line drawn. Several months later he stabbed a fellow inmate, in a dispute over a card game, with a "knife" he had fashioned from a spoon.

STROKE

Alschuler and Hattwick[1] found that children who drew with long strokes stood out for their controlled behavior, whereas children who worked with short strokes showed more impulsive behavior.

Mira[24] also writes, "In general, the length of movement of a stroke tends to increase in inhibited subjects and decrease in excitable ones."

Krout[19] found that straight lines were associated with aggressive moods. Jagged lines (which incidentally appeared as the symbol of the most aggressive unit in Hitler's army) were associated with hostility, usually overt and acted out.

DETAILING

Children or adults who have the feeling that the world around them is uncertain, unpredictable and/or dangerous tend to seek to defend themselves against inner or outer chaos by creating an excessively-detailed, rigidly ordered, highly structured world. The drawings of these subjects will be very exact. These people tend to create rigid, repetitious elements in their drawings. There is nothing flowing or relaxed in the lines, the drawings, or in their total presentation. Everything is put together by force, as though they feel that without this pressure everything would fall apart.

Too perfect a drawing performance, executed with unusual, exacting control and care, is offered by patients who range from obsessive-compulsive to incipient schizophrenics or early organics. But whatever the diagnosis, the "too-perfect" performance reflects the effort of these patients to hold themselves together against the threat of imminent disorganization. It is a direct manifestation of their hyper-vigilance, and implies the presence of a relatively weak ego, so afraid of acting out a breakthrough of forbidden impulses that it dares not relax its constant vigilance.

The most frequent emotional accompaniment of the excessive detailing of one's drawing is a feeling of rigidity. Stiffly drawn trees or animals parallel the same quality in the drawn person. In this regard, the latter may be presented as standing rigidly at attention, with body and head very erect, legs pressed closely together, and arms straight and held close to the body. The kinaesthetic emphasis, in these projections, is on the erect posture and on the rigid tension with which the posture is held, keeping impulses in. These drawing performances often express a most unfree, and hence uncertain but rigidly-controlled defensive attitude. This is the characteristic drawing performance of people to whom spontaneous release of emotions is an acute threat. Impulses, when they are released, are not smoothly integrated, but tend toward the eruptive and uncontrolled.

SYMMETRY

Symmetry has long been regarded as one of the most elemental Gestalt principles. It is not surprising, therefore, that drawings which display an obvious lack of symmetry have been found to indicate equivalent feelings of personality imbalance, diminished integration, and hence increased chances of acting out.

PLACEMENT

In regard to placement on the horizontal axis of the page, Buck[8] hypothesizes that the farther the mid-point of the drawing is to the right of the mid-point of the page, the more likely is the subject to exhibit stable, controlled behavior, to be willing to delay satisfaction of needs and drives, to prefer intellectual satisfactions to more emotional ones. Conversely, the further the mid-point of the drawing is to the left of the mid-point of the page, the greater is the likelihood that the subject tends to behave impulsively, to seek immediate, frank and emotional satisfaction of his needs and drives, and to act out. Koch[16] independently, on the basis of his projective drawing work on the "Tree Test" in Switzerland, identifies the right side of the page with "inhibition," which is consistent with Buck's concept of emphasis on the right side of the page suggesting control. Wolff's[30] finding that subjects who were attracted to the right side of the page in their drawings showed introversion, and those to the left side of the page extroversion, is also consistent with Buck's findings, in that introversion is associated with the capacity to delay satisfaction, and extroversion the seeking of more immediate gratifications.

DISSOCIATION

Suggestions of dissociation, which are offered by incongruities between the graphic drawing and the verbal description of it (i.e., a clash between the two communication media) are perhaps the most pathognomonic of the clues to acting out tendencies.

This can best be conveyed by an example.

The patient, a 17-year-old, white male, was referred to the clinic because he had been arrested for involvement in fights on the beach on several occasions and charged with felonious assault during racial riots. He had been transferred from high school to high school because of inability to relate to the African-American population in school, and hence was referred to the clinic with the idea of appraising his potential assaultiveness.

The essential problem for which we were asked to appraise this youth, namely his dangerousness, gains focus as we examine his performance as he moves through the projective drawing figures. He draws his first person, a female, as an extremely puny figure, and then comments that it is "pretty skinny." He had left the top of the head out, and it now comes through that this was so that he could delay choosing whether to make it a male or a female. He decides to refer the question to the examiner and asks, "It doesn't matter, does it, whether I make it a male or a female, does it? . . . Which shall it be?" When this question was referred back to the patient, he elected to make it a female and added a curlicue of hair and earrings below. He then commented, "Holy Sweat, *it* looks like *it* went through the mill." Here, in addition to the feeling of debasement, we note that he chooses the neuter gender in which to refer to the figure.

The feelings of insufficiency, punyness, unimpressiveness, and confusion about psychosexual identification which come through in the first person drawing are then handled in a passive-aggressive, compensatory maneuver in the following Person drawing (Fig. 3-11). He emphasizes the shoulder muscles and then opens the person's mouth wide in a sort of savage roar, where facial muscles strain, the arms go out to intensify the energy he is expelling, and the teeth are bared. To add to the aggressive quality, he then makes the nose quite sharp. The demonstrative efforts to convey himself as angry, noteworthy, and certainly someone to be reckoned with are somewhat denied by the subtleties of the figure being empty, and thus without substance or the power he attempts to convey, and the fact that one arm appears as if grafted at the elbow. Thus we get an image which is essentially empty and attempts to play a role of aggressive savagery and anger.

In regard to the question concerning his potential aggressiveness, the important quality which comes through is not so much the aggressiveness of his character armor but rather the *dissociated* aspects of this aggression. This dissociated ingredient is discerned when he describes the drawn figure. When asked what the figure is doing, the subject commented, "just standing there." This comment cannot be dismissed as mere evasiveness, for the subject is frank, even vividly expressive, in his graphic communication. It is as if, rather, consciousness does not recognize the clearly angry quality which comes through around the edges of his awareness. When we then move on to a consideration of his drawn tree, we find a sharp and somewhat unintegrated branch structure exists in among the foliage. This sharp, hostily-pointed branch is not blended with the tree but rather again appears to be a thing apart. Once more we get the feeling that aggressive qualities can be dissociated in him and surge outward, away from his control. In summary, then, the uncertain quality conveyed in the first person drawing gives way to the compensatory masculine posturing of the second. This posturing is reenforced by

Figure 3-11.

anger to make it all the more impressive. But this rage is, in turn, handled by dissociation—unfortunately making it all the more dangerous and prone to be acted out.

Sometimes the clues to a state of dissociation of hostile impulses will come through within the drawing level alone, without involving a disharmony between the drawing and its verbal description. Figure 3-12, with its massive, highly-aggressive, and mechanical-like hands, attached as mere appendages at the end of the arms, illustrates this type of projection. The automaton quality, particularly in the area of the aggressive urges, suggests that these impulses are acted-out automatically and without adequate integration with the personality proper.*

CHROMATIC DRAWINGS

Now for the last, and perhaps most dramatic, of the variables. The introduction of color to the projective drawing task, by asking for a new set of drawings, this time in crayon, adds an additional affective element.

---

*The highly aggressive fingers suggest dissociation by appearing metal-like rather than flesh-like, and by being separated off from the body proper by the lines between fingers and hand, between hand and arm, between arm and double-lined body.

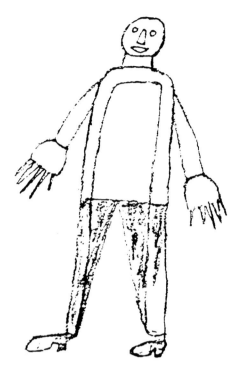

Figure 3-12.

It has long been established that color symbolizes emotion. The many experiments establishing this are too numerous to mention singly. The most abbreviated sample will have to suffice.[1,3,5-7,9,11,13,15] Common parlance supports the experimental data. We speak of someone "red with rage," we associate "yellow" with cowardice and fear, "blue" as depression, "green with envy," and refer to someone as "colorful" if he is in various ways freer in expressing unique personality ingredients and is generally at the opposite pole from the emotionally subdued or constricted personality.

Color stimulates people, as every fine arts painter or even advertising person well knows. Asking a patient to draw in crayon tends to supply an additional affective impact, and thus moves closer to sampling reactions to, and tolerance for, emotional situations—just those situations in which acting out, if it is to be released, is apt to be triggered.

Moreover, the chromatic series of drawings is designed to supplement the achromatic series, to take advantage of the fact that two samples of behavior are always better than one. But the chromatic series is more than a second H–T–P sample because the subject who produces it must, I believe, be in a somewhat more vulnerable state than he was when he produced his achromatic drawings. Even to the best adjusted subject, the achromatic H–T–P and the subsequent searching Post-Drawing-Interrogation are an emotional experience, for many memories, pleasant and unpleasant, are aroused, at the least.

Thus, the chromatic series becomes a behavioral sample that is obtained with the subject at a level of frustration that is different from that which obtained when the achromatic series was sought. If the achromatic (as it frequently is for the well-adjusted subject) was a welcome catharsis, the subject may be far less tense than he was at the beginning. In the average clinical case seen for differential diagnosis, however, this will scarcely be the case. Such a subject will almost inevitably be emotionally aroused enough so that his chromatic series will reveal still more about his basic needs, mechanisms of defense, etc., than the achromatic.

In the achromatic series, the subject is afforded every opportunity to employ corrective measures: he may erase as much as he likes, and the pencil is a relatively refined drawing instrument. In the chromatic drawings, the only corrective measure available is concealment with heavy shading, and the drawing instrument, the crayon, is relatively crude.

Thus, at the beginning, with the subject in relatively fuller possession of his defensive mechanisms, he is given tools which permit expressive defensiveness; in the second phase, by which time the subject will be more likely to have lost at least part of his defensive control (if he is going to lose it at all), he is provided with a grosser instrument, and with an opportunity to express symbolically (through his choice and use of color) the emotions, the controls, and lack of controls which have been aroused by the achromatic series and Post-Drawing-Interrogation.

Thus, when aggression is *relatively* more mildly conveyed in the achromatic rendition, as in Figure 3-13, but is then presented by the subject in his chromatic expression (Fig. 3-14) in frank and unvarnished fashion, our experience has been that such subjects can more-or-less get by in ordinary relations but tend to erupt into violence in emotionally-charged situations.*

---

*The patient had been charged with sexual assault, following a necking and petting session with a girl he had met at a dance and was now taking home. As he tried to advance to slipping his hand under her

Figure 3-13.

As we follow this particular subject from his achromatic to his chromatic person drawing, we observe that the facial expression becomes more menacing, the hands now become so large that they are elongated, pointed, spear-like entities which fairly shriek "hostility." This time the shoes turn into a sort of Army boots affair, with excessively elongated and tapered sharpness and which go up to almost the knees in conveying a feeling of brutality. All in all, the body-image gives way to the pressing forward of a chromatic depiction of a monster with snarling mouth. His raw feelings of aggression and rage are similarly apt to come charging forward in emotional situations.*

blouse, the girl objected; he, in an excited state, drew a knife and threatened her. The Probation Officer's report described the incident as follows: "He asked her to open her blouse, and she refused again. At this point the defendant ripped open her blouse with his hand. With the knife he cut her brassiere in the middle and fondled her breast. He made her bend down and he put his finger in her vagina. During the whole episode he made threats, and at one point banged the complainant's head against the side of the building. This knocked her down. He pulled her up and wanted her to open his zipper." At this point the victim was able to break away and run to safety. It is of interest that the particularly aggressive finger in the drawings coincided exactly with the acting out, a "finger rape" as it were.

*Implications of guilt and of superego, and of positive prognosis (i.e., readiness) for therapy, are suggested by the ten-commandment-like encasing of the achromatic body and prisoner-like stripes on the chromatic one.

Figure 3-14.

A CASE ILLUSTRATION: SUICIDAL IMPULSES

The next case is a particularly appropriate one with which to draw this presentation to a close. A psychiatrist referred a 52-year-old man to me for a diagnostic assessment around the possibility of suicidal issues: Is a suicide impulse present? If so, is it intense enough to be taken seriously? And is it imminent?

As the data unfolded, the picture quickly took an ominous tone. The pencil Tree drawing (Fig. 3-15) speaks of the patient's subjective bleakness and barrenness of life. It is experienced as finished? The poignancy of the two last leaves of life being shed, and dismally drifting to the ground suggest a resigned sense of "it's all over," of forlorn despair, of giving up life, of "going quietly into this good night."

If this was the magnitude of negative feelings, of the pervasiveness of gloom this man suffered, it was with foreboding that I administered the chromatic phase of the projective drawing experience. I expected all the

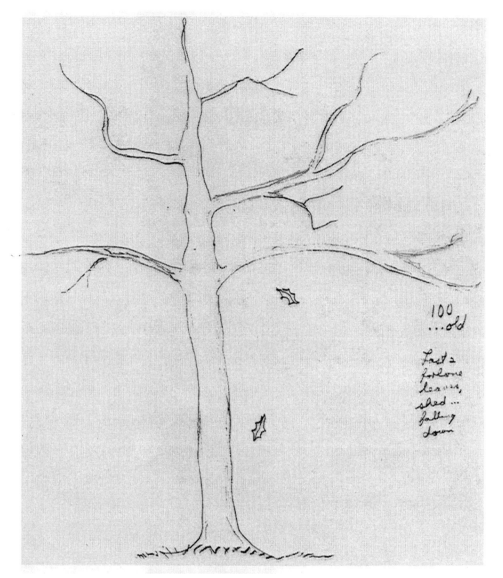

Figure 3-15.

more of the unhappy mood to come cascading out, to drench the projections in their tone.

With what surprise, with what reassurance I witnessed this patient's reaching down into himself to mobilize a healthy desire to live. His chromatic Tree drawing (Fig. 3-16) turns back toward life, it bursts out in a display of spring, of growth and youth and joyful green. Where the subject's achromatic Tree was 100 years old (at the end of life), his chromatic one now is 20 (closer to its beginnings), at the arrival point of adulthood.

What is now expressed is a fullness, a richness of existence. The chromatic statement—from the depths below the achromatic one—is of rejuvenation, is of affirming, not of abandoning, life, of blooming! And the flying birds add further to the liveliness, freedom, and carefreeness.

Here one is with, or needs, or can connect with, others; rather than is, as with the first drawing, desolately alone. The benefits of adding Group Therapy to the treatment program thus become suggested, and was recommended.

To return to the reasons for which the patient was referred, is he suicidal? Well, yes and no. Superficially (on the layers of personality tapped by the achromatic expression), yes; but underlyingly (tapped by the chromatic), no. Is it imminent? Because the patient's hold on life is, underlyingly, strong, the answer is again no.

The diagnosis is of a Reactive Disorder, in which the deeper chromatic level is healthier than the more surface, achromatic level. As to the recommendations, in addition to drawing on the support of Group Therapy to help see this man through his struggle against his despair, are his suicidal impulses deep enough to require the protective setting of institutionalization? Here, the projective drawing examination offers a sense of security that treatment can successfully, and safely, be conducted on an out-patient basis.

This professional advice was extended, and the course of the patient's therapy in the years since have demonstrated its soundness, and the absence of the need to hospitalize and deprive this man of his liberty.

It is this, as alluded to when introducing it as an appropriate illustration to end with, which gives the case its happy ending.

A word of caution: Examples here were presented as illustrations, as samples only. In actual clinical practice, the dangers of basing interpretative deductions on isolated bits of data are obvious. In practice, confirmation of interpretative speculation on the basis of one drawing must be checked against not only the other drawings, but the entire projective battery, the case history, the clinical impression gleaned during the interview with the subject, and all other available information.

Figure 3-16. **Chromatic Tree.** Outpouring of green, enlivened by touches of orange and yellow and red. Birds (brown) suggesting freedom and lightness.

SUMMARY

Clues to the possibility of acting out may be reflected in projective drawings by strong, open, and unsublimated expression of impulses breaking through to flood the drawing page; by strained or insufficient controls; by too large a size of the drawing so that it presses out against the page's edges as the subject himself will similarly tend to act out against the confines of the environment; by sequential movement from expression of controls to exaggerated expression of impulses (in contrast to the opposite sequence); by pressure and savage digging of the pencil at the paper; by stroke; by detailing, dyssymmetry, placement, evidence of dissociation, and by the triggering-off of the impulses in the chromatic expression.

As to the type of impulses apt to be released in the acted out behavior, this can be discerned in the content more than in the structure of the drawings, whether aggressive, exhibitionistic, suicidal, and so on.

The pencil or crayon stroke, at the moment of contact with the paper thus carries, in the words of the American artist Robert Henri, "the exact state of being of the subject at that time into the work, and there it is, to be seen and read, by those who can read such signs."

REFERENCES

1. Alschuler, A., & Hattwick, W. *Painting and personality.* Chicago, University of Chicago Press, 1947.
2. Anastasi, A., & Foley, J. A survey of the literature on artistic behavior in the abnormal. *Psychol. Monographs,* 1940, *52,* 71.
3. Anastasi, A., and Foley, J. P. An analysis of spontaneous artistic productions by the abnormal. *J. Gen. Psychol.,* 1943, *28,* 297–313.
4. Bellak, L. A study of limitations and "failures": Toward an ego psychology of projective techniques. *J. Proj. Tech.* 1954, *18,* 279–293.
5. Bieber, I., & Herkimer, J. Art in psychotherapy. *Amer. J. Psychiat.,* 1948, *104,* 627–631.
6. Brick, M. The mental hygiene value of children's art work. *Amer. J. Ortho.,* 1944, *14,* 136–146.
7. Buck, J. N. The H–T–P technique: A quantitative and qualitative scoring manual. *Clin. Psychol. Monogr.,* 1948, *5,* 1–120.
8. Buck, J. N. Richmond Proceedings (mimeographed copy) Calif., Western Psychological Services, 1950.
9. England, A. O. Color preference and employment in children's drawings. *J. Child. Psychiat.,* 1952, *2,* 343–349.
10. Fox, R. Psychotherapeutics of alcoholism. In Bychowski, G. and Despert, J. L. (Eds.). *Specialized techniques in psychotherapy.* New York: Basic Books, 1952.
11. Hammer, E. The role of the H–T–P in the prognostic battery. *J. Clin. Psychol.,* 1953, *9,* 371–374.
12. ———. A comparison of H–T–P's of rapists and pedophiles. *J. Proj. Tech.,* 1954, *18,* 346–354.
13. ———. *The clinical application of projective drawings.* Springfield, IL: Charles C Thomas, 1958.
14. Hetherington, R. The effects of E. C. T. on the drawings of depressed patients. *J. Ment. Sc.,* 1952, *98,* 450–453.
15. Kadis, A. Finger painting as a projective technique. In Abt, L. E., and Bellak, L. (Eds.). *Projective psychology.* New York: Knopf, 1950.

16. Koch, C. *The tree test.* Berne: Hans Huber, 1952.
17. Korner, A. Limitations of projective techniques: Apparent and real. *J. Proj. Tech.,* 1956, *20,* 42–47.
18. Kris, E. *Psychoanalytic explorations in art.* New York: International Universities Press, 1952.
19. Krout, J. Symbol elaboration test. *Psychol. Mono. A.M.A.,* 1950, *4,* 404–405.
20. Landisberg, S. Personal Communication, March 1951.
21. ——. Relationship of Rorschach to the H–T–P. *J. Clin. Psychol.,* 1953, *9,* 179–183.
22. Lindberg, B. J. Experimental studies of colour and non-colour attitudes in school children and adults. *Acto. Psychiat. Neurol,* 1938, *16.*
23. Machover, K. Human figure drawings of children. *J. Proj. Tech.,* 1953, *17,* 85–91.
24. Mira, E. *Psychiatry in war.* New York: Norton, 1943.
25. Murray, H. Uses of the Thematic Apperception Test. *Amer. J. Psychiatry,* 1951, *107,* 577–581.
26. Napoli, P. Fingerpainting and personality diagnosis. *Genet. Psychol. Monogr.,* 1946, *34,* 129–231.
27. Payne, J. J. Comments of the analysis of chromatic drawings. In Buck, J. N. The H–T–P techniques: A quantitative and qualitative scoring manual. *Clin. Psychol. Monogr.,* 1948, *5,* 1–120.
28. Precker, J. Painting and drawing in personality assessment: Summary. *J. Proj. Tech.,* 1950, *14,* 262–286.
29. Schafer, R. *Psychoanalytic interpretations in Rorschach testing.* New York: Grune & Stratton, 1954.
30. Wolff, W. *The personality of the pre-school child.* New York: Grune and Stratton, 1946.
31. Zimmerman, J., & Garfinkle, L. Preliminary study of the art productions of the adult psychotic. *Psychiat. Quart.,* 1942, *16,* 313–318.

Chapter 4

THE POSSIBLE EFFECTS OF PROJECTIVE TESTING UPON OVERT BEHAVIOR*

THE PROBLEM

Recently the following theoretical questions have been raised by a number of clinicians: Can projective testing be expected, upon occasion, to precipitate an acting out of conflicts? Does projective testing tend to lower, at least momentarily, the repressive or suppressive defenses erected by the subject to control the expression of forbidden behavior? Does the period in which these defenses are lowered extend beyond the testing session? Can the consistency of projective data in highlighting certain conflicts or stress constellations be taken as a clue that the material in question is close to consciousness? And if this last is so, does it tend to prognosticate a proneness toward the acting out of behavior related to the stress producing feelings, in the near future? Can a supportive psychotherapy session, following the projective testing period, operate to avert the acting out of culturally condemned behavior, where projective techniques catalyzed greater awareness in the subject of his anxiety-producing dynamisms?

These questions appeared to have little more than academic interest until recently when a 28-year-old male subject was seen by the writer. The richness and consistency of the material produced by projective testing, and the subject's dramatic behavior immediately following the examination period, served to bring these questions into sharper focus and to suggest certain possible hypotheses as answers to them.

---

*Reprinted from *The Journal of Psychology,* 1953, 36, 357–362, with permission of the Helen Dwight Reid Educational Foundation, Heldref Publications, 1319 18th St., N.W., Washington, D.C. 20036.

PERSONAL HISTORY

The patient was born in a small town in a Mid-Atlantic state in 1923. He was the youngest of four children. Little more than the following could be discovered concerning his early background. He finished four years of elementary school, and was there described as, "a nervous, sickly, underweight child, given to temper tantrums." After finishing school he held various jobs but never worked steadily, and was never satisfied with his job.

Six years earlier the patient received a head injury when he was thrown through the roof of a car during an accident. No fractures or neurological evidences of brain damage, however, were found. He began to suffer from headaches and about two months later had his first seizure, which was described as being of the typically grand mal type. Neither tongue-biting, incontinence, nor injury to himself, however, has been observed during a seizure. In spite of the seizures, the patient enlisted in the army in 1945 and remained in service for two years. He was successful in concealing his seizures for this extended period. When the epileptic condition was discovered he was discharged, and he then worked intermittently at odd jobs.

On one occasion he was arrested on a charge of attempted rape, and after three months in jail he was transferred to the hospital because of his epileptic condition.

Shortly before the car accident, the patient, while on a neighbor's property, was threatened that he would be shot if he didn't leave. The patient told the neighbor that he didn't believe him, and then bent down offering his buttocks as a target. The neighbor fired, and the patient reports: "The bullet went through my rectum and came out through my penis." The content of this statement, in spite of its delusional flavor, turned out to be essentially true. The medical report reveals that there is a healed bullet hole on the inside part of one of the buttocks as well as injured testes and bladder. The penis itself, however, has not been affected. The patient reports that occasionally urination and sexual intercourse are so painful that he has to "scream and stop."

PROJECTIVE TESTING

His somewhat contaminated concept of an injured bladder and penis is clearly reflected in his response to Rorschach card No. X: "It looks

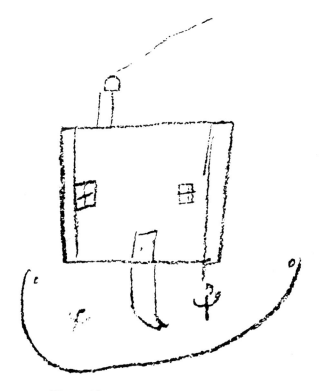

Figure 4-1.

like a tree with water underneath in a hole in the ground; the water hole is under the roots and insects are swimming in the water."

Although strong feelings of castration showed up rather clearly on all the projective techniques, they were most markedly evidenced on the H–T–P. In his chromatic drawing of the House, the chimney was depicted in distinctly phallic style with the head of the phallus displaced to the right of the chimney proper as if ready to fall off. The chromatic drawing of the Person depicted a man wearing a hat which was also displaced off the vertical axis. His story to *TAT* card No. 17BM involved a man climbing down a rope which suddenly broke. On Rorschach Card III he saw the upper red area as "a snake ready to fall." His wish for, and feeling of futility concerning, a more adequate phallus was reflected in his story to *TAT* Card 14 (silhouette of a person in front of a window) in which a man stands wistfully at the window watching an airplane "fly by."

The picture presented by the integration of the projective data suggests that the injury to his genitals found fertile ground in an unresolved Oedipal constellation so as to result in the castration feelings so prevalently revealed above. The patient's father died when the patient was 14, a time when the patient's erotic reawakening was presumably at its height. Guilt and fear of retribution were caused by the unconscious feeling that the omnipotence of his hostile wishes toward his father had resulted in the latter's death. The patient has dreams of his mother which are never finished; evidently the superego steps in and interrupts the dream before any forbidden action can take place. The injury to his genitals inflicted by the elderly neighbor was susceptible to unconscious interpretation as retribution for erotic desires toward his mother and death wishes toward his father—a retribution consisting of castration at the hands of an elderly father-figure.

Figure 4-2.

Feminine identification combines with castration feelings to cause this person seriously to contemplate giving up of the masculine rôle. Contemporary females are viewed with hostility. His repressed tendencies toward homosexuality produce the paranoid symptom consisting of the feeling that people stare at him: "Some people look at your personality—to see if you're clean." One cannot help hypothesizing that this man's homosexual tendencies were unconsciously operative during the shooting incident previously referred to. When the neighbor lifted his rifle and threatened to shoot, the patient responded to the phallic symbol in the neighbor's hands by offering his buttocks—a symbolic homosexual gesture.

Two other bits of behavior fit into the picture. One, the patient's attempted rape may be viewed as a last ditch attempt to convince himself and others of his masculinity. As his object he chose a young girl, a less challenging female whose lack of experience would operate to keep his sexual inadequacies from becoming evident, a girl whose naivete would lead her to be impressed by the masculinity of his attack. Two, some time ago when the patient was unable to find a job—another situation interpreted as a reflection on his masculinity—he contemplated suicide.

Structurally this man's personality is constricted and dependent. In

Figure 4-3.

his choice of a Christmas tree, when asked to "draw a tree," he indicated that he has regressive tendencies and longs for childhood again; that he desires to return to a period when everything was given to him and he was called upon to give nothing in return other than the privilege of allowing himself to be admired by a doting, worshipping mother. The Christmas tree further reflects his exhibitionistic tendency.

He is presently handling his personality problem by withdrawing into a schizoid, possibly preschizophrenic, state. He has made his personality inaccessible to others and lacks adequate contact with reality. That part of his relationships with people which remains is fundamentally barren and cold. ("Snow" and "ice" are projected to areas on the Rorschach where humans are popularly seen.) Possible delusional material is hinted at in his protocols.

POSTTESTING BEHAVIOR

Of unfortunate consequence to the patient, although of theoretical interest to the psychologist, was the confirmation of the patient's castration feelings found on the behavioral level. After leaving the psychologist's office, the patient stopped on the road leading to his ward and exposed himself to a group of females.* This act was evidently precipitated by his castration feelings having risen closer to consciousness during projective testing.† The patient apparently found it necessary to expose himself and elicit a reaction from a group of females so as to prove to himself and to others that his genitals had not been castrated. It was as if he unconsciously said: "Convince me that I have a penis by reacting to it."

CONCLUSION

This case appears to be of very definite theoretical interest because of the following reasons: All projective test material emphasized the presence of profound castration feelings within the patient. Following the intensive examination session, the patient for the first time, so far as we know, resorted to frank exhibitionism. From this it appears that the following hypotheses are tenable.

---

*At an institution for mental defective and epileptic patients.

†No interpretations or even reflection of feelings had been given the patient.

1. Where interprojective test consistency is very great, the likelihood of frank acting out of hitherto suppressed material may be anticipated because of the heightened reactivation of the conflict material within the patient.

2. In such instances, the clinician's job—even when he is functioning as a diagnostician only—is not terminated with the recording of the last response. He will probably be wise to conclude the interview with a supportive psychotherapy session in which the patient might achieve emotional release and reassurance before leaving the sheltered atmosphere of the examiner's office. This might well prevent the acting out of conflicts which, in turn, might lead the patient into difficulty with the law, the community, or his family, as well as his own conscience.

Chapter 5

DIAGNOSTIC TOOLS:
THE CHROMATIC H–T–P, EXTENDING THE
DEPTH PLUMBED IN PROJECTIVE TESTING

Perhaps the most exciting of all the recent decade's developments in projective assessment is the extension downward into the lower layers of personality tapped by the addition, to the conventional battery, of chromatic projective drawings. In the chromatic (crayon)-achromatic (pencil) comparison, a hierarchal personality portrait emerges, one in which the defenses are relatively more laid bare in the achromatic expression, and what is defended against revealed in the chromatic expression. The use of this development for a refinement of a diagnostic and a prognostic tool is discussed and illustrated with representative case examples, and then bolstered by an experimental follow-up study which adds reassuring support to the clinical data.

What is new, and of arguably the most reassuring and most rigorous of all the experimental studies in the domain of projective techniques, is the follow-up study. This is new, and may be found in the last section of the chapter.

What was published before (in the companion volume, Hammer, *The Clinical Application of Projective Drawings,* Springfield, IL: Charles C Thomas) is the first section of what follows, the clinical cases, and that is here reproduced (plus several new cases) in order to present the integrated gestalt, the cases and the experimental data together all of a piece, thus the full tapestry.

Consideration of the concept of "levels" of personality structure, as they come through in the projective battery, has moved into the center of clinical concern as the use of projectives has gained in sophistication (Bellak, 1954; Eysenck, 1947; Hammer, 1953; Klopfer et al., 1954; Murray, 1938; Piotrowski, 1952; Rapaport, 1946; and Schafer, 1954). As both personality theory and the projectives have become more refined, the clinician has addressed himself to gaining a picture of not only the patient's conflicts and defenses, but more often of their hierarchical relationships.

For example, when an excess of both hostile and tender feelings come through, how can the clinician decide whether the hostile feelings are used to ward off people in an effort to avoid the danger of experiencing

87

affection with others, or whether the tender feelings are exaggeratedly employed to deny the underlying hostility.

One might answer that, in everyday practice, projective protocols are not interpreted "blindly," and the behavioral picture tells us which of the opposing traits is on the surface. But in terms of understanding our projective tools, in terms of refining our theory around the projective techniques, it is important to clarify our thinking concerning the way in which the protocols reflect the imprint of surface versus underlying dimensions. Also, frequently we must differentiate between sub-surface and sub-sub-surface layers of feelings, and here the case history or clinical interview is not always helpful.

When a projective protocol reveals feelings of both deadness and also eruptive emotions, how do we decide when the deadening and dampening of affect is in the service of controlling volatile, eruptive potentials, or when a seeking of excitement and "kicks" is employed in an effort to get a sense of life, to taste affect?

To take another example, how do we decide from a protocol whether expansive, grandiose feelings are a compensation for feelings of insignificance and lack of worth, or whether feelings of humbleness, humility, and modesty are a form of leaning over backward to deny underlying arrogance?

Or, how do we distinguish, when both passivity and aggression flood a projective protocol, between the two situations:

(A) passivity as a cloak for underlying aggression, and

(B) aggression as a disguise for inner passivity.

When two common denominators are apparent—helpless inadequacy, on the one hand, and ambitious need for status, on the other hand—what are the clues we go by to differentiate the status-striving which is a compensation for feelings of insufficiency, from the outer role of innocuousness and ineffectuality, which is a protective disguise for secret ambitiousness and forbidden competitiveness?

In the projective protocol of a child, we may frequently find marked ambivalence toward a parent. How do the records differ in the case of the child who employs hate and bristling antagonism in an effort to push off his mother because of unacceptable dependency on her, as opposed to a situation in which the dependency side of the coin is uppermost as a covering and screening for the forbidden feelings of hatred?

When we find a clash between anger and feelings of being easily exploited or controlled by others, when might we predict that the patient will fight off the therapist with antagonism in an effort to avoid his fear of being dominated, and when might we predict that the patient will be docile in accepting interpretations because he will perceive disagreement as a forbidden aggressive act?

The most frequent fault I find in reports written by the interns and psychologists I supervise is that while a patient's defenses are described, their *place* in the total picture is not delineated. If we find a patient relying to excess on the defensive mechanism of "denial," we want to know what he will resort to when this mechanism is blocked by the therapist confronting him with certain of his feelings. Which of his defenses will he give up first, because it is superimposed upon which other one? *What is the order in the series of buffer systems or layers of defense which guard the approach to that which is repressed?*

The point is to avoid chain-like interpretations in which each trend is simply juxtaposed to other trends, and no *hierarchy* of importance, push and restraint, is established.

Personality may be regarded as encompassing a number of organizational levels, "varying in the degree of accessibility to observation from the outside and to self-observation" (Hanfmann & Getzels, 1953). It is, after all, this concept of levels upon which our earliest psychoanalytic understanding is based. The existence of conscious, preconscious and unconscious areas, the phenomenon of repression which is rather central to all dynamic systems of personality theory, and the clinically observed mechanism of reaction-formation are all based upon a hierarchical view of personality structure.

The concept of layers is used, not in the form of stratified rock—immobile, sedentary, and with no fluidity of permeable membranes between—but rather in a form more like a river, with warm currents at the surface and colder currents beneath, which at times flow juxtaposed—and because of this contact, influence each other, reacting and interacting, and at times reversing, sometimes one uppermost and sometimes the other.

In this chapter, the writer intends to share a series of clinical observations, to the end that further study by investigators in various institutions can eventually more firmly establish, or refute, the deductions forced upon the writer, first in an atmosphere of skepticism and ultimately in an atmosphere of increasing empirically-based conviction.

The data, a liberal sample of which is presented here, suggest the deduction that the achromatic (pencil) and chromatic (crayon) drawing phases of the H–T–P actually tap somewhat different *levels* of personality. The chromatic H–T–P cuts through the defenses to lay bare a deeper level of personality than does the achromatic set of drawings, and in this manner a crude hierarchy of the subject's conflicts and his defenses is established and a richer personality picture derived.

The chromatic series is designed to supplement the achromatic series, to take advantage of the fact that two samples of behavior are always better than one. But the chromatic series is more than a second H–T–P sample because the subject who produces it must, I believe, be in a somewhat more vulnerable state than he was when he produced his achromatic drawings. Even to the best adjusted subject, the achromatic H–T–P and the subsequent searching Post-Drawing-Interrogation are an emotional experience, for many memories, pleasant and unpleasant, are aroused, at the least.

Thus, the chromatic series becomes a behavioral sample that is obtained with the subject at a level of frustration that is different from that which pertained when the achromatic series was sought. If the achromatic (as it frequently is for the well-adjusted subject) was a welcome catharsis, the subject may be far less tense than he was at the beginning. In the average clinical case seen for differential diagnosis, however, this will scarcely be the case—such a subject will almost inevitably be so emotionally aroused that his chromatic series will reveal still more about his basic needs, mechanisms of defense, etc., than the achromatic, and point up the disparity between his functioning and his potential pattern of behavior.

But I shall allow the data to speak for themselves; this they do rather eloquently, I think:

CASE ILLUSTRATIONS

A Brief Description of the Chromatic H–T–P Administration

After the achromatic set of H–T–P drawings has been completed, the examiner substitutes a fresh set of drawing blanks for completing the set, and a set of crayons for the pencil. The pencil is taken away so that the subject is not tempted to do the outline of the drawing in pencil, and then color in the drawing as one might in a coloring book. A set of

Crayola®* crayons are employed; the set consists of eight crayons, colored respectively, red, green, yellow, blue, brown, black, purple and orange.

The initial instructions are, "Now, will you please draw a House in crayon," with parallel requests then following for Tree and Person. The subject is purposely not asked to draw another House, another Tree or another Person, for to most subjects the word "another" would imply that they must not duplicate their achromatic drawings. The intent is to provide the subject with the widest latitude of choice.

Figure 5-1. **Case A: Achromatic House.**

The subject is allowed to use any or all of the eight crayons, with all questions as to how he should proceed handled in a nondirective manner, thus maximizing the subject's self-structuring of the task.

In the achromatic series, the subject is afforded every opportunity to employ corrective measures: he may erase as much as he likes, and the pencil is a relatively refined drawing instrument. In the chromatic drawings, the only corrective measure available is concealment with heavy shading and the drawing instrument, the crayon, is relatively crude.

Thus, at the beginning, with the subject in as full possession of his defensive mechanisms as he will presumably be, he is given tools which permit expressive defensiveness; in the second phase, by which time the

---

*A popular commercial brand put out by the American Crayon Company, Sandusky, Ohio, and easily obtained at any children's toy counter or stationery store.

subject will be more likely to have lost at least part of his defensive control (if he is going to lose it at all), he is provided with a grosser instrument, and with an opportunity to express symbolically (through his choice and use of color) the emotions which have been aroused by the achromatic series and Post-Drawing-Interrogation.

Figure 5-2. **Case A: Achromatic Female.**

Case A: A Pseudo-Energetic Neurotic Man

The subject, a thirty-one-year-old, married male, had had two and one-half years of college and was employed as a draftsman.

For his achromatic House he drew a slightly pretentious and showy House, suggesting a degree of status consciousness. His achromatic female Person is depicted as dancing, conveying buoyancy and activity. The achromatic male Person is likewise a picture of energy and action. The suspicion may arise in the clinician's mind as to whether or not the

Figure 5-3. **Case A: Achromatic Male.**

Figure 5-4. **Case A: Chromatic House.** Roof and chimney shaded black; walls—brown and black; ground—brown and green.

subject, in Shakespeare's words, "doth protest too much" by his so emphatic underscoring of the components of energy and activity in his projections.* On the other hand, it is still conceivable that this may actually be a man of outstanding vitality and buoyancy, and the clinician is uncertain as to whether to take the drawings at face value or to view them as a defensive personality blanket.

Figure 5-5. **Case A: Chromatic Female.** Hair—brown, blouse—green, skirt—red.

The introduction of the chromatic phase of the H–T–P resolves the issue as neatly as it does dramatically.

On the deeper chromatic level, a crude log cabin replaces the elaborate, overadorned, and impressive achromatic House. The patient's pretentious front collapses into a portrayal of insufficiency and, by comparison, almost abject insignificance. The picture of wealth and "have" is replaced by poverty and "have not," comfort is replaced by bare essentials, ornateness by barrenness, and an expansive, many-roomed home by a tiny, one-room log cabin. The patient's prestige-hungry front, conveyed

---

*Particularly when we note the spindly shank protruding from the trouser cuff and the fact that the suit—the cloak of social behavior—fits very badly. The latter conveys the strong implication that his role is not an essentially satisfying, comfortable one.

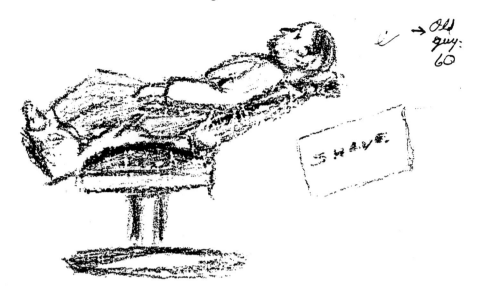

Figure 5-6. **Case A: Chromatic Male.** Hair—brown and black, beard—shaded brown, pants—brown and black, chair cushion—green.

by the achromatic drawing, which compensates for his essential lack of worth (deserving no better than a crude log cabin as a home), was also supported by his flashy dress, conspicuous jewelery, and his use of pedantic vocabulary.

His chromatic female collapses into a sitting position, and even then has not the strength to keep her head erect, but must lean it against something. A sapping of energy and drive may thus be seen to actually exist beneath the patient's energetic front. By the time the patient comes to the task of drawing the chromatic male, his basic feelings of the futility of overstriving come to the fore and he depicts a Person who reclines still further to a horizontal position, and one who is described as "sixty years old," thus reflecting a mixture of feelings of impotency, decline and decreptiude along with his underlying passivity. On deeper symbolic levels, we note that he will lose his beard and possibly be in the hands of a razor-wielding adult.

We haven't yet reacted to the patient's Tree drawings. I've purposely held these for last, in that they convey deeper subtleties, and are more easily understood if we have the advantage of profiting from the earlier inspection of House and Person projections.

But we are, first off, struck with the less than subtle aspects, the hard and upward striving, many layered, and closely held or closed (as a

Figure 5-7. **Case A: Achromatic Tree.**

flower is closed) layers, of not one but two Trees; two drawn in response to the request to draw *a* Tree. In regard to gender, these shapes are suggestively "masculine." In regard to thrust, it is decidedly more upward than outward. This is a man who doesn't reach out to others so much as to whom what matters is accomplishment (as also conveyed in the status of the higher socioeconomic House).

The rendering of two Trees may be multidetermined. In line with the patient's achievement needs, he is asked to make one drawing and, as with the graduate student who is asked for a 15-page term paper and brings in a 30-page piece of work, he delivers twice as much as asked for. At the same time, it may reflect dependency needs. This is particularly so since the Tree stands in a barren, lonely environment, and so it now, at least, does not stand alone but with another, with a companion, as it were.

What supports the latter dependency interpretation is what I've referred to above as the complexity of the projection, the subtlety, here: the bimodal hills in the background. Introduced bimodal hills usually, in projective drawings, take on the shape of a breast-like configuration. The need to have "breasts" in one's picture has been found to express dependency needs for a mothering figure.

But here, what kind of a mother-figure is it that our patient experiences? Distant. Harsh. And meager. (The breast symbols are far off. One is crag-like. The other is minimal, unample, and "flat chested.") Thus, the implications are consistent with the patient's frustrated dependency needs, for which he so *energetically* compensates and tries thereby to escape.

The same dependency needs are supported by the chromatic female leaning over onto whatever that is that supports her body and head, and the chromatic male all the more flat on his back, and furthermore dependent on someone else (getting a shave). As the man rests on his back, the figure must be uncomfortable, even strained, as the cushion line of the plush pillow-like seat, for the subject who draws so ably, doesn't come anywhere close to supporting the Person's backside. The cushion line, the heaviest and most emphasized line in the drawing, is noteworthy in withholding from its function: supporting.

To return to the drawn Tree, its roots appear to "hungrily" reach to Mother Earth, as the rest of his world is essentially empty, bleak and unnourishing.

To advance to a more speculative level: While the achromatic Trees convey essentially so "masculine" a quality, where the legs of the Trees meet its body, we note on one and then again on the other, a circular (vaginal?) opening. Is there a feminine underpinning beneath the dominant masculine presentation?

Certainly the deeper-tapping chromatic Tree, with its softer, rounder, fluffy, more gentle connotations, give a distinctly "feminine" impression.

Thus, all in all, the pencil set of drawings and the chromatic set, when taken together, convey a psychological truth: *sometimes even the apparent contradictions in life can be seen to possess an inner harmony.*

The chromatic House and two Persons are devalued concepts which mirror the subject's depression and depreciated self-concept beneath his three achromatic projections.

The underlying picture of the patient's pathology might have been largely lost without the chromatic redrawings. Similarly, the compensatory front of energy and activity, as the other side of the personality coin, is clearly demonstrated in the achromatic, more superficial, level. It is in the integration of the two levels, that the richness of the personality picture is derived.

Figure 5-8. **Case A: Chromatic Tree.**

Case B: A Prepsychotic Female

The subject, a thirty-six-year-old unmarried female, was referred for a psychological evaluation because the psychiatrist was in doubt about the differential diagnosis. He wished a projective examination done to help evaluate a neurotic, against a latent psychotic, picture.

Her achromatic House is presented as insecurely anchored to an amorphous *cloud-like* ground line. The presentation thus suggests that contact with reality, as symbolized by the ground, is at best uncertain.

The achromatic drawing of the House implies the presence of a latent psychotic condition, but it does not do so with any of the dramatic certainty of the chromatic drawing. The subject's lack of firm contact with reality on the achromatic level gives way to an obvious and catastrophic loss of emotional equilibrium when a deeper personality level was tapped with the chromatic phase of the H–T–P. The House, now presented as frankly toppling over, suggests that the latent psychotic condition is of the incipient or prepsychotic, rather than of a stabilized, chronic, form. Although the person may now be adjusting on a borderline level with the psychosis not being overt, the indications are

Figure 5-9. **Case B: Achromatic House.**

that in the immediate future there will be a clear-cut loss of contact with reality.

The patient's subsequent confinement to an institution, four months after the administration of the psychological examination, provided empirical proof of the deeper, and prophesying, level of the chromatic drawings.

Case C: A Prepsychotic Male

The subject, a twenty-three-year-old, single, male, was also referred for purposes of establishing a differential diagnosis.

This case also illustrates the thesis that personality clues hinted at in the achromatic drawings, often come through full-blown, in more clear-cut fashion, in the chromatic drawings. The tenuous contact with reality, as suggested by the choppy groundline and the drawn Person's spotty contact with it, in the achromatic drawings, gives way (as with the case of the previous pre-psychotic) to a more frank loss of personality balance under the impact of color. (Also noteworthy as pathology indicators are

Figure 5-10. **Case B: Chromatic House.** Sun — red, house — brown, ground — orange.

the absolute profile and the progressively less realistic proportion from massive head to tiny feet.)

A large number of sets of drawings, which Cases B and C illustrate, have served to convince the writer that *incipient or latent psychopathological conditions are most frequently presented by being hinted at in the achromatic drawings and then more vividly and dramatically overtly portrayed in the chromatic expression.* (Also see extra Case X, described under Figs. 5-13 and 5-14).

Case D: An Overtly Psychotic Patient

A comparison of the achromatic and chromatic sets of drawings produced by the patient, a twenty-eight-year-old male, confined to an institution, again illustrates the relatively stronger stimuli represented by the chromatic phase and its greater efficacy in cutting through the patient's defenses.

In spite of the psychotic process, strongly suggested by the gross distortion of reality apparent in the depiction of smoke blowing simul-

Figure 5-11. **Case C: Achromatic Male.**

taneously in two directions and the window shades extending outside the window down the front of the building, a degree of personality intactness is suggested by the over-all integration of the remaining achromatic drawings which are of a progressively healthier quality. The only evidence of frank psychosis apparent in the achromatic Tree is the unusual similarity between root network and branch structure; psychotic patients occasionally offer a drawing such as this which just as appropriately represents the concept asked for if it is viewed upside down. The desperate clutching grip of the roots is suggestive of a fear of losing one's hold on reality. The personality picture which evolves from a consideration of the achromatic drawings only is one of severe maladjustment of probably psychotic proportions with certain delusional areas, but a degree of personality integration and some fair defensive resources upon which to

Figure 5-12. **Case C: Chromatic Male.** Entire drawing in brown.

fall back. There appears to be a degree of "give" to his personality structure, and the clinician may wonder whether when the patient is driven over the line into the borderlands of psychosis he is not able to recover and return to reality once again.

The later introduction of the chromatic drawings into the clinical consideration, however, shatters the clinician's prognostic optimism by revealing the patient's defenses to be actually paper thin.

Under the emotional impact of color, the patient's defenses do not strengthen, but totally crumble. The House disintegrates entirely, the stones composing the pathway to the door appear to float up off the ground, and the patient himself may be presumed to fall apart on the spot. The patient projects this inner feeling verbally by commenting

Figure 5-13. **Case X: Achromatic Male.** His self is stiff, postured and rigidly maintained; it seems to be all that is keeping him together, or stable.

spontaneously that the branches of the chromatic tree are "falling off." Chaotic emotional impulses are clearly indicated by his inability to contain his coloring within the outline of the drawn Tree as well as by his choice of clashing red, green, orange and yellow heaped helter-skelter onto the page. The Tree itself topples. The wind is bizarrely described as blowing not from the left and not from the right, but straight down upon the Tree from above; reflecting the terrible feelings of pressure which beset the patient. Thus, the projection of himself clinging hard to reality, as conveyed by the overemphasized roots of the achromatic Tree clutching at the ground, is replaced by the self-portrait of total personality collapse and disintegration on the chromatic level.

Case E: A Mentally Defective Psychotic

Still another example of the chromatic drawing phase bringing forth into fuller relief that which generally comes through in less intense

Figure 5-14. **Case X: Chromatic Male.** Here he loses it and topples.

fashion in the achromatic drawings, is offered by a seventeen-year-old male psychotic functioning on an intellectual level of mental defective.

His face-like achromatic House reflects the anthropomorphism with which psychotics will frequently endow inanimate objects. The achromatic House (Figure 19) is doused so heavily in anthropomorphism that it seems to leave no latitude for any more human quality to come through on the chromatic level. But the crayons can, and do actually, stimulate a still more anthropomorphic House: two twin, ear-like chimneys, now complete the face (Figure 20).

Case F: An Exhibitionist

The subject, a forty-two-year-old, married male, had gotten into trouble with the law by exposing his penis to a group of twelve-year-old girls who were playing across the street from his window.

Figure 5-15. **Case D: Achromatic House.**

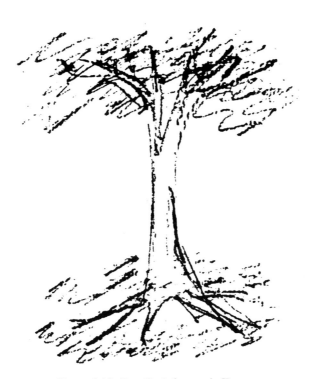

Figure 5-16. **Case D: Achromatic Tree.**

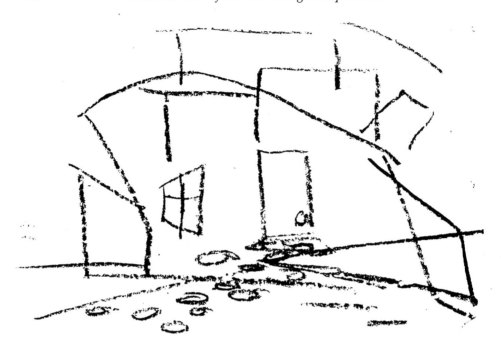

Figure 5-17. **Case D: Chromatic House.** Roofline in bizarre purple; chimney, walls and windows in green; rock path in brown.

In the achromatic House, his need for drawing attention to protuberances is hinted at by the somewhat oversized chimney. In his drawing of the chromatic House, however, his exhibitionistic needs are thrown into fuller relief by the tremendous full-length chimney, with smoke pouring forth, presented as the focus of the drawing. His choice of colors follows the same pattern of spot-lighting the phallic symbol. Black crayon is employed to devalue everything but the chimney, which he then colors in a bright, erotic, attention-getting red.

All of the above cases have been presented to carry the thesis that the chromatic level brings forth the deeper personality picture, as a rather direct contrast to the achromatic level. The cases thus far have all been examples of deeper pathology surging beneath the relatively more calmly rippling surface.

Perhaps an even more important clinical yield occurs when the chromatic drawings uncover relatively greater health, rather than sickness, within. Case H is later presented as illustrations of this type of clinical finding. (But first, one more Exhibitionist.)

Figure 5-18. **Case D: Chromatic Tree.** Splashes of orange, purple, yellow, brown, green seeping out of the Tree into the very air!

Case G: Another Exhibitionist

Presenting cases of the same symptomatology consecutively allows one to more easily discern the common denominators of a syndrome.

The achromatic House drawing of a second exhibitionist (Case G) demonstrates the phallic emphasis of a noteworthy, attention-getting, enlarged chimney. When we get to the chromatic House, this becomes even more so, and, at the same time, we note an additional element, a noteworthy clue to what this symptom is all about.

But, first, we note the frequent common denominators for exhibitionists: the emphasized, full-length chimneys are focused with a high-lighting RED, while the House is receded into the background with black or brown. As to what the exhibitionism is all about, the chimney separates off from the House in a clear suggestion of—literally—underlying "castration anxiety." Unconsciously fearing that his penis is impaired, damaged, unimpressive, or even falling or cut off, the patient draws the chimney likewise on the H–T–P, and "flashes" in behavior, in order to

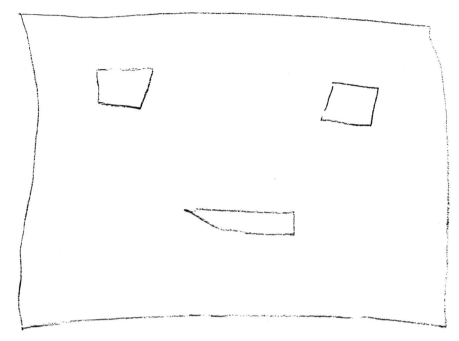

Figure 5-19. **Case E: Achromatic House.**

reassure himself by the screams or cries of the female(s) to whom he exhibits, that the penis is indeed there and noteworthy. The exhibitionist, hence, more often than not, for his audience, chooses high school girls, those who are more prone to histrionically and loudly shriek than are other females, and thus by their more intense reaction carry comparatively greater reassurance.

As an interesting aside, psychoanalytic theory has often been criticized for finding behind many nonsexual symptoms, sexual motives. Exhibitionism, for one, is a symptom in which the opposite is true. The penis is used here for nonsexual purposes. There is almost never a sexual approach toward the female(s), neither along with, nor following, the "flashing." Sometimes the act is engaged in from behind a closed window. Or sometimes the act is on a subway platform, addressed to women on a train which is pulling away. And the masturbating is not so much in the service of pleasure as for the functional purpose of gaining an erection in order to have something more to display. Thus, exhibitionism is not for libidinal, so much as for Ego-reassurance, purposes.

To return to the drawing, one more element deserves understanding. The walls of the Chromatic House conspicuously buckle. As the basic

Figure 5-20. **Case E: Chromatic House.** Walls and windows—blue, chimneys—orange.

Figure 5-21. **Case F: Achromatic House.**

structure of the drawing of a House, particularly its walls, experience informs us, stand for the subject's Ego, its buckling implies an Ego collapse—and a Borderline or Preschizophrenic state.

Figure 5-22. **Case F: Chromatic House.** Walls and smoke—black, chimney—red.

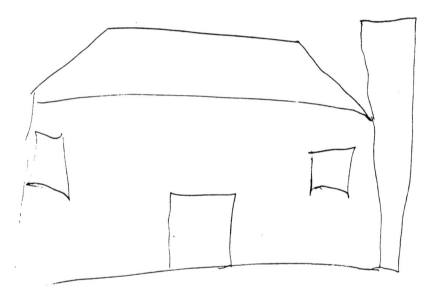

Figure 5-23. **Case G: Achromatic House.**

Case H: A Reactive Condition

The patient, a twenty-three-year-old male, was referred by a psychiatrist for personality evaluation because of recurring nightmares following an elevator accident. The accident, which occurred eight months earlier, had resulted in the loss of the patient's right leg. The achromatic House, reflecting the more recent and superficial personality picture, reflects the patient's feelings concerning precariously attached appendages by the placement of the chimney overhanging the roof in a position

Figure 5-24. **Case G: Chromatic House.** House — black; chimney attention-drawing red.

Figure 5-25. **Case H: Achromatic House.**

Figure 5-26. **Case H: Chromatic House.** Chimney — red, walls and roof — yellow, windows — green.

easily susceptible to toppling. On the deeper, chromatic level, he moves his chimney into a position of more secure footing away from the dangerous *edge* of the roof. Thus, it is suggested that the anxiety he is discharging in his nightmares is rooted in a relatively reactive, rather than earlier developmental, situation. This was subsequently supported in the psychiatrist's later therapeutic collaboration with the patient, as well as the case history data indicating loss of the patient's limb during adulthood.

Case I: A "He-man" Character Disorder

The subject, a twenty-eight-year-old male, presents a set of drawings of a type not infrequently obtained from adolescent males.

Subjects of the adolescent age group, frequently convey, in their drawings, their need to demonstrate virility as compensation for their lack of full maturation and growth, and for their delayed attainment of status. In a subject of the patient's age, however, the persistence of such a need reflects immaturity, as well as the same compensatory character-armoring suggested by his various vocational choices which included truck driving, boxing, and during the war, volunteering for paratrooper duty.

The projective drawings were administered five years after the patient had been in service; hence his achromatic drawing of a soldier conveys his clinging to the self-concept of a warrior as a badge of virile manliness. His defensive masculine strivings then intensify and become still more

Figure 5-27. **Case I: Achromatic Person.**

frank in his chromatic drawing of a muscular weight-lifter exhibiting his prowess. Beneath the compensatory muscles of the drawn Person, however, exists a somewhat short and organically less adequate frame, a hint of the inner doubts beneath the patient's virility strivings.

Whereas the achromatic soldier suggests the twin possibilities of either virility strivings or aggressive impulses, the chromatic data throws the evidence on the side of the need to demonstrate manliness.

Whereas this subject's defenses deepen on the chromatic level (showing a consistency with the diagnosis of character disorder), the next case presented is one whose defenses, in neurotic fashion, give way rather than intensify as the subject proceeds from the achromatic to the chromatic levels.

Figure 5-28. **Case I: Chromatic Person.** Entire drawing in black crayon.

Case J: A Child in the Cloak of a Warrior

The subject's drawings proceed from the achromatic surface of an Indian brave whose conspicuous headdress testifies to his being a leader among hunters and warriors, to the deeper chromatic level which eloquently conveys the core of his self-concept: a little boy masquerading in the garb of a virile adult (i.e., wearing a sailor suit). On the achromatic level, some hint at lassitude and passivity beneath the virile front comes through in the position of the drawn Indian, who sinks into a sitting posture.* But it is in the chromatic phase that the basic person —a child playing at being a man—is seen. The "shrinkage" in size of the figure is as striking as the change in content. Once again, a hierarchy of

---

*His inner doubts concerning his virility and sexual adequacy are also reflected in his Unpleasant Concept Test where he draws what he later describes as: "A judge telling a man his wife is an adulteress. The judge has just found this out from a lab report indicating that the husband did not really conceive the child."

Figure 5-29. **Case J: Achromatic Person.**

conflict and defense has been contributed to the clinical picture.

Case K: A Case of Don Juanism

The patient, a 30-year-old, married male with two children, entered psychotherapeutic collaboration because of a heavy sense of guilt which pervaded a recent onset of extramarital activities.

The subject, for his achromatic male Person, drew a well-dressed person in a nonchalant pose, whom he then described as about his own age, or leaning a bit on the younger side (i.e., "twenty-six to thirty"), and as "sophisticated, dapper and self-assured." From merely the achromatic level, one would get little impression of the extent of the basic problem

Figure 5-30. **Case J: Chromatic Person.** Entire drawing in green.

lying beneath the surface (and brought up by the impact of color). Beneath this surface impression of himself, the chromatic male which he later drew indicates that the patient is beginning inwardly to entertain grave doubts concerning his youth, vigor and virility. In the chromatic drawing, the male figure loses his confident and self-assured casualness of pose. The hands are held in a position of helpless ineffectuality, and the facial tone changes to a pathetically empty and depressed one. The achromatic Person's smile is replaced by a morose frown and his bright, alert facial expression gives way to a vacuous one. A premature fear of decline, impotency and decrepancy, associated with "old age," is dramatically conveyed in his description of the chromatic male: "This is the same man years later, his hair is gone, his money is gone, his waist is gone, and his poise is gone. (The drawing is complementary to the Rorschach response the subject gave on Card VI, of a "penis with a beard on it.")

The inner doubts generated by this self-concept appear as the motivational mainspring behind this attempt to recapture his earlier "sophisti-

Figure 5-31. **Case K: Achromatic Person.**

cated, dapper, self-assured" picture of himself through extramarital activities with his twenty-two-year-old secretary, his nineteen-year-old clerk, and another twenty-one-year-old woman.

In his achromatic and chromatic drawings of Trees, the two levels of his self-concept again are graphically and dramatically portrayed. Thus, his Tree drawings parallel his Person drawings. For his achromatic Tree he drew a sturdy oak which he then describes as "full-grown, stately and very solid." Beneath this surface impression of himself, he apparently inwardly harbors a self-concept actually possessed of just the opposite traits: for his chromatic Tree he draws a weeping willow (conveying his underlying depression) which he then describes as "weak-looking."

The patient is presently panicked by the cracks he is beginning to

Figure 5-32. **Case K: Chromatic Person.** All in purple.

experience in his self-esteem. The conspicuous sawed-off limb protruding from his otherwise sturdy and intact achromatic Tree might suggest that he is beginning to experience his feelings of impairment, inadequacy and "castration" on increasingly closer-to-conscious levels.

Case L: Neurosis vs. Deeper Pathology

We have seen, in a preceding case, where the more surface achromatic level emphasized an impressive masculine figure (an Indian chieftain), but the deeper chromatic conveyed an immature counterpoint (a boy, in sailor suit, merely playing at the equivalent of the achromatic hero).

The present case does more-or-less a similar thing. He presents, in pencil, a boxer, and then, in crayon, a young child. Both cases emphasize a compensatory defense, and beneath that an identity of clear inferiority — inferiority of masculinity and of maturity.

But let's step closer. Whereas the Indian was a realistic, flesh-and-

Figure 5-33. **Case K: Achromatic Tree.**

blood figure, the current drawing, the boxer, is exaggerated: a grossly exaggerated figure of blown-up muscles, maybe as if composed of balloons with more air in them than necessary to give it real dimensions. Muscles become twice their natural size (note shoulders, biceps and thighs), the waist thinner than is humanly possible.

Here grandiosity moves toward only borderline marginal reality testing and hints of borderline feelings of depersonalization. In this context, the drawn Person then has unseeing (pupilless) eyes and no ears.

The reality testing is again suspect in that the gloved hand raised in victory does not prove enough, but the boxer then *incongruously* wears what looks like a cowboy hat on his head.

After the inflated self of the achromatic projection, on the chromatic

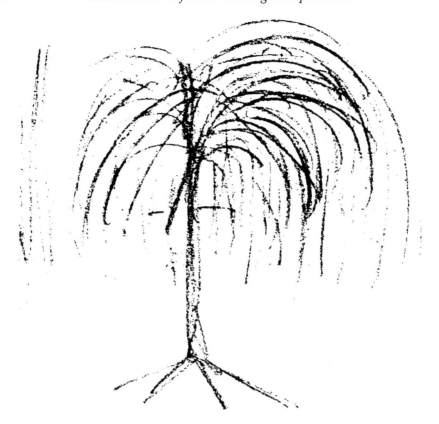

Figure 5-34. **Case K: Chromatic Tree.** Foliage—green and brown, trunk—brown.

projection the subject slides down the human scale to almost as far as the sense of self can go: Though he says it's a 6-year-old, it actually looks like an infant, in diapers, with one curlicue of hair, first learning to walk, trying out his wobbly legs and uncertain balance.

While the diagnosis rests on the principle I propose in this book, of neurosis being indicated by a clash of oppositeness of theme between the pencil and crayon drawings, this particular case may be more complicated. The impaired reality testing, unleashed grandiosity, unseeing eyes and marginal feelings of depersonalization introduce the consideration of possible deeper pathology.

In passing, this case brings to the fore another principle regarding the achromatic-chromatic comparison of a subject's drawings. There is a concept we may formulate of *distance* between the polarities of the achromatic and the chromatic projective self. For example, comparing the distance of masculinity (and maturity) between, first, the drawn Indian

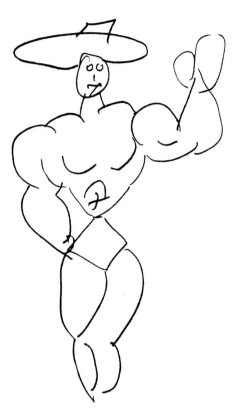

Figure 5-35. **Case L: Achromatic Male.**

and the perhaps 8-year-old boy in a sailor suit, and, second, the distance between the inflated masculinity of the exaggeratedly muscular boxer with hand raised in victory and the infant in diapers just stumblingly learning to walk, the latter *distance* is greater. The compensatory level of the way the boxer is exaggerated is more than the Indian, on the one hand, and the immaturity and insufficiency of an infant is more than that of a boy, on the other hand. So the distance between boxer and mere infant is wider than that between Indian and 8-year-old boy.

A general rule we may then formulate is that the greater the achromatic-chromatic *distance* of projected selves, the more "sick" is the patient's diagnosis (i.e., the more severe, and less reconcilable, the conflict) and the more guarded the prognosis.

Figure 5-36. **Case L: Chromatic Male.**

Case M: A More Obvious and Borderline Schizophrenic

To carry this continuum further, the next case is one in which the subject, a 28-year-old woman, for her achromatic projective drawing of a female offers a clearly reality-based figure, proportions, perspective, and detailing are quite good.

The projection is of a woman with arms tucked close to her body, eyes looking down, shyly or depressively, at the ground, and with the line quality suggesting the possibility of some depression or anxiety. The only hint of anything more comes at the bottom of the drawing where the feet seem vague, undetailed or amorphous, suggesting, perhaps, some feelings of uncertain stability emotionally.

But the posture is upright, and the overall communication is of an essentially stable and intact subject.

However, when she is hit with the impact of color, reality testing

Figure 5-37. **Case M: Achromatic Female.**

disappears and the functioning of her Ego is significantly, acutely, thrown off. The drawn figure just, eerily, floats off. And depersonalization is signaled by the dropping off of any hint, even, of seeing eyes.

The impaired reality of this woman is further supported on the verbal level. The subject looks at her chromatic drawing, and when asked what the drawn Person is doing, merely describes, "She's a rather silent person." When pressed further, she only adds, "She's not standing up." Still further questioning no more than elicited "Just waiting." The examiner echoed, "Just waiting?" and the patient responded, "No particular position." Only another minute of silence from both sides focused the reality a bit for the subject, who then finally saw, "Just floating."

This, then, is a patient who in emotional situations (represented by the chromatic impact) readily loses both her hold on reality and her emotional balance, suffers depersonalization and crosses the line to a schizophrenic reaction. But, on the other hand, when not emotionally buffetted (the achromatic level), sees reality, holds her balance, and

Figure 5-38. **Case M: Chromatic Female.**

suffers no depersonalization. Both conditions are clearly anchored (in their respective spheres), and this case represents a more or less classic instance of Borderline Psychosis—and more severe than the preceding case.

Case N: A Feminine Character Structure

This adult male's achromatic Person is drawn with narrow shoulders and dressed in rather effete, dandyish clothing. It leans toward the unisex, and thus hints of feminine identification, but subtly and only marginally so.

But the color rendition, next, elicits a bolder, franker, richer, fuller and more ornate rush of uncontained feminine identification. It is now no longer subtle, no longer hinted at, but loudly advertised and shown off, flauntedly and uncontainedly. His femininity is not just his business, but is intruded into everyone's attention. He now parades his femininity —as the vernacular has it—as a "screaming" homosexual. There is also, thus, a lot of narcissism and exhibitionism orchestrated in with the female identification.

Figure 5-39. **Case N: Achromatic Male.**

This is evident from head to toe, from the plumed hat, the long hair, the woman's blouse, the "petticoat britches," the unmasculine legs in high heels and bows at the ankles. The drawn male is dressed all in "feminine" purple; and the subject has to cruise down the long corridor of history in order to find a *Louis XIV* costume in which to express his identity.

The fact that this identity deepens as the subject descends from pencil to crayon expression, rather than there being a clash between the theme of the two levels (as so many of the neurotic subjects revealed), suggests the subject affirms, rather than is at odds with, his femininity. Thus, it is ego syntonic, or characterological. In fact, the quality of every aspect of the chromatic drawing conveys that beyond affirming it, he *celebrates* it!

Figure 5-40. **Case N: Chromatic Male.**

DISCUSSION

In its concern with the deciphering of the symbolic meaning of the different individual colors in various projective art techniques, psychodiagnostic psychology has by-passed an awareness of the perhaps richer clinical yield: the tapping of the generally deeper level of the personality by chromatic, as compared to achromatic, projective drawings. The two levels thus contribute to a more definite picture of the stratification of the subject's personality structure.

The chromatic drawing phase strips away the closer-to-conscious personality layers; it more easily raises the deeper layers of the unconscious to eye-level.

Observation of subjects engaging in the achromatic and chromatic drawing tasks suggests a three-factor rationale to go along with the empirical data presented.

First, the crayon drawing task tends to elicit reactions to, and tolerance for, emotional stimuli. In this manner it supplies an impact similar to the Rorschach chromatic cards in getting beneath the subject's defenses.

The second factor probably operative in the chromatic phase of projective drawings, which enables it to dig down deeper into the personality structure, is the associative value of the crayons, which tends to elicit childhood adjustment levels in adult subjects. It seems almost as if crayons appeal in some degree to the residue of childish layers in the adult's personality, and cut-through to tap this level.

The third factor which probably contributes to the efficacy of the chromatic phase, in descending deeper beneath the subject's defenses than the achromatic phase, is a temporal factor. As routinely administered, the chromatic H–T–P is asked for after the subject has produced an achromatic set of drawings and has been questioned at length concerning them. Thus, by the time he is asked to enter the chromatic phase, he may be psychologically in a more vulnerable position, with his conflicts stirred up, his emotions aroused and, as is the case with some subjects, his defenses ajar. It is through this chink in his armor that the chromatic phase penetrates.

Thus, a three-factor hypothesis is offered in explanation of the clinically-observed phenomenon that chromatic drawings reveal a deeper personality picture than achromatic drawings: (a) the emotional impact of colors, (b) the childhood associations to crayons, and (c) the repetition of the drawing task* (after a questioning period),

With colored pencils, crayons that leave a pencil line (achromatic), and a procedure in which the chromatic drawing phase precedes the achromatic one, the writer is presently following through a research design which attempts to separate the three factors and thus evaluate their relative contributions to the, as presently conceived, more potent chromatic clinical instrument.

COLOR SYMBOLISM ON THE H–T–P

In the foregoing section, the chromatic drawings were discussed as if they were merely deeper-tapping pencil drawings. In the present section,

---

*This last factor is the basis upon which the Eight-Card Redrawing Test (see Chapter 17 of Hammer, E. *The Clinical Application of Projective Drawings*, Springfield, IL: Charles C Thomas, 1958.) is effective in providing successively deeper personality pictures.

a consideration of the specific use of different colors will be added to round out the total picture of the chromatic contribution.

Some subjects approach the crayons with the hesitant anxiety so characteristic of their customary everyday patterns of behavior. Their crayon lines are faint and uncertain with the color choices restricted to the safer black, brown, or blue. They reveal their personality constriction and interpersonal uncertainties by not daring to open up with the bolder reds, oranges and yellows. This color usage reveals those subjects to be at the end of the personality continuum where overcautiousness in exchanging feelings with others prevails.

Psychologically healthier subjects, by contrast, plunge more deeply into the chromatic task, confidently employ the warmer colors, utilize a firm, sure pressure on the crayon, and thus reflect their greater self-assurance in the emotional areas that colors represent.

On the other side of this healthier range in the continuum, are those subjects who employ an almost savage pressure (frequently bearing down so heavily that they snap the crayons) and a clash of inharmonious hot colors. Excessive lability, turbulent emotions and jarring inner needs, in a tension-laden setting, characterize the psychological state of the subjects in this group.

From a normative standpoint, the use of from three to five colors for the House represents the average range, as does two to three for the Tree, and three to five for the Person.

An inhibited use of color, below this average range, is exhibited by subjects unable to make warm, sharing personal relationships freely. The most "emotion-shy" subjects tend to use crayon as if it were a pencil, employing no coloring-in whatsoever.

A more expansive use of color than the normative middle range, particularly if combined with an unconventional employment of the colors, occurs most frequently in those manifesting an inability to exercise adequate control over their emotional impulses. One psychotic recently indicated his inadequate control, as well as his break with conventional reality, by drawing each of the eight windows in his House a different color.

Anastasi and Foley[3] found that an extensive variety of color usage occurred almost exclusively among schizophrenic patients and manic-depressives in the manic phase. Both Lindberg[14] and Eysenck[9], among others, demonstrated a decrease of number of colors employed with increasing age in children, evidence in accord with the increase of emotional control with age. England[8] differentiated problem children from normal children by the former's inappropriate use of color. Since the younger, more uncontrolled child and the adult with lessened control (schizophrenics and manics) manifest a more expansive color usage, they supply support for the projective drawing hypothesis relating this type of color employment with inadequate control over emotionality.

John Payne[17] offers an interesting and fruitful four-fold scheme for the classification of the color output on the H–T–P:

(a) "Empathic intensity" is defined as color emphasis of a particular item, and is reported to occur in the drawings of normal, flexibly-adjusted subjects.

(b) "Tensional intensity," which refers to repeated reinforcement of a color by going back over it again and again, is found in the drawing productions of anxious subjects in the normal and neurotic ranges, particularly in anxiety states.

(c) "Clash intensity," an intensification of conventionally inharmonious color combinations, is evidence of a disturbance of a more profound degree, approaching and within the psychotic range. The schizophrenic patient, previously mentioned, who drew each of his eight windows a different color illustrates this classification. Manics also frequently exhibit "clash intensity."

(d) "Pressure intensity," refers to improperly modulated and excessively heavy pressure on the crayon. Payne finds this in the chromatic H–T–P's of mental defectives and organics. The present writer finds "pressure intensity" occurring also with two other groups of patients: aggressive "psychopaths" and paranoids.

In regard to the specific symbolic connotations of the individual colors, research in the area is in general agreement that the use of reds and yellows is a more spontaneous form of expression[22] than an emphasis on the blues or greens, which are more representative of controlled behavior.[1,2,12]

Black and brown are more common to states of inhibition,[5] repression,[16] and possibly regression.[19]

Brick,[6] in his study of 200 children between the ages of two and fifteen, found an overemphasis upon yellow to be significant as an expression of hostility and aggression. This finding may be related to the study of Griffiths,[10] in which yellow was found to be the preferred color at the earliest stage of a child's engaging in drawings. This may be viewed as consistent with Brick's finding, in that young childhood is the stage of the freest experience of rage and open release of hostility.

Buck[7] has found purple to be the preferred color of paranoids and regards any considerable use of it as presumptive evidence of strong power-striving drives, usually paranoid-tinged. Whether the grandiose need of the paranoid taps the same associative stream which links purple with royalty is not presently known. The idea, even if highly speculative, is certainly engaging.

SUMMARY

Empirical data has been presented which suggests that by the addition of the chromatic phase to the projective drawing task, the clinician is provided with an instrument which taps a deeper personality layer and, hence, when taken with the achromatic drawings, provides a richer and more accurate picture of the hierarchy of the patient's conflicts and defenses. A three-factor rationale, offered along with the empirical data, views the emotional impact of color, the childhood association with crayons, and the repetition of the drawing task as all working in the same direction to enable the chromatic drawings to penetrate deeper beneath the patient's defenses and bring the more basic personality levels to view.

Inhibited or expansive color usage has been related to the corresponding personality correlates. Overemphasis upon any of the eight colors has been discussed and the research correlating color preference with personality traits has been presented. Much more research, it goes without saying, needs to be done.

EXPERIMENTAL FOLLOW-UP STUDY

On an empirical basis, the foregoing data are rather impressive; but can an experimental design yield equally demonstrative data in support of the central hypothesis, i.e., that the drawings produced in crayon tend to emanate from a relatively deeper region than those produced in pencil?

For the experimental phase of the study, sixty cases were accumulated over the years. These were individuals who had been initially referred for projective technique assessment, and had then been treated by a therapist, in the majority of cases by the psychiatrist who had referred the case for diagnostic evaluation.

The writer administered the H–T–P, made and recorded his H–T–P derived diagnosis on the basis of a comparison of the pencil and the crayon drawings, and only then proceeded to administer the remainder of the projective battery. The guideposts he employed for the diagnosis based on the achromatic-chromatic H–T–P comparison were those distilled, on an empirical basis, from the sort of cases presented in this chapter. The following rules of thumb, derived from the hypothesis that chromatic drawings tend to tap deeper personality "levels" than do achromatic drawings, were employed:

Neurotic conditions will be reflected in relatively opposite personality polarities elicited by the chromatic and the achromatic H–T–P, respectively (with the latter representing defenses and the former, what is defended against). (See, for example, Cases A, G and J.)

Character disorders will reflect themselves in the same defense (and drawing theme) appearing and deepening as the subject progresses from the achromatic to the chromatic rendition. (See, as illustrations, Cases F and I.)

Latent conditions (latent psychotic, ambulatory or preschizophrenic conditions) will yield dramatically sicker chromatic than achromatic H–T–P's, with the achromatic almost "passing" as non-psychotic. (See Cases B, C and X.)

Schizophrenic reactions will produce evidence of frank pathology in both the achromatic and the chromatic drawings, with the chromatic H–T–P's being even more pathological than the achromatic. (See Cases D and E.)

Organicity: Confusion, perseveration and organic flavoring* will not become worse on the chromatic than on the achromatic drawings (as things, on the contrary, do get worse on the chromatic drawings of neurotic, pre-schizophrenic, and schizophrenic patients).

Relatively healthy or "essentially normal" people will reveal relative personality resiliency, stability or effectiveness which will not diminish on the chromatic drawings, and will be more or less integrated and undisrupted on both levels.

Because the psychotherapists required a report from the psychologist, almost invariably during the first five sessions, the psychotherapist's

---

*For a listing of such signs of organic flavoring on the H–T–P, see pages 11 and 12 of Hammer, E. F., *H-T-P Clinical Research Manual*, Los Angeles, California, Western Psychological Services, 1954, and the more recent findings presented in Chapter 2 of the current book.

diagnosis of each case was not the original one formulated during the first phase of treatment, because it was felt that that diagnostic impression might well have been influenced by the psychological report. Instead, the psychotherapist was contacted six months later and asked for his final diagnosis in the case. The psychotherapist was asked to place patient into the category in which the patient most essentially fit: Neurosis, Character Disorder, Reactive Condition, Latent Condition, Schizophrenic Reaction, Organic, or Essentially Normal. By thus obtaining the diagnosis six months after treatment had been inaugurated, the writer hoped to minimize, if not almost eliminate, the influence of the original psychological report on the diagnosis. Presumably, after a psychotherapist has been working with a patient for a full half year, his clinical impression will be founded on his observations and intimate knowledge of the patient himself rather than on earlier diagnostic impressions of others. This, at least, is the assumption upon which the experimental section of this study is based.

The basic operational hypothesis, stated in null form, is that the diagnoses based on a comparison of the achromatic-chromatic H–T–P will agree no better than chance with the criteria of the psychotherapist's diagnosis on the same patient after six months of treatment.

Of the sixty cases, we find, when the data is accumulated, that agreement of the H–T–P derived diagnosis with the later psychotherapists' diagnoses occurs in forty-eight cases, or in 80 percent of the instances. In computing the statistics, the more parsimonious assumption was employed that by pure chance the diagnoses derived from each source had an even or fifty-fifty chance of agreeing with one another. In actuality, pure chance would produce agreement in much less than half the cases, since there are seven categories, rather than two from which each diagnostician can choose. But on the other hand, it is not a case of chance allowing one chance out of seven either. The respective diagnosticians are not equally prone to employ any one of the seven diagnostic alternatives, in that in general practice the diagnosis of neurosis, as one example, occurs much more frequently than does an organic or essentially healthy diagnosis. The situation thus becomes more complicated.

However, even with the parsimonious base of pure chance yielding agreement in thirty of the sixty cases, the Chi square obtained is 21.60, statistically significant at the .001 level of confidence. In addition to the Chi square results, the face value of exact "correlation" over seven categories in forty-eight out of sixty instances is confirming. Here we obtain encouraging experimental support for the empirically-derived view that the addition of the chromatic H–T–P to the achromatic H–T–P provides a diagnostically useful extension of the projective drawings, probing relatively deeper into the underlying personality regions.

Table 5-1.
Comparison of Psychiatric Diagnosis Made Six Months After Therapy Began
and the Initial Projective Drawing Hypothesis

| | CASES | |
	Agreement	Disagreement
NEUROSIS: Opposite personality polarity comes out on chromatic H–T–P as opposed to achromatic (with the latter representing defenses and the former, what is defended against)	14	4
CHARACTER DISORDER: Same defense (and drawing theme) deepens from achromatic to chromatic	4	1
REACTIVE CONDITIONS: Healthier looking chromatic than achromatic drawings	3	1
LATENT CONDITIONS: (Latent, ambulatory, and preschizophrenic conditions): Dramatically sicker chromatic than achromatic, with achromatic almost "passing" as non-psychotic	12	3
SCHIZOPHRENIC REACTIONS: Pathology frank on both levels, although even more overt on chromatic level	9	2
ORGANICITY: Confusion, perseveration and organic flavoring* do not become worse on the chromatic than on the achromatic drawings, (as things do get worse on the chromatic drawings of neurotic and schizophrenic patients)	3	0
HEALTH ("ESSENTIALLY NORMAL" DIAGNOSIS): Personality resilience, stability and effectiveness do not get worse on chromatic, and are relatively integrated and undisrupted on both levels.	3	1
	48	12

As for the particular *subgroup* of a diagnostic entity, each is really so small that it does not make sense to individually employ statistical treatment with one or another separately. But *purely for descriptive purposes* we may turn to Table 5-1 for a breakdown of the various diagnostic entities, as they were numerically represented in the overall study. We find that with each one of the diagnostic groups, the data is in the predicted directions. With the category of *Neurosis* there is agreement in fourteen out of eighteen cases; with that of *Character Disorder* in four of five cases; with the *Reactive Conditions* in three of four cases; with the *Latent Conditions* in twelve of fifteen cases; with the *Schizophrenic Reactions*

*See Chapter 2.

in nine of eleven cases; with *Organicity* in three of the three, and with the *Essentially Healthy* agreement occurs in three of the four cases. These four "Essentially Normal" cases, it later turned out, were two actors and two psychiatrists. Each of the actors had sought a psychoanalytic experience in the interest of deepening his awareness or of liberating greater richness or creativeness for his artistry, and the two psychiatrists were in analysis as a part of their psychoanalytic training.

Discussion

In its concern with the deciphering of the symbolic meaning of the different individual colors in various projective art techniques, psychodiagnostic psychology has by-passed an awareness of the perhaps richer clinical yield: the tapping of the generally deeper level of the personality by chromatic, as compared to the achromatic, projective drawings. The two levels can produce a more definitive picture of the stratification of the subject's personality structure, and, as both the clinical and the experimental data vividly demonstrate, provide clear-cut differential diagnostic (and prognostic) criteria.

The chromatic drawing phase strips away the closer-to-conscious personality layers; it more easily raises the deeper layers of the unconscious and its impulses to eye-level.

REFERENCES

1. Alschuler, and Hattwick, W.: Easel painting as an index of personality in preschool children. *Am. J. Orthopsychiat., 13:*616–625, 1943.
2. Alschuler, and Hattwick, W.: Painting and personality. Chicago: University of Chicago Press, *I* and *II:*590, 1947.
3. Anastasi, A., and Foley, J. P.: An analysis of spontaneous artistic productions by the abnormal. *J. Gen. Psychol., 28:*297–313, 1943.
4. Bellak, L.: *The Thematic Apperception Test and the Children's Apperception Test in Clinical Use.* New York, Grune & Stratton, 1954.
5. Bieber, I., and Herkimer, J.: Art in psychotherapy. *Amer. J. Psychiat., 104:*627–631, 1948.
6. Brick, M.: The mental hygiene value of children's art work. *Amer. J. Ortho., 14:*136–146, 1944.
7. Buck, J. N.: The H–T–P technique: A quantitative and qualitative scoring manual. *Clin. Psychol. Monogr., 5:*1–120, 1948.
8. England, A. O.: Color preference and employment in children's drawings. *J. Child Psychiat., 2:*343–349, 1952.

9. Eysenck, H. J.: *Dimensions of Personality.* London, Kegan Paul, 1947.

10. Griffiths, R.: *A Study of Imagination in Early Childhood.* London: Kegan Paul, Trench, Trubner & Co., 1935.

11. Hammer, E. F.: The role of the H–T–P in the prognostic battery. *J. Clin. Psychol.,* 9:371–374, 1953.

12. Kadis, A.: Fingerpainting as a projective technique. In Abt, L., and Bellak, L.: *Projective Psychology.* New York: Knopf, 403–431, 1950.

13. Klopfer, B., Ainsworth, M. D., Klopfer, W. G., and Holt, R. R.: Developments in the Rorschach Technique. In Vol. I, *Technique and Theory.* New York: World Book, 1954.

14. Lindberg, B. J.: Experimental studies of colour and non-colour attitudes in school children and adults. *Acto. Psychiat. Neurol., 16:*1938.

15. Murray, H. A.: *Explorations in Personality.* New York: Oxford University Press, 1938.

16. Napoli, P.: Fingerpainting and personality diagnosis. *Genet. Psychol. Monogr., 34:*129–231, 1946.

17. Payne, J. J.: Comments of the analysis of chromatic drawings. In Buck, J. N.: The H–T–P techniques: A quantitative and qualitative scoring manual. *Clin. Psychol. Monogr., 5:*1–120, 1948.

18. Piotrowski, Z. A.: Sexual crime, alcohol, and the Rorschach test. *Psychiat. Quart. Suppl., 56:*248–260, 1952.

19. Precker, J.: Painting and drawing in personality assessment. *J. Proj. Tech., 14:*262–286, 1950.

20. Rapaport, D.: *Diagnostic Psychological Testing.* Chicago: Year Book, *I* and *II:* 1946.

21. Schafer, R.: *Psychoanalytic Interpretation in Rorschach Testing.* New York: Grune & Stratton, 1954.

22. Zimmerman, J. and Garfinkel, L.: Preliminary study of the art productions of the adult psychotic. *Psychiat. Quart., 16:*313–318, 1942.

Chapter 6

PROJECTIVE MOTHER-AND-CHILD DRAWINGS*

JACQUELYN GILLESPIE

As the newest addition to the drawing family, by extending the projective probe into a request to draw a Mother-and-Child, Jacquelyn Gillespie (1994) has recently created a fresh and rewarding innovation to the battery—one which moves to illuminate central dimensions of personality and its development. As with most of the contributions to this book, Gillespie takes a psychodynamic approach and uncovers unconscious promptings and defenses. But, in addition, her devised technique is particularly useful in bringing to eye-level issues of early development and its delays, symbiosis, merger, separation, and individuation. Thus, it is tailor-made for Object Relations assessment and use with Borderline states.

THEORETICAL ISSUES

Current theoretical explorations in object relations and other psychoanalytic thought focus in various ways and with varying emphases on the early relationship between the mother and child. The importance of mother in the psychological development of the child has always been a fundamental tenet of classical psychoanalysis and has been further developed through the object relations work of Melanie Klein (1975) and her followers, Winnicott (1971/1982) and the "middle school" in analysis, and the foundation work in ego psychology as developed by Anna Freud (1965), Hartmann (1964), Jacobson (1964), and Spitz (1965).

The work of Mahler, Pine and Bergman (1975) has served to give an impetus to the consideration of mother-and-child issues by others than those steeped in the psychoanalytical traditions. For one thing, the work of Mahler et al. is based on practical, clinical observation of mothers and children behaving toward each other in ways that can be monitored and objectively assessed. Through their graphic descriptions of children

---

*Reprinted from *The Arts in Psychotherapy*, Vol. 16, Gillespie, J. "Object Relations as Observed in Projective Mother-and-Child Drawings," 163–178, 1989, with kind permission from Elsevier Science Ltd., The Boulevard, Langford Lane, Kidlington OX5 1GB, UK.

clinging, pulling away, moving toward and/or *against mother,* leaving her to explore and then rushing back again—all in definable developmental sequences based on satisfyingly large samples—we are presented with a reality of a mother-child developmentally sequential relationship rather like that found in the Piagetian child development literature. The solid ground of observation lends credibility to and provides new interest in Mahler's psychoanalytic formulations concerning early child development.

The major theme of the Mahler et al. (1975) work is the complementarity of symbiosis and individuation in the very early psychological development of the child. They posit a universal initial symbiotic phase that is developmentally normal and that slowly gives way to a separation-individuation phase, which is then followed in the normal course of things by other steps toward an individual sense of self and object constancy. Developmental disruption, particularly in the separation-individuation phase, results in identity conflicts that may be reactivated through eliciting events at any stage of life. These conflicts may become the focus of many clinical hours of psychotherapy.

But the observations and theoretical formulations of Mahler et al., which have given so much support to the fields of ego psychology and object relations, pertain to the events in the lives of small children. How do we move from our understanding of those experiences to the issues confronting therapists and patients in the consulting room? How can we verify the existence of symbiotic and separation issues in older children, adolescents, and adults?

In recent years there have been a number of attempts to validate psychoanalytic concepts through the techniques of experimental psychology. Perhaps the most important of those for the issues raised here are the detailed studies of Silverman, Lachmann and Milich (1982) summarized with critiques by them in 1984 for an analytic audience, and summarized more generally in Silverman and Weinberger (1985). Through the medium of tachistoscopic presentation of a subliminal stimulus of the phrase "Mommy and I are One" along with a pictorial image of two human figures joined at the shoulders, the researchers were able to evoke changes in behavior and test response in schizophrenic and other patient groups.

Designed specifically to test the notions of merger and fusion between mother and child inherent in the concept of symbiosis through the use of a "oneness" stimulus, the results of the primary study with schizophrenics found that "more differentiated" patients showed improvement, whereas "less differentiated" patients showed no reduction in pathology. The more differentiated patients were presumably able to maintain separateness while profiting from the oneness experience; the less differentiated patients, on the other hand, were unable to do so because of what seemed to be a threat to the sense of self. Differentiation, in this study, was described as "level of differentiation from mother" and defined through patient rating scales of self and mother and the degree to which the ratings coincided (Silverman, et al., 1984).

This ingenious study of schizophrenics and subsequent work with a number of other patient and nonpatient groups provided evidence that issues of symbiosis can be explored usefully in an experimental fashion. The portion of the Silverman material described here, however, has identified the differentiation of self from mother as a relevant variable in the examination of issues of symbiosis and suggests its validity as a clinical concern. It is the Silverman thesis that "oneness gratifications enhance adaptation only if a sense of self is preserved (Silverman & Weinberger, 1985, p. 1300).

If Silverman and his colleagues have been able to demonstrate issues of symbiosis and differentiation through the use of rating scales and responses to subliminal stimulation, then is it not possible that such concerns may also be clinically accessible through the use of projective mother-and-child drawings?

THE MOTHER AND CHILD IN ART

The mother-and-child theme in art is a primary one. Not only is the Western Christian culture exposed to numberless presentations of the Madonna and Child in every conceivable style, but nonreligious artists of all periods also turn to the mother-and-child relationship as a favorite subject. That body of work provides indications of the variety of ways in which the mother-child relationship is experienced.

Walk through any art gallery; note the frequency of the mother-child theme and the variations of its expression. Note babies in arms, sometimes held close, even greedily, in mutual absorption—sometimes held loosely or listlessly in a perfunctory fashion. Toddlers exploring, but not too far from a watchful, smiling mother. Other little ones facing away from a mother absorbed in something or someone else. Note the cool, distant mother-child relationship in one picture and the warmth and intensity of the interaction in another. Some artists have explored the theme more than once; Picasso has done so in different styles. Which of the Picasso pictures, for example, is the "right" one in its presentation of his notion of the mother-child relationship? It is obvious that the question is an absurdity. It does not occur to us to look at pictorial details for indications of pathology. However, there is a personality in those Picasso paintings, often clearly absorbed in technical problems that are understood only by other artists, but often exuberant and carefree, enjoying the mastery of technique and the presentation of content. His mothers seem calm, strong, capable; his infants are large and robust and demanding. Powerful pictures. Now wander over to a Mary Cassatt exhibit and see her bright, delicate, careful mother and child, or to a Gauguin, simple, powerful, restrained in its primitive strength.

Do we assume that the painting style represents the personality of the painter? If so, in what way? We watch the evidences of mental deterioration in van Gogh's work, which we are told about in basic art classes. But what of other material that seems at least as disorganized to the undiscerning eye? How, then, can we present interpretations of patient drawings with more understanding than we bring to the work of artists, who are able to use their talent, training, and skills to convey their meaning without hesitation? A tentative answer to that question lies in the superior ability of artists to use their skills defensively, to present only what they intend to present, in a style that is their chosen way of communicating themselves to others. Nevertheless, they tell us about themselves in their choice of subject matter, their styles, and what they avoid. Issues of this sort are particularly relevant in patient drawings and, quite probably, account for a good deal of the discrepancy noted in work with the interpretation of drawings.

PROJECTIVE DRAWINGS

Patient drawings have been used as expressions of self-concept, affective states, and various kinds of pathology since the original work of Karen Machover (1949), who used draw-a-person figures to evoke evidence of "the impulses, anxieties, conflicts, and compensations characteristic of that individual" (p. 35). Machover's book was subtitled "A method of personality investigation," and she did not hesitate to draw quite specific conclusions concerning personality dynamics from the characteristics of drawings.

During the many years since Machover's work there have been many attempts to validate it, many different approaches to the use of drawings in personality assessment, and many studies attempting to find specific drawing characteristics in delimited populations. The work of DiLeo 138(1973) and Kellogg (1979) with children, and Schildkrout, Shenker, and Sonnenblick (1972) with adolescents have received attention. Koppitz (1968) developed a scoring system that yielded "emotional indicators" that have been the subject of a number of replication attempts. Results have been inconsistent. In fact, Anastasi (1982) has suggested "that the D–A–P (Draw A Person) can serve best, not as a psychometric instrument, but as part of a clinical interview, in which the drawings are interpreted in the context of other information about the individual" (p. 580).

Some of the work on drawings has been done on the basis of unconscious content, whereas other material deals primarily with manifest content and/or cognitive issues. Most of the work seems to lack focus on theoretical perspectives and assumes the existence of one-to-one correspondences between characteristics of drawings and specific personality or behavioral disturbances. It seems that the use of drawings in a clinical fashion has been developing from and directed toward a number of different settings and purposes. Yet the use of drawings in assessment and psychotherapy remains popular, and it is testimony to the sense of drawing as valuable communication of the self that seems to underlie its place on the psychological scene. It seems reasonable to accept Anastasi's evaluation of the utility of drawings and to consider them as one source of useful communication about unconscious attitudes toward self and others that is the focus of so much clinical work, avoiding cookbook-style interpretation of details in drawings.

This paper presents an overview of the use of mother-and-child drawings as a projective technique, based on the extensive work with projective person drawings in the clinical literature. The mother-and-child drawing, however, may be used specifically to gain a sense of an individual style of object relatedness.

PROJECTION IN PATIENT DRAWINGS

Patient drawings, like those of acknowledged skilled artists, are creative works of nonverbal imagination. They are completely subjective, and therein lies their projective significance. However, like the work of artists, they also project wishes and fears, and they often deny unpleasant realities. It is not unusual, for example, for children who are known victims of parental abuse to draw pictures of very smiling children and attentive smiling mothers. It would be disastrous for examiners to take such pictures as evidence that nothing is wrong in the home.

Splitting, as well as denial, may be presented in pictorial form. That is, a mother who is in treatment to conquer habits of verbal abuse frequently directed toward her children may draw a sweetly smiling child with an angry, screaming mother, or a furious child with a blandly serene mother. In such a situation the discrepancy between the figures suggests the need to explore issues of splitting and projective identification as well as the actual home circumstances that may lead to verbal abuse. Here we have not positive differentiation but a sort of negative differentiation in that it is not appropriate to have one party to a relationship smiling in the face of so much anger. In such a clinical situation it would be particularly helpful to have drawings from the child as well as the mother, to compare and contrast their presentations of self and other.

MOTHER-AND-CHILD DRAWINGS

The use of mother-and-child drawings in projective assessment is a logical, almost inevitable outgrowth of immersion in ego and self-psychology and object relations theory. As the clinician investigates the quality of object relations and the nature and structure of ego development in a patient, it seems to be an easy next step to observe the presentation of the self and object representations in drawings. As Silverman (1982) has pointed out, it is possible to obtain indications of levels of mother-child differentiation through rating scales that have implications for treatment.

Mother-and-child drawings should present something of the self in both figures, as well as the quality of the perceived relationship. If the differentiation is gradual, as theory proclaims, then younger children should draw children and mothers as much alike. Differentiation in the figures should follow a developmental sequence, with drawings typical of adolescence differing in style from those of younger children. The drawings of adults should be well differentiated.

INSTRUCTIONS FOR MOTHER-AND-CHILD DRAWINGS

It is important that whatever a person produces in the way of a mother-and-child drawing be simply accepted, without either disapproval or effusive delight. Psychologists experienced in clinical assessment learn to focus on the material presented either verbally or in other ways with careful but nonjudgmental interest and attention in an attempt to understand it as fully as possible.

The drawings may be presented as a task at any age after a child is old enough to produce representational drawings, usually by age five or six. Children tend to enjoy drawing. Adults are more cautious, usually because drawing is no longer a familiar activity and they may feel less than competent.

The instructions, as was mentioned, are simple: "Draw a mother and child." Note that the instructions do *not* ask for *your* mother, or for a mother and *her* child, or a mother and *a* child. These apparently small differences tend to alter the focus of the individual who is establishing a mental set for the drawing task. Each approach to the task is completely individual and seems to reflect both the universality and the specialness of the mother-child relationship.

A child will often ask, "My mother?" which immediately suggests that the distinction is already being drawn between "my" mother and a generalized abstraction of "mother" as a concept. Other children, who have not yet drawn that distinction, immediately proceed to draw their own mothers, as their comments during the drawing often indicate. There is no problem in this task approach. It simply reflects the individual's conceptual organization of the mother-child relationship, which is still personal and specific. Those with intellectual impairments at all ages also typically draw "my mother," since the concrete aspects of their thinking lead them in that direction. The projective aspects of the drawings, of course, are the inclusion of aspects of the personal mother-child relationship and the self within the more abstract formulation.

It is important to separate the concept of the mother-and-child drawing from that of a personal family drawing, which will evoke the cognitive attempt to produce a likeness and an effort to portray events in the family life. The mother-and-child drawing is deliberately designed to move to the unconscious content of the internalized self and object representations, which often have little to do with lifestyle and current events.

To return to the child's question: "My mother?"—the response should be nondirective. Repeat the instructions; perhaps add "However you wish to do it."

DEVELOPMENTAL DRAWINGS

The normal developmental process finds children under age eight or nine portraying the mother and child in very similar fashion, with the mother usually somewhat bigger than the child. The drawing in Figure 6-1 was done by a six-year-old girl.

By latency age, drawing skills have usually improved considerably. The little girl (age 10) who drew Figure 6-2 is experiencing pleasure in her ability to admire mother and identify with her while seeing her as a separate individual.

However, latency age boys need to work a little harder at establishing their firm separation and differentiation from mother. Note the drawing (Fig. 6-3) by an 11-year-old boy, with the exaggerated emphasis on the "son" label, the round bicep muscle, and the phallic gun, which he does not yet seem able to control. There are still a number of identical aspects to the two figures, however, suggesting some not unexpected residual dependencies.

By adolescence some individuals exhibit real artistic talent. Figure 6-4 is a 16-year-old girl's drawing that reflects a difficult pose. However, note the sad look on the infant's face and the inattention of the mother.

In contrast, the teen-age girl who drew Figure 6-5 has little talent for drawing, but notice the happy baby basking in the mother's delighted gaze.

The teen-age boy who drew Figure 6-6 is certainly artistically competent, but this scene is different from the others. Now we have an additional member in the group. Mother dragon is trying to protect her baby, but the knight in armor is a powerful figure and may well win the battle. This boy is the child of a father in therapy for physical abuse of the boy. Perhaps we have the early indications of "identification with the aggressor" and the possibility that the abused child may become an abuser himself.

This next young teenage boy is not working out his power needs very well (Fig. 6-7). From his sad expression, it seems that his Superman suit is not working. He has no hands to make him competent, but he is beginning to get his feet on the ground in the clearest and most firm part of the drawing. Note the mother's empty body and the emphasis on large mouths and eyes in the figures, suggesting control struggles with a good deal of arguing and little nurturing. Mom is probably winning at present, but perhaps not for long.

By adulthood the young mother in Figure 6-8 is able to present her

Figure 6-1. **Mother and Child.**

mothering role with confidence and pleasure. Her drawing skills are also well developed.

Men tend to be more reluctant to try out their drawing skills. They tend to do more abstract representations than women. These two interlocking simple shapes (Fig. 6-9) nevertheless manage to communicate closeness and caring.

SEVERE PATHOLOGY

One of the notable features of the mother-and-child drawing seems to be that it does not reliably differentiate kinds of behavior disorders. Apparently, as seems obvious from clinical experience, there are many ways to manifest inadequacies in self-concept and poor interpersonal skills. Nevertheless, there are some drawings that are almost breathtakingly and painfully atypical.

Figure 6-10 is an example of a sadly pathological drawing done by a young disturbed child. Note the lack of body shapes and the blackness of what appears to be the child in the drawing. The blackness and destruc-

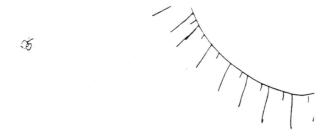

Figure 6-2. **Mother and Child.**

Figure 6-3.

tion of the child figure appears to reflect severe depression and lack of positive self and object representation. Yet the child figure clings in a sort of primitive way, suggesting the continuing search for the object.

Figure 6-4.

Figure 6-5.

The exhibition of genitalia in projective drawings is generally considered to be an indication of severe pathology. This drawing (Fig. 6-11) was done by a young adult male with a diagnosis of paranoid schizophrenia.

Figure 6-6.

Figure 6-7.

In spite of the deliberate overemphasis on sexually differentiating characteristics, there seems to be little real sexual identity for these figures.

Figure 6-8.

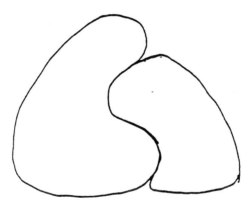

Figure 6-9.

SUMMARY

Contemporary object relations theory and the use of projective drawings have been presented to provide some clinical access to the symbolic aspects of the initial mother-child relationship. That relationship becomes

Figure 6-10.

Figure 6-11.

the prototype of subsequent relating styles in later life and a major focus of psychotherapy. The role of artistic expression as a vehicle for communication of fundamental personal symbols and meanings is explored, and the uses and limitations of projective drawings are presented. The use of mother-and-child drawings as a projective technique is described. A series of sample drawings reflecting various aspects of primary relationships and clinical concerns illustrate the material.

REFERENCES

Anastasi, A. (1982). *Psychological testing* (5th ed.). New York: Macmillan.

DiLeo, J. H. (1973). *Children's drawings as diagnostic aids.* New York: Brunner/Mazel.

Freud, A. (1965). Normality and pathology in childhood. In *The writings of Anna Freud* (Vol. 6). New York: International Universities Press.

Gillespie, J. (1994). *The projective use of mother-and-child drawings: A manual for clinicians.* New York: Brunner/Mazel.

Hartmann, H. (1964). *Essays on ego psychology.* New York: International Universities Press.

Jacobson, E. (1964). *The self and the object world.* New York: International Universities Press.

Kellogg, R. (1979). *Children's drawings/children's minds.* New York: Avon Books.

Klein, M. (1975). *Love, guilt and reparation & other works, 1921-1945.* New York: Delacorte Press.

Koppitz, E. M. (1968). *Psychological evaluation of children's human figure drawings.* New York: Grune & Stratton.

Machover, K. (1949). *Personality projection in the drawing of the human figure.* Springfield, Ill.: Charles C Thomas.

Mahler, M. S., Pine, F., & Bergman, A. (1975). *The psychological birth of the human infant.* New York: Basic Books.

Schildkrout, M. S., Shenker, I. R., & Sonnenblick, M. (1972). *Human figure drawings in adolescence.* New York: Brunner/Mazel.

Silverman, L. H., Lachmann, F. M., & Milich, R. H. (1982). *The search for oneness.* New York: International Universities Press.

Silverman, L. H., Lachmann, F. M., & Milich, R. H. (1984). Unconscious oneness fantasies: Experimental findings and implications for treatment. *International Forum for Psychoanalysis, 1*(2), 107–152.

Silverman, L. H., & Weinberger, J. (1985). Mommy and I are one. *American Psychologist, 40*(12), 1296–1308.

Spitz, R. (1965). *The first year of life.* New York: International Universities Press.

Winnicott, D. W. (1982). *Playing and reality.* Middlesex, England: Penguin Books. (Original work published 1971).

Chapter 7

CRISIS ASSESSMENT:
THE PROJECTIVE TREE DRAWING BEFORE,
DURING AND AFTER A STORM

Michael J. Miller

The Draw-a-Person-in-the Rain technique, from which the battery below takes off, taps one's sense of self when experiencing a condition of stress. But left untapped is the patient's degree of awareness and, related to this, capacity for insight. Into this gap has flowed the fertile imagination of Michael Miller, while at the same time advancing the stimuli *rain* up an octave to *storm*.

In his richly innovative projective technique, Dr. Miller has shaped a valuable tool for simultaneously assessing four intertwined dimensions: (a) a patients' sense of the acuteness of crisis he/she is in, (b) its related disruption of the self-concept, and its integrity, (c) resiliency and recoverability (personality strength), and (d) as mentioned above, degree of awareness and, by implication, general capacity for insight.

By focusing on the Tree drawing, Miller capitalizes on the deepest tapping entity in the triad, House-Tree-Person. At the same time, as both an elemental living entity and one not experienced as close-to-home as a projection as is the Person drawing, the Tree drawing can more readily and less defensively receive the projected more negative aspects of self—i.e., broken, damaged, mutilated, destroyed, etc.—with less ego—threat and less need for evasion, disguise, or camouflage.

INTRODUCTION

Born in a crisis atmosphere—an acute psychiatric inpatient ward— the Projective Tree Drawing Battery provides a rich clinical yield of projections of the self when experiencing a crisis. This technique gives patients the opportunity to vent their sense of danger and the consequences of it for the integrity of their personality.

In its administration, the technique requests of the patient, three drawings and his or her associations to them. Using a number 2 pencil with eraser and an 8½ by 11 sheet of paper for each drawing, the patient is requested to:

1. Draw-A–Tree
2. Draw-A–Tree-In-A–Storm
3. Draw-A–Tree-After-A–Storm

followed by the:

4. Post-Drawing Inquiry
5. Projective Responsibility Inquiry

Coming after the Post-Drawing Inquiry (Buck, 1980) and concluding the Battery, the Projective Responsibility Inquiry confronts the patient with his projections. (The procedure and contents of this Inquiry are presented in the section, Crisis Awareness: An Inquiry into Projective Responsibility.)

Patients in crisis are particularly responsive to the Projective Tree Drawing Battery. In their crisis projections, such patients give vent to their despair and desperation. Torn from the earth and buffeted about by the "storm," they desperately try to hang onto the "ground." Fearful lest they be uprooted, they desperately reach out for help. Their very survival is at stake. Spiritual salvation may be sought. The patients' angst over their fate is paralleled by the clinician's confrontation with the question of crisis prognostication. As the question of fate hangs heavily over the patient, the question of prognosis confronts the clinician. What does this crisis portend?

Implicit in this question of crisis prognosis is that of psychotherapeutic prognosis. This is the question of psychotherapeutic treatability. The patients' level of crisis awareness as well as their sense of projective responsibility will be telling as to their treatability. The Projective Tree Drawing Battery addresses these clinical issues of crisis projection, crisis prognostication and crisis awareness.

Sequentially, coming after the Pre-Storm Tree which establishes a baseline for the patient's condition, the Tree-In-A–Storm enables an assessment of the patient's present sense of crisis. Most impressively, one can be witness to the internal experience of agitation as patients thrust themselves into the graphomotor depiction of the storm. The intensity of inner turbulence of these patients becomes palpable. (Clinical examples may be found in the Crisis Projection and Crisis Prognostication sections.)

The felt consequence of such crisis for the integrity of the patient's personality is provided expressive outlet through the drawing of a Tree-After-A–Storm.

Simultaneously, one can look backward, comparing the tree in crisis to the Pre-Storm Tree, and look forward to the consequences of the crisis with the Tree-After-A–Storm. What is the impact of the storm on the tree? How does it "weather" the storm? Does it "survive" relatively unscathed? Or, is it damaged? If so, how badly? Irretrievably so? Or, can it be "restored"? As one outpatient, who had been discharged from the hospital, put it, "This is after the storm. I do notice that the trunk. . . . its grounded. The sun is bigger, brighter."

Valuable prognostic data may be culled from such a technique as this which encourages patients to give full expression to the impact of crisis on the integrity of their personality. (Clinical data with their implications for crisis prognostication are presented in the Crisis Prognostication section.)

To enhance prognostication, an inquiry has been developed to directly explore the patients' awareness of, and responsibility for, their crisis projections. Although the patient is encouraged to externalize crisis on to the environment (i.e. the storm), the technique, at the same time, intensifies consciousness of such crisis projections. As one patient put it, "I'm like that tree, Doctor." As another one said, "That's my life in a nutshell." Those that are aware typically sense that the storm projected is very much the storm in their own life. "The worse a storm is, if you really want to, it makes you stronger after. There are three times as many rays from the sun after the storm. I feel better. I overcame a lot of the storm. I'm coming through." Such verbalizations were elicited in the Projective Responsibility Inquiry (P.R.I.), an inquiry designed to more directly explore the patients' sense of responsibility for their projections and, at the same time, their general capacity for insight.

Finally, the concluding section draws forth the social implications of the Projective Tree Drawing Battery's findings in regard to the ubiquity of crisis. Methodologically, the Battery's contribution to the understanding of crisis, both social and personal, is promising in the context of the psychotherapeutic relationship. We close with the recommendation of the Battery's psychotherapeutic utilization.

CRISIS PROJECTION

Patients in the grips of crisis and able to express the experience give us every opportunity to feel their fright. They allow us to enter the inner world of crisis. We get to know what it feels like to be in the midst of a crisis struggle. Clinical examples, illustrative of such crisis projections elicited by the Projective Tree Drawing Battery, follow.

Case A: "Torn From The Earth"

For the expression of sheer, stark terror in a crisis-ridden patient, we turn to a 45-year-old female, diagnosed as suffering a bipolar disorder, going in and out of manic-depressive mood swings over the course of the Projective Tree Drawing Battery. In response to the Post-Drawing Inquiry of her Tree-In-A–Storm, she came forth with the following:

> Its all uprooted. It fears that its going to be blown away. Its torn from the earth. Its no longer attached down here. It's frantic. It's in despair. It's flying in all different directions. Its world is falling apart, because it's torn from the earth. It's screaming for help. . . .

The emotional intensity of this woman's inner turbulence is gripping. She hangs on for dear life. Her very psychic survival is at stake, and her

Figure 7-1. **Case A: Pre-Storm.**

Figure 7-2. **Case A: Storm.**

world is going to pieces. In a state of abject despair, she desperately cries out for help. The personalization of the tree, imbued with human qualities, bespeaks a loss of ego boundaries consistent with psychosis. Such psychotic manifestations were already evident in her associations to her Pre-Storm Tree Drawing:

> A dick tree. Ha! Ha! . . . A maple tree about 100 years old. It looks to me like a dick. Ha! Ha! This part looks like the balls. The trunk is the dick itself. It's kind of bare, except it has two birds sitting there. Two friends.

Although attempting to dismiss the seriousness of it all, she is giving us every reason to believe that we are dealing with a psychotic process. However, the nature of this patient's psychosis, as well as the depths of her despair, with a subsequent manic mood swing, did not become fully apparent until her Tree-In-A–Storm and Tree-After-A–Storm drawings. These drawings allow us to enter into a manic-depressive patient's mood swing.

Figure 7-3. **Case A: Post-Storm.**

The Tree-After-A–Storm actually takes on a human form. The foliage is transformed into a head; the trunk into a neck; the roots into a chest and shoulders. Such anthropomorphism signals schizophrenic ingredients. Coming out of her depressive phase into a manic and perhaps still more pathological state, she imbues the Tree with human motivation and mobility:

> It's happy that the storm is over. It's feeling on top of the world. It has birds singing in it. It's branches are going in an upward direction. It's in the summertime. It plans to go to Wildwood in Atlantic City because those are its playgrounds. It also escapes over there. . . .

Such projective test data enable the clinician to witness, first hand, the clinical phenomenon of a bipolar disorder caught at the very moment of a manic-depressive mood swing; and possibly worse. In this instance, the patient's drawings and verbal associations capture the profound turbulence of labile emotions and thought process reaching psychotic proportions.

Figure 7-4. **Case B: Storm.**

Case B: "Swept Away"

In our next case it will become apparent how the Tree-In-A–Storm taps into the graphomotor depiction of tumultuous emotions. Encouraged to ventilate internal crisis, patients have, often, been observed to eagerly express such crisis through visual imagery. This Hispanic woman of limited English thrusts herself into the task, spontaneously coming forth with, not one but, two drawings of a Tree-In-A–Storm. Figures 7-4 and 7-5 graphically display the magnitude of her crisis, which reaches traumatic proportions. In Figure 7-4, we witness an enormous tree under a darkened sky with leaves cast to the wind and limbs truncated. Birds are darting. The wind is blowing. Under a downpour of rain and threatened by a heavily shaded cloud, even a house is cast about. As if this drawing were not enough, she goes on to depict a second storm scene more ominous than the first. Swept away in response to the simple

Figure 7-5. **Case B: Storm.**

request to Draw-A–Tree-In-A–Storm, this patient puts on paper a truly traumatic scene. A fierce storm reaches hurricane proportions. A heavily shaded sky looms overhead. The scene is dark. Most foreboding, danger and threat are everywhere. The rain is a torrential downpour. Trees are uprooted. A frightened cat is on the run. Birds are darting through the sky. People in the house look terrified. Outside, a person is laid out. The scene is one of devastation!

Such drawings were found to reflect, all too well, her mental condition. Psychiatrically hospitalized, she appeared to have been traumatized. Although graphomotorically thrusting herself into the task, she could not really put her feelings into words. She had to excuse herself from group therapy. Visibly shaken, she could not verbally participate. A Post-Drawing Inquiry was not attainable. However, the drawings speak for themselves as to the magnitude of her traumata.

This points to the value of the technique when applied to the verbally inaccessible. Such patients can best, and sometimes only, be reached

Figure 7-6. **Case C: Pre-Storm.**

through such a projective technique which encourages the non-verbal depiction of internal agitation.

Case C: "Paul the Failure"

The theme around which crisis projections revolve is, frequently, one of devastation and despair. The patient's very world is shaken to the core. Is there hope? Is there salvation? The crisis can take the form of a spiritual one. Such was found to be the case in "Paul the Failure," which dramatically depicts the spiritual crisis of a schizophrenic inpatient. Self identified as "Paul the Failure", he weaves a story around the same tree through all three drawings. His associations are as follows:

Tree

Tree in the dead of winter. In the park. Dead of winter. No one around. Snow flakes falling off the tree. Nobody there. Nobody to see what it looks like. Nobody's out. (?) must have been standing there for a very long time. But nobody took notice of it. (?) winter time. So, the tree is sleeping . . . in hibernation. Protecting itself in the wintertime. So, it don't get destroyed.

Figure 7-7. **Case C: Storm.**

Figure 7-8. **Case C: Post-Storm.**

Tree-In-A-Storm

> Storm is raging in the same tree. Around the tree its very cold, windy. Heavy snows are blowing around the tree. The Tree, itself, has no life becau- se . . . The sign of the cross is protecting itself . . . protecting the Tree to let all those who look on know that one day the tree will be saved . . . eventually. Cold wind with snow and sleet mixed in through the Tree. The cross has a heart to protect the trees that are sick. It will be protected. It won't let nothing happen to it.

Tree-After-A-Storm

> The storm has stopped. It's grey. But the sun is trying to break through the clouds. That's the sun with clouds. (The Tree) is still asleep. Too cold to bear leaves or fruit. But, eventually, when the sun does shine upon it . . . with any luck, the Tree will perhaps produce green leaves and fruit.

As the drama of this Tree unfolds, the issue of its very salvation presents itself. "In the dead of winter," the Tree needs to protect itself "so, it don't get destroyed." In a raging storm, "Paul the Failure" spontaneously draws a cross on it "protecting the Tree to let all those who look on know that one day the Tree will be saved . . . The cross has a heart to protect the trees that are sick."

In his Tree-After-A–Storm, he draws a barren, split tree (a test sign consistent with schizophrenia (See Hammer, 1980 and Chapter 2 of this book) which, though suggestive in his first two drawings, did not become fully "split" until this drawing). "Too cold to bear leaves or fruit", the Tree stands under a darkened sun. Struggling against despair, "Paul the Failure" verbally projects out hope with " . . . eventually, when the sun does shine upon it . . . with any luck, the Tree will perhaps produce green leaves and fruit." This series of Tree Drawings allows one to witness, first hand, the spiritual struggle of a schizophrenic patient in a profound crisis. Clinically, the patient presents visual and auditory hallucinations. In group therapy, he witnessed the presence of his dead father and heard the sounds of his wedding. Plagued with a bad conscience, he "confesses" to having abandoned his wife. In deep despair, "Paul the Failure" struggles for his very salvation. This series of Tree Drawings allows him to give poetic expression to his spiritual struggle as well as to sensitize the clinician to his (the patient's) abject despair and longing for salvation.

Both patient and clinician are presented with the very real concern of the future outcome of this crisis. For the patient, hopefully "one day the

Tree will be saved." For the clinician, the question of the prognosis of this crisis and its consequences for the personality integrity of the patient cannot be avoided (i.e., the open split of the tree after the storm). To this clinical question of crisis prognostication, we shall presently turn our attention.

CRISIS PROGNOSTICATION

The perennial question presented by the patient is, simply put, "What is to become of me?" Stated or otherwise, the patient's pressing concern is one of fate. Apprehensive about the future, the patient presents to the clinician the question of prognosis. How will this crisis turn out? Fate hangs heavy over the patient. Crisis prognostication confronts the clinician.

Figure 7-9. Case D: Pre-Storm.

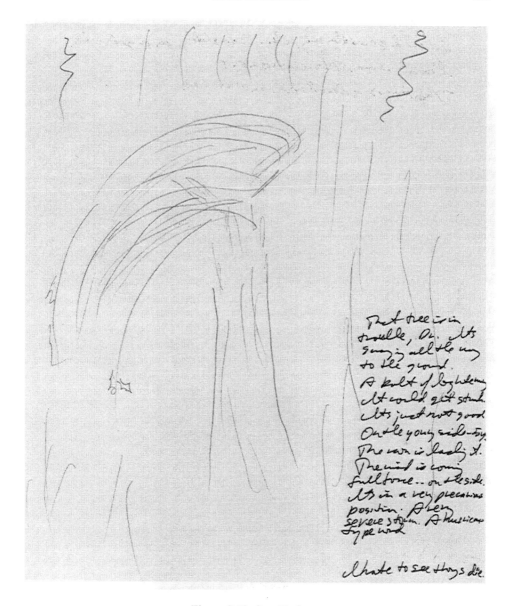

Figure 7-10. **Case D: Storm.**

Case D: The "Troubled" Tree

The next case is a 67-year-old female patient, in a severe depression, concerned with the fate of the Tree throughout her three Tree drawings. In association to her tenuous Christmas Tree, she came up with . . . "maybe

It lost a lot of leaves in the storm. The rain + the wind. Its got a hole in its bark. Its damaged like. But its survived the storm. But its going to take time to get back in top shape the way it was before the storm came. But the bark fell off, the wind was so bad

Figure 7-11. **Case D: Post-Storm.**

it will be chopped down for Christmas, if anybody wants it. I hope not because its happy in the forest where it is." Although "alive" and "happy," there is an undercurrent of concern. Although innocuous in its appearance as a Christmas Tree, there is a note of apprehension. Although the drawing, by itself, is not fully suggestive of what is to come, the patient's verbal association of apprehension about its fate is foreboding.

The value of the Tree-In-A–Storm and the Tree-After-A–Storm is that they bring out in full detail the seriousness of this woman's crisis and its potential consequences for her personality. In her Tree-In-A–Storm, we are witness to a "precarious" Tree buffeted about by an overwhelming storm. In the patient's own dramatic words:

> That tree is in trouble, Dr. Its swaying all the way to the ground. A bolt of lightening. It could get struck. Its just not good.... The rain is lashing it. The wind is coming full force... it's in a very precarious position. A very severe storm. A hurricane type wind. I hate to see things die.

Through this Tree in a storm, the clinician can experience the "storm" in this woman's life. Her crisis becomes palpable. One can see the "bolt of lightening"; one can feel the "lashing" rain and the "hurricane-type wind"; one can experience the "swaying all the way to the ground." Both Tree and patient are "in trouble." Both are "in a very precarious position." Her closing association, "I hate to see things die," fully expresses her apprehension about the Tree's fate. The clinical question of crisis prognostication is directly before us. For both patient and clinician, alike, the question is one of the consequences of the "storm." The request for the patient to draw a Tree-After-A–Storm is an attempt to directly address this question. Her Post-Storm Tree was found to be clearly damaged and split. In her own words, "It lost a lot of leaves in the storm. It's got a hole in its bark. It's damaged like. Part of the bark fell off, the wind was so bad." The damage suggests depression which is consistent with the clinical picture. Susceptible to morbid moods, she has yet to recover from the death of her sister. Preoccupied with death, she thinks of joining her sister. Consistent with the split tree is a grim susceptibility to psychosis. Reality offers little in the way of gratification for this woman. Life is grim. The fact that this damaged, split tree goes off the top of the page suggests that she has to reach out into fantasy for whatever supplies of gratification can be obtained (E.F. Hammer, personal communication, November 18, 1995). Sorely deprived, feeling damaged, and fragmented in personality, her crisis prognosis is bleak.

Case E: The "Uprooted" Tree

The Tree-After-The-Storm gives patients every opportunity to project out their sense of the consequences for them of their crisis. There are cases where it provides the only clue as to the crisis' after-math. In Case

Figure 7-12. **Case E: Pre-Storm.**

E, we examine the series of Tree drawings of a 37-year-old, psychiatrically-hospitalized, army veteran who had gone through a series of traumas, including his "failure" as a soldier and the death of his war hero father. The Pre-Storm Tree and the Tree-In-A–Storm give no indication of the patient's crisis and its possible consequences. His associations to the former were, "A big old oak tree. I would like to have one so I can use it for shade in the summer. 100 years old." His association to the Tree-In-A-Storm were. . . . " The rain still coming down. And the birds are coming back. Good (condition)." In neither of these drawings did the patient express a sense of crisis or apprehension about the consequences of crisis. The Trees were intact. The storm was negligible. In no way did these drawings anticipate what became evident in the Tree-After-A-Storm; an "uprooted" Tree that stimulated an association to his past military involvement. "That's the tree that fell over in the storm. We destroyed a lot of trees in the military because we needed to make a clearing. It's got to be still alive. It just got uprooted." The patient went on to talk about his failed career as professional solider. Unable to follow orders in the shooting of a civilian, he is a "traitor to his county." Unable to live up to the high military standard of his dead father, he is a

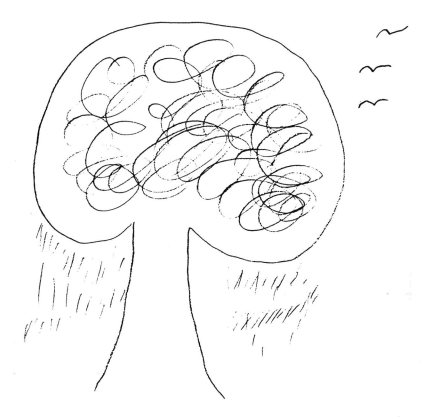

Figure 7-13. **Case E: Storm.**

profound disappointment. Apparently having been traumatized, he was diagnosed by the army psychiatrist as posttraumatic stress disorder. His Post-Storm Tree drawing served to express his posttraumatic condition. "Uprooted," he feels his life to be "past tense." Verbalizing as much in group therapy, he claimed to have "lived my life." Although his "tree has got to be still alive," it is "uprooted" and thus, traumatized, will not survive. Here, timing of testing is critical. One reading of the relative absence of crisis in his first two drawings is the possibility that he is not presently in a crisis. Rather, we are witnessing a man in a posttraumatic condition. It is only in his Post-Storm Tree drawing that we have a true reading of his posttraumatic stress disorder. The implications for the interpretation of these projective findings is that the clinician must take into consideration the timing of testing. Prognostication requires some clinical knowledge of where the patient is in regard to crisis at the time of testing. More specifically, the timing question for the clinician is

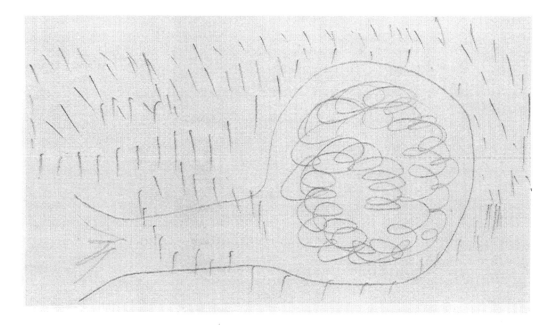

Figure 7-14. **Case E: Post-Storm.**

whether testing is done prior to, during, or after crisis. The results and their correct reading will vary accordingly. To demonstrate this point, we turn to our next case.

Case F: The "Tormented" Tree

In this case, testing was done at two different times—prior to, and during, crisis—over a nine month period of time. Dramatically different, the results speak for themselves as to the patient's respective conditions prior to, and during, crisis. There is no question as to which drawings were done while in a crisis state. Their prognostic implications become apparent.

This 37-year-old female patient, initially tested at a time of relative stability, drew a Tree with the following associations (see Fig. 7-15):

> It looks like a fairly healthy tree . . . it looks like it has a strong trunk and a strong base and a good set of roots. It's trying to put out new growth. You can see signs of new growth around the edges but the middle of the tree is filled with struggle. A pretty old tree. 100 years (old). The heart shaped leaves represent hope. The other leaves around the edge represent the tree trying to put out new life, new growth. All the jagged edges in the middle are the struggle.

Although she was not in a crisis at the time of this testing, she was definitely in a "struggle." A struggle for what? Hammer's interpretation

Figure 7-15. **Case F: Pre-Storm.**

Figure 7-16. **Case F: Storm.**

is most suggestive: "The tree is striking in its greater horizontal than vertical dimension. Trees generally grow upward more than side ways. This patient even has to turn the page 90 degrees to accommodate to the tree's expanding—greatly expanding—width. This may express the

Figure 7-17. **Case F: Post-Storm**.

patient's hunger for social gratification, by reaching outward into the environment (rather than grow and/or stretch upward toward achievement). But the tree's lateral openendedness suggests that this social gratification can't be maintained or made one's own. The patient needs more and more, because the satisfaction of such contact with others is ephemeral. This is all the more apparent when the conspicuous omission of closing the sides are viewed against the compulsive detailing of all the leaves" (E.F. Hammer, personal communication, November 18, 1995).

In point of fact, this patient has described herself as "emotional," "dependent," and "needy." She wrote, regarding her relationship with her father, "I'm so weak and emotional . . . I can't get his (father's) attention . . . (but) he'll love me and pay attention to me because I'm like a bird with a broken wing who can't help it, my wing, just got broken, it wasn't my fault, now please love me and help me and pay attention to me." Struggling to secure these emotional supplies, she is susceptible to the downward pull of helpless dependency. At the same time, she struggles against such vulnerability, defensively compensating with a display of strength and growth. Her Tree, "filled with struggle," is torn between weakness and strength. At the time of this testing, she was outwardly presenting herself, as in the case of her Tree projection, alive, vital, and hopeful. Looking "like a fairly healthy tree," she projects "a strong trunk and a strong base and a good set of roots." Representing the Tree as "trying to put out new life, new growth," she presents a picture of hope. However, nine months later, this picture dramatically changes. The Tree-In-A–Storm, reflective of this patient's crisis, has lost its identity in the storm. "Tormented" and "consumed," she associates (Figure 7-16):

> You probably can't tell where the tree leaves off and where the storm begins. So, I tried to define the Tree, make it darker. So, I made the storm darker, too. The tree is almost part of the storm. It is being consumed by the storm. It doesn't have any real roots to speak of. It's a very tormented tree. This tree doesn't have an age. It doesn't have an identity. . . .

Lost in the storm without roots to anchor it and threatened by lightening, this patient's crisis projection bespeaks a life threatening situation. Her very psychic survival is at stake. Directly confronting the question of crisis prognostication, the clinician asks her to draw a Tree-After-A–Storm, to which she responds with the following associations (Figure 7-17):

> That tree is alive but just barely. It is completely spent. . . . I wanted to say it's a very young tree. But, I'm not sure. It looks like it's so young and so tentative that it may not make it. (What is the impact of the storm on the tree?) Complete devastation, with a little hope of renewal. Uncertain hope of renewal.

Her true vulnerability and fragility are captured in this drawing. The "complete devastation" of this Tree-After-A–Storm, sequentially following the "tormented" Tree-In-The-Storm, sends off a warning signal to the examining clinician. The drawings are prognosticating imminent collapse. In point of fact, they did anticipate a "breakdown" in her condition. Eleven days after these Tree drawings, she came into the emergency room of a general hospital in a state of emotional collapse. Seen by the resident psychiatrist on call, she was immediately hospitalized.

Although this patient had sought out psychotherapy and had actually been in psychotherapy for some nine months, her condition did not improve. To the contrary, she regressed. Her crisis reached the breaking point. By having done so, it begs the question of psychotherapeutic efficacy and treatability.

Overwhelmed by crisis, the patient, herself, is questioning her "uncertain hope of renewal." Can she be helped? Although experiencing "complete devastation," she preserves "a little hope of renewal." The implicit question for the clinician is one of treatment prognosis. Is she amenable to psychotherapy? Crisis prognostication invariably confronts the clinician with the task of assessing the patient's psychotherapeutic treatability. For an inquiry into this pressing clinical question of treatment prognosis, we turn to our next section.

CRISIS AWARENESS: AN INQUIRY INTO PROJECTIVE RESPONSIBILITY

For over three-quarters of a century, this question of psychological treatability has been before us. Back in 1914, Freud had already drawn attention to the specific problem of negative therapeutic reactions. Noting the phenomenon of "deterioration during treatment" in *Further Recommendations in the Technique of Psychoanalysis: Recollection, Repetition and Working Through"* (Freud, 1914), Freud spelled out such negative therapeutic reactions as patients luxuriating in their symptoms, intensification of conflicts, secondary gain, acting out of conflicts, etc. Certain patients were observed to deteriorate in therapy; others, to improve. Why? What makes for the difference? For Freud, patient awareness was critical. Addressing "the patients conscious attitude towards his illness," Freud cited the necessity of the patient to pay "attention to the phenomena of his illness." Certainly, patient awareness of illness is necessary. That's why they come to therapy in the first place. Some of our patients are acutely aware; they do cry out for help. Nonetheless, they vary in their therapeutic response. Some prove responsive; others not. Awareness is not enough. Freud would be the first to acknowledge the limitations of awareness. He saw, first hand, the "aware" patient "luxuriating" in symptoms, wallowing in distress, clinging to illness and squeezing out every ounce of "secondary gain." Above and beyond awareness, what essential ingredient is necessary? Freud's 1914 paper is most suggestive. Drawing forth its implications, we will return to this Freudian text at the end of this section.

Twenty-three years later in *Analysis, Terminable and Interminable* (Freud, 1937), Freud elaborated on those difficulties and resistance's that make for the "negative therapeutic reaction." Presenting a veritable catalogue of such obstacles to successful treatment, ranging from repetition compulsion ("all that has once lived clings tenaciously to life"), to the "adhesiveness of the libido," to the need for punishment, to the instinct of destruction, to patient inertia, Freud cautions the clinician making a treatment prognosis. Treatment can be for better or worse.

A considerable amount of research confirming Freud's clinical impressions of "deterioration during treatment" has been conducted (Rogers, 1967; Tomlinson, 1967; Bergin, 1967; Garfield, 1986). Although this is not the place to review that literature (See Garfield, 1986, for such a review), a brief summation with implications for the question at hand can be provided. Rogers (1967) found that some of the patients in his psychotherapeutic research project actually declined. Tomlinson (1967), commenting upon this finding of therapeutic deterioration, noted that "... if therapy is cited as the agent of positive change in the more successful patients, then presumably it must also be cited for the negative change in the less successful patients ... this study provides evidence of the harmful as well as the salutary effects of psychotherapy." Bergin (1967) found that "psychotherapy can and does make people worse than their control counterparts (p. 137)." He concluded that "Those engaged in this field (of psychotherapy) should be more cautious and critical of their own practices, carefully eliminating any ineffective or harmful techniques. They should find out whom they are making worse or better, and how, with all due speed (p. 137)." Richmond (1992), in attempting to identify patient characteristics of those who prematurely terminate treatment, draws attention to the all too frequent problem of "psycho-therapy drop-outs." Finally, Tomlinson (1967) highlights the importance of "client selection" in psychotherapeutic prognostication: "The problem of client selection is now expanded to include identifying and selecting out those who may be expected to react adversely to a given type of therapy experience.... (pp. 333–334)." All of this leads to the compelling question before us of exactly what is it that makes for the difference between the successful and unsuccessful psychotherapeutic candidate. We know that "awareness of illness" brings people into treatment. We also know that such awareness, by itself, does not guarantee treatment success. Specific to our patients, what is it, above and beyond crisis awareness, that makes for psychotherapeutic success? Faced with a patient in crisis, the clinician's task of identifying the characteristic(s) which makes for treatability is all the more urgent. Sometimes, simple clinical clues can point the way. Projective drawings offer such clinical simplicity. The sheer poetry of expression, the visual imagery of symbol and the graphomotor expressiveness of stroke can be most suggestive. Such proved to be the case in the following example.

CASE G: The Tree That "Flowered"

This naive subject with little in the way of education and less in the way of cultural sophistication demonstrated remarkable "projective" intuition. Coming from an impoverished background in Puerto Rico, she had never heard of the projective technique process, nor had she ever read a page from the works of Sigmund Freud. Nonetheless, this 30-year-old female intuitively grasped the projective hypothesis. She readily gave poetic expression to her own past trauma. She spontaneously sensed the implications of her drawings for her own personality. Her Tree drawings, with the associations given prior to the development of the Projective Tree Drawing Battery, stimulated the very idea of drawing a Tree in, and after, a storm. In Figure 7-18, this 30-year-old female, while in psychotherapy, drew a Tree that had been traumatized and, now, was in the process of recovery. She associates to her Tree as follows:

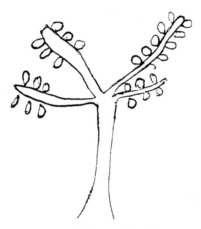

Figure 7-18. **Case G1: Tree.**

Just a tree. The regular tree that you find in the park. Middle-aged. Lived half its life. 25 (years old). It's losing its leaves, but its alive . . . When (a tree) loses its leaves, it rests and then new leaves fill it up again. (E: Tell a story about your Tree.) Well, you see, that was a regular tree. A couple of people planted it. It grew into a nice tree and there was a forest fire. The tree looked dead, but after all the leaves fell off it rested for a while and then it got new leaves and the tree was okay. (E: How does your story end?) It has a happy ending because it looked dead and everything but it got new leaves so that meant it didn't die after all (E: How old was the Tree at the time of the forest fire?) Oh gosh, it was about 20 (Figure 7-18).

Figure 7-19. **Case G2: Tree.**

Symbolically, this young woman is giving vent to a trauma that happened some five years ago. In point of fact, she had been raped five years prior to this testing, resulting in psychiatric hospitalization with the diagnosis of catatonic schizophrenia. The tree's relative barrenness and its subtle pull toward a split suggests vestiges of the depressive after-math persisting within a vulnerable personality susceptible to ego fragmentation. However, hopeful for recovery, she was found to reach out for psychotherapeutic help.

Some four months later, while in psychotherapy, she was tested again, coming up with the Tree drawing in Figure 7-19 and the following associations to it:

> Oh gosh! Well, that tree didn't have any flowers on it. And this is the first time that it ever flowered. It was never given the opportunity to flower because the people that had it didn't take care of it. (They) kept it in the shade. Then the tree was moved some place else and taken care of and it flowered." (E: How does your story end?) "Oh gosh. Its a good ending. I guess the seeds from the flowers fell and other little trees will grow next to it. And the moral of that

story is. sometimes there's nothing wrong with the plant. It's the people around it. Its the pollution that kills it.

As the Tree came alive and "flowered," she similarly blossomed in psychotherapy. Sensitively attuned to her past crisis, keenly aware of her present development and poetically expressive of her future possibilities for new growth, perhaps she has something to teach us. Amenable to psychotherapy, she may provide us with a clue to what contributes to such treatability. She certainly possesses the necessary therapeutic ingredient(s). She certainly demonstrated an awareness of past trauma. She certainly seemed to be aware of the implications of her Tree drawings with their revelatory associations for her own personality. In response to a direct inquiry into her awareness of the projective implications for self, she said:

> I feel like I'm waking up from a deep sleep. Being around a lot of people—talking to them—made me see things differently . . . open my eyes up a lot." "It (the tree) has leaves and it has flowers and it's the first time it ever had them and, I guess, that's how I feel, too.

The last sentence captures the very essence of the projective hypothesis. Acutely aware of her projection, she claims it as her own. It is her very self. In assuming projective responsibility, is not this patient demonstrating the capacity for self-responsibility? In owning up to her projection, is she not likely to own up to herself in psychotherapy? Is she not likely to prove receptive to psychotherapy. Is she not treatable? If such is the case, why not directly inquire into the patient's capacity for projective responsibility? Can patients acknowledge the projection of feelings into drawings (experiential projection)? Do they see any of themselves in their drawings (personality projection)? Can they learn anything about themselves from their drawings (projective exploration)? In order to probe into such experiential projections, personality projections, and the value of projective exploration, an inquiry has been developed to assess the patients' capacity to assume responsibility for their projections.

Procedurally, the Projective Responsibility Inquiry (PRI) follows the Projective Tree Drawings and their Post-Drawing Inquiry. After the patient completes the three drawings and associates to them, all are then laid out in front of the patient in the order in which they were drawn. The following Projective Responsibility Inquiry into the patient's experiential projections, personality projections and the value of projective exploration is then conducted:

PROJECTIVE RESPONSIBILITY INQUIRY
(A SAMPLE OF QUESTIONS)

I. Inquiry Into Experiential Projections:

Questions probing the patients' experience such as: "What was your experience of this exercise? How did you feel as you were doing the Tree drawings? Do you see any of your feelings in your drawings?"

II. Inquiry Into Personality Projections:

Questions probing the patients' awareness of their projections of self such as: "What do your drawings say to you about yourself? Do they have any meaning for you? Do you see any parts of yourself in your drawings?"

III. Inquiry Into The Value Of Projective Exploration:

Questions probing the patients' appreciation of projective exploration such as: "Is there anything to be gained from this exercise? Is there any value for you in doing this? Did you learn anything about yourself in doing this?"

One rather striking finding that emerges from the Projective Responsibility Inquiry is the high percentage of patients (two out of every three in this sample) who disavow responsibility. There are a goodly number of patients who simply reject the projective implications of their drawings, out of hand. Culled from the protocols of the following psychiatric inpatients, all of whom were in a crisis of one sort or another, are PRI responses devoid of any sense of projective responsibility. Such patients responded to the PRI's questions probing experiential projection, "How did you feel as you were doing the tree drawings?" and "Did you see any of your feelings in your drawings?" with the following:

> How do you mean? What do I feel?
> I feel retarded.
> Inept. I wish I had greater capacity. I have no ability whatsoever.
> Very nervous and not able to (draw). Hopeless its very belittling.
> I don't like doing this.
> I was expressing myself in a normal way.
> I feel its terrible. Cuz I can't think. My memory is gone. I think it's horrible. A tree doesn't look like that.
> I felt that 'myself' was not in the drawing.
> Anger. Frustration. I hate doing drawings ... Anything that I do that I do badly, I get upset.
> I never pretended to be an artist. My creativity involves accounting and record-keeping and measurement of financial data.
> I've got a lot of feelings for a tree. Like it's human. When they chop it up, I get sick.

Well, I don't like to draw. I don't draw well. But I did the best I could. And, I'm just co-operating.

I didn't have no feelings. Just did it. I drew three trees—in the rain and storm and a plain tree. I like the rain.

These patients responded to the PRI's question of personality projection, "What do your drawings say to you about yourself?" with the following:

Nothing cuz I'm always scribbling.
They say, I can't draw well.
That I have no capacity for drawing.
That I'm not capable of doing any art whatsoever.
I just don't like doing it. It says that I get frustrated easily.
The trees that I drew mean something about nature.
No. Not much.
I don't see myself in the drawing.
No. What they say is (that) I love art but I was so bad at it. I wish I could do it better.
These drawings don't say anything about myself.
I see that I can't draw well. I wish I could draw better but I don't know how.
I'm a very poor artist (Do you see any parts of yourself in your drawings?) No. (Do they have any meaning for you?) Just the rain. I walk in the rain. I like the rain.

In response to the P.R.I.'s question probing the value of projective exploration, "Did you learn anything about yourself in doing this?", these patients came up with:

No.
Hardly. If one has capacity, there may be some benefit.
No.
It has no value.
This art work was fun.
Not much. (?) Nothing at all.
Nothing further can I say about myself at this time.
No. I'm going to punish Dr. Miller for putting me through this.
This experiential exercise does not hold any real meaning (for) me on any level.
Yes. I'm going to be much, much better to nature than I am now.
No.
No. I always knew I liked the rain.

Although all of these patients were psychiatrically hospitalized and, presently, in varying degrees of crisis, they demonstrated little in the way of crisis awareness and less in the way of projective responsibility. Not only were they unreceptive to projective responsibility, they actively repudiated it. Feeling inadequate to the task, some of these patients turned on the task, itself. For them, responsibility resides outside of themselves. Their active repudiation and externalization of projective responsibility bespeaks a poor therapeutic prognosis.

In marked contrast to this repudiation of projective responsibility were those patients, previously presented, who struggled to assume responsibility for their projections. Acutely aware of their crisis, they did own up to their projections. For example, the female patient (Case A) diagnosed as a bipolar disorder whose manic-depressive mood swings were captured in her drawings and associations, responded to the PRI's personality projection questions of "What do your drawings say to you about yourself?" with:

> I'm a very intense person . . . I see features of depression. The downward strokes, heavy. A combination of depression and pleasure seeking . . . I have a tyrannical streak. And against people who don't know me I could turn extremely malicious. I could be vicious . . . And then again, it has something to do with depression. ("Is there any value for you in doing this?") "I learned about the make-up of my personality. Some of the make-up and traits.

In response to the PRI, "Paul the Failure" (Case C) was struggling to achieve projective responsibility as suggested by the following response to the experiential question of "How did you feel as you were doing the Tree drawings?":

> I feel that with my personal life, maybe I did not try hard enough and maybe there's no reason why the Tree wants to flower because I'm not working. But, then again, when I was drawing I heard noises telling me not to do anything rash. Not to say nothing that isn't true. But, this is the truth—that the Tree has no life to it now." ("What do your drawings say to you about yourself"?) . . . They're a reflection of what's on my mind. But, I seem so confused. People don't know the turmoil that goes on inside me.

Although apprehensive about his condition and what the future holds, "Paul the Failure" as well as Case D, The "Troubled" Tree, did acknowledge responsibility for their projections. Case D responded to the PRI with "I'm like that tree, Dr. I could go either way, Dr. . . . completely down or get better. I'm all alone." Even more succinctly, the army war veteran (Case E: The "Uprooted Tree), diagnosed as a posttraumatic stress disorder, responded to the PRI with "My life in a nut shell!" Although shell-shocked, in six brief words he owns up to his "up-rooted" projection in his drawings.

These patients, in their crisis awareness and assumption of responsibility, are likely to prove receptive to psychotherapy. We know that, in our sample, qualities that they possess are in the minority of patients. They are hard to come by.

And, yet, even with them, patients can "go to pieces." Although aware and receptive, such patients do not necessarily prove successful in psychotherapy. A case in point is that of Case F: The "Tormented" Tree. Acutely aware of her crisis, fully capable of owning her projections, most receptive to psychotherapy and actually being seen for psychotherapy at the time of crisis, she still regressed to such a state as to require hospitalization. She definitely was not getting better. And, yet, in response to the PRI, she demonstrated a considerable capacity for self-exploration. Her record was reflective and revealing. Her protocol reads as follows:

Case H: Projective Responsibility Inquiry

I. Inquiry into Experiential Projections:

"Anxiety. Real sadness. Real Sadness. Wanting to cry. Profound fear. The tree represents me, definitely. And I don't know what the future holds."

II. Inquiry into Personality Projections:

"That I'm feeling very desperate. I have a sense that I failed life, somehow. That, I can't do it. That, its too much a struggle to try and fight that storm." (Patient in distress. She goes from sniffles to tears).

III. Inquiry into The Value of Projective Exploration:

"I didn't expect the drawings to be that intense. I would have thought the tree would have been drawn more carefully and precisely and instead it was like a scrawl. An angry scrawl. Or desperate. I'm talking about the Tree in the storm, right now. The other one (After-The-Storm). The lack of faith that it portrays. It was as though I didn't even want to spend any effort on drawing it, much less being it. It did surprise me. When I do anything artistic I just let my feelings come out. I don't try to control it . . . "

We see a woman who demonstrates an acute awareness of her crisis and assumes a ready responsibility for her projections. We know her to be receptive to psychotherapy. And yet, it soon becomes apparent that she is in dire distress, on the edge of collapse. As we know, psychiatric hospitalization was imminent. This was not and has yet to be a psychotherapeutic success. Awareness of crisis and ownership of projections, although necessary for receptivity to psychotherapy, are not guarantors of success. Something more is necessary. What is that "something more"? What is the missing ingredient? To approach an answer to this question, we turn to Dr. H., the admitting psychiatrist of Case F.

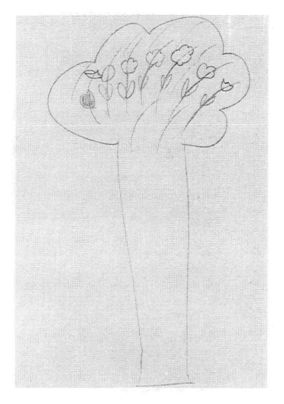

Figure 7-20. **Case H: Pre-Storm.**

Case H: The Tree That Will "Prevail"

Dr. H. presents us with the opportunity to expand the results and implications of our study. This is not so much because of what she has to say about Case F (in her immediate recognition of her crisis) as it is because of what she has to say about herself. For, interestingly enough, we have available Dr. H's own Projective Tree Drawing Battery protocol. This 62-year-old female resident in psychiatry had gone through a crisis of her own in her thirties—a serious bout of depression. She went into psychotherapy and has made a successful life for herself. She is presently in group therapy. At a time of stress, she consented to this present testing while in the middle of a two day psychiatry exam. Rather hastily produc-

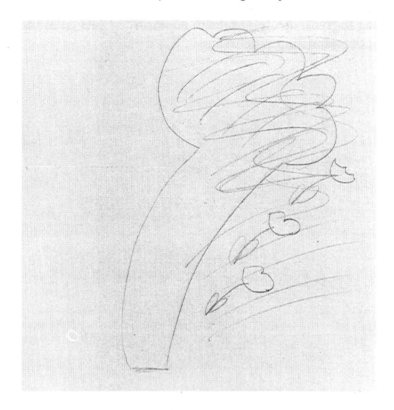

Case H: Storm

Figure 7-21. **Case H: Storm.**

ing the drawings (see Figs. 7-20, 7-21 & 7-22), she made frequent reference to her drawing performance inadequacies. Her drawings were simple;
her associations to them, sparse. They concluded on a theme of barrenness.
To her Tree, she associated, "It has flowers on it. It's blooming. It's tall.
It's got a straight trunk. It's a spring tree. I don't know how old it's
supposed to be." To her Tree-In-A–Storm, she associated, "Its a bad
storm. So, that the trunk is going over to the right side. The branches are
going off to the right side. All of the flowers have fallen from the tree.
They are coming down from various layers." To her Tree-After-A–Storm,
she associated, "Well, the Tree trunk is still bent over from the storm.
The tree is bare. Everything has been stripped from the tree. No flowers.
Its still alive. It's not flowering any more. The trunk is still to the side. It
has straightened out from the storm."

Although these drawings and associations are telling as to the impact

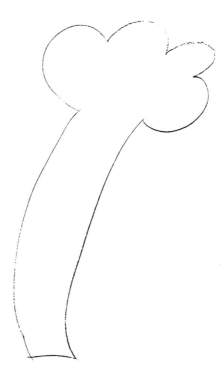

Case H: Post-Storm

Figure 7-22. **Case H: Post-Storm.**

of crisis, which is real enough, and as to the consequence of crisis, which is significantly experienced, they are not richly elaborated. To the contrary, they are underdeveloped.

Simple, sparse and unelaborated, they suggest a simplicity and immaturity of mind. There is something child-like about the drawings. One cannot quarrel with her self-described inadequacy in drawing ability. One might go on to infer a similar inadequacy and simplicity in mental development if one did not have the opportunity to explore her self-reflexivity through the inquiry into projective responsibility. Although seemingly running through the drawing task with very little thought given to it, the matter is otherwise, as we shall soon discover. Far from being mindless, this a woman who gives considerable thought to her actions. Far from being simple, this is a woman given to introspection. Assuming responsibility for what she feels to be "performance" inadequacy, she comes up with the following responses to the Projective Responsibility Inquiry:

Case H: Projective Responsibility Inquiry

I. Inquiry into Experiential Projections:

"Anxiety. Feelings of knowing that I can't draw. Feeling that I was going to be not a good performance. Wanting to do better and knowing that it was going to be a simple thing. Plus coming from the exam (Psychiatry). I haven't settled down yet. I can't really do this the way it should be done but I'm going to try and not make it a big deal. (?) What are you going to think of me with this effort."

II. Inquiry into Personality Projections:

"I have to go to this one (Post-Storm Tree). It is bare because everything is blown away. But it's still standing. I'm still standing. I'm ready to bloom again. I might be blown away a little bit but . . . It represents that the tree is strong and I am. I have fortitude and tenacity. I will prevail."

III. Inquiry into the Value of Projective Exploration:

"Yeah, I have allowed myself to be exposed even though I'm not proud of my effort. I'm glad that I could do it anyway. I know you're not going to criticize me. Nevertheless, I feel that you are going to judge me somehow. Obviously, I trust you because I wouldn't have done it otherwise. Mostly, I'm glad I could do it and not be afraid of how it was going to come out. Probably, it was a freedom, I wouldn't have allowed myself several years ago."

So, even though Dr. H. has been shorn of her "flowers," she is "ready to bloom again." Even though she is "bent over from the storm," she is "still standing." She may bend, but she does not break. She may feel less than capable, but she perseveres. She has weathered much, but, to this day, she stands "strong."

This is a woman who is engaged in the projective task. She struggles to assume responsibility for her projections. She is willing to expose herself to the implications of her performance for her personality. Although feeling inadequate, she does not run away from responsibility. She does not externalize blame. She does not attack the task. To the contrary, she confronts it. She affirms the struggle required in grappling with it. This affirmation of struggle characterizes her Projective Responsibility Inquiry. It sets her apart from Case F. It may well be the critical distinction between them.

For, otherwise, they both share in common, awareness of crisis and ownership of projection. They are, similarly, engaged by the "storm" and the consequences of it for the Tree. They both know what it feels like to be "blown away." However, whereas the "tormented" Tree ends up in a state of "complete devastation," the Tree that will "prevail" is "still standing" . . . ready to bloom again." One is in a state of imminent collapse; the other, prepared for growth. Dr. H., in her struggle to assume projective responsibility, affirms crisis as a test to demonstrate "fortitude and tenacity." Echoing Emerson's "Adversity is the prosperity of the great" and Nietzsche's "What doesn't destroy you will make you stronger," Dr. H. proclaims "I will prevail."

Freud: "He Must Find The Courage. . . . "

This case of Dr. H. brings us back to Freud's (1914) paper. We return to, and end, this section with the very passage wherein Freud addresses patient responsibility for engagement in treatment. It is a high task Freud sets before the patient who:

> . . . . must find the courage to direct his attention to the phenomena of his illness. His illness itself must no longer seem to him contemptible, but must become an enemy worthy of his mettle, a piece of his personality, which has solid ground for its existence and out of which things of value for his future life have to be derived.

To be fully responsible, the patient need possess courage. Awareness of illness requires courage. Ownership of illness requires courage. The patient is struggling with and against an enemy—the enemy within— that must be courageously confronted. This confrontation tests the patient's responsibility. Such responsibility is at the very heart of the battle being waged. The "enemy" within must be owned up to. " . . . a piece of his personality, which has solid ground for its existence and out of which things of value for his future life have to be derived." Not only need the patient become aware of illness and assume ownership of such illness, he must also find a way to affirm the struggle as well as the very illness itself. Implicit in such patient responsibility is valor. Up against an enemy worthy to be fought, the patient is put upon to valiantly struggle to achieve responsibility for the derivation of value from illness. Is the patient up to such a task? Is he capable of assuming such responsibility? This is the question addressed by the Projective Responsibility Inquiry. By directly inquiring into patient awareness of, ownership of, and valuation of his projections, we are assessing patient capacity to assume such responsibility.

SUMMARY, CONCLUSION AND RECOMMENDATION

This study has presented the Projective Tree Drawing Battery used in crisis assessment. Clinical cases, illustrative of crisis projection, crisis prognostication, and crisis awareness have been presented. Addressing the question of psychotherapeutic treatability, the issues of crisis awareness and projective responsibility have been explored. Clinical data, specific to projective responsibility, have been provided with their implications drawn for treatability. Projective responsibility has been presented as an integral part of crisis assessment serving to unify the inquiry into patient's awareness of crisis, patient's responsibility for crisis projection, and patient's valor in struggling with the crisis.

Although born and bred in an inpatient psychiatric ward, the Projective Tree Drawing Battery, as we have seen, is not restricted to psychiatric patients. The emergency room meeting between Case F and Dr. H was fortuitous. Although the patient came to the doctor in a state of crisis, the doctor, herself, had her own past experience with psychiatric crisis. Both patient and doctor shared, in common, the experience of crisis. As Terrence, the philosopher, put it, "Nothing human is alien to me." And, as Dostoevsky observed, "There is nothing I have ever read of in the newspapers, no matter how heinous, that I cannot find the same tendencies in myself" (E.F. Hammer, personal communication, November 18, 1995). Psychiatric patients do not have a monopoly on crisis. On coming out of confinement, one confronts the larger crisis of our times. As one patient, recently discharged, who had spent years in mental asylums, said, "It looks like everyone is out on pass."

Not only are our patients in crisis. So, too, is society. The social fabric is shaky; the moral structure, precarious. Symptoms are widespread. People, in and out of the psychiatric hospital, are in trouble. Addiction. Alcoholism. Homelessness. Illegitimacy. Criminality. Psychopathy. Malaise. The symptoms list is long. The distress, profound. The desolation, deep. Families go to pieces; communities dissolve. Rootlessness is the rule. The wasteland grows. In this age of angst, psychiatric symptomatology proliferates. People feel isolated, alienated, lost. Bereft of meaning in their lives, they sink into despair. Spiritually impoverished, they lack purpose. Depressed, they present symptoms of exhaustion, apathy, futility, suicide. Lacking insight, there is little in the way of crisis comprehension. All of this is of particular concern to the clinician, whether in or out of the hospital, who is besieged by such people in distress. One needs every tool available to diagnose and to prognosticate if one presumes to treat. It is suggested that the Projective Tree Drawing Battery is one such tool. It is no less relevant for assessing those in the larger society, many of whom, as enumerated above, experience "crisis," than it is for assessing psychiatric patients.

This does not mean that it is capable of addressing the larger crisis questions of this "modern eclipse" (Nietzsche, 1984). One does not presume to provide a causal explanation for the symptomatic consequences of modernity's "nihilism" (Nietzsche, 1884), "decline of the west" (Spengler, 1928), "flight of the gods"... "time of destitution"... "endless winter" (Heidegger, 1972), "revolt of the masses" (Ortega, 1957), "civilization and its discontents" (Freud, 1930), etc. However, one cannot avoid the living human casualties of these ills. They bring their crisis symptoms to us. We have seen them in this study. We have witnessed their struggles. Undefended, they are highly reactive to their world. Sensitized, they provide us with an emotional barometer of the times in which we live. Acutely aware, they are attuned to the modern distress. They bring us uncomfortably close to the pathology of nihilism diagnosed by Nietzsche in 1884, at which time he wrote in his notebook:

> My friends, it was hard for us when we were young: we suffered youth itself like a serious sickness. That is due to the time into which we have been thrown—a time of extensive inner decay and disintegration, a time that with all its weaknesses, and even with its best strength, opposes the spirit of youth. Disintegration characterizes this time, and thus uncertainty: nothing stands firmly on its feet or on a hard faith in itself; one lives for tomorrow, as the day after tomorrow is dubious. Everything on our way is slippery and dangerous, and the ice that still supports us has become thin: all of us feel the warm, uncanny breath of the thawing wind; where we still walk, soon no one will be able to walk.

Today, a century later, our patients give expression to this experience of collapse in their Projective Tree Drawings Battery's depiction of the Tree as:

> ...in trouble...in a very precarious position...sick...in the dead of winter...(having) no life to it now...(not having) an identity...(not having) any roots to speak of...so tentative that it may not make it...consumed by the storm...completely spent...very tormented...blown away...all uprooted ...in despair...frantic...flying in all different directions...(having) uncertain hope of renewal...(in a state of) complete devastation...torn from the earth...screaming for help...(in a world that is) falling apart...(portraying a) loss of faith.

Do not these patients bring us into the very heart of the crisis experience? Do we not come away with a fuller appreciation of the meaning of being in crisis? This "hands on" clinical study of live human beings in the throes of crisis enables us to penetrate more deeply into the experience. Those expressive ones, aware and responsible, are particularly illuminating.

Unhappily, the majority of our patients, although in crisis, were inclined to deny it. Not unlike the society at large, they were not able to confront it. Such crisis escapism represents a flight from responsibility and from the reality of their experience.

In this study, psychiatric inpatients, clearly hospitalized for good reasons, were inclined to repudiate responsibility for their projections. Some two out of three patients did so. In attacking the task, they externalized responsibility for their own performance. Perhaps, something akin to this is going on in the larger society. In repudiating responsibility, people are all too quick to blame "society" and/or the "system." It is not their personal crisis; it's "society's." Raging away against the perceived external causes, they do not look within.

Projective responsibility, whether amongst our patients or in the society at large, is hard to come by. And, for good reason. It is a hard task, a difficult task. Owning up to crisis is frightening. Assuming responsibility for one's predicament can be terrifying. Yet, unless crisis is looked at in the face, one will never face oneself. Unless one realizes that one is lost, one will never find oneself. The stakes are high. Lost at sea, one will, out of necessity, seek rescue. Salvation is in the balance. For a depiction of the self-acknowledged "shipwrecked" whose projections are "... the only genuine ideas," see *The Revolt of the Masses* (1957) where Ortega captures the very essence of projective responsibility.

Albeit rare, such a sense of responsibility holds forth great possibilities in a psychotherapeutic context. Does not psychotherapy, itself, request of the patient, awareness, responsibility, and valor? Is not psychotherapy a confrontation, of the "shipwrecked," with oneself? Applying Freud's (1914) text and its appeal to patient "courage," we are asking of the patient to pay attention, to acknowledge, to face up to, to assume responsibility for, and to derive future value from his/her crisis. If this is psychotherapy, then the Projective Tree Drawing Battery with its Projective Responsibility Inquiry could well be applied as a psychotherapeutic procedure—let us call it *projective therapy*. Such a *projective therapy*, in its confrontation of the patient with his crisis projections, will reap its greatest dividend from those capable of a fully developed projective responsibility. A flood of associative material specific to struggling with crisis may be anticipated.

This is not an altogether novel idea. Molly Harrower, an original contributor to *The Clinical Application of Projective Drawings* (1980), presented a similar idea 40 years ago in her 1956 article, "Projective Counseling—A Psychotherapeutic Technique" (1956). Using a variety of projective techniques, she presented patients with their projective productions—"raw material" (i.e., their own Rorschach responses, T.A.T. stories, or projective drawings)—as a therapeutic tool to elicit patients' associations. In addition to the elicitation of valuable associative material, she found it to result in the lessening of patient anxiety. Patients eagerly amplified and explained their feelings of relief. It was and is a good therapeutic idea. Patients in crisis could well benefit from it.

As a projective therapeutic technique, the Projective Tree Drawing Battery could be used in either an individual or group psychotherapeutic context. Most easily utilized in an individual therapeutic relationship, the technique could be applied as has already been presented. In a small group, the drawings as well as the inquiries could be done in an art therapeutic context. In traditional group therapy, the patients would be requested to do their drawings outside of and prior to a given session and come into that session with drawings in hand. With each patient taking his/her turn in group and presenting the drawings, the leader would conduct the inquiries. Fellow patients would be given every opportunity to present their feedback to a given patient. Therefore, patients in group would be exposed to therapeutic confrontation of their projections by, both, patients and therapist, as well as by themselves.

Needless to say, such a projective therapeutic approach possesses a potent potential. It should only be handled by competent psychotherapists, well qualified and trained. Such therapists should know their patients. They should be alert to potential dangers such as patient susceptibility to psychotic regression and/or traumatization. Many patients would not be receptive, such as those repudiating projective responsibility. This projective therapeutic technique must, of course, be handled with care.

However, in the right hands and with the right patients (who are capable of projective responsibility), both patients and therapist(s) stand to benefit. For the patient, there is a heightening of awareness of one's crisis situation. The patient comes face-to-face with the struggle. A searching examination of how one copes with adversity is encouraged. In this confrontation, the patient is called upon to employ one's resources. It represents a challenge. It is a test of one's strength. It provides an opportunity for the patient to give poetic expression to the internal struggle. In the process, a ventilation of pent-up affects in regard to crisis is facilitated.

The consequence for the therapist of such patient projective confrontation is a rich harvest of data serving to both prognosticate and guide the treatment. It cannot help sensitize the therapist to patient resources and vulnerabilities. It provides an internal view of patients' coping with crisis. The patient's experience of crisis, as well as resiliency in the face of same, is provided the opportunity for expression. Gaining entré into the inner world of crisis, the therapist is presented the opportunity to learn from the patient about this. For, after all, our patients, in this study, displayed a remarkable expressivity in regard to crisis. Both personal and sociocultural crises were tapped. The potential projective yield is considerable.

We have much to learn from our patients. They have much to teach us, particularly, those expressive ones capable of a realized projective responsibility. These give voice to the crisis experience. They picture it for us.

REFERENCES

1. Bergin, Allan E. (1967) "Some implications of psychotherapy research for therapeutic practice." *Int. J. of Psychiatry 3(3):* (pp. 136–160).
2. Buck, John N. (1980) "The case of R: Before and after therapy." In Emanuel F. Hammer (ed.) *The Clinical Application of Projective Drawings,* Springfield, IL: Charles C Thomas (pp. 276–308).
3. Freud, Sigmund. (1914). "Remembering, repeating and working through (further recommendations on the technique of psychoanalysis II)." In J. Strachey (ed.), *The Complete Psychological Works of Sigmund Freud. (Standard Edition) Volume XII,* pp. 145–156). London: Hogarth Press.
4. Freud, Sigmund. (1930). Civilization and its discontents. In J. Stachey (ed.) *The Complete Psychological Works of Sigmund Freud. (Standard Edition) (Vol. XXI,* pp. 64–145). London: Hogarth Press.
5. Freud, Sigmund. (1937). Analysis terminable and interminable. In J. Strachey (ed.) *The Complete Psychological Works of Sigmund Freud. (Standard Edition) (Vol. XXIII,* pp. 209–254). London: Hogarth Press.
6. Garfield, S.L. (1986). Research on client variables in psychotherapy. In S.L. Garfield and A.E. Bergin (eds.). *Psychotherapy And Behavior Change* (pp. 213–256). New York: Wiley and Sons.

7. Hammer, Emanuel F. (1980). "The House-Tree-Person Projective Drawing Technique: Content Interpretation." In Emanuel F. Hammer (ed.), *The Clinical Application of Projective Drawings,* Springfield, IL: Charles C Thomas (pp. 165–207).

8. Hammer, Emanuel F. (1980). *The Clinical Application of Projective Drawings.* Springfield, IL: Charles C Thomas.

9. Harrower, Molly. (1956). Projective counseling—a psychotherapeutic technique. *American J. of Psychotherapy, 10,* (pp. 74–86).

10. Heidegger, Martin. (1972). "What are poets for?" in *Poetry, Language And Thought,* (pp. 91–142). Quoted in Michael E. Zimmerman (1990) *Heidegger's Confrontation With Modernity: Technology, Politics Art.* Bloomington, IN: Indiana University Press.

11. Nietzsche, Friedrich. (1884–86). History of European nihilism. In *The Will To Power.* New York: Vintage Books (1968) (p. 40).

12. Ortega, José Y Gasset. (1957). *The Revolt Of The Masses.* New York: Norton (pp. 156–157).

13. Richmond, Raymond. (1992). Discriminating variables among psychotherapy dropouts from a psychological training clinic. *Professional Psychology.* 23, No. 2, (pp. 123–130).

14. Rogers, C.R. Gendlin, E.T., Kiesler, D.J., & Truax, C.B. (Eds). (1967). *The Therapeutic Relationship and Its Impact: A Study of Psychotherapy with Schizophrenia.* Madison, WI: University of Wisconsin.

15. Spengler, Oswald. (1928). *The Decline Of The West.* 2 vols. trans. Charles Francis Atkinson. New York: Alfred A. Knopf.

16. Tomlinson, T.M. (1967). The therapeutic process as related to outcome. In C.R. Rogers, E.T. Gendlin, D.J. Kiesler and C.B. Truax (Eds) *The Therapeutic Relationship and Its Impact: A Study of Psychotherapy With Schizophrenia.* Madison, WI: University of Wisconsin Press.

Editor's Comment:

Miller's point about the prevalence of distress in the general population suggests that with the non-hospitalized out-patient, his battery is also appropriate. We might specify, this is certainly so with the anxious and/or the depressed patient. But with the out-patient, I would suggest the stimuli *storm* be changed to *rain,* asking for Pre-Rain (which would already have been obtained in the H–T–P), Rain, and Post-Rain drawings, followed by Miller's devised fruitful suggested inquiry.

E.F.H.

Chapter 8

MISCELLANEOUS TECHNIQUES: THE DRAW-A-GROUP, AND THE INDUCTION OF MOVEMENT —VIA THE KINETIC FAMILY DRAWING AND THE KINETIC H–T–P TEST

The House-Tree-Person and the Draw-A–Person are unanimously, and certainly, regarded as the core of the projective drawing battery. In addition to the tool presented in the immediately preceding chapter, the Draw-A–Person-in-the-Rain, which received such substantial experimental support, and the Mother-and-Child Drawings with its illumination of object relations, other miscellaneous drawing tools which have recently come into being are the Draw-A–Group Test, and the *induction of movement*, this via the Kinetic-Draw-A–Family ("Please draw a family with everyone doing something") and the Kinetic-H–T–P ("Please draw a House, Tree and Person all on one page and with each in action").

DRAW-A-GROUP (DAG)

The specific possibilities of projective drawings for the evaluation of personality in a group context, whether group therapy or other group structures, was seen by N. J. Ferin who devoted his doctoral dissertation to this issue. Mining this vein in his study of groups of children, he uncovered four personality roles reliably reflected in the drawings: *dominance, dependence, aggression,* and *isolation.* Evident in Ferin's work is that the DAG is useful to the task of eliciting a subject's preferred or characteristic social role, and at the same time his phenomenological place in a group setting. Immediately apparent is this tool's value for selecting members for composing an effective or productive Group Therapy unit, and later down the road for evaluating changes in the members in response to the group therapy process, or at termination.

Investigating whether interpersonal role behavior of adults (as well as children, which Ferin demonstrated) are reliably and validly reflected in this drawing technique, Sandra McPherson (1969) established confirmation along the four dimensions (defined in observable terms) of dominance, dependence, aggression, and isolation. The findings were reassuringly confirmed at the .01 level of confidence.

THE INTRODUCTION OF MOVEMENT

Kinetic-Family-Drawing

Projective drawing techniques have become a bridge, of late, uniting psychologists and art therapists with a shared instrument of clinical assessment and of research. Buck's House-Tree-Person and Machover's Draw-a-Person techniques parented a rich progeny of projective drawing devices of which the Draw-a-Family and, in turn, its offspring, the Kinetic Family Drawings (K–F–D), now constitute the second and third generations. Robert Burns' book, *Kinetic Family Drawings* (1970), constituted this latter innovation's debut; *Actions, Styles and Symbols in Kinetic Family Drawings* (1972) offered a more detailed and rigorous shaping of the technique. The latest work (1982), while it does contain some basic material, constitutes more of a casebook to supplement the earlier books.

The instructions for using this tool are simple: "Draw everyone in your family doing something." The results, however, are often rich and dramatic, bringing forth, for instance, a child's panic in interaction with an alcoholic father, feelings of isolation in a stepfamily, or massive withdrawal from the threatening others in the household. The clinical yield, and the zeroing in on problem areas, are all the more impressive considering the short time expenditure needed to administer the technique.

The K–F–D's basic focus, and its special contribution when embedded in the psychologist's projective technique battery or in the art therapist's patients' free artwork, lies in the principle that how an individual sees himself within a family may be somewhat different from how he sees himself outside the family. It, hence, constitutes an available tool for diagnosis and ongoing assessment in individual and in family therapy. Practical uses include the K–F–D's contribution to decision-making concerning custody disputes, to determining if a child should be removed from his parental home and placed in a foster one, and to demonstrating to parents how their tensions and bickering may be specifically detrimental to the child-patient examined.

Dimensions elicited by the procedure regarding self and regarding family interactions are those of physical intimacy or distance, emotional tone in the family, pleasantness or unpleasantness in the home setting, and feelings of who is closest to whom. Are family members touching or are they isolated from each other? Which member is facing which other member? Are certain family members, or the self-figure, using one's activity to show off, or to hide, or lure, or become protected by a parent or sibling? Which family member is ascendant and which descendant? Which are sad, happy, suffering, bored, cruel, rigid, detached, enraged, subservient, or trusting? How do family members relate? Are they comfortable or strained with each other, and what are their messages, manifest versus latent, toward each other? Burns suggests, as hints to reading a K–F–D, that the clinician ask himself, and I would add we ask the subject, the following: "What if the drawing could come to life? What would be happening? Who would go, Who would stay? Who would nurture? Who would hate? Who would love? What feelings are flowing from the father, or mother, or siblings, or self?"

Burns uses his latest book to develop two central ideas. The first postulate is that the self-figure in the family setting drawing reflects the inner self whereas the Draw-a-Person figure depicts a layer of personality covering up the former more basic self-image. The K–F–D self is felt to represent an expression of the self as formed in early family life, i.e., the nuclear self. The clinical data sustaining this hypothesis are rather thin, one case, among others, even contraindicating it: The Draw-a-Person figure, in this case, radiates feelings of insufficiency and effeminacy and dandyishness, whereas the self-figure in the family setting assumes an impressive pose, lifting heavy barbells. The underlying doubts reflected in the Draw-a-Person (D–A–P), with the compensatory defenses suggested by the K–F–D self, appear to be layered, contrary to Burns' hypothesis, with the D–A–P the deeper and the K–F–D depiction the more surface appearance for which the subject strives. His fetish for women's shoes, in contrast to his pattern of excelling in sports, supports and parallels this in its implications of deeper and private effeminacy beneath the more public athleticism.

The author's second postulate, intertwined with the first, involves the view that the K–F–D self more closely portrays the child, while the Draw-a-Person portrays the adult, level of the subject. In support of this,

Figure 8-1.

we find the argument "We know, for example, if we score the mental age of the K–F–D self as compared with the mental age of the D–A–P self, the K–F–D self will score significantly younger." This leaves us, I fear, with a spurious deduction from observable data. The reason for the younger mental age of the K–F–D self figure may be found, more parsimoniously, in the fact that the Draw-a-Person is given more attention and detailing, as the single entity addressed on the page. This causes it to score a higher mental age than is achieved by each individual drawing (including the self drawing) of the family gestalt when usually four, five, or six people are included and each is given less time and attention than is the single figure of the Draw-a-Person. Approximately five minutes, I find, is usually expanded on the D–A–P and similarly on the K–F–D. As such, the former is given the full five minutes of detailed attention while, on the average, the K–F–D self-figure, as one of approximately five figures, is handled in only about a minute. Or should the K–F–D run ten minutes, that's still just two minutes for each figure.

Another issue now joins this line of discussion. Burns, according to his illustrations, administers the drawings in the sequence of Draw-a-Person, House-Tree-Person, Draw-a-Family, and Kinetic Family Drawing, a process that a subject enters freshly when engaging in the Draw-a-Person and often comparatively more impatient, fatigued, and bored with the repeated drawing requests by the time he comes to the K–F–D. He is, hence, prone to throw the latter off with less care or IQ-point-acquiring attention.

A smaller quibble: Reproduction of the drawings in Burns' book leaves something to be desired. All are printed with the same line pressure. There is no variation from the faint and tentative line through the firm and sure one, on to the heavy bearing down on the pencil which widens the line and gives the clue, in these extremes, to a digging at the paper. What is hence missing is a dimension of authenticity. The result is not only the loss of expressive data, but also an absence of a feel of the real drawings as the reader relates to the visual material.

Drawing inferences occasionally veer toward the arbitrary, as when the self-figure, facing the mother-figure, is interpreted in one drawing as the child "looks at the mother for guidance," whereas the same data are elsewhere interpreted as "looking to the mom for nurturing."

On the positive side—and I save this for the end because of its strong, rather than incidental, valence—the book shows an imaginative approach, at times even a playfulness which orchestrates with the serious intent. The work is essentially sensitive in clinical quality, sophisticated in research thinking, and rich in case illustrations.

> In Figure 8-1, 16-year-old George depicts a complicated picture. He appears to compete with the older brother, who is larger and dominant.* One notes However, that George repeats himself and is close to the father, who is "giving" him the pants in the family. The pants seem to be the symbol of manhood to George. The father is smiling and benevolent and facing his son. The strong, nurturant mother is witnessing the transaction and perhaps giving her approval. Again, the drawing suggests a closeness to the father and a willingness to "follow in his footsteps" and to copy him by accepting the gift of manhood.

Kinetic-House-Tree-Person (K–H–T–P) Variation

After Burns innovated upon the Draw-A–Family projective technique by devising its immediate, natural heir, the Kinetic-Family-Drawing (K–F–D), he next attempted to do the same with the House-Tree-Person

---

*We may also observe that the object in the brother's hand, while objectively a football, is altered somewhat toward an aggressive, missile shape to which George responds by raising his hands, not so much outward or forward as if to catch a ball, but straight up in the air as if *surrendering and complying* when being held up. This may be his relationship to his brother, and, eventually, predictively toward peers— whom, in turn, he experiences as threatening, exploitative and extractive. Thus, he submits, rather than as Burns says "competes," with brother figures.

(the subject is asked to draw the H–T–P all on one page and with all the entities in motion); but on two counts this becomes a strained affair.

His procedure of having the subject draw all three entities, House, Tree, and Person, on one sheet rather than each on its separate page is not new. We tried that, John N. Buck and I, as far back as the 1950s, and found it gained something (the relationship between drawn House, Tree, and Person), but lost something more; it lost the larger, more detailed projections, richer in subtleties and emotional nuances invited by more total time devoted to the three drawings, each on its own page, than to the one composite drawing with each of its three entities treated more briefly.

As for the attempt to add action to the H–T–P, this is theoretically certainly a productive idea, but in practice not very applicable. Houses don't move; trees can only sway (or maybe drop fruit). Let us survey next what happens with the Person, using the sample of K–H–T–P's in Burns' (1987) book, illustrations presumably chosen to make his point. Even here, when subjects are instructed to include "some kind of action," in the majority of cases the drawn person is not depicted in motion. Only 16 of 48, i.e., one-third, are drawn in any action—the single most frequent one consisting of sitting in a swing hanging from a tree, a choice determined presumably not as likely psychodynamically, as cognitively, i.e., determined by the task of thinking up an action linking a Person and a Tree or House.

The basic rationale of projective techniques also is to be considered here and suggests it may be better to leave the option of projection of movement open to the patient. The clinician is interested in whether the subject, when given no structuring from the examiner, projects himself as either an in-action, or as a static, being: with its pivotal identity, as well as energy, implications.

As one reads in Burns' (1987) book from one case to the next, one feels the hard sell of self-promotion. In each and every case, all 48 of them, the K–H–T–P is said to out-perform the H–T–P as the more revealing. Is there not a single instance of the opposite ever occurring? The data seem selectively assembled and/or interpreted biasedly. To take just one example, Burns says of the illustrated case, a woman with agoraphobia: "The House in this case is a place for survival and protection . . . Peggy prefers to be in her own territory and safe in her home." (This is the long and short of all the interpretation offered in this case, and adds nothing not already known from the symptom of agoraphobia itself—although to go the other way, the symptom does confirm the validity of the K–H–T–P with its depiction of the person hiding indoors and merely looking out the window.)

Figure 8-2. **Peggy's K–H–T–P.**

Figure 8-3. **Peggy's H–T–P.**

It is the H–T–P, in this case, which proves the more revealing. As the larger, more detailed Person drawing reflects, behind the phobic symptomatology, an underlying more ominous diagnostic integration is to be understood and addressed in the treatment: the schizoid. A wooden, lifeless identity defines the patient in her Person drawing. There we also note that without legs to stand on, without hands with which to contend with the environment or the issues in her life, without some of the necessary facial features, she suffers intense feelings of social inadequacy which, in turn, feed her agoraphobia. At the same time, the omitted essentials of nose and ears, reveal defective reality testing. This interpretation is backed up by the autism hinted at in the anthropomorphic H–T–P Tree with the suggestion of legs rather than trunk.

The bleak mood of the Person, with black, unseeing eyes and darkened body join the depression-indicating weeping willow drooping its branches, all adding a mood of despair and dysphoria also to be engaged in the therapeutic collaboration.

Burns is annoying when he takes a pejorative tone toward alternate techniques to his own, referring, for example, to the "stiff" Draw-A-Family (as opposed to the kinetic one). Why not call it the *standard* D–A–P?

The reviewer joins Louis Bates Ames, who provides the Forward to the book, in two of her reactions:

> (1) The author, one assumes, intends some of his fascinating but unusual interpretations as possibilities rather than as guarantees. One hopes that some of his interpretations will not be taken too literally. (2) Many of the author's unsubstantiated interpretations may be reacted to with wonder or even disbelief.

At times, Burns' statements grow confused, confusing, and contradictory. For example: "Buttons suggest a certain self-sufficiency. Buttons are often dependency symbols; when placed on the self, they usually indicate a person who takes care of himself." Which is it, dependency *or* self-sufficiency? They are opposites. So it can't be both.

At other times, he is simply wrong. Drawing the Person sitting indicates, he states: "Usually, persons trying to *get on* with their lives and trying to detach themselves from expectations or problems associated with the house (body/family/power)." Actually, clinical experience instead finds the sitting-Person drawing goes along with passivity, real or yearned for, or lethargy—particularly when this response is to the author's request for an *action* drawing.

Even more eyebrow-raising than much of the above is the author's version of Freud, whom he faults as inferior to his own champion, Abraham Maslow, whose "open system with its scope...yields more hypotheses than the relatively closed, unchanging, reductionistic Freudian system for so long applied to the H–T–P."

Maslow, of course, is more derivative of Freud than otherwise, so I don't see any conflict here. But, who more than the protean figure of Freud teaches us to unravel the multilayers of defense and impulse. No one's sense of personality illuminates for us as ably, the creature of lusts and of aggression inside the gray flannel suit. And without Freud (and Jung) the exquisitely subtle language of symbols—tapped by the projectives, by art, and by dreams—is virtually preliterate.

Is Burns' latest book all weakness and flaws? Not at all. Its positive quality is given, deservedly, the prominence of ending this evaluation.

Regarding the notion of the three drawings all on one page, while not the first to use it, Burns is the first to comprehensively study this variation and to document it. Here an extra dimension of the *relationship* among the three symbolic entities is elicited.

Adding a request for action in the drawings, when the subject does comply, may enliven the projective process and embody it with more dynamic quality, as it more clearly does with Burns' Kinetic-Family-Drawing technique.

A bottom-line evaluation: Readers would be wise not to be nudged by this book into by-passing the use of the standard H–T–P—with its larger, more detailed, close-up projective portraits—for the K–H–T–P. But if the latter supplements the former, one more dimension may at times be added, making the personality assessment all the more variegated and richer.

REFERENCES

1. Burns, R.C. *Kinetic Family Drawings.* New York: Brunner/Mazel, 1970.
2. ———. *Actions and Symbols in Kinetic Family Drawings.* New York: Brunner/Mazel, 1972.
3. ———. *Self-Growth in Families: Kinetic Family Drawings (K-F-D), Research and Application.* New York: Brunner/Mazel, 1982.
4. McPherson, S.B. Role behavior and group concept in drawings. *J. Proj. Tech. & Pers. Assessment,* 33, 1969, 45–48.

CHILDREN'S
PROJECTIVE DRAWINGS

Chapter 9

DRAWINGS BY CHILDREN AND ADOLESCENTS*

It is hard for us when we are young: we suffer youth itself like a serious illness.
                                                                    —Nietzsche

T he drawings of children, in addition to doing service as a projective
    technique, attain value on a larger plane. They reflect universal,
basic, primitive, representational processes of symbolization in man and
at the same time, in this manner, constitute *art* in its own right. It was in
recognition of this universal, basic dimension that Pablo Picasso honored
children's creations by commenting: "Once I drew like Raphael, but it
has taken a whole lifetime to learn to draw like a child (again)."

By looking back and forth at children's artistry and at Picasso's, we
resonate to their mutual magic in full flower, at least in some and in
certain of the children's work. Picasso knew which compass to turn to in
directing his own artistic development. By going back, he learned to go
forward.

In returning to childhood, in the world of art, Picasso was not alone.
Marching along with, and in step with, him we find Fineberg (1995)
(indicates in his aptly titled *The Innocent Eye*), Dubuffet, Klee, Kandinsky,
Matisse, Miro, and others.

Garry Trudeau (1995), the creator of the comic strip *Doonesbury*,
turning his talents to a more academic topic, is also interested in the
above process. As a parent, he reports, he was totally unprepared to be so
charmed by his children's art, which he had earlier come to praise as a
mere matter of devotion. Noting the "astonishing art" that "explodes"
between the ages of six and eight, he observed: "Vibrant, rhythmic,
balanced and, above all, expressive, the art of the young does more than
delight; it can—and often does—inspire."

Children have a way of getting to the heart of a situation, and projective drawings have a way of getting to the heart of the child. Hence, we

*Reprinted, with major revisions and additions, with permission from Rabin, A. & Haworth, M. (Eds.),
Projective Techniques with Children, 1960, Thiese Med. Pub.

are struck with the tendency for child projective drawing case studies to be particularly fascinating. They are so comparatively rich, so open, undefended and revealing (note, for example, Dr. Finger's child case).

Children like to draw! When projective drawings are included in the battery, they take quite readily to this task, since drawing is a favorite play activity. For the child, the request to draw is very likely to reduce tension in the psychological examination. He or she responds to it with pleasure and enthusiasm as well as with feelings of security, for it is an activity in which youngsters feel at home.

FUNCTION OF DRAWINGS

Within the projective battery, drawings thus serve a special function by providing a minimally threatening yet maximally absorbing introduction to the testing procedure. If employed as the first projective technique in the battery, drawings serve as an easy bridge to the clinical examination; the drawing task allows uncomfortable subjects to exclude the examiner, in a relative sense, during the initial phase of getting used to the new surroundings and to the stranger on the other side of the desk. To borrow from the observations of a nonprofessional psychologist, one may note that Winston Churchill[23] speaks of drawings as "complete as a distraction." He continues, "I know of nothing which... more entirely absorbs the mind.... All one's mental light such as it is, becomes concentrated on the task."

The writer has found that children with emotional difficulties can be led more easily from drawing to verbal expression. Drawings also serve as a means of more easily establishing rapport and are a good "ice breaker" with the children—especially the shy ones. Or the negativist ones.

The psychologist, Howard Gardner (1980), at Harvard, that keen observer of children, reports in his book *Artful Scribbles: The Significance of Children's Drawings,* in congruence with Churchill, that children engaged in drawing are by and large quite "engrossed." The sense Gardner makes of this absorption is that via drawings children are "trying to make sense of their world, and of their own thoughts and feelings" (p. 12); and again, "The child who first wields a marker (pencil or crayon) is learning, in many areas of his young life, about tool use" (p. 14).

While Churchill's words pertain to the adult who is into drawings, most adults are not. But, on the other hand, most children are. Thus, with adult subjects—subjects tending to feel inept, awkward, uncomfortable, and hesitant when asked to draw—when administrating the projective technique battery, I put the verbal tools, Rorschach and Thematic Apperception Test, first, and then follow with the projective drawings. With children, on the other hand, I customarily reverse the sequence starting off with drawings where there is less relationship and verbalizing required to the other person in the room on the other side of the desk. An adult and an unfamiliar one at that. And in charge! Thus, for this reason, with children, I try to avoid the title *doctor.*

Both children and primitive people consistently draw elements which they consider essential and drop out others which do not concern them. They then include aspects which are known to be there but are not visible. The goal, thus, of both child and primitive (and also, we may note, of the genius, Picasso) is not "objective realism" but what Luquet calls "mental realism."[22]

As for Picasso and other artists, and children as well, the poet William Carlos Williams speaks of them extending the immediate and lasting personal expression to a universal dimension that often deepens art: "It is ourselves we seek to see on the canvas, as no one ever saw us, before we lost our courage and our love."

PROJECTIVE ASPECTS OF DRAWINGS

The drawing page serves as a canvas upon which the subject may project a glimpse of his or her inner world, traits and attitudes, behavioral characteristics, personality strengths and weaknesses. Children find it easier to communicate through drawings than through the verbal projective techniques much that is important to them and much that troubles them.

Projective drawings, basically a nonverbal technique, have the obvious advantages of greater relative applicability not only to young children but to the more poorly educated child, the mentally defective child, the non-English-speaking child, the mute, the painfully shy or withdrawn child, the child with a predominantly concrete orientation and the child from a relatively barren and underprivileged sociocultural background who frequently is wracked by feelings of inadequacy concerning his capacity for verbal expression. In addition, we may add to this list the case of the child referred for a psychological evaluation because of remedial reading problems. Bender[2] points out that children with reading difficulties often show compensatory adeptness in artistic ability to make articulate their emotional and social problems and needs.

Some children draw parent figures and use as their emotional palette their feelings toward mother or father, portraying that portrait which proclaims the child's affections and also transmutations of the youngster's conflicts and hostilities. The drawer transforms the portrait, as to some degree all artists do, in the painter Rubens' words, "from a purportedly objective document into a frankly subjective one."

At first, drawings were employed by clinicians as a form of intelligence scale based mainly on the number of details put into the drawings. Soon, however, it became apparent that the drawings were tapping personality factors in addition to intellectual capabilities. In fact, emotional factors even more than intellectual ones were constantly pressing into view.

The writer recalls a child who had to walk with the aid of crutches. When asked to draw a Person, although he did not draw someone leaning upon crutches, he did draw an extra line suggesting a long spike extending from the heel of the shoe into the ground, as if through this device to gain greater stability of posture than the subject himself experienced. While the subject was not consciously drawing himself, he nevertheless projected his inner feeling that one cannot stand without the help of something additional upon which to lean. His need for physical bolstering pressed forward onto the drawing page.

Another subject, who was born missing his left arm, though he did not draw a one-armed Person, did give a distinct treatment to the left arm of the drawn Person which rendered it withered, foreshortened, crippled and conspicuously less effective than the right arm. When asked to draw a Tree, he drew one in which a truncated limb protruded from the trunk of the Tree. And if additional support for the projective thesis be needed, the amputated limb of the tree appeared on the same side as both the missing limb of our subject and the crippled arm of the Person he drew.

We have observed that obese children tend either to draw obese-looking Persons or else to fly to the other extreme—representation of an extremely lithe, slim and/or athletic looking Person. The depiction of an ego-ideal represents a more positive prognostic indication. Such children, it has been found, still actively entertain ideas of conquering their weight problem and have not yet given in to a self concept involving sluggishness, passivity, and overweight.

We find in children, actually, the same principles of interpretation, the same language of symbolism, as pertain in adults' drawings. Only the frame of reference differs. Thus, for example, the signs of dependency, including a large or otherwise emphasized sun (representing a warmth-giving entity from above as a parent might be), or exaggerated detailing of buttons (emanating from the meaning of the belly button as the umbilical, primary, earliest connection to one's mother), to mention two such signs, are indicative of such dependency needs in both children's and adults' drawings. But, normative perspective tells us that such dependency signs are normal in the former drawings but neurotic in the latter, i.e., reflective of normal dependency in childhood and of excessive and neurotic dependency in adulthood where this should have been long since outgrown, generally by preadolescence.

In terms of expressive aspects, children's movements have diagnostic potential whether they are gross (as in the play therapy room) or confined (as on the drawing page). A child may withdraw into a corner of the room or sit on the edge of the chair, as though he were ready to run away; if he is given a big sheet of paper, he may follow suit by drawing cautiously in one corner of the page only. At the other extreme, a child may sit at a table as though he wished to occupy the whole space, showing no consideration for the other children there. No paper is big enough for him either, and his drawings expand beyond the drawing sheet. Projective drawings thus "capture" and record expressive movements on paper.

The size of drawings is a particularly important variable with children. Those children who draw small, or even tiny, objects and Persons tend to suffer from intensified awareness of the fact that they live as pigmies in a world of giants. Their Persons are drawn as weak and insignificant and are protected or reinforced by guns, canes, etc. Feelings of inferiority and insignificance have been more deeply ingrained, via interpersonal experiences, in such children than in those who draw with adequate size. Whereas the aggressive child draws big, dangerous arms with long fingers, the inadequate or withdrawn child forgets to draw hands at all—as though the subject had not experienced helping hands when he needed them, or as if one's own hands were guilty things which may be used to do something which is labeled as taboo in our culture.

With adolescents, we find their projective protocols are characterized by two striking emphases more than any other: they are more earthy and they are more flooded with the expression of the impulses, as is the adolescent him or herself. As a function of the impulses, often raw and unvarnished, the drawings also reveal more potential for acting out, again as is possessed by the adolescent him or herself (see Chapter 3).

As a reflection of their virility strivings, (adolescent males) frequently draw soldiers or cowboys as symbols of status attained through the use of force and aggression. One child who was referred to the writer because of excessive truancy, the flaunting of rules in school and generally rebellious behavior reflected his characteristic role in life in his drawing of a Person. As a reflection of the subject's need for greater status, prestige and recognition than he felt he possessed, the drawn male was dressed in a soldier's outfit with his back turned on the world, bigger and better than he inwardly felt, looking more masculine and snubbing the needs and expectations of others.

Adolescent girls project themselves in gowns, or in bathing suits, as shapely, or particularly during prepuberty, carrying flowers.

With adolescents, drawings assume the character of an overemphasized, exaggerated portrait of strength or importance. Within the normal range, adolescents tend to draw persons as more forceful, more glamorous, bigger, or older than they themselves actually are—a depiction indicative of their own wishes about themselves. They put into the picture a promise of that reality which they desire and toward which they strive.

Before leaving the topic of size, Figure 9-1 may serve as an example of a drawing reflecting acute feelings of psycholog cal tininess. The figure is so small that the reader may have trouble locating it; it will be found at the very bottom, center, of the drawing page.

Whereas some children portray small figures as a graphic reflector of feelings of inadequacy, Figure 9-1 reflects feelings of total insignificance. Not only by the miniscule size, but also by the light line pressure* which causes the drawn Person to all but fade from view, our subject conveys to us his feelings of being wholly without worth, status or recognition as a person. He feels painfully constricted and in danger of being totally overlooked by others.

Figure 9-1 was made by a 12-year-old boy with fully an IQ of 150. His father held a Ph.D. in one of the social sciences, and his mother a master's degree in an allied area. They so pushed the child to attainments above even his clearly superior capabilities that he soon crystalized the self concept of someone who was, by comparison with these high

---

*The actual drawing was considerably fainter than was reproduced by the photographer in his efforts to make it more visible.

Figure 9-1. **Person, by 12-year-old boy.**

standards, clearly inadequate. Obvious preference was shown to the subject's younger sibling, which served to reinforce the subject's feelings of insignificance as a person. Also, his parents held to the philosophy that watching TV, reading comic books or drinking a soda would spoil the child. Here, too, their behavior led him to believe that his needs were to be forever overlooked, just as the drawn Person he rendered is so easily overlooked. Close inspection of the drawing reveals inadequate, puny arms that cannot accomplish anything for himself, a head that is looking down in dejection and a sad facial expression.

ADMINISTRATION

A No. 2 pencil and a sheet of paper are handed the subject. His or her drawing of a House is requested with the longer axis of the sheet placed horizontally before the subject. The child's drawings of a Tree and Person, in turn, are then obtained on separate sheets of paper with the longer axis placed vertically. The subject is asked to draw as well as he or she can, but is not told what kind of House, Tree and Person to draw. If the subject protests that he or she is not an artist, the child is assured that the H–T–P is not a test of artistic ability at all but that we are interested, rather, in how one does things. Any questions asked are reflected back to the drawer in such a way as to indicate that there is no right or wrong method of proceeding but that one may do the drawing in any manner one wishes.

After drawing the Person, the subject is then handed another sheet of paper and this time told to draw a Person of the sex opposite to that of the first Person drawn. In addition, in pencil again, the subject may be asked to draw the most unpleasant thing he or she can think of, to draw a person in the rain, or to complete or make a drawing from certain lines which serve as stimuli (The Drawing Completion Test). With children, we may occasionally also ask for a drawing of a family and/or a drawing of an animal (Hammer, 1958).

HOUSE

The House, as a dwelling place, has been found to arouse within the subject associations concerning home life and intrafamilial relationships. In children, it has been found to tap their attitudes concerning the home situation and their relationships to parents and siblings. One child drew a House with profuse and very heavily shaded smoke pouring forth from the chimney as a reflection of the hot and turbulent emotional atmosphere this youngster experienced in the home situation.

TREE

The drawing of the Tree appears to reflect relatively deeper and more unconscious feelings about oneself, whereas the drawn Person becomes the vehicle for conveying the closer-to-conscious view of oneself and one's relationship to one's environment. In this manner, the elicited conflicts and defenses may be assigned to levels in the hierarchy of the subject's personality structure.

The view that the Tree taps more basic and long-standing feelings is supported by the fact that the Tree is less susceptible to change on retesting.[4,11] Whereas psychotherapy of a nonintensive kind will frequently bring improvement as indicated by the decrease of pathologic signs in the drawn Person, only deep and extensive psychoanalytic collaboration (or highly significant alterations in a life situation) will produce any but minor changes in the Tree.

Clinical experience also suggests that it is easier for a subject to attribute more conflicting or emotionally disturbing negative traits and attitudes to the drawn Tree than to the drawn Person because the former is less "close to home" as a self portrait. The deeper or more forbidden feelings can more readily be projected onto the Tree than onto the Person, with less fear of revealing oneself and less need for ego-defensive maneuvering.

A subject may, for instance, more readily and unwittingly portray a feeling of emotional trauma by scarring the drawn Tree's trunk and truncating its branches, than by a parallel mutilation of the drawn Person's face and body and similar distortion of the drawn Person's arms.

The clinical finding that forbidden feelings can be projected more readily onto the Tree than onto the Person is similar to the rationale behind Blum's Blacky Picture Test, Bellak's Children's Apperception Test and the Despert Fables. The animal figures in these thematic techniques seem to lend themselves to the projection of deeper and more negative feelings (with less threat to the subject) than do the human figures of the TAT.

Thus, a comparison of the subject's responses to the animal as opposed to the human TAT-type stimuli and a comparison of the subject's drawn Tree with the drawn Person provide data which enable the clinician to appraise the relative levels from which the subject's different projected feelings come.

Adolescents often draw aggressive Tree drawings. Some, in contrast, depict beaten-up, mutilated, damaged, or scarred entities. The former expresses an image of oneself as the initiator of hostility, the latter as the victim, occasionally masochistically, of it.

A noteworthy instance of scarring that the writer encountered was offered by a 12-year-old boy. He placed a ravaging wound approximately half-way up the height of the Tree trunk. Subsequent psychotherapeutic collaboration with the youngster revealed that his mother's death, occurring when he was five years of age, was unconsciously felt as an abandonment and left him with a deep hurt. This feeling of an aching wound was etched deeply into the self portrait which his drawn Tree represented.

If the projective examination occurs some weeks after the initial phase of psychotherapy has begun, it is frequently found that the Tree trunk itself is truncated and that tiny branches grow from the stump. This type of Tree drawing reflects stunted emotional growth, but with beginning — although tentative and rather feeble — efforts at regrowth, stimulated by the initial phase of the therapeutic relationship. Some of these children, at the completion of therapy, render Tree drawings whose full bloom express their regained feelings of capability, fulfillment and optimism regarding future, continued growth.

In children's drawings particularly, branches are sometimes drawn as if reaching appealingly to the sun. This has occurred with those youngsters who have shown other evidence of marked and frustrated needs for affection. The Tree stretches out its arms hungrily for warmth from some significant authority or parent figure.

Occasionally a child will draw a Tree as bending away from a large and low-placed sun, which seems to be bearing down upon it. This depiction is offered by subjects who shy away from domination by a parental or other authority figure who makes the subject feel painfully controlled, subjugated and inadequate.

PERSON

In regard to theme, the drawing of a Person tends to elicit principally three types: a self portrait, an ideal self, or a depiction of one's perception of significant others (parents, siblings, etc.).*

---

*(This is touched upon in the Section "Research Studies and Research Issues" but bears summary here.)

Self Portrait

The subject draws what he feels himself to be. Body contours, whether obese or thin, areas of sensitivity such as a hooked nose, a cauliflower ear, a pockmarked skin, or a club foot are often reproduced faithfully and exactly in the drawn Person. Subjects of average or below average intelligence will usually reproduce these features upon their drawn Persons in mirror image, i.e., if the subject has a withered right hand, he will reproduce this condition on the drawn Person's left hand.* Abstract ability allows the nonmirror image depiction, i.e., the subject's right side to be portrayed by the drawn Person's right side, and is seldom found in subjects of less than high average intelligence.

It has been noticed, however, that physical flaws or disabilities are reproduced in the drawing of the person *only* if they have impinged upon the subject's self concept and have created an area of psychological sensitivity.

Along with his projection of feelings of physical defects, the subject *also projects his assets:* broad shoulders, muscular development, attractive physiognomy. This is done to the point at which an amazing likeness frequently results, even in artistically incapable individuals.

In addition to the physical self, the subject projects a picture of the psychological self into his drawing of the Person. Subjects of adequate or superior height may draw a tiny figure, with arms dangling rather helplessly away from the sides and a beseeching facial expression. Here the subject is projecting his psychological view of himself as tiny, insignificant, helpless, dependent and in need of support, his physical self notwithstanding.

Other examples are: the toppling Person, losing equilibrium, offered by a preschizophrenic child; the manikin-like clothes dummy suggesting feelings of depersonalization; the adolescent's drawn Person carrying a baseball bat in one hand, a tennis racket in the other and wearing a mustache on his lip, revealing by his yearning for so many badges of virility his underlying feelings of inadequacy in this area; the drawing of a clown as a fusion of the child's attempts to depict the harmlessness of his instinctual impulses and the secondary use of this concept as an attention-getting maneuver; the reduced energy and drive suggested by the drawn Person slumped into a chair or sitting on the curb of the

---

*As if looking in a mirror.

street—all these themes support the thesis that the drawn Person represents a psychological self portrait, not only a physical one.

Ego Ideal

Rather than a picture of what the subject presently feels him- or herself to be, the child may draw an ego ideal.

A slender, rather frail, intensely paranoid boy drew a boxer whose shoulders, before he was through, extended to the dimensions of a Hercules.

An unmarried, pregnant, 15-year-old girl, suffering feelings of terrible shame in regard to the stomach contour which was so revealing of her condition, drew a lithe, graceful, slender dancer twirling unencumbered by any burden.

Adolescent boys frequently draw muscular athletes attired in bathing suits, and adolescent girls draw female movie stars wearing evening gowns—the ideal states often longed for by adolescents. Healthy children tend to draw Persons two or three years older than their own ages as an index of their striving for forward growth.

Significant Others

The subject depicts a significant person in his contemporary or past environment, usually because of that person's strong positive or negative valence for the subject. This pressing forward into the drawing page of the subject's perception of significant figures in the environment, in contrast to the perception of one's self, occurs more often in the drawings of children than of adolescents or adults. (At times the same drawing may yield a fused image of self and others.) The "other" Person children represent in their drawing is almost invariably a parental figure and represents the great importance of the parent in the child's life and the need for a model to identify with and to incorporate into one's self concept. The kind of mother or father figure the child reveals in the drawing is often a prophesying element and predicts the traits which retest drawings, years later, frequently indicate the child incorporates.

One 8-year-old boy, referred because of excessive bullying of his classmates, drew a man who was menacing in every aspect: bared teeth sharpened to a point, a club in one hand, the other hand coming to an end not in conventional fingers but in a clear depiction of what looked like the ends of scissors—a weapon which might shear off and do damage to vital parts of the subject. The social worker's investigation of the father revealed that he was a despot in every way, cruel, punitive and domineering. The bullying attitudes the subject had picked up suggested that he had already begun to defend himself against the threat of the destruction-invested father through the mechanism of incorporation. In an understandable self-protective maneuver, he donned his enemy's cloak so that he could put himself out of harm's way. He became the bully, rather than the bullied. The process of incorporation became the bridge across which the subject sought to travel to comparative safety.

In this manner, projective drawings tend to reveal the felt self, the ideal self and—one is tempted to say—the future self (barring the intervention of psychotherapy or significant changes in the environmental situation).

USE OF CRAYONS

The chromatic phase of the H–T–P involves a new set of drawings, in that the clinician collects the drawings previously made with pencil and now presents new sheets of paper and crayons. Some children approach the crayons with the hesitant anxiety characteristic of their customary everyday patterns of behavior. Their crayon lines are faint and uncertain with the color choices restricted to the safer black, brown or blue. They reveal their personality constriction and interpersonal uncertainties by not daring to open up with the bolder reds, oranges and yellows. Such color usage places these subjects at the end of the personality continuum at which overcautiousness in exchanging pleasure or pain with others prevails.

Psychologically healthier subjects, by contrast, plunge more deeply into the chromatic task, confidently employ the warmer colors, utilize a firm, sure pressure on the crayon and thus reflect their greater self assurance in the emotional areas that colors represent.

On the other side of this healthier middle range in the continuum are those subjects who employ an almost savage pressure (frequently bearing down so heavily that they snap the crayons) and a clash of inharmonious, hot colors. Excessive lability, turbulent emotions and jarring inner needs in a tension-laden setting characterize the psychological state of the subjects in this group.

From a normative standpoint, the use of from three to five colors for the House represents the average range, as does two to three for the Tree, and three to five for the Person.

An inhibited use of color, below this average range, is exhibited by subjects unable to make warm, sharing personal relationships freely. The most "emotion-shy" subjects tend to use crayon as if it were a pencil, employing no coloring-in whatsoever, and usually one color only, and that black or brown.

A more expansive use of color than the normative middle range, particularly if combined with an unconventional employment of the colors, occurs most frequently in those manifesting an inability to exercise adequate control over their emotional impulses. One psychotic subject indicated his inadequate control, as well as his break with conventional reality, by drawing each of the eight windows in his House a different color.

Concerning the particular colors and the emotional states with which they tend to correlate, my four decades of experience with chromatic drawings has suggested the following. Overemphasis or inappropriate use of a color (inappropriate use, for example, might be purple for the Tree trunk, green for the Person's face, orange for the House's chimney) tends to go along with, if:

BLACK, the one achromatic color in the 8-crayon *Crayola®* box, the emotion-shy or emotion-avoidant child, as the severely obsessive-compulsive or highly intellectual youngster.

BROWN, the next least chromatic choice, the depressed, or sometimes the anal-personality-structured (punctual, parsimonious, retentive) child.

GREEN, the color of grass, and trees, and by implication of nature, if strongly emphasized, a *need* for tranquility or security (if mildly emphasized, the *presence* of feelings of tranquility and security).

YELLOW, hostility and/or negativism (this is especially so if the entire drawing is made in only yellow, which says, in effect, "I'll comply with your request,* but I'll be darned if I'll let you be able to see it"). Yellow is also the preferred color at two years of age, the negativistic phase).

RED, if mildly emphasized, suggests warm, sharing affect; if highly stressed reveals the emotionally "hot" conflict areas, like the heavy red coloring of the genital area by a child in trouble for exhibiting his penis, or the child suffering obesity who shaded the entire stomach in red.

ORANGE, a jarring color when used in an inappropriate setting, as one borderline schizophrenic boy did for the trunk of the Tree, suggesting his sense of marginal depersonalization and unreality.

---

*to draw.

BLUE, from mild overemphasis to very heavy, reflecting relatively comfortable feelings of self-control all the way to strained uncertainty and need for more exaggerated control of oneself as in the excessively heavy laying on of blue in the drawings of an adolescent just arrested for assault.

PURPLE, a "royal" color, is associated with coronations, and kings and queens, has, in keeping with this, empirically been found to be overused excessively in the projective drawings of grandiose, paranoid subjects or manic ones.

There is interesting support for some of the above relationships coming from outside the area of projective drawing. For experimental psychology's contribution, consult Chapter 4. But there is further interesting verification coming from, respectively, such diverse fields as medicine, sports, and advertising.

In medicine we have the experience in England where a placebo was given to two groups of patients, one suffering *anxiety* and the other suffering *depression.* Neither patients did any better than before. Then the placebo was first given to both groups in a yellow pill, daily for a month, and then next for another month in a green pill.

The results were statistically significant by a wide margin. The anxiety patients made no improvement under the program taking the yellow pills, but were tranquilized and felt better, losing their anxiety, when taking the green pills.

The depressed patients didn't respond to the green stimuli, but were energized and significantly became less depressed when taking the yellow pills.

In sports, the coach of a college football team, having read a sport psychology text, painted his own team's locker room yellow, and the visiting team's dressing room, green. When reporting this "experiment," the coach, who could note no other intervening variables, noted that comparing the win-lose record of the five years before this painting of the two dressing rooms with the five years after, a positive and statistically significant favoring of the aggression-instilling yellow stimuli, over the tranquil-inducing green.

If I may be permitted a personal anecdote, I was playing tennis one day and we were using yellow balls, hitting out at them energetically and aggressively. When the man whose balls they were left, he took them with him, and another of us opened a new can. But these were pink balls, and I observed a change. My game became more gentle. And so too did the other players'. I felt not a desire to *hit* the balls, but, as I experienced an association, the image of wanting to *"pet"* the balls.

The advertising area: A detergent was given to two groups of fifty housewives. The detergent was the same, but one group was given it in a yellow box, and the other group in a blue box. After two weeks, interviewers questioned the subjects. Those who used the detergent out of the yellow box reported it to be too aggressive, it "attacked" their clothing, it was "too harsh" and "too strong."

The detergent in the blue box was said to be overly "controlled," it "didn't do the job," it "didn't clean."

So then the advertising people made up a third box, with splashes of blue and yellow, and gave it out to a third group of housewives. They, in turn, found it "just right," "does the job," a "good soap."

There is confirmation from other areas as well, but these from medicine, from sports, and from advertising are varied enough to suffice.

Illustration of a Child's Chromatic Expression

An 8-year-old boy, referred for misbehavior at home and continual disruption of class and outbursts at school, revealed his symptoms and at the same time what they were in the service of, its cause, in his House drawing (Fig. 9-2).

The emotionality of this boy and its outpouring are each directly revealed in the drawing. The overemotionality is abundantly evident in the many colors employed: black, brown, blue, purple, green, yellow, red, and orange. And its outpouring may readily be seen in the way the emittance from the House (in this case the smoke) emerges as one color after another after another. It comes out yellow, then chaotically turns green, red, purple, orange, black, green, blue, orange, black. This child's behavior must be not only chaotic, but confusingly and disturbingly unpredictable in the extreme.

As to its underpinnings, or in a way its cause: the hint to this may be picked up in the hollow beneath the colors, the empty space at its center. This boy's development, the drawing tells us, has left him with a void inside. His feeling of emptiness at his center must lead him to overreact to things emotionally to drum up affect in order to feel; to try in this way to stir a sense of sensations, to try in this manner to quicken the sluggish emotional tone from which he inwardly suffers.

In short, he misbehaves, and he emotes, in order to feel more alive.

Figure 9-2. **House.**

At the same time, there may be simultaneously another pay-off to this personality structure the boy has evolved. The outer layers of overemotionality may also serve to buffer and protect the vulnerable, inner self. His overreactive emotionality may hold others off, and thereby help him feel safe.

There is still something further to be inferred from this drawing. We see the beginning of yet another defensive style starting to develop to handle his impulsiveness and overaffect, that interpreted in the child's overly rich resort to color. While there is an overabundant chromatic outpouring, there is at the same time a certain orderliness which controls it, thus a counterpoint of perhaps mobilizing some compulsiveness. For the walls of the House he chose first one color, then the next, and so on, until in a careful and orderly way, he used all of the crayons in the box provided (but each only once and none more than once). And, too, there is another orderliness in the sequence from the most achromatic, the black and then the brown at the center, and one by one on to the more and more chromatic blue, purple, and green at the middle, to then terminate with the most vivid colors, yellow, red, and orange, at the periphery.

Thus, on the favorable side, this boy may be in process of beginning to develop controls. On the unfavorable side, it is important that, in the long run, he not become overcontrolled and compulsive as an adult.

Psychotherapy might provide a balancing influence to this ongoing process and future outcome, as well as to assist this child with his current difficulties at home and school.

Psychotherapy, thus, is evidently indicated. And Relationship Therapy is its particular prescription. Also desirable would be a counseling and/or therapeutic collaboration with the parents to discover, and resolve, how their son's core emptiness came about.

AN EMPTY HUSK OF A CHILD

The next case, a 9-year-old, Asian-American boy of 120 IQ, in interview was detached and distant and for a child seemed flat in affect, interpersonally listless and lacking a child's usual spontaneity. Compared to the preceding case, this next one appears to be further along the continuum of the severity of a child's sense of feeling an inner void, a core emptiness. Here we find a dread that one doesn't even exist, a marginal sense of depersonalization, of being not so much a flesh-and-blood person as only a near-person, an almost-person, a mere *silhouette of a person* (See Figs. 9-3, 9-4, 9-5, 9-6, 9-7, 9-8, 9-9, 9-10).

Figure 9-3. **House.**

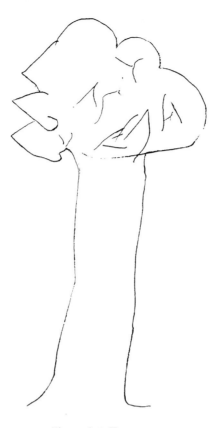

Figure 9-4. **Tree.**

This boy's self exists without eyes, without ears, and without a mouth, in all without the essentials to connect with others, to communicate, in short, to be in contact with the human world.

And if this wasn't pathology enough for a youngster to suffer, we regretfully see that he is also troubled by another symptom of serious derangement: gross distortion of body image. Here, note the asymmetry of the shoulders and arms and feet, arms at times hung from closer to the waist than the shoulders, arms drastically foreshortened, no feet and all the more importantly, no hands and no fingers at all, and still more striking, the alarmingly displaced head and neck.

Inner feelings of emptiness—even of nonexistence—were also sensed by the *way* he did his drawing, in one continuous line, to thus circle the emptiness within, to not deal with any detailing of body parts, of anything. There is thus again nothing within his barely stated outline, no substance, no actuality.

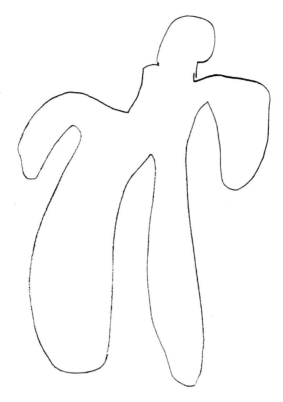

Figure 9-5. **Male.**

As a baseline for this youngster's drawing ability we have the Tree projections which, although immature, are adequate enough. It is when he gets to the "closer to home" self-representing Persons that his undifferentiated, unformed, and amorphousness of self come forth more directly.

When asked to draw a Kinetic Family Drawing, he stated he couldn't think of the family members "doing something," so he was then asked to merely draw them even if not doing something. He drew a family of a brother and sister (as he has) but with no parents (as he experientially has?) and then, perhaps even more meaningfully, he omitted himself entirely. He doesn't exist in the family, as he doesn't exist in his own skin (Fig. 9-10).

He then, for the first time, puts a little—very little—detailing on his Persons, mere hair, but nothing meaningful, like communication capacities of eyes, or ears, or mouth, or the other ordinarily conspicuous facial feature, the nose.

How did a child—we must ask ourselves—get this way? How did he

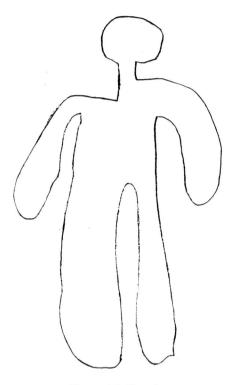

Figure 9-6. **Female.**

end up so undeveloped? So socially, so interpersonally, and so intra-psychically nonexistent?

A small but meaningful set of hints emerged during, or rather periph-eral to, the examination. The mother, a stock analyst and a workaholic, kept very late hours, when home, obsessed about work, and was essen-tially an absent parent. And the father, a very controlling parent, seemed to live the patient's life for him. He arrived later after the mother brought the boy, and I already had him in the office talking to him. The father loudly knocked on the door interrupting the examination to ask if the boy, a 9-year-old, "had to pee," explaining the boy usually had to urinate after school. (I was seeing the child at 4:00 o'clock on a school day.) The father's view that a 9-year-old was not sufficient enough, nor autonomous enough his own person to know if, and when, he had to go to the bathroom, or capable enough to say so to the examiner, suggested that the father, a particularly controlling parent, in living the child's life even as to bodily functions, had more or less poured himself into, and displaced his son from, the latter's own skin.

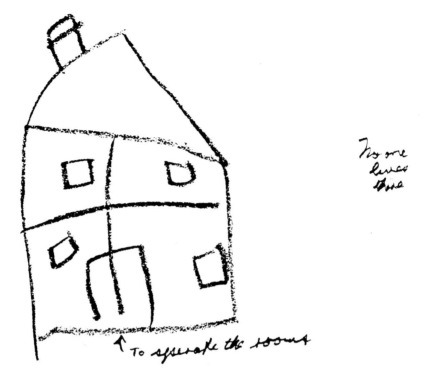

Figure 9-7. **Chromatic House, in red.**

This is just what the projective drawings looked like, that the subject's experience of himself was that he was no more than an empty skin, a mere hollow blob.

As a postscript, it may be of interest to see what the child did on the Rorschach, when we shifted to a verbal modality as opposed to the graphomotor one of the H–T–P. Here his performance was similarly empty. He rejected fully five of the ten inkblot stimuli, showing his imagination was as meager and barren as the projective drawings revealed he himself to be.

On the remaining five cards, he offered an unrevealing and unelaborated, simple, single response ("butterfly," "bat"), thus dismissing it. Where children his age tended to see an average of three or four images to each card, the patient thus offered only a single response, and that to only half the cards. His was a mere five-response Rorschach where his peers give a more comprehensive, expanded one of about 30 to 40 with the responses' content qualitatively more complex, detailed, and imaginative—far, far richer than our present subject's.

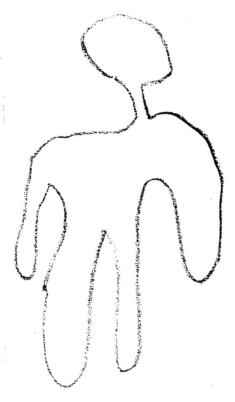

Figure 9-8. **Chromatic Male, in brown.**

Lastly, to return to the drawings, it is interesting that the House contains a cross-hatching which the subject explains is "to show the different rooms." This treatment is often introduced by children who experience one or both parents as intrusive, and metaphorically need their space, to psychologically have their own room, so to speak.

At the same time, transposing a floor plan onto the outside front of the House demonstrates confused thinking and impaired reality testing: supportive of the pathology elsewhere seen in the record. When such pathology advances from affect emptiness to a thinking disorder, the condition is becoming more ominous.

On the other hand, there is another possibility to consider. The superimposed "floor plan" onto the front of the House (backed up by the frequent drawings with only one crayon, and that used as a pencil more than as a chromatic expression) may suggest a referral to a neuropsychologist to rule out a possible secondary contributing factor of some organicity further complicating this child's struggle to cope.

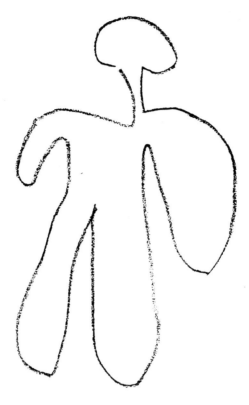

Figure 9-9. **Chromatic Female, in brown.**

A CASE STUDY

Although some clinicians interpret each drawing of a Person as a projection of the body image or self concept, the writer's experience has been that not all such drawings involve self portraiture. A figure drawing may at times, particularly with children, be a reflection of perceptions of significant people in one's environment, as indicated here.

The case of Leonard, a 12-year-old who stayed away from school because he felt the teachers were picking on him, may serve as illustration (Fig. 9-11). The tensions within the boy were reflected behaviorally in his doubting eyes, taut face, unceasing and jerky chatter and complete self centeredness. Knowing no other way to establish himself, he tried to do it by bravado, belligerence and a refusal to abide by the rules. It was for this latter reason that he was referred to the writer. Lenny soon earned from his peers the nickname of "Rocky." Behind Rocky's ten-

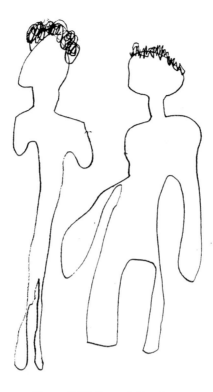

Figure 9-10. **Draw-A-Family**.

dency to misinterpret the actions of people in authority was a series of childhood traumatizing experiences with a cold, harsh and often brutal set of parents; his mother was bitingly sarcastic and his father physically abusive.

This perception of his parental figures is expressed in the subject's two figure drawings. The mother is clearly presented as orally aggressive and capable of inflicting severe damage with her mouth. The hands are absent, reflecting Rocky's perception of his mother as not reaching out to him—ungiving and rejecting. She is perceived in unappealing and frightening tones. Rocky's father figure, on the other hand, while not orally aggressive, is apperceived as capable of inflicting severe physical damage to one's vital parts. The scissor-like fingers seem capable of cutting off anything that protrudes from Rocky's body. The implications of castration anxiety are supported by the drawing of a House in which Rocky projects onto the chimney his feelings that any protrusion from his own body is likewise flimsily attached and vulnerable to separation

Figure 9-11. **Drawing by a 12-year-old boy.**

from the body. The chimney hangs onto the body of the House by a mere thread; it is as unattached as one can draw a chimney and still keep it part of the House. Rocky's feelings of vulnerability are also expressed in the House drawing by its quality of thinness, lack of substance and lack of capacity to withstand the pressures and forces of the environment. On one side the House already buckles.

It should be noted that the subject dresses the male drawing in the authoritarian role (military uniform of the Russians) in which he apperceives his father to parade. He then adds the dictatorial aspects of his father image by labeling the drawn male "Stalin." From the facial expression of the male figure, it is apparent that Rocky, somewhere within himself, perceives the underlying passivity and ineffectuality of his father beneath his father's authoritarian cloak. The projective drawing looks not so much like a dictator, as Charlie Chaplin playing *The Great Dictator*.* Rocky appears to have some awareness, perhaps only unconsciously, of the compensatory nature of his father's aggressive role.

Apparently Rocky's experiences with his parents have torn a deep gash in his feelings of adequacy and have left him with no one to turn to for help in tending the aching wound. The drawings suggest the intensity of the dowry of antagonism with which Rocky had to start off in life. And once a boy has suffered rejection, he will find rejection even where it does not exist. The boy's fear of, and expectation of, mistreatment at the hands of authority figures rippled outward to include the teachers with whom he had so much trouble. So Rocky built a wall of isolation and toughness around himself, strong enough—he hoped—to defend himself against the world.

In response to the request to draw an animal, he began by drawing what he described as "a timid rabbit running away" on one side of the page; he then appeared displeased with the drawing, turned the page over and on the other side drew what he described as "a little wildcat." Here we see the two sides of the coin of Rocky's inner view of himself. His basic feeling of fearfulness and lack of adequacy ("a timid rabbit running away"), he attempts to hide behind the tough-guy facade of "a little wildcat."

One of the early dreams the patient reported after about six therapy sessions was a nightmare in which he tried to kill someone and then fell out of bed. He reported, "I'm always trying to kill someone in my dreams. I was beating up a guy in this dream. I had him on the floor and was kicking him, almost killing him." He then followed this with a

---

*With cap turned, Skippy-like, to the side.

degree of insight: "I was afraid of the guy, but I just hit him. When I hit him, I wasn't afraid any more." Thus, in his dreams, Rocky offers us support for the interpretive deductions made on the basis of his animal drawings, in which he attempts to hide his feelings of being the "timid rabbit" behind the cloak of "a little wildcat."

As our last illustration for the chapter, we come to the point made at its beginning: that the principles of projective drawing interpretation for the drawings of children, and of adolescents, hold to the same language of symbolism operative with adults, only the frame of reference shifts. So, as earlier stated, the signs of dependency are the same for the adult and for the child; it is just that they are normative in the projections of the latter while neurotic when appearing in those of the former.

Emphasized, attention-getting, elongated chimneys were seen in the Houses drawn by the adult exhibitionists in Chapter 3. The current adolescent subject, a 13-year-old, also in trouble for an act of "flashing," whose projective House drawing is here shown (Fig. 9-12), is similar in essence to that offered by the adult. But it is more so; it is an enlarged phallic symbol, as is the adult's. But, the point is, it is even more so—more *dramatic,* more *compelling,* more *extreme,* more *fantasy* enriched, and more *bold* in its statement. It stretches the concept of chimney to its outer limits. A lighthouse is not a chimney, it is only like a chimney, and it is more unsublimated, more unvarnished, more insistent as a phallic structure made for, clamoring for, demanding attention.

Also, the drawn House here is secondary to the chimney, and via the perspective, we look down on it (although almost up on the lighthouse). The lighthouse is figure to the house being ground.

EXPERIMENTAL STUDIES

Space limitations permit only the briefest passing mention of experimental studies in the area of projective drawings.

Central to the core thesis of drawings as a projective device are the studies by Lehner and Silver,[19] indicating that one's own age tends to be projected in drawings; by Hammer,[13] suggesting that one's felt or subjective psychomaturational age tends to be projected; by Lehner and Gunderson,[18] finding that the height of the drawing is related to the degree of feelings of bodily adequacy; by Lyons,[20] showing a correlation between age at which psychic trauma was experienced and height up the Tree trunk where a scar is placed; by Kotkov and Goodman,[17] demon-

Figure 9-12. **Chromatic House.**

strating more "obese" drawings by the more obese subjects; by Berman and Laffel,[3] who reported significant correlations between body type of the subject and figure drawn; by Hammer,[9] finding significantly more indices of castration anxiety in the drawings made by subjects after sterilization than before they knew of the impending operation; by Barker et al.,[1] who reported greater hostility toward women in drawings by homosexuals than in drawings by heterosexuals; by DeMartino,[6] who found more feminine features in homosexuals' drawings of a male person; by Fisher and Fisher,[7] who uncovered a relationship between the femininity expressed in females' figure drawings and their psychosexual adjustment; by Hammer,[10] who showed the H–T–P to differentiate aggressive from control groups; by Tolor and Tolor,[24] who showed that popular and unpopular children projected associated traits into their drawings; by Cook,[5] who substantiated Machover's hypothesis that the drawing of the head area reflects the degree of social dominance of the subject; and by a number of investigators[6,12,16,21,25] who demonstrated that subjects, when asked to draw a person, drew a person of their own sex.

For a more complete presentation of research in the area of the

H–T–P, and for a presentation of the H–T–P reorganized into a tool for research purposes, the reader is referred to *The H–T-P Clinical Research Manual.*[14]

SUMMARY

Armed with the knowledge that man's deeper needs color his creative efforts and show an affinity for speaking in pictorial images, the clinician and/or experimenter has at his disposal a rapidly and easily administered technique for eliciting submerged levels of feelings. Basically, the subject's relative emphasis of different elements within his drawings, in addition to his global drawing performance, tells us a good deal of what matters to him, what it does to him, and what he does about it.

By examining the creative art work of a number of individuals, we have observed that subjects tend to express in their projective drawings quite unwittingly (and at times, unwillingly) their view of themselves *as they are, as they fear they might become* or *as they would like to be.*

Drawings represent a form of symbolic speech which taps a relatively primitive layer within the subject. In the words of Tunnelle, "The artist does not see things as they are, but as he is." Hubbard, another artist, expressed it in much the same way: "When an artist paints a portrait, he paints two, himself and the sitter."

REFERENCES

1. Barker, A. J., Mathis, J. K., & Powers, C. A. Drawings characteristic of male homosexuals. *J. Clin. Psychol.,* 1953, *9,* 185–188.
2. Bender, L. *Child psychiatric techniques.* Springfield, IL: Charles C Thomas, 1952.
3. Berman, S., & Laffel, J. Body types and figure drawing. *J. Clin. Psychol.,* 1953, *9,* 368–370.
4. Buck, J. N. The H–T–P technique: A quantitative and qualitative scoring manual. *J. Clin. Psychol. Monogr. Suppl.,* 1948, No. 5.
5. Cook, M. A preliminary study of the relationship of differential treatment of male and female headsize in figure drawing to the degree of attribution of the social function of the female. *Psychol. Newsletter,* 1951, 34, 1–5.
6. DeMartino, M. F. Human figure drawings by mentally retarded males. *J. Clin. Psychol.,* 1954, *10,* 241–244.
6a. Fineberg, J. *The innocent eye.* New York: Little Brown & Co., 1995.
7. Fisher, S., & Fisher, R. L. Style of sexual adjustment in disturbed women and its expression in figure drawings. *J. Psychol.,* 1952, *34,* 169–179.
8. Fox, R. Psychotherapeutics of alcoholism. In Bychowski, G., & Despert, J. L.

(Eds.) *Specialized techniques in psychotherapy.* New York: Basic Books, 1952, pp. 239–260.

8a. Gardner, H. *Artful scribbles: The significance of children's drawings.* New York: Basic Books, 1990.

9. Hammer, E. F. An investigation of sexual symbolism—a study of H–T–P's of eugenically sterilized subjects. *J. Proj. Tech.,* 1953, *17,* 401–413.

10. ——. Frustration-aggression hypothesis extended to socio-racial areas: comparison of Negro and white children's H–T–P's. *Psychiat. Quart.,* 1953, *27,* 597–607.

11. ——. The role of the H–T–P in the prognostic battery. *J. Clin. Psychol.,* 1953, *9,* 371–374.

12. ——. Guide for qualitative research with the H–T–P. *J. Genet. Psychol.,* 1954, *51,* 41–60.

13. ——. A comparison of the H–T–P's of rapists and pedophiles: III. The "dead" tree as an index of psychopathology. *J. Clin. Psychol.,* 1955, *11,* 67–69.

14. ——. *The H–T–P clinical research manual.* Beverly Hills, CA: Western Psychological Services, 1955.

15. ——. *The clinical application of projective drawings.* Springfield, IL: Charles C Thomas, 1958.

16. Jolles, I. A study of the validity of some hypotheses for the qualitative interpretation of the H–T–P for children of elementary school age. I. Sexual identification. *J. Clin. Psychol.,* 1952, *8,* 113–118.

17. Kotkov, B., & Goodman, M. Prediction of trait ranks from Draw-A-Person measurements of obese and nonobese women. *J. Clin. Psychol.,* 1953, *9,* 365–367.

18. Lehner, G. F., & Gunderson, E. K. Reliability of graphic indices in a projective test (DAP). *J. Clin. Psychol.,* 1952, *8,* 125–128.

19. ——, & Silver, H. Age relationships on the Draw-A-Person Test. *J. Pers.,* 1948, *17,* 199–209.

20. Lyons, J. The scar on the H–T–P tree. *J. Clin. Psychol.,* 1955, *11,* 267–270.

21. Mainord, F. B. A note on the use of figure drawings in the diagnosis of sexual inversion. *J. Clin. Psychol.,* 1953, *9,* 188–189.

22. Naumburg, M. Art as symbolic speech. *J. Aesthetics and Art Criticism,* 1955, *13,* 435–450.

23. Ray, M. B. You can be an amateur painter. *Coronet,* 1954, *35*(5), 82–104.

24. Tolor, A., & Tolor, B. Judgment of children's popularity from human figure drawings. *J. Proj. Tech.,* 1955, *19,* 170–176.

24a. Trudeau, G. Out of the crayons of babes. *The New York Times Magazine,* January 22, 1995, 34–45.

25. Weider, A., & Noller, P. A. Objective studies of children's drawings of human figures. I. Sex awareness and socio-economic level. *J. Clin. Psychol.,* 1950, *6,* 319–325.

Chapter 10

SEX DIFFERENCES IN THE DEVELOPMENT PATTERNS OF CHILDREN AS SEEN IN HUMAN FIGURE DRAWINGS

KAREN MACHOVER

Among the things for which readers should be grateful to Karen Machover are her creative innovations, independence, and high artistry with which she has, over her prolific decades, contributed so richly to our field. Here she is at her best, her finest work in her strongest genre.* In it she addresses lines of development, comparatively in the two sexes—and to this gives compelling and subtle description.† In what follows, she uncovers the drama of boys pursuing the myths of manhood and success, of girls pursuing theirs of womanhood and attractiveness, of the more recent overlap between the two, the shriek of the agony of growing up, the effort to flee the weight of parental pressure and demands, but also the revelation of gratification along the way; thus, both the inferno and the joys. In all this, Machover's chapter carries psychoanalytic punch and is expressed in a wry style which is delightful.

This chapter will be devoted to a major area of consideration (i.e., sex differences) that has emerged from a comprehensive normative study. Human figure drawings were obtained from middle class, white, urban children of ages five through twelve, who were of at least average intelligence. Comparative studies of different cultural and racial groups are in progress. It was anticipated that the drawings not only would provide concrete normative guides but, considering the intimacy of body image projection, might well shed light upon known theories and behavioral facts of child development while, in addition, perhaps raising new questions.

*Reprinted with permission from Rabin, A. & Haworth, M. (Eds.), *Projective Techniques with Children*, 1960, Thiese Med. Pub.

†The author is indebted to Helen Anderson, assisted by Alvin Wolf, whose ingenuity and persistent efforts have made available the mass of data upon which the study is based. She also extends her gratitude to the New York City Board of Education for their generous cooperation.

239

One hundred sets (male and female) of drawings (50 boys and 50 girls) obtained in group classroom situations from children at each age level were classified with regard to 45 major graphic variables covering structural and content aspects of the figures drawn. These were organized into personality syndromes sufficiently comprehensive to offer a fairly solid picture of prevailing age trends. Principles of interpretation followed those developed by the author. It is assumed that the reader has sufficient orientation in the special language of body image and body function terms, indigenous to the method of human figure drawing interpretation, to follow references to specific drawing features made in the course of discussion.

In processing the drawings, it was discovered that differences between the sexes at each age were not only as important as age level differences, but often were more striking and dramatic. It is not my intention to persuade the reader that there are sex differences and that they are here to stay, but rather to point out that, despite the persistent encounter of these differences in daily clinical practice, they have, heretofore, not been taken into serious account in the development and application of such dynamic instruments as projective techniques. Statements of biologic differences are mostly buried in actuarial statistics, and sex differences, when noted, are dismissed with "boys will be boys" (when the boy is aggressive) or "that's a woman for you" (when a woman changes her mind, which was never really hers, since it was often made up for her).

GENERAL DEVELOPMENTAL PATTERNS
IN BOYS AND GIRLS

The group trends that will be discussed briefly for each age group will, to be sure, not account for the individual child. As usual, it has been difficult to select a single drawing that would, in detail, portray composite group trends. A brief overview of the findings place the prepubertal girl in a highly privileged and triumphant position with regard to her less fortunate brother of similar age, intelligence and background. Her advantages in maturity, efficiency and prestige are most prominent at the peak of "latency" of the boy, at ages seven and eight, and they register least at periods of high physiological loading and urgency, such as at Oedipal periods of 4 and 5 and pubertal thresholds of eleven and twelve. In general, it may be said that when the environment is most regulated, persistent and demanding, the growing girl prospers with this structure, while the boy squirms with restless incoordination or else "plays possum," offering a deflated, ineffectual and harmless version of himself. The data suggest that the boy, although often reacting with disorganization and even panic to the pressure of his impulses, derives greatest ego strength at the "energetic" periods when he keeps active contact with his impulses, such as at five, eleven, twelve, and thirteen.

From the earliest years, with accelerated differential, the drawings of girls are more mature in body concept, are more realistic and detailed, and express greater fluency, more flexibility and composure than do those of boys. Orderliness, tidiness, emphasis of facial features, cosmetics and clothing display mark the well groomed girl child in both drawing projection and in behavior. With such competent use of surface defenses, the girl can afford to draw sexual characteristics and show male-female differentiation more actively and at an earlier age than do the boys. A mood of apologetic compromise is often communicated in the relatively deflated and frequently crude and diffuse productions offered by the boys in early school years. Their self drawings shrink drastically in size, are hidden at the bottom and side of the page (timid or self-conscious) and are singularly lacking in vigor of limbs, posture or extension. Limbs are short, often weak, cut off and poorly integrated with the trunk. Substituting for the vitality of hair growth there is most often a silly or oversized hat in a feeble attempt to offer social stature. The female is most often given hair, more clothing detail and is made larger and more forceful. Since it is clearly a female government at home and at school, the girl displays her supremacy by drawing her self figure with greater detail and skill, while not neglecting the male of the pair in these respects. Although she may draw him smaller, less mature in appearance and perhaps give him a "beanie" rather than a prestige hat, she seems, after a spurt of rivalry at five, to show increasing interest in cultivating him as a sex object. She gives him wide shoulders, crotch formation, strong limbs, appropriate coiffure, clothing, ties, belts and buckles, earlier and more frequently than the boy gives it to his own sex.

The boy, after his bold and often reckless self assertion at four and five, seems to settle down to a career of female domination with varying degrees of resentment and various methods of coping with the constant threat. There is throughout, even in the early school years when he offers the most deflated drawings, some subtle or meek warning that the fires are only banked. They are not out. In dealing with the evidence offered by body projection, it is difficult to see latency as anything but a description of comparative shifting of balance of forces between the inner pressures and the environmental demands, for which the boys offer the major battlefield. The struggle is paced unevenly through the school years. There is constant graphic evidence of either biding time or gathering courage for the "putsch" against the domination of the female. While the girl is free to cultivate the male figure as a potential love object, the boy, in his constant struggle to liberate himself from libidinal dependency upon his mother, is most likely to build up exaggerated hatred toward the female. His campaign has two aspects. One is to project upon, to punish and to denounce the female, and the other is to accumulate (and test out) his powerful masculinity, which, by sheer force, will overcome female authority. The drawings suggest that, despite the tumult that is associated with pubertal development, the biologic and cultural advantages, for the first time in the growing boy's career, are basically his. The increase of physical magnitude and power, though frightening, seems more positive and growth-inspiring for the boy. The girl, however, approaching the exciting, yet frightening responsibility of sex and reproduction, retreats from "the curse." She has lost her emotionally subsidized childhood, in which she reigned supreme. She perhaps clings to the "princess" enchantment in her daydreams.

PSYCHODYNAMIC AND CULTURAL CONSIDERATIONS

Before proceeding with a more detailed age level discussion of boy-girl differences seen in the drawings, it may be useful to inquire about the "why" and the "wherefore." Ego goals of the male in our culture revolve mostly about opportunities to use his potentials (intellectual, physical, sexual) in competitive masculinity. He constantly doubts his capacities "to measure up." In terms of space dynamics, it may be seen, in line with masculine play and interest patterns, as vertical ego striving. The girl, on the other hand, is generally more horizontal and involving-of-others in her play, interests and ego extensions. She is more concerned about her competitive power, not to achieve, create or fulfill potentials, but rather to seduce and command possessions, love, prestige and power. Rather than herself making any effort for attainment and distinction, she will insist that her man work for it. In her marriage vows, the female is instructed to love, honor and obey (as she did her mother); but whom? Not herself! Her self respect is measured only by what she can get. Goals for the female are essentially geared to building up a source of supply that is plentiful and secure, and to developing a sort of king-father figure, who will select her as a mate and thus offer a perfect Oedipal solution. It is in such rich and unrealistic fantasy soil that seeds of fears, depression, sexual frigidity, anxieties, postpartum reactions and suicides breed into the grave emotional disorders that beset the adult female. The male who "cannot make it" is more likely to veer off into ego-alienating symptoms, into addictions and/or antisocial behavior. In dealing with his ambition, the male may reap the somatic consequences of heart disease and in coping with his angry dependencies he may pay with ulcers.

So much for the differences in adult patterns. In childhood, the benefits of cultivated dependency are many for the girl and dangerous for the development of the boy. In many cases, the hazards of "receiving" interfere with the process of learning. The boy shows more difficulties in modification and control while the girl develops more indirect and subtle expression of countering or passively resisting authority. She will "throw up," refuse food or "faint" when overcome with an impulse. The boy, on the other hand, is more likely to submit or to rebel more openly, thus placing himself more frequently in the path of apprehension and punishment. Techniques of self expression must, for the boy, usually develop independently and subterraneously, since they are bound to be met with sharp disapproval. In drawings, as well as in behavior, the boy lunges into self assertions and fearful retreats more bluntly and ineffectively than does the girl. She traverses a well practiced middle ground, with her eye constantly fixed on authority (mother or teacher). The boy gives more trouble to the community in every area. In his body symptomatology the boy expresses primarily the consequences of restraint of aggression. Thus enuresis, nailbiting, stammers and tics are more common in boys, as are the physical acting out and learning difficulties that constitute our "problem" children. Even the allergic symptoms (such as asthma) for which boys are frequently referred are most often mixed with behavior disorders. It seems that the boys never fully lose contact with their raw impulses and the mandates of their growing bodies. Although this creates troublesome problems of control and discipline in childhood, it may constitute a source of ego power and creativity that is culturally appropriate for the adult male and not for the female.

For the girl, child or adult, aggressive and sexual drives are never appropriate as areas of enjoyment or self expression, while orderliness, control, display and surface talents are cultivated as her major social currency. She is thus more naturally coordinated with the passive values of *childhood,* while the male is more coordinated with the culturally more aggressive values of *adulthood.* The girl glides through childhood smoothly with approval and rewards, while the boy stumbles through, always the victim of conflicting standards. Expected to achieve the divergent goals of independence and power on the one hand, and full submission and organization on the other, it is no surprise that the boy, in his drawing and in his behavior, achieves neither. He is thus more awkward, slower to learn, more of a social problem and less mature in development of sexual interests. Considering the sources and background, opportunities for role identification are, unlike those for the girl, sporadic and confusing for the boy. His childhood government is all female. What is a man? What is his task, and how does he learn to perform it? In our urban, middle class culture, the father is often a weak, shadowy figure who may, on occasion, behave like a competitive big brother or as the executioner of a sentence substantially imposed by the mother. He is often a mechanical source of provisions and is accorded only token respect and prestige. Unlike the girl, the boy does not have a concrete model of manhood and thus, most often resorts to stereotyped figures such as policemen, cowboys, soldiers or spacemen (each with individual dynamic significance). The persistence of unrealistic fantasy models of a masculine ego woven in childhood, usually rigid and exaggerated, may produce lasting neurosis in adulthood.

In contrast to the boy, sex-role identifications for the girl are, in most middle class families, concrete, direct and rewarding. The girl most often assumes the position of first lieutenant to "the boss," and is encouraged to follow an established and consistent set of standards modeled continuously, and in detail, by her mother or her teacher, with the ever implicit promise that some day she will be given the reins. Actually, she is a perpetual "mother's helper" and is never trained for independent decisions or authority. The girl participates in accepting (with conflict) this role of safe security. She rehearses with house and doll play, and details are always subject to correction. She learns too well the lesson of gaining love and recognition by doing what mother and teacher ask of her. Her own sensations and feelings are unimportant and unladylike, and her personal decisions are usually regarded as inadequate. For childhood, this silent agreement seems satisfactory. Having the gratifications of love and effective sublimation in learning experiences, the girl does not seem to be under as great inner pressure as does the boy. The girl can secure love and possession equivalents by just being decorative, quiet and useful. It is in marriage, when she is told to make independent decisions and to accept such "sinful" impulses as sex, that panic and anxiety may ensue. On the one hand, she demands to be given the authority she had accorded her mother, and on the other, she looks to her husband to reward her as her mother did, thus she is feeding marital disharmony with her inconsistent demands to be both mother and child.

Since weakness is a quality that is rewarded, the girl has learned to make a positive virtue of it by cosmetization and display. In her drawings, she will, for example, often shape a dependent, concave mouth into a cupid bow. Instead of the dark, irascible line the boy draws to separate the sexual area of the body from the chest, the girl more often will deftly convert her restraint into a fashionable and seductive tight waistline. Dependency upon the mother, symbolically expressed in a navel button, is wrought into a socialized buckle which the girl offers at an early age. Disarray of the hair suggestive of sexual excitation, may be offered by the young girl with a crown, a bow, a fancy hat or a feather to top off the display. Similarly, sexual preoccupation conveyed in shading of the skirt, will most often appear as decoratively designed shading with flowers and plant themes on the skirt, perhaps, to suggest active pregnancy fantasies. The boy does not have the girl's subtlety or talent for socialization. He chafes with his weakness and dependencies and hides his struggles or inadequacies in profile evasion earlier and more often than does the girl. There is a more persistent rumble of his body impulses, and the boy cannot use the niceties of clothing or detail as a source of pleasure or defense.

At this point, it may be well to outline briefly the sexual differences as they are reflected in the developmental picture at successive age levels. Since, as has already been noted, it is the boy who is constantly gaining the attention of authorities (usually negative) and who reflects a more stormy pattern of development in his drawing projections, it will be he that gets more attention in this study than the girl. The girl continues to gain steadily in goals and methods that are established quite early in development. Minor retreats and adjustments, as well as differences in the pace of improvement, punctuate the growth record. It is only at twelve when the girl, under the threatening impact of puberty, finds her defenses strained and her resources not too adaptable that the boy-girl pattern shifts against her favor. At this age, the boy is seen looking to his own strength as a means of transcending female authority.

Figure 10-1A. Male and female figure drawings produced by boys and girls 4 to 12 years of age:

Figure 10-1B. Continued.

Male I   Female II

Twelve-year-old boy

Female I   Male II

Twelve-year-old girl

Figure 10-1C. Continued.

FOUR- AND FIVE-YEAR-OLDS

Children of four and five, who are not as yet members of the outside or school community, exhibit less differences between the sexes than at any other age. The familial Oedipal drama, exaggerated by the imminence of school placement and loosening of family ties, is reflected in a rather "excited" body-image projection for both the boy and girl. For the *girl,* the projections are, in accordance with her more passive disposition, less bold, less assertive, less disorganized and more self conscious and insecure. Although both sexes draw fairly large figures, shade them with pressureful anxiety and guilt and are concerned with body extensions, the *girl* will draw more small figures, with lighter lines, place them more to the left of the page, introduce multiple figures for support and place them in toppling stance. In terms of control, she will attempt some clothing, accessories, give more double dimension arms, legs and fingers and more frequently draw hands with which to grip things. Arms of her figures extend from a more controlling area of the trunk and are less mechanical in extension than are those drawn by the boys. The *boy,* on the other hand, having more interest in his body stimulations and less of an eye for integration with the environment than does the girl, projects his figures in larger size, heavier line, in middle or right, acting out placement and with more aggressive and disorganized shading. Arms are flung out in single dimension, mechanically, often from the lower (impulse) level of the trunk, ending in heavy and long, spanning, stick-fingers. There is poor modification and control. Rarely is there a neck with which to integrate the raucous body needs with the controlling head, nor are there hands to direct the manipulating fingers. The boy does not avail himself of clothing with which to cover his needs but rather, in stark display of his anxious dependency, he often draws large shaded buttons down the middle of the trunk, balanced by a hat for stature. Sexual stimulation is conveyed through voyeurism (transparent or shaded skirt, popeyes) or passive sensual enmeshment in disordered hair. Oversized noses, exactly "counted out" five fingers, and large extensions constitute restitutive repair. The head, as a self signature, is large and misshapen with bulging fantasies and with tortured attempts to resolve the unrealistic aspirations for masculinity characteristic of the Oedipal storm. The female of the set will often be drawn with a larger and ovverticalized head, adding a note of menace.

The *girl* also draws large heads for control, but they are more round, more even in contour and enhanced with decorative or cosmetic touches. She, too, makes the female more important. Although the girl does not deface or mutilate her male figure, she may express her contempt by making him much smaller, more childish, putting a dunce cap on him, or depicting him as a clown. Envy of the boy is reflected in the fact that the five year old girl draws the opposite sex first more often than at any of the school ages until the age of twelve. Also she assigns an older age to the male figure of the set more frequently than in succeeding years. Even at this rivalrous age, her figures are better integrated and controlled than are those of the boy. Like the boys, she may display oral aggression by drawing teeth, but while the boy scatters his teeth in a large, overactive and loosely drawn mouth, suggesting primitive eating habits and profanity, the five-year-old girl, drawing teeth, stacks them neatly in a reserved mouth as if to create a deliberate barrier against "intake" (of food?).

SIX-YEAR-OLDS

After five, when the acuteness of the Oedipal excitement has subsided in varying degrees with the boy and more promptly for the girl, whose reaction was milder initially, the conspicuous difference in self concept and style of expression between the boy and the girl enters a decisive phase which is best described as a capitulation to female supremacy. This supremacy continues throughout the early and middle school ages with mild rebuffs imposed by the boy's sporadic, restless breaking of his restraints and by feeble efforts to declare himself as a male. At six and seven, as if in resolution to settle down to learning and regulation and to make room for 40 or more children in their class, boys and girls draw smaller, more controlled tidy figures in more reserved or withdrawn placement. Action potentials are all minimized. The *girl,* with her gratifications from control and from modelling after the teacher as she does after the mother, learns readily with pleasure and reward. The *boy,* on the other hand, having retreated or been thrown back from his bold self projection, views learning from the sulky dissatisfaction of defeat. The figures, though meek, are quiet and composed, raising the possibility of secondary gains being derived from the position of protected retreat. Judging from subsequent trends, the small figure in a quiet corner, with a small dot eye, may be studying the field and assessing the tolerance of the school environment as compared with his home. Emphasis upon limbs and bold or acting out placement diminish sharply, while the female of the set is drawn larger, more mature and given the wider, more assertive stance. Venturing so little, there is little expression of conflict. A feeble attempt is made to hold the line by attributing either the same or even older ages to the smaller and weaker self sex figures. An increase in phallically extended hair coiffure on the female figure suggests consolidation of sex and aggression which, at five, was expressed more bluntly. The six year old boy seems pleasantly disposed toward the more powerful female figure, while giving anger, fear and worry to his deflated self figure. Active, oversensitized ears appear less frequently as does the deep, wide arc mouth of contrived placation. Even the distorted head shapes (and fantasies) of the five year phase have faded out.

The six-year-old *girl* accepts the surrender, thus creating a wide gap in confidence of self projection between the two sexes—a gap which continues to widen for several years. Her drawings, particularly of her own sex, are now larger, more skilled, placed more boldly on the page, heavier in line and wider and firmer in stance. Although the girl has less to tidy up from the five year phase, she too is more controlled. Not only does she give the male a hat as she did at five, but she now adds a hat and a pocketbook to her self figure as if ready to go out and command the world. She is now a full-fledged member of the female club. In her self-confident stride, the six-year-old-girl sharpens her passive techniques of seductive display while adding action features, such as strong limbs, active postures and outward (toward action) foot direction. Sensuality is underplayed. She either overtightens her hair in corkscrew style or gives outline indication of curly hair, avoiding the substance. She draws more mature and intense eyes and accents them with the social commentary of brows more often. Mouths are less frequently concave and are set in a moderate arc line, suggesting the determined congeniality of contained pleasure of the triumphant. She is more attentive to the clothing, hair, and sexual characteristics of her male figure, while often drawing him smaller, younger, with a "droopy" crotch, or dunce cap. She is clearly in conflict.

SEVEN YEAR OLDS

Although all seven year olds, at the peak of learning and "receiving," offer small and passive drawings, boy-girl differences continue. The *boys* draw one-third opposite sex first, and play down such assets as body vigor, aggression and boldness even more than they did at six. Their figures are unlively images, more shrunken in size and hug the bottom of the page. They are lacking in sensuousness. Arms are weak, tentatively attached to more controlling areas of the trunk, and sockets are closed off. Feet point in all directions as if the figure is without a rudder. Facial features are brief and noncommittal, suggesting defensive social exchange. The seven-year-old boy watches himself and the female from a distance. An increase in short and mildly designed skirts betrays a simmering sex interest, while an increase in "father-replacement" heads and a tendency toward geometric object and clothing-equivalents of phallus-like forms give suggestion of restless stirring. His interest in external symbols suggests a greater readiness for learning.

The *girl* of seven advances further in her displayful, detailed, and ordered self presentation. She seems content with her age and shows less interest in parent ages or "parent-replacement" heads than does the boy. She gives her male figure more sexual characteristics, more ties, hats, and more masculine clothing. The masculine strength features she borrowed at six are now returned to him. Less of a rival, he is being cultivated for a role suitable to the pregnancy fantasies and princess daydreams which she rehearses in her doll play at this age. The seven-year-old girl manages rather well the integration of her childhood competency with stimulated fantasies of being grown up. She puts crowns and bows on her hair often, as if to signal her success. One cannot, however, help but see in her drawings such evidences of strain as increase in brittleness of control, more frequent defensive arm position, more inquiring head tilting, more sober eyebrow emphasis and more expressions of worry and sadness. It may be said that at seven the girls seem to control too much, and the boys to repress too much.

EIGHT-YEAR-OLDS

Although at eight the *boy* continues to draw passive and weak body forms, he gives fewer unrelieved apologetic figures than he did at seven. He draws fewer round, passive heads on the self sex and revives the more active and distorted head (full of ideas) seen at five. The body parts are still weak. The eight-year-old boy draws more circular body forms, more buttons, more small and round feet, more small noses, small and concave mouths and empty eyes, but he is beginning to pack a gun "in case." In contrast to the apparent submission at seven, the boy of eight is beginning to serve notice that he is dissatisfied with the balance of power and intends to do something about it. There is much labeling, balloon talking and strident humor with which he announces verbally his declaration of rights. There is still reliance upon outer symbols of stature and activity such as hats, heels and holding of sticks as at seven, but more active postures and shoulders for strength and responsibility do appear on the self sex, bringing in their train more conflict and anxiety. Thus, we find the eight-year-old boy reviving background, multiple figures, holding things and active erasures in his drawings. His female figure, still drawn larger, is given the more assertive stance, is indicated as the older of the set more often and is drawn first more than at any other age (40%). She is revived, though not as vividly as at five, as an object of threat and stimulation and is handled with greater sex detail, aggression, anxious and guilty shading and restless erasures. More control features such as neck, hand (to grip with) and waistline and hemline demarcations enter to cope with the added stimulations. Despite the greater disarray and diffusion on the female figure, the drawings offered by the eight-year-old boy are more mature and skilled. He has literally gotten off the ground, exchanging his "sunken" bottom placement for a more cautious but active left placement on the page. He is now less amiable toward the female and more frequently gives her angry expressions to replace the contrived pleasantness given her at six and seven.

The eight-year-old *girl* consolidates her gains. She takes hold of her superior position, adding sturdiness and physical activity at the same time that she cultivates further the more feminine assets such as clothing, jewelry, hair coiffuring, shaded lips, horizontal and intense eyes and emphatic brows. She takes herself quite seriously, and rather than being disorganized by a growth spurt, as the boys are, she increases her controls and her efficiency, leaving the boys behind more than ever. This age probably is seen as the height of differential between the adjustment of the boy and the girl in school and at home. The girl seems less preoccupied with themes of marriage and babies than she was at seven and, on the whole, shows greater realism. Her interest in the male as a potential sex object is increased. There is least evidence of rivalry. On her self figure, she draws fewer fanciful costumes, less dress and skirt designs and shows less hemline emphasis. She is well sublimated. In general, the eight-year-old girl shows less body arousal than is evident in the boy. She seems more highly satisfied with herself, more firmly controlled and is deriving more gratification from her positive achievements. This burden of adequacy does, however, produce an increase in expressions of worry and fear on the self sex.

NINE-YEAR-OLDS

Following the verbal notice and restless sniping at the dominant female at eight, the *boy* of nine presses further into the struggle. Although the female is still strong and there is an increase in aggressive and sexual interest in her, the boy introduces himself more vigorously as a worthy contestant. While at eight, the primary emphasis centered around protest and anger against the female, and the drawings tended to get "noisy" and disorganized, the nine year old boy balances his attack upon the female with more active explorations of his own body strengths. With this positive approach, the drawings become more varied and less shallow than in previous ages, and improve in skill. More open sockets, more flexibly extended arms (integrated at the shoulder level) and more hair shading add to the flavor of self expressiveness. More active themes underscore the impression of a heated campaign. There is, as at eight, still much labeling and "talking." Graphic features of dependency offer contradiction to manifestations of manliness. Thus, along with "father replacement" heads, parent ages, heavier lines, more dignified hats and brief cases, heels, cigarettes, and phallic objects, we see much emphasis on food, sucking, and talking. Mouths, in fact, become larger and more uncontrolled, teeth reappear, and more midlines and buttons enter as evidence of increase in body sensitivity. The female continues to be presented as sexually exciting with wide stance, diffusely shaded and erased hair and skirt, phallically extended hair, and a cigarette, stick, or broom frequently stuck in her hand. Whereas, at seven and eight he draws a meek phallic object symbol with his self sex figure, at nine the boy seems more actively fighting the female for his phallus. Judging from the graphic evidence of noisy, orally aggressive, attention seeking and disorganized behavior, nine is a troublesome disciplinary age. While toying with father roles, he offers, rather gratuitously, the theme of a tree, solid in trunk, whose branches are bare and sharply truncated, with a self sex figure beside it, holding a hatchet as if he has just chopped down the mother tree. (It was not Washington's birthday.) The balance of power is being challenged energetically, although the move is essentially a "bootstrap operation" with the feet of the figure going in all directions. Figure 10-2A presents inquiry responses of a nine-year-old boy.

The nine-year-old *girl* is not unaffected by the mounting disparagement and active challenge of the boy. She, too, is becoming more interested in body functions and is no longer content with just reading and spelling better than the boy. The nine-year-old girl is less smug and composed under the impact of the boy's assertiveness and increasing awareness of her own developing body. She draws smaller figures than at eight and now gives the male figure more active recognition for the special qualities of physical sturdiness, some of which she would previously appropriate for the self figure. The male figure is, at nine, more often given the wider stance, more bold placement, heavier line, is made larger and indicated as the older of the set. At eight, the girl was secure in her superiority. At nine, with an increase in respect for the male figure, she mingles envy with anger. Thus, while giving him a crotch

1. *What is she doing?*   standing
2. *How old is she?*   22 year old
3. *Is she married?*   No
4. *Does she have children?*   No
5. *How many girls?*   0
6. *How many boys?*   0
7. *What kind of work does she do?*   college work
8. *What class is she in?*   11B
9. *What does she want to be when she grows up?*   Nerce.
10. *How smart is she?*   very smart
11. *How healthy is she?*   regular
12. *How goodlooking is she?*   very pretty
13. *What is the best part of her body?*   Her face
14. *What is the worst part of her body?*   Hair
15. *How happy is she?*   very happy
16. *What does she worry about?*   nothing
17. *What makes her mad?*   nothing
18. *What are the three worst things she ever did?*   nothing
19. *What are the nicest things about her?*   Her legs face build up
20. *How many girl friends does she have?*   60
21. *How old are they?*   20 and 21
22. *What do people say about her?*   nice things
23. *How much fun does she have with her family?*   she doesn't have a family
24. *How much does she like school?*   very much
25. *How many boy friends does she have?*   75 to a 100
26. *What does she call a good time?*   reading
27. *Will she get married?*   Yes
28. *How old will she be when she gets married?*   23
29. *What kind of a boy will she marry?*   a nice boy
30. *What are her three best wishes?*
        1. nothing   2. nothing   3. nothing
31. *Is she like somebody you know?*   no
32. *Who is she like?*   No Body
33. *Would you like to be like her?*   no   *Why?*   she is a girl I am a boy

Figure 10-2A. Inquiry responses given by a nine-year-old boy to the female figure.

more frequently, she will either draw it low, scooped out or make it like a skirt. She may give him a "beanie" for a hat. Her greater insecurity is reflected in an increase in use of background as well as the defensive, overcontrolled self sex figure that she offers, with arms frequently at side or glued to body walls. Eyes are more often small and intense, while the mouth, contrary to the mouth of the boy, is most often small, cosmetized and faintly placating. In this sober mood, she places more figures toward the "magical" upper part of the page, and dresses her figures more primly. On occasion, she will engage in a "princess" daydream lingering from or returning to the seven year phase. This fails, however, to relieve

1. *What is he doing?*   He is standing.   2. *How old is he?*   He is 37 years old
3. *Is he married?*   No, He isn't.   4. *Does he have children?*   no
5. *How many boys?*   0
6. *How many girls?*   0
7. *What kind of work does he do?*   He makes blouses.
8. *What class is he in?*   He is not in eny class.
9. *What does he want to be when he grows up?*   He is grown up already
10. *How smart is he?*   very smart
11. *How healthy is he?*   very healthy
12. *How goodlooking is he?*   very goodlooking.
13. *What is the best part of his body?*   His whole body is good
14. *What is the worst part of his body?*   He has know worst part
15. *How happy is he?*   very happy.
16. *What does he worry about?*   a private house.
17. *What makes him mad?*   fight's make him very mad
18. *What are the three worst things he ever did?*   yelled fought got C in homework
19. *What are the nicest things about him?*   He's very good.
20. *How many boy friends does he have?*   50
21. *How old are they?*   20, 21, 22 and ma more
22. *What do people say about him?*   very nice things.
23. *How much fun does he have with his family?*   He doesn't have a family
24. *How much does he like school?*   He's out of scool already
25. *How many girl friends does he have?*   55 girl friends
26. *What does he call a good time?*   playing baseball.
27. *Will he get married?*   yes
28. *How old will he be when he gets married?*   38
29. *What kind of a girl will he marry?*   tall, dark and pretty
30. *What are his three best wishes?*
        1. sucses   2. Happunes.   3. and children
31. *Is he like somebody you know?*   No, He isn't.
32. *Who is he like?*   No Body
33. *Would you like to be like him?*   No.   *Why*   He is too nicelooking.

Figure 10-2B. Inquiry responses given by a nine-year-old boy to the male figure.

the tension. There is evidence of brooding body concern. Eyes look to the side for approval, and overemphasized ears on the male testify to her sensitivity concerning his opinion of her. The male is a more serious contender. To handle her increased tension, the girl resorts to more overcompulsive detail, while sharpening her techniques of passive seduction.

TEN-YEAR-OLDS

While the eight-year-old boy served warning, and the nine-year-old boy combined high rebellion against female supremacy with a search for his masculinity, the ten-year-old shows a definite advance in the direction of concentration on self assets. When the focus is largely upon outside points of reference, the *boy* presents a rather tame and constricted image. When it is upon his own feelings, graphic expressions of conflict become more numerous. Judging from the large increase in restless erasures, impatient reinforcements and islands of heavy shading on the figures, both sexes seem to be carrying a heavy load of body growth and sex sensitivities. There is, too, massing evidence of masturbatory tension. Increase in sexual arousal is seen in the greater number of diffusely shaded or near transparent skirts, emphasized waistlines and disordered hair on the female figures drawn by the boy. Occupied with the problem of building up his own stature, the boy appears to be less threatened by the sexually provocative female than he was in weaker states. He ventures more. He is free to indicate more sex characteristics on both figures and draws his self sex figure with greater maturity, skill, and detail than he did at nine. Though he displays a substantial interest in body development and does not look to a large head or a tight bottleneck for control as he did in earlier years, the ten-year-old boy, still lacking in body confidence, experiments with outer credentials of manhood, such as uniforms, insignia, elaborated belts and buckles, impressive hats. He draws his figures at an active postural slant as if they are in a hurry to get there. His figures are larger, placed more boldly toward the middle and are more detailed. Moreover, the self sex is given larger feet, wider stance, shoulders and more open sockets, and is cast in an active theme. He is beyond the gingerly testing of ground seen at nine, and "talking" protests of the eight year boy. He is now involved in actively mapping out his manhood. The boy seems to be catching up with the girl in many respects, and draws fewer of the opposite sex first.

Although the ten-year-old boy thrives on this display of self-assertion, and the girl takes appropriate notice of his challenge and makes room for him, the enterprise increases conflict and fear. The limbs may be stronger, but they are smudged with erasures or heavy shading. With the more frequent indication of crotch formation comes disturbance in that area. In his energetic attempts at masculinity, the boy needs to draw a line under the figure more frequently to sustain him. He no longer involves clouds, rain, cut-off trees, people, or objects for support as the nine-year-old did. His fight is beginning to be more consciously with himself than with his environment. The burden shows in the increase in negative expressions, worry lines and turning aside to evasive profile more often. The developmental sequence may be described as follows: The seven-year-old boy draws quiet phallic object replacement of his emasculation. The eight-year-old boy is planning an offensive, mostly with "Am I going to tell her off!" fantasies. The nine-year-old is talking tough and becomes offensive to the female while beginning to inquire about his masculine strength, and the ten-year-old seems to be actively trying out roles for manhood and is less oriented toward sheer rebellion.

The ten-year-old *girl* views her growing body with more threat than promise. She vies less for stature, physical power or prestige and seems to cling more to her practical feminine virtues. She focuses increasingly on grown-up and seductive clothing, jewelry, special coiffure styles, bangs, cosmetized mouths and lashes. More hips are drawn, hemline problems (growth implicating) increase, and the breast area receives more attention, albeit in still indirect forms such as pockets, reinforced chest walls, and such bilateral symbols as bows or Peter-Pan collars. Under the stress of heightened body sensitivities, the girl tightens her controls and increases detail. She tightens and elaborates her waistline and designs her skirt more actively, rationalizing her anxiety about sex. She reserves for herself more of the small, weak, and demure body features, except for still giving the girl wider shoulders (responsibility?). Some strong legs enter to suggest a prepubertal athletic thrust. She clothes her male more and shows more interest in sex characteristics and differences, but continues to express rivalry along with her respect by wrapping the boy up in a tight collar, giving him a weak tie, mostly immature crotch formation and frequently has his trousers too short for his legs. She imposes upon him the midline body sensitivity and button indications of dependency as if in sullen scapegoating. At ten, the boy is more challenging and the girl less amiable.

ELEVEN-YEAR-OLDS

The strained, heroic and often poorly organized attempts at manliness projected by the ten-year-old *boy* continue at eleven with more realism than the stereotype models with uniform offer. This sobering up brings into its wake a more manifest conflict between growth strivings and powerful dependencies which inevitably stir up the ever-present problems around the infantile patterns of sex and aggression. Body tensions press the environment into the background, except for increasing anger at the female whom he holds responsible for his growth difficulties. Both sexes strongly identify with their own, resisting the influence of the other. Sex differences between the male and female figures are more actively indicated. Stronger body parts and more fluency in self-assertion are apparent, but there are false starts, and many of the figures withdraw toward left, self-conscious placement, must use a line for ground support and are heavily erased. More frequent midlines attest to increased sensitivity to body processes. More hair and fewer hats appear. An increase in clothing, collar, and neckline demarcations add control features. Sex characteristics are more frequently indicated. The crotch formations are, however, essentially immature or disturbed. The mood has, for the eleven-year-old boy, quieted down. Overlarge heads, bottlenecks, arms up and at side and more rationalization of shading mark the greater control and reserve. It seems that throughout this process of emancipation seen in the later school years, the rhythm of self assertion wavers in its forcefulness. Disorganized advance may be followed by a reflective pause. Thoughts point to growth ahead. The eleven-year-old boy assigns older ages to his self figure. Although the figures look more active, the feet positions are static and the figure is most often described as doing nothing, standing, or just looking.

The *girl* of eleven is also extremely aware of her growing body and communicates increased disturbance by her many erasures, areas of tightly controlled shading, disturbed lines and strong masturbatory tension, as revealed by mutilated fingers and repetitive clothing designs. If the girl has reached puberty, her disturbance is generally more severe. Legs may be pressed tightly and defensively together and hands are often hidden behind the back. In a hurry to grow up, the girl intensifies seductive features while fearfully looking to see the effect. She fights dependency and fears sensual involvement, drawing more empty hair (while the boy gives hair more substance than previously). She gives most items pertaining to physical vigor to the male of her set, more often casting him in athletic roles, giving him suits and manly ties. In other respects, she will express her rivalry by giving the male of the set the immature eyes and weak crotch formation, imposing upon him the midline and buttons, and presenting him as childish and carefree. It is as if she were taking advantage of the slightly less aggressive posture of the eleven-year-old-boy as compared with that of the 10-year-old.

TWELVE-YEAR-OLDS

The twelve-year-old *boy* continues to battle with the twofold task: (a) he must free himself from female domination and its libidinal complications, and (b) he must examine, assess and construct a self image adequate to the task of manhood—a task that is confused and inflated in its standards. These central themes are presented in various balances and interplay from the age of nine. As the crisis ripens, patterns of the balance of forces and the methods of coping become numerous and variegated. Conflict continues to rise in intensity, and repressions, useful in former years, are less effective. There is, however, underlying the struggle a positive growth striving. After a brief pause at eleven for self-accounting, the twelve-year-old gives more large drawings and places them more boldly in the center of the page, as if ready to do battle with the enemy. The line is active and disturbed. Extension is of primary concern and much conflict is expressed in what type of arms to make and where to place them. Often they are thrust out rigidly in phallic extension. With the rapid pace of physiologic changes pressing upon his awareness, the twelve-year-old boy presents particularly disturbed and disorganized projections. Line is shredded with lack of clear boundaries of head and trunk, shading is diffuse, joining and integration are careless, and the drawings are smudged with critical erasures and anxious, often diffuse, shading. Facial features are frequently uncomposed and overactive, and the face bears many marks and scars as if in the thick of an uncompromising battle. The "elements" are menacing with clouds and rain, and there is active background for thematic emphasis. Badges, merit ribbons, athletic letters and verbal balloon threats add to the heat and noise of the struggle. The picture bears a similarity to the surge at ten, but is more intense. It is as if it were a combination of all the efforts at self assertion made in previous years. Large, active mouths reappear, as well as a groundline for support, and figures are often holding "something." This dependency and need for support always enter in the height of battle and may be viewed as a mobilization of deeper and more primitive sources of strength for the critical task of ego survival.

The female of the set is also jolted out of the relative reserve with which the eleven-year-old boy drew her. She now is presented as a worthy contender to justify the display of injury shown on his self figure. She is often angry, the skirt area is actively erased, diffusely shaded, or almost transparent, and hair is drawn roughly and disordered, conveying acute sexual excitement. To return to the boy's self presentation, we find the male in two major stages of the battle. He is either castrated with broken limbs, disturbed crotch, perhaps small in size, or else he is a compensated figure of large size, often in the battle array of a two-gun cowboy, a marine with a sharp bayonet, a prizefighter, or a weight lifter. The self figure is now drawn larger more often and is given the wider stance of the set. Despite improved male-female differentiation, the boy tends to masculinize his female and the girl feminizes her male, perhaps as a reflection of their acutely egocentric self reference at this age. The boy's drawings, though more disorganized, do advance in maturity and in strength of body features. Fewer weak noses, weak legs, small feet and more shoulders and crotch formations are drawn on the self sex. Necks with which to control appear more frequently. There is also control by evasive hiding of the commotion, as reflected in an increase of profiles.

The twelve-year-old *girl* struggles primarily with her own growing body sensations. Her drawings differ, depending upon her pubertal status. The girl, unlike the boy, does not project her "storm" upon background "elements." Nor can she use the reassurance of the environment in which, as a child, she was dominant. A decrease in object interest parallels her increased concern about body processes. Fewer hands with which to grasp are drawn. The twelve-year-old girl falters markedly in her poise and is worried about her future. In her drawing of 36 percent opposite-sex first, in contrast to the usual five percent, she expresses protest against her role. Her mood is essentially sober. She draws relatively large figures, suggesting active self-esteem elements, but they are placed on the left of the page. Her growth task, unlike that of the boy, is not to overthrow female domination and to build masculine strengths. She must preserve the mother as a model while attempting to differentiate herself from her as an individual. Her effective childhood adjustment gave her contrary training. The drawings reflect uncertainty, depressive brooding and some withdrawal. Under stress, she increases her controls and most often reacts intrapunitively, while the boy disorganizes and often acts out upon others. The girl continues to persist in her interest in maturity. She displays determination, intense viewing, feet forward and outward, although her controls are under strain. The neck is often tense and erased and fingers compressed. Her clothing is, however, more mature, she depicts hips and breasts, and will assign teen ages to her figures.

Compulsive detail, binding, legs tightly pressed together, combine with the unstable line and nostril emphasis to suggest temper outbursts. No longer does she unload her dependency upon the male figure, but rather accepts upon her own figure the burden of her weakness. Mouths become more immature, with a small line-arc suggesting truce. She now seems to have less confidence in the seductive detail. She draws shorter, narrower skirts, prim, Peter-Pan collars and sleeves, as if suddenly ashamed of her body. She gives herself fewer curls, bangs, lashes, cosmetic lips, fancy dresses, jewelry, or seductive poses. Sensuality, as reflected in hair substance, cannot be evaded or denied by suggestive outlines as it was by the eleven-year-old girl. As with the boy, hair is now heavily shaded. There is much fussing with hair at this age.

Sexually she is, as in earlier years, more interested in her peers than are the boys who rather fear girls since their fantasies and arousals are more linked with revived Oedipal problems. The 12-year-old girl accords to the male less grudgingly the advantages of strength, self assertion and freedom from load. She reinforces his figure, dresses him more with suits and ties, assigns an older age to him, shows more sexual interest in him and emphasizes his ears. She is much concerned about his opinion of her and seeks out approval from her father at this age.

REFERENCES

1. Frank, L. K., Harrison, R., Hellersberg, E., Machover, K., & Steiner, M. Personality development in adolescent girls. *Monogr. Soc. Res. Child Develpm.*, 1951, *16*, Serial No. 53.
2. Machover, K. *Personality projection in the drawing of the human figure.* Springfield, IL: Charles C Thomas, 1949.
3. ———. Drawing of the human figure: A method of personality investigation. *In* Anderson, H. H., & Anderson, G. L. (Eds.) *An introduction to projective techniques.* New York: Prentice-Hall, 1951, Pp. 341–369.
4. ———. Human figure drawings of children. *J. proj. Tech.*, 1953, *17*, 85–92.
5. ———. The body image in art communication. *J. Proj. Tech.*, 1956, *19*, 453–460.
6. ———. A destructive juvenile delinquent. *In* Burton, A., & Harris, R. E. (Eds.) *Clinical studies of personality.* New York: Harper, 1955.
7. Witkin, H. A., Lewis, H. B., Hertzman, M., Machover, K., Meissner, P. B., & Wapner, S. (Eds.) *Personality through perception.* New York: Harper, 1954.
8. Wolff, W. *Personality of the preschool child.* New York: Grune & Stratton, 1946.

Chapter 11

CHILD CASE STUDY
ALan, BEFORE AND DURING THERAPY

Dennis R. Finger, Ed.D.

This child case, as children's projections tend to be, is refreshingly revealing and consequently engrossingly dramatic.

At the same time, their communicativeness renders these H–T–Ps particularly sensitive and an instrument *par excellence* for test-retest appraisal of changes due to psychotherapy—as this case's gratifying responsiveness, under the talented hands of Dr. Finger, is richly demonstrated. The drawings here are interpreted with both sympathy and with insight. With this case, which tells so emotionally compelling a story, Dennis Finger establishes himself as a wise, unsentimental portraitist of children.

IDENTIFYING DATA

Alan was almost seven and a first grader at the time of intake. His parents were divorcing after being separated for ten months. He had no siblings. An earlier psychoeducational assessment placed Alan in the average range of intelligence.

PRESENTING SYMPTOMS

Alan was having much difficulty in school. In reading, he could not associate a letter with a sound nor do any decoding; and he did not like to read on his own although he liked being read to. Alan could not do simple beginning arithmetic. He did not want to do any writing. Alan would freeze if he found something difficult and seemed very fearful of failure. However, he was able to do the same work if he was given assistance. His teacher reported that Alan had considerable self-doubt and seemed generally anxious. He had trouble retrieving information, answering questions and working. Overall, he had poor academic functioning.

Alan's mother reported separation problems and general tension at home. He did not want to be alone nor sleep by himself. Alan complained of waking up due to bad dreams, but he could not remember any dream content. He was very concerned about his mother leaving him and became very anxious about daily arrangements made for him while his mother worked. When his mother became angry at him, he feared her leaving. He frequently followed his mother around the house.

Alan seemed quite sad and terribly missed his father. At the time of the initial assessment he had not seen his father for a full month, although his father had been his primary caretaker for Alan's first six years.

THE PROJECTIVE DRAWING BATTERY

The projective drawing battery consisted of three approaches: the House-Tree-Person Projective Drawings (H–T–P–P), achromatic and chromatic (Hammer, 1958); the Kinetic Family Drawing (KFD) (Burns & Kaufman, 1970); and the Levy Animal Drawing Story (LADS) (Levy & Levy, 1958).

Children like to draw and usually enjoy the opportunities provided. These three techniques are utilized to gain a more comprehensive picture of the child and to present several different opportunities for the child to project inner issues, conflicts, and strengths.

INITIAL BEHAVIORAL OBSERVATIONS

At the first session I asked Alan to enter the consulting room, but both his mother and Alan stood simultaneously and then proceeded forward. Alan had a great deal of difficulty separating from his mother. As a compromise, the office door was left open for the first half-hour, then closed with Alan's permission. Alan spoke occasionally, and in a baby voice, and was evidently very tense.

PRETHERAPY H-T-P-P

Achromatic

Alan wanted to make a "humungus house, big house." "It's a mansion. It has lots of Nintendo® games in the living room, but it still needs more games." When asked the House's worst part, Alan spontaneously drew a rug on the front steps. Upon questioning, he replied, "You could fall down and slip, there are banana peels on the rug."

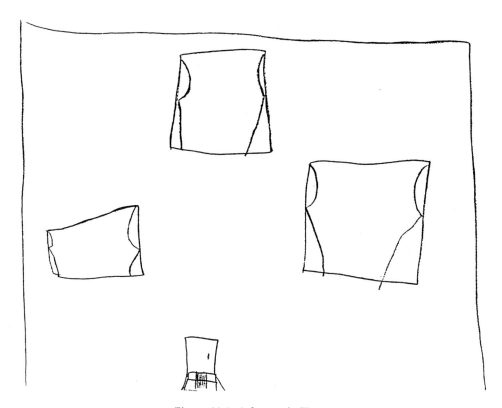

Figure 11-1. **Achromatic House.**

The whole House is awkward looking. There are very large windows and a very small door. It makes it hard to reach Alan through the door, but large windows show a ready and strong need for environmental contact. Perhaps he wants others to connect with him, but he is afraid to let them get close. Grandiose expressions of "big humungus house/mansion" may be seen as a compensatory defense for feeling small, inadequate, and inferior. He draws what he wishes his House to be, a mansion filled with Nintendo games, but it still falls short. The house needs more Nintendo games.

During the inquiry phase of the Tree drawing, Alan mentioned that the rest of the tree was gone. There is a hole in the tree, and a front door. When asked about the top of the tree, Alan said that "Someone came and chopped it down, an awful man who hated all trees." Someone "punched the tree" and made the hole. At that moment Alan inserted quickly, "This is a cartoon, some roadrunner cartoon, and you could run through the door." He stated that "the tree is hollow, tweety bird made it hollow." Just then he said, "There's the monster bird right now and he blew up the tree," and drew circling lines emanating from the giant claw to the tree. Alan shared that the tree is dead, "That's what the man thinks who hates trees wanted."

The Tree, compared to the Person, reflects the subject's relatively deeper and more unconscious feelings about himself (Hammer, 1958). It is easier for the subject to project deeper or more forbidden feelings onto the Tree with less fear of revealing himself. Children tend to draw (a) that Tree toward which they feel the most empathic identification, or (b) that Tree which symbolizes their mothers.

The Tree drawing depicts graphically and powerfully Alan's own experience. He feels massively traumatized, chopped down, killed. The world is very scary. The monster bird claw is only the tip of this huge creature. The great difference in size between the enormous monster bird and the small tree stump reflects the tremendous threat of awful damage Alan feels. He is terrified of being hurt, and already feels badly injured, punched.

As a defense mechanism, in order to handle the intense feelings associated with his projection, Alan tries turning the drawing into a mere "cartoon" dissociating himself from this jarring experience.

Alan was stumped when first asked to draw a picture of a Person. Then he remarked, "I'll draw a weirdo, a snow monster, he wears a jacket." As he worked he made heavy, dark dots on the figure explaining, "He has chicken pox, he's in his own bed. There's a force field around him." Responding to further questioning, Alan related that the snow monster has "rocks for a pillow," and "he's dying, he just is." The snow monster feels "awful."

The drawn Person becomes the vehicle for conveying the subject's closer to conscious view of himself than does the Tree, and his relationships to his environment (Hammer, 1958). As a self-portrait, the subject draws what he feels himself to be.

The snow monster represents Alan's own feelings of rage and impotence. He is a monster that melts. Alan's sense of self is not of a solid and whole person, but one who is more amorphous and weird. Further, this snow monster has chicken pox, skin scars, and is ill, feelings which Alan has

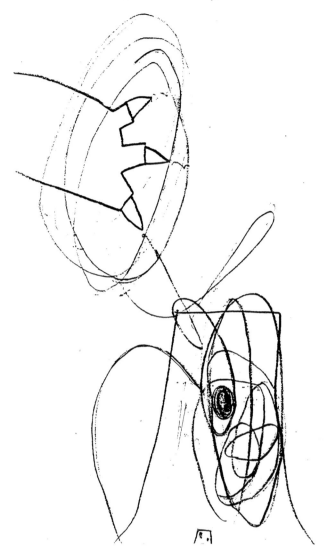

Figure 11-2. **Achromatic Tree.**

about himself. Additionally, there is a force field around him. The force field represents magical thinking in that a shield will protect him from being hurt, chopped down like the Tree. He is lying down in his bed on a pillow of rocks dying and feeling awful. Alan feels very depressed, living a hard life, extremely low, just awful.

The emphasis on buttons underscores his strong dependency yearnings.

This drawing shows evidence of some, at least marginal, depersonalization. Alan does not draw a human being, but a snow monster. Also, the

Figure 11-3. **Achromatic Person.**

force field represents a phobic, perhaps paranoid construction, mixing his feeling terribly threatened with his magical, unreal, solution.

Alan's second drawing of a person is an 87-year-old female who is "just standing there." "She's a painting, with long hair, thinking nothing, feeling pretty good."

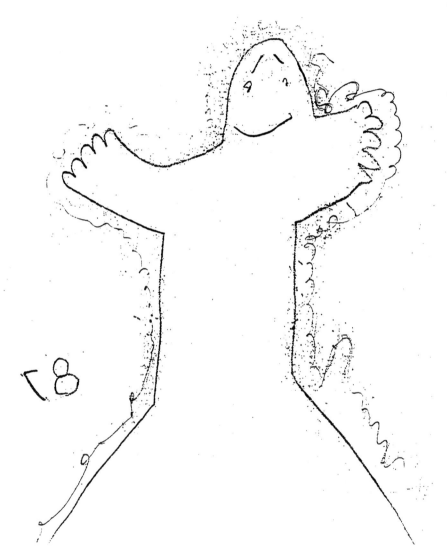

Figure 11-4. **Achromatic Person.**

Again, Alan does not draw a real person, only a *painting* of a person, a person not in the flesh but one step removed. We have further evidence of depersonalization. He is detached from people, and here from the female figure. The form begins to lose humanness with wing-like hands and no differentiated bottom. The painting is an immobile, passive, lifeless, inadequate object. Also, the female in the painting has a beseeching look, as if asking to be picked up like a helpless child. The whole drawing has a very regressive quality. Alan cannot identify with human beings, only secondary representations of persons. Besides the intense adjustment reaction Alan is experiencing to his parent's divorce, loss of his father, and the loss of his family life, there are indications of a deeper pathology characterized by depersonalization, paranoia, and magical thinking.

Chromatic

The achromatic and chromatic drawing phases tap somewhat different layers of the personality (Hammer, 1994). The chromatic drawings cut through the defenses to lay bare a deeper layer of the personality. Pencil drawings may show the way the subject wants to be, the strength and intactness, the defenses. The crayon drawings may show what the subject wants to hide, the secret recesses of human nature below the defenses. The pencil taps the overt, surface defenses; the crayons give the deeper, covert layer of the personality.

Alan's crayon drawing of a house is only a "cave, there's darkness." At that instant, Alan turned the paper over so we could not see the drawn cave. The only elaboration he would make was, "Nobody lives in there."

The house becomes only a bare cave, and further, a cave of darkness which he does not want to face. It is empty, without life. The cave is small and placed on the very bottom of the page. The cave of darkness denotes withdrawal and regression. He does not want to feel his intense reactions to the cave as home. The choice of colors is also meaningful. Brown is often used by depressed subjects and the use of black is associated with emotional constriction (Hammer, 1994). So the cave has a constricted, feelingless core surrounded by depression. The choice of a cave also shows a need to regress to the first enclosed dark world, the womb, the ultimate dependency in which nothing is required of a person and all needs are met fully. Alan is showing a movement toward a deep regression.

The chromatic Tree is "the tree before it got chopped down, a big tree." During the inquiry phase, Alan shared that no part of the tree is dead. "It's healthy and safe, it didn't fall yet, no leaves fell yet." When

Figure 11-5. **Chromatic House.** Boundary is brown, interior is black.

asked what the tree needs most, Alan responded, "water, it has no water, I don't know why."

His drawing gives evidence of Alan's health before the trauma. This is an important indicator for a positive prognosis. Still, the tree is starving for nourishment and care. The bottom of the tree looks like an oral cavity hungrily opening up to Mother Earth for sustenance. Alan is emotionally famished, needing the psychological equivalent of water.

Alan's first chromatic Person is a "woodman." The whole body is made of wood and there is again a force field around it, this time of wood. "Wood is everywhere so no one can kill him." Here the defense, and the fear of total destruction behind it, are both quite evident. In response to questioning, Alan described the woodman as "sleeping, dreaming about sleeping, and feeling good."

Again, there is depersonalization and not a human figure. The brown color is again associated with depression.

Everything is merged: the woodman, the force field, wood is everywhere. Alan is removing himself as a separate person and becoming part of his surroundings. A lack of individuation and differentiation is evident, and like the depersonalized feelings, denotes pathology.

Even though he is made of wood, that is still not enough to protect

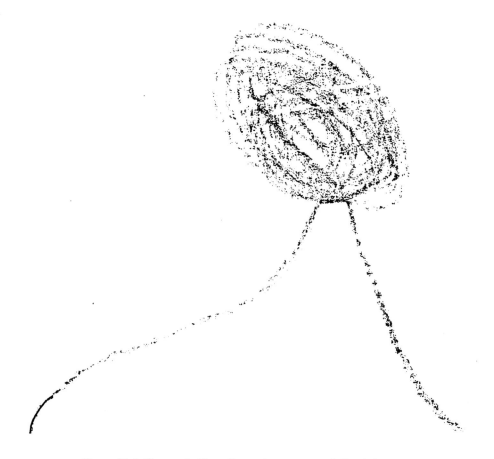

Figure 11-6. **Chromatic Tree.** Crown is green, trunk line is brown.

him. He still needs a force field, but this too is not enough for safety. The woodman is sleeping, and even further, dreaming about sleeping. Even in sleeping, the height of withdrawal, Alan wants more withdrawal, dreaming about sleeping. His sense of self is strikingly diminished. He is terrified of being hurt. The depiction of the woodman sleeping gives further support for depression, including a low energy level and passivity. Alan uses the defense mechanisms of avoidance and denial.

Alan's second drawing of a Person is a "grass lady," whose whole body is made of grass. There is "a grass force field, a bunch of grass." During the inquiry, Alan said, "That's Mother Nature, she's a girl." "She's just staying there. . . . She feels good."

Once more, everything is merged. Not only is there no flesh-and-blood human figure, but there is again not even a separate object with

Figure 11-7. **Chromatic Person.** Woodman and forcefield are brown.

boundaries. Alan is not separated from the mother; and he is very regressed with no sense of self. This finding corresponds with the way Alan and his mother simultaneously rose when Alan was initially called into the consulting room.

PRETHERAPY KINETIC FAMILY DRAWING (KFD)

In his drawing, Alan is alone, "walking downstairs to have breakfast and watch TV and go to school." Just then he wanted to play with clay, and he began to knead it. When Alan was reminded that he was asked to draw a picture of a *family* doing something, he became enraged and said emphatically, "My dad doesn't live here anymore! Does that answer your question!"

For the first time, Alan is able to draw a person, himself. This ability is a good prognostic indicator. But his sense of family is shattered; there is no family now for him. "Going downstairs" again represents feeling down and depressed. He feels alone and estranged from his father. Once more Alan tries to avoid looking at the emotional issue at hand, but then is able to grapple with it when he is prompted. Alan expresses strong

Figure 11-8. **Chromatic Person.** Grass lady is green with black, yellow, red, brown and orange lines.

Figure 11-9. **Kinetic Family Drawing.**

anger appropriately. He is able to assert himself, another good prognostic indicator.

PRETHERAPY LEVY ANIMAL DRAWING STORY (LADS)

After drawing the picture, in the inquiry phase, Alan told the following story:

> Once upon a time there was a dog named Copin and he was walking to his dog house. He's going to eat dinner. Then he went on another walk and he met an alien who had lots of lollypops, cookies, jellies, and cupcakes.

When asked how the story ended, Alan responded, "The alien is sad. Copin feels pretty good; he brought them back to his family."

Figure 11-10. **Levy Animal Drawing.**

Rather than looking like a dog, Alan's drawing resembles an animal that might burrow into the ground and live in Alan's chromatic cavehome. This dog is starving, hungry for emotional nurturance. He needs to be given to, to be fed. There is a striking oral need, suggesting very early deprivation and regression. He meets an alien, again not a fully realized person, who has many goodies. The sense is that the alien is the therapist who has lots of toys and games (used for play therapy). While telling his story, Alan slipped into baby talk, reinforcing the interpretation of his regression to babyhood. Alan's dog is named "Copin," and perhaps that is just what Alan is straining to do: "cope."

At the end of this session, Alan held up the piece of clay which was now rolled into a ball. He looked directly at the therapist and warned, "This is a dangerous creature; you must stay out of its way; it lives underground." Alan seemed to be symbolically strongly cautioning the therapist as if to say, "Watch out! Beneath the surface, I am enraged and dangerous! Proceed with caution!"

DISCUSSION

In terms of diagnosis, at the least, we find a severe adjustment reaction with depression, anxiety, and academic inhibition. However, there are also features associated with deeper pathology: indications of a lack of differentiation between self and environment (a loss of ego boundaries), depersonalization (a loss of "me-ness,"), and paranoia. His extreme academic troubles may be attributed, in part, to his terror about moving ahead and his strong pull to regress.

The prognosis is guarded. There are, however, elements of health in the projective drawings, including the relatively healthy chromatic tree, and his ability to draw himself as a real, flesh-and-blood person on the KFD. He has presenting strengths consisting of a good social life; a concerned mother; a capacity for self-assertion and appropriate expression of anger; artistic skill; the capacity for the healthy use of his imagination; and the hunger for, though fear of, a close, ongoing, nurturing relationship. He has also many ideas and a willingness to share them.

One essential initial goal was to enable the boy to reestablish contact with his father, to get the latter involved with Alan. The importance of regular contact between father and son was emphasized to the parents, as well as the establishment of a working relationship between the therapist and Alan's mother. On going therapy was recommended for Alan and for his parents, and begun.

PROJECTIVE DRAWINGS AND THERAPEUTIC CHANGE

As a clinical tool, projective drawings may be used to look at changes that occur as a result of therapeutic intervention. Progress in therapy can be evaluated along its course through the multiple use of a projective drawing battery, each administration showing a snapshot of the child's psychological world at that moment in time. Oster and Gould (1987) noted, "Because of their brevity, nonthreatening nature, ease of administration and interpretative product, drawings are frequently used in the evaluative process."

PROJECTIVE DRAWINGS: DURING THERAPY

Projective drawings were used to evaluate Alan's progress after two and one-half years of therapy which had involved individual play therapy, joint child-parent sessions, and parent guidance sessions. Besides the therapy, other variables have impacted on the child including maturation, a changed family situation, school interventions, and other uncontrolled variables. Thus, these factors also need to be considered in explaining change.

DURING THERAPY H-T-P-P

Achromatic

During the inquiry phase Alan described the house as having "a sundeck and a sliding door." It's a one-family home; there are dome windows. "The House is built good; there are two bedrooms and stairs to the roof. There's a weathervane, a chimney with smoke, and a car outside." When asked what the House needed most, Alan replied, "a new paint job; it has no color; it's a plain gray."

Alan's previous achromatic house was rigid and basic, while this house is imaginative. Immediately may be seen a more appropriate use of size, a more advanced use of content, and more complexity. There is direct and more open accessibility to him, and reduced grandiosity. A sundeck denotes the ability to relax and enjoy, and further, it may indicate an openness to take in the sun's warmth overhead. This may relate to taking in his parents' warmth and adults' warmth from overhead. The car depicts that he can be more mobile. The dome windows show a more advanced conception as well as letting in more light from the outside. The emptiness shown in his first achromatic House drops away. The weathervane may be viewed as an appraiser of the emotional climate around him. He is attuned to reading the parents' moods, looking for the winds of emotional conflict in the air. The easy smoke coming from the chimney suggests that he feels able now to express his feelings.

His Tree is "the tallest tree in the world; it's one year old with leaves on the top and a branch." The season is summer, the tree is alive, and no part is dead. Alan remarked, "There used to be more limbs, but they got chopped off. A big bad wolf wanted to use them to fry a pig." The tree is healthy and "rain goes on it." The best part is the branches, and the worst

Figure 11-11. **Achromatic House.**

part is the the whole middle. "It used to be wide, it got skinny." When asked what the tree needs most, Alan answered, "sunshine."

Alan's first achromatic tree was massively damaged, reflecting an acutely damaged sense of self. Currently, there is more fullness. Some grandiosity is still apparent. There are still feelings of trauma and perhaps castration, though considerably milder. There previously were more limbs chopped off. However, now one branch is growing out, a sign of health as he dares to stick out, reach out. Also, given the location of the branch and its penis-like structure, it may be that Alan is coming of age and regarding his penis as a pleasure producer.

Discussing his first, the achromatic, Person, Alan now says, "He will be a tall, skinny man, about 30 years old.... He's watching a parade, thinking he's happy because he likes the parade."

Like the tall tree that's skinny, this man is shaped similarly. There is an exaggerated sense of self (so very tall) and a weak sense of self

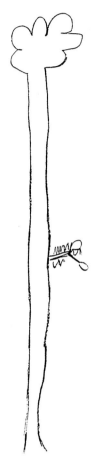

Figure 11-12. **Achromatic Tree.**

(skinny). Both are apparent expressions of his developing selfness. The force field has dropped out and there is a fleshed-out, real person. The depersonalization has been overcome.

More pleasant or positive things are now going on in his life. There's a parade; in his House drawing there is a car. Life is less threatening. Now there is even enjoyment, a parade. The parade has replaced the force field. He can now enjoy his environment instead of concentrating on protecting himself from harm in it. No nose may represent continued although less castration fear. There are still, carried over from the first set of drawings, only three fingers, suggesting his continued feelings of inadequacy.

Alan's second achromatic person is a woman age 30. "She's little. She's watching the parade. She likes it and feels happy."

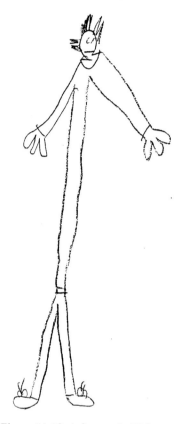

Figure 11-13. **Achromatic Male.**

There is a real flesh-and-blood person, not a mere painting. There is more differentiation as a person, the wings become hands. The female picture is about one-fourth the size of the male figure. Perhaps he keeps the female figure small to be able to relate to her. He makes the female into a nonthreatening figure. Alan may also be entering the world of sexuality and girls (e.g., the tree "penis.") Symbolically, Alan may be saying, "I am big enough to handle sexuality with girls."

Chromatic

For his chromatic house Alan stated, "I'll make my house. This is my room (lower right). It's raining out (it *was* raining outside). It's with other houses. It's built well and looks happy." The best part of the house is "the whole thing." The worst part is "Nothing," and the house needs "Nothing."

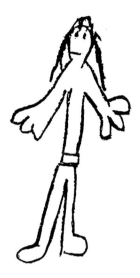

Figure 11-14. **Achromatic Female.**

He moves from a dark cave to now a real house. It's raining out, so there's residue from the dark cave. There is still rain in Alan's life. Now it was raining hard that night; he was aware of it and brought the rain into his drawing. The womb-like implication of the cave is gone, as is the intense withdrawal and regression. The color has changed from a combination depicting depression and constriction to a more emotional blue. Whereas blue may have some depressive connotations, it is considerably lighter in tone than the heavier dismal black of the cave.

Alan chose to make an orange tree. "The season is winter and the tree is next to a real house. The tops are branches, and it's old, a century. It's with other trees, it's alive, no part is dead and it's healthy." Alan related that the best part is the whole thing and there is no worst part. When asked what the tree needs most, Alan replied, "leaves, it doesn't get leaves in the winter (this drawing was done in the actual winter season).

The Tree is centrally placed, no longer shifted to the side. It now stands straight and tall. There is also a change in the base of the tree. Whereas the initial chromatic Tree had a large, wide, mouth-like base hugging onto Mother Earth, very oral looking and its shape associated with feelings of insecurity, now there is a proper base. The Tree reflects a child who is more secure and steady. He now adds branches; the first chromatic Tree had none. Alan is currently able to reach out into the environment more, showing a capacity to connect to others and to deal with his surroundings.

Figure 11-15. **Chromatic House.** House and rain are blue.

After drawing his first chromatic Person, Alan looked up and said, "It's you." He described the person as "about 30 years old, standing there, waiting to cross the street to go home." The Person is thinking, "It's too rainy and you want it to stop. You're feeling happy."

He draws a real person, and also shows differentiation of self from the environment. Consistently now the depersonalization has dropped out. The picture is affirming of humanness and developing growth with an open, full stance. The hands are overemphasized. He is taking karate and has become more active with utilizing his hands. Alan has become more healthily aggressive, and is testing out his new hand skills.

He draws the therapist, suggesting he is incorporating the new parent/therapist into himself, a favorable process in therapy. At his current age of 9, he is still incorporating a model, which is age appropriate. Hammer (1958) stated,

A subject may depict a significant person in his/her life because of the person's strong influence for the subject. The drawing of a significant other is found frequently in children's drawings and often represents a fusion of self and

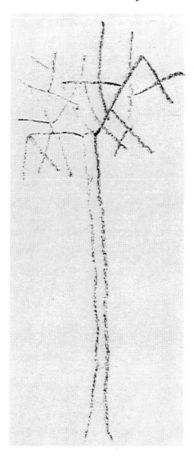

Figure 11-16. **Chromatic Tree.** Tree is orange.

other. The "other person" children represent in their drawings is almost invariably a parental figure and probably represents the great importance of the "significant other" in the child's life and the need for a model to identify with and to incorporate into his self-concept. The kind of significant figure the child reveals in his drawing is often a prophesying element and predicts traits which retest drawings, years later, frequently indicate the child incorporates. In this manner, projective drawings tend to reveal, one may say, the future self.

Alan's second chromatic Person is his mom, age 44. "She's putting on her coat and thinking what she'll do at work today. She's happy."

In the first assessment, the Grass Lady was merged with the environment without boundaries or a sense of a coherent self. Here now the female figure, the mother, once again is a fully real, not a near-person. However, we see more improvement with the male authority figure perhaps because of the patient's positive experience with a male figure.

Figure 11-17. **Chromatic Person.** Therapist is orange.

The female is depicted as more aggressive than the male, with threatening sharp fingers. She looks a bit out of control, especially in terms of the hair and the ballooning chest and arms. With emotionality added, the female figure becomes large and intimidating. There is also an overemphasis on the top half of the figure and a deemphasis below the waist. Alan also puts pants on the female figure. Does she wear the pants at home? Or is there a need to diminish her sexuality? Or does he put up a defense against, and feel uncomfortable with, his sexual feelings?

All of the drawings, past and present, sink to the bottom of the page, to come to rest paper-based. Depression was, and is still, a problem—and remains to be addressed in the subsequent treatment. His frequent use of only one color (rare for children) supports the depressive inference. And an orange tree and orange people suggest that what emotional tone is present is experienced as uncomfortable and jarring.

Figure 11-18. **Chromatic Person.** Mother is orange.

DURING THERAPY KFD

Telling about his drawing of a family doing something, Alan stated, "The only person I do things with is my mom. I have long sleeves over my hands, and my mom is leaning back." When asked what they are doing, Alan responded, "We're going on Mr. Toad's Wild Ride in Disneyworld. Yeh, we're having fun and feeling happy."

Alan now sees himself as having at least a part of a family. He is no longer shattered, utterly depressed, and alone. He and his mom are having fun together. Perhaps life has been a "wild ride" for Alan, but he is handling it and starting to enjoy it more. His hands are covered, yet situated near his mother's breast. Once more there may be an indication of sexual feelings arising, specifically toward his mother.

Figure 11-19. **Kinetic Family Drawing.**

THERAPEUTIC PROGRESS

Alan made much progress during his therapy. Three significant changes were: his reexperiencing a separation-individuation crisis and moving from a merged state with mother to being a more separate person able to progress in school and enjoy a more independent life; his movement from a dissociated, unowned anger to a more owned and integrated anger and mastery with the ability to channel and utilize his aggression; and his working through his mourning of the loss of his intact family to an adaptation to, and an enjoyment of, his new changed family situation.

Alan is enjoying writing and often writes about personal experiences. He has been asking many questions about the world. Alan has strong arithmetic skills and is a good problem-solver. He has excellent listening comprehension and is an active class participant. Alan is happy with his friends and enjoys school, participating now in all activities. His work habits have shown more maturity and focus. He seems calmer and more confident trying new things. Alan has, all in all, come a long way.

Overall, clinicians may better understand and empathize with the inner experience of children (and adults) through the use of projective drawings. The drawings present a unique opportunity for seeing, and hearing, a child's innermost struggles, which cannot, or will not, yet be put into words.

REFERENCES

Burns, R.C., & Kaufman, S.H. (1970). *Kinetic family drawings (KFD): An introduction to understanding children through kinetic drawings.* New York: Brunner/Mazel.

Hammer, E.F. (Ed.). (1958). *The clinical application of projective drawings.* Springfield, IL: Charles C Thomas.

Hammer, E.F. (1994). Annual projective drawing workshop, New York City, July.

Levy, S. & Levy, R.A. (1958). Symbolism in animal drawings. In E. F. Hammer (Ed.), *The clinical application of projective drawings.* Springfield, IL: Charles C Thomas.

Oster, G.D. & Gould, P. (1987). *Using drawings in assessment and therapy.* New York: Brunner/Mazel.

RESEARCH STUDIES
AND RESEARCH ISSUES

Chapter 12

ISSUES CONCERNING RESEARCH FINDINGS
AND FUTURE DIRECTIONS

Projective drawings have been attacked and defended vigorously, with a sizable literature resulting. The balance of positive vs. negative research results has not changed much since previous reviews. But what has emerged are more promising directions of research and an increasing sophistication concerning the defects of previous research designs. These promising directions may be seen in the following:

1. Levy, Minsky, and Lomax (1977) found that the accuracy or inaccuracy of the proportions within the figure drawings correlated highly—and in the expected direction—with the degree of pathology of the subject executing the drawing. Thus the relationships between the elements of the drawing, more than the individual details, may prove to be the validating dimensions. This promising lead, of comparative dimensions within the sets of drawings of an individual, is illustrated by the carefully scored and analyzed work of Irgens-Jensen (1971). Comparing the male and female human figure drawings of male problem drinkers, he found that alcoholics, to a statistically significant degree, more frequently drew male figures with abnormal (blurred, disturbed, or omitted) heads and caricatured eyes. Thus, using the heads of the female figures drawn by alcoholics as a baseline, Irgens-Jensen could discern the emergence of distortions concerning the self-figure. These male subjects also drew female figures, again to a statistically significant degree, larger than male figures. The females were drawn in an obscene manner and were rated by judges as more typically a sex object, in the style of drawings in men's rooms. Based on this cluster of findings, Irgens-Jensen engaged in a multivariate analysis which accounted for 60 percent of the variants associated with alcoholism. The direct interpretations from the projective drawings revealed the problem drinker as having hostile and conflicted attitudes toward females, a less differentiated and articulated conception of his own body, a diminished lack of self-confidence, a

reduced control of emotional impulses, and a reliance on both punitive and crude defense mechanisms. The study stands as an example of how careful research with projective drawings can be done, with mutual illumination of the subject population and of the validity of the projective instrument.

The central findings of this study concerning validity of several dimensions of projective drawings are consistent with findings of Craddick and Leipold (1968), who also investigated the hypotheses that alcoholics will draw same-sex figures smaller than will a control group and that male alcoholics will draw male human figures smaller than female figures since more anxiety is attached to their own body image (and, according to my own work with alcoholics, because of their feeling threatened by females). The statistical differences were significant at better than the .01 level. The more impressive difference was within the sets of each subject's drawings, between the comparative size of his male and female drawings.

2. The introduction of dynamic stimuli (rather than the investigation of static relationships), by intensifying the reactions caught by projective drawings, puts the variable in question under a magnifying glass, as it were, to enhance the emergence of data for validity studies. Ludwig (1969) investigated the relationship between one's self-image and one's projective drawing of a person. Negative feedback, in the form of criticism of a male subject's physical abilities, produced a highly significant corresponding decrease in the height of the male figure drawn. That criticism from "experts" resulted in constriction of the height of the person drawn underscores the validity of height of drawing as a reflection of self-esteem.

An interesting collateral effect was the significant increase in the athletic appearance of the male figure drawn as the height decreased. The threat to the ego that a lowered self-image produces seems to give rise to a compensatory increase in the athletic quality drawn onto the person. This suggests, we may read from the data, that the deeper feelings about the self will be expressed in the more basic qualities of the drawing, such as height, whereas the secondary or defensive maneuver—in this case, compensation—will be projected via secondary qualities such as the exaggeration of muscles and the introduction of athletic equipment.

Another core hypothesis involved in projective drawing assessment was also verified: the higher a subject's state of self-esteem the more likely a "happy" mood will be drawn on the projected figure, and the lower the self-esteem the more likely a dysphoric mood will be projected.

In a study investigating the hypothesis that extensive shading in the drawing serves as an index of anxiety, Goldstein and Faterson (1969) showed films to male subjects; these included an anthropological one, from Geza Rohein's study of Australian aborigines, depicting a subincision rite. The film showed an incision being made on the surface of the penis with a sharp stone, the bleeding penis being held over a fire, and the faces of the initiates reflecting their pain. The control situation included nonstress films, one a travelogue of the Far West and one of London. The findings dramatically supported the hypothesis of the relationship between anxiety and shading for the self-sex figure. This study illustrates the principle of dynamic stimuli in research and, at the same time, the earlier principle mentioned involving comparative assessment within the set of drawings. In terms of the latter, the proportionately greater anxiety concerning the self was directly correlated with the greater shading laid onto the self-figure in contrast to the opposite-sex figure.

In experiments such as these, the issues of ethics and immediate alleviation of the induced anxiety or of the negative feedback (as in the experiment before the current one cited) are self-evident. Employing the dynamic stimuli already provided by eugenic sterilization, Hammer (1953), without subjecting individuals to negative stimuli for the purpose of the experiment, found striking support for the hypothesis of sexual symbolism. Elongated objects in the House-Tree-Person drawings, such as chimneys, branches, arms, nose, and feet, were utilized as phallic symbols. Circles, triangles, and objects with a vertical split down the center were employed as vaginal symbols, and served as reflections of felt castration in the drawings of males. Feelings of genital inadequacy were presented via the phallic symbols drawn as damaged, cut through, broken, or otherwise impaired.

3. Studies which avoid the hazards of employing the pigeonholes of psychiatric diagnosis (themselves lacking in established reliability and validity) have better chances at establishing projective technique validity. Griffith and Peyman (1965) found support for the hypothesis that eye and ear emphasis in the drawing of a person is associated with ideas of reference. This study is memorable in drawing to our attention the superiority of actual overt behavior to official psychiatric classification in attempts to validate projective techniques. Had psychiatric diagnosis been the criterion in this study, nonsignificant rather than statistically significant results would have been yielded. Also avoiding psychiatric

diagnosis as the criterion, Schmidt and McGowan (1965) demonstrated the relationship between drawn Persons and the traits of the subject offering the drawing; judges operating "blindly" could distinguish figure drawings by physically disabled persons from figure drawings by physically normal persons.

4. Content and global dimensions are proving more valid as projective drawing indicators than are formal or expressive characteristics. In a noteworthy study, Coopersmith, Sokol, Beardslee, and Coopersmith (1976) obtained figure drawings from 97 preadolescents who differed in self and behavioral assessment of self-esteem. The figure drawings were scored for formal characteristics, content, and global-interpretations of the total drawings. Content and global-interpretive categories proved more differentiating between self-esteem groups than did the formal qualities. The advantage of content interpretation over the scoring categories has clearly been emerging in studies of the Rorschach, and as Klopfer (1972) summarized, "It has become amply evident that content is that aspect of the Rorschach which has shown the greatest success as a predictor of other behavior."

5. The validity of projective drawing hypotheses is being established in children's drawings in advance of adults' drawings. In addition to the study by Coopersmith et al. on preadolescent subjects, one by Vane and Eisen (1965) may serve as illustration. In this study, kindergarten children served as subjects. Those rated as showing poor adjustment in school produced figure drawings differentiated, to a statistically significant degree, from the other children's on four signs: "grotesque" (the drawing has gross distortions), "no body," "no mouth," and "no arms." A follow-up the next year, with first-grade teachers' ratings, served to validate all four signs. These qualities in children's drawings thus have predictive value as indices of maladjustment (and as clues for consideration of referral for preventive therapy).

In a study of samples of disturbed and of normal children, disturbed youngsters showed considerably greater tendencies toward barrenness in their drawings and toward the inclusion of only minimal details (Davis & Hoopes, 1975).

A series of studies was undertaken by Koppitz (1968) to select a list of valid "Emotional Indicators" for children's drawings "from the hypotheses of Machover (1949) and Hammer (1958)." Comparisons of the Emotional Indicators on the projective drawings of well-adjusted pupils with those of clinic patients validated the Emotional Indicator technique for spotting emotional difficulties. As one example, shy children drew tiny figures more often than did others. Another study showed that anxiety or threat, too, produced constriction in the size of drawings (Craddick, 1963). Generally, we are finding that experiments on validity of projective drawings employing child subjects more easily establish the hypothesis in question. This may be because children's drawings, as with children's behavior in general, are more transparent and less defensively covered. As we find important leads about adults by studying children, and as we find out much about the universal in people by studying neurotic and psychotic behavior, we may initially seek those situations where the issue is more obviously laid bare. More concentrated research efforts with the young subject first may be the wisest sequential program to pursue at this point of development of our understanding of the language of projective drawings.

6. Apfeldorf, Walter, Kaiman, Smith, and Arnett (1974) focused on the affectively toned associations that occur when an observer first sees a drawing, and from this developed a system for measuring two components: emission of emotional associations and evaluation of affective associations. This method was applied with significant success in studying individuals who had represented in their drawing an image correlated with their actual physical appearance. The research suggested that the affective tones and their evaluation may contribute more to the assessment of the subject who did the drawing than do the usual components focused on. It is for this reason, of course, that the Post Drawing Inquiry, with its many emotionally toned searching questions, is traditionally employed to obtain the subject's emotional and associational elements to enrich the drawing analysis.

7. We are learning to separate the data within any study for possible sex linkage operating in the study. One such finding occurred, for example, in a study (Roback, 1966) of the relationship between figure drawing size and depression. In this investigation, there was a significant difference (.01) in the height of drawings between depressed and control-group females, although not in their male counterparts. Keeping the male and female data combined in an aggregate had obscured the significant difference for female subjects. We similarly don't know whether keeping the data in one mass may in many other studies have spuriously masked the significant validity of the investigated dimension for one sex or the other.

8. The use of a battery of drawings is suggested for research purposes,

as it is used clinically by those who employ the House-Tree-Person-Person (one of each sex), both achromatic and chromatic, and the Draw-a-Family technique combined as the minimal drawing battery, rather than only the drawing of a male and a female Person. A drawing of just two people is, after all, a very small sample. This might be much like testing the validity of a Rorschach examination by employing only the first two cards. The conflicting results of research studies based merely on the Draw-a-Person technique suggest that for a more valid test we should employ a wider projective drawing net than just the paired drawings of the human figure. Caligor (1952) found that paranoid trends could be detected in only 25 percent of a group of paranoid schizophrenics when only one drawing was used but could be detected in 85 percent when a series of eight drawings was employed.

We know—not only as clinicians but as readers of novels, as play watchers, and as viewers of art (think, for example, of Kafka, of Tennessee Williams, and of Van Gogh, particularly his later work)—we know, in our bones, that every creative product draws in part from the psychic innards of the creator. We receive, and resonate to, the person revealed in the work, the tenderness of J. D. Salinger, the sympathy of Rembrandt, the strength of Michelangelo as well as his bisexuality, the gloom of El Greco, the fury of Beethoven, the macho of Hemingway, the agony of Toulouse-Lautrec, or the wit of Picasso. Nor does it have to be art to embody the artist, for even more apparent is the sadism in the nonart novels of Mickey Spillane.

Shy children draw shyly, aggressive children aggressively, impulsive people impulsively, and controlled people tightly. Part of the difficulty revealed in our experiments is expressed in the truth offered by Saul Bellow. The recent Nobel laureate tells us, in *Herzog*, that human life "is far subtler than any of its models."

Many of our experiments do not catch the elusive variables because these clues do not always appear in the same place. A person may reveal trait X in the type of line with which he draws, another may reveal the same trait in the contents he draws, another person in the placement of the drawing on the page, another in its size, another in the color employed, another in the pressure, i.e., the savage digging of the pencil into the paper vs. the hesitant, uncertain, timid line pressure, and so on. In one set of projective drawings a diagnostic hint emerges, in another a personality need, in still another psychodynamics, and in still another something of expressive personality style. It is the rare experiment that can throw out so fine and so comprehensive a net as to catch such complexity for which the clinical approach is, thus far at least, more flexibly geared. It is, perhaps, in part for this reason that studies employing global analysis of projective drawings prove more effective than those resting on item analysis.

Lastly, there is the sterling answer to those naysayers among the research psychologists, the innovating response Burley and Handler come up with from their study of "Personality Factors in the Accurate Interpretation of Projective Tools: D–A–P." This study appears later in this book, so I will not steal their thunder by here mentioning the pivotal essence of their investigation. But their imaginative chapter is exciting reading, and might well influence our subsequent research work.

As we continue with our research efforts, the above guideposts may point the way toward a more sophisticated and more refined program for future efforts.

SUMMARY AND DISCUSSION

Meaningful gains have emerged in research areas by the arrival of more promising directions of research and of a growing sophistication concerning the inadequacies of previous research designs. These include focus on relationships between the dimensions within the drawings rather than on isolated details in drawings; the introduction of dynamic stimuli* into the drawing experience; the avoidance of psychiatric diagnosis as the accepted criteria since psychiatric diagnosis itself constitutes an unvalidated set of pigeonholes and also varies from institution to institution and from geographic region to geographic region, to say nothing of from psychiatrist to psychiatrist; a drift to the more promising variables of content and global evaluation, more preliminary work on the more direct and forthright expression in children's drawings before moving up the scale; affect associations to the drawings; studies focusing on a battery of drawings not on single drawings; and separation of the data of studies by sex rather than allow the data of males and females to cancel each other out as has been observed, all too often, to happen.

In sum, to reconcile the affirming positive clinical findings with the ambiguous, mixed research results, it is particularly on the point to

---

*The Kinetic Family Drawings, for example.

consider here the judicious assessment once made by Gordon Alport: "The problem facing psychology today is to prove that which it simply *knows* to be true."

In line with this, up against the mixed research findings, we have the perceptions of the professional artists, as for example no less a genius than Leonardo da Vinci, for one, who noted the projective phenomenon in that regardless of the subject who sits for him, "the artist always paints himself."

The weight of still another genius, Picasso, may be put alongside of Leonardo, and intrinsically in his prodigious work itself. In his rich stream of variegated portraits, we note how often his subjects were perceived through the filter of projection, and thus so many of the paintings are flooded by the self of Picasso. Patterson Zims, in *Picasso and Portraiture* (1996), points out that Picasso's "head and stance can be detected—in works (of) portraits of others, in overlays or conflations of his facial features or his body." And so Zims finds, particularly in the later of the portraits, Picasso's "unrelenting, mordant and noble" traits portrayed.

REFERENCES

Abel, T. M. Figure drawings and facial disfigurement. *American Journal of Orthopsychiatry*, 1953, *23*, 253–261.

Apfeldorf, M., & Smith, W. J. The representation of the body self in human figure drawings. *Journal of Projective Techniques and Personality Assessment*, 1966, *30*, 283–289.

Apfeldorf, M., Walter, C., Kaiman, B., Smith, W., & Arnett, W. A method for the evaluation of affective associations to figure drawings. *Journal of Personality Assessment*, 1974, *38*, 441–449.

Bender, L. Psychological principle of the visual motor gestalt test. *Transactions of the New York Academy of Sciences*, 1949, *70*, 167–170.

Buck, J. N. Personal communication, 1970.

Caligor, L. The detection of paranoid trends by the 8 Card Redrawing Test (8 CRT). *Journal of Clinical Psychology*, 1952, *8*, 397–401.

Cauthen, N., Sandman, C., Kilpatrick, D., & Deabler, H. D–A–P correlates of *Sc* scores on the MMPI. *Journal of Projective Techniques*, 1969, *33*, 262–264.

Coopersmith, S., Sokol, D., Beardslee, B., & Coopersmith, A. Figure drawing as an expression of self-esteem. *Journal of Personality Assessment*, 1976, *40*, 368–374.

Craddick, R. Size of Halloween witch drawings prior to, on, and after Halloween. *Perceptual and Motor Skills*, 1963, *16*, 235–238.

Craddick, R., & Leipold, W. Note on the height of Draw-a-Person figures by male alcoholics. *Journal of Projective Techniques,* 1968, *32,* 486.

Cramer-Azima, F. J. Personality changes and figure drawings: A case treated with ACTH. *Journal of Clinical Psychology,* 1956, *20,* 143–149.

Cutter, F. Sexual differentiation in figure drawings and overt deviation. *Journal of Clinical Psychology,* 1956, *12,* 369–372.

Davis, C., & Hoopes, J. Comparison of H–T–P drawings of young deaf and hearing children. *Journal of Personality Assessment,* 1975, *39,* 28–33.

Goldstein, H., & Faterson, H. Shading as an index of anxiety in figure drawings. *Journal of Projective Techniques and Personality Assessment,* 1969, *33,* 454–456.

Goldstein, K., & Sheerer, N. Abstract and concrete behavior. *Psychological Monograph,* 1941, *43,* 1–151.

Goldworth, S. A. A comparative study of the drawings of a man and a woman done by normal, neurotic, schizophrenic, and brain damaged individuals. Doctoral dissertation, University of Pittsburgh, 1950.

Gray, D. M., & Pepitone, A. Effect of self-esteem on drawings of the human figure. *Journal of Consulting Psychology,* 1964, *28,* 452–455.

Griffith, A., & Peyman, D. Eye-ear emphasis in the DAP Test as indicating ideas of reference. In B. I. Murstein (Ed.), *Handbook of projective techniques.* New York: Basic Books, 1965.

Gutman, B. An investigation of the applicability of the human figure drawing in predicting improvement in therapy. Unpublished doctoral thesis, New York University, 1952.

Hammer, E. An investigation of sexual symbolism: A study of H–T–P's of eugenically sterilized subjects. *Journal of Projective Techniques,* 1953, *17,* 401–413.

Hammer, E. (Ed.). *The clinical application of projective drawings.* Springfield, IL: Thomas, 1958.

Hammer, E. Critique of Swensen's "Empirical evaluation of human figure drawings. *Journal of Projective Techniques,* 1959, *23,* 30–32.

Irgens-Jensen, O. *Problem drinking and personality: A study based on the Draw-a-Person Test.* Oslo: Universitetsforlaget, 1971.

Kamino, D. K. An investigation of the meaning of the human figure drawing. *Journal of Clinical Psychology,* 1960, *16,* 429–430.

Klopfer, W. "Will the real Rorschach please stand up?" *Contemporary Psychology,* 1972, *17,* 25–26.

Koppitz, E. M. *Psychological evaluation of children's human figure drawings.* New York: Grune & Stratton, 1968.

Lakin, M. Formal characteristics of human figure drawings by institutionalized and non-institutionalized aged. *Journal of Gerontology,* 1960, *15,* 76–78.

Landisberg, S. Personal communication, 1973.

Levy, Minsky, and Lomax. In preparation, 1978.

Lord, M. Activity and affect in early memories of adolescent boys. *Journal of Personality Assessment,* 1971, *35,* 418–456.

Ludwig, D. Self-perception and the Draw-a-Person Test. *Journal of Projective Techniques,* 1969, *33,* 257–261.

Machover, K. A case of frontal lobe injury following attempted suicide. *Rorschach Research Exchange*, 1947, *11*, 9–20.

Machover, K. *Personality projection in the drawing of the human figure.* Springfield, IL: Thomas, 1949.

Neal, J. *Encephalitis: A clinical study.* New York: Grune & Stratton, 1942.

Niebuhr, H., Jr., & Cohen, D. The effect of psychopathology on visual discrimination. *Journal of Abnormal and Social Psychology*, 1956, *53*, 173–177.

Phillips, L. *Human adaptation and its failures.* New York: Academic Press, 1968.

Proceedings of the 16th International Congress of Psychology, Psychological testing in diagnosing cerebral pathology. 1960, 811–812.

Roback, R. Depression and size of the drawn human figure. *Journal of Abnormal Psychology*, 1966, *71*, 416.

Schmidt, L. D., & McGowan, J. F. The differentiation of human figure drawings. *Journal of Consulting Psychology*, 1965, *23*, 129–133.

Shaskan, D., Yarnell, H., & Alper, K. Physical, psychiatric and psychometric studies of post-encephalitic Parkinsonism. *Journal of Nervous and Mental Disorder*, 1943, *96*, 653–662.

Stoer, L., Corotto, L., & Cormutt, R. The role of visual perception in the reproduction of Bender-Gestalt designs. *Journal of Projective Techniques and Personality Assessment*, 1965, *29*, 473–478.

Swensen, C. H. Empirical evaluations of human figure drawings. *Psychology Bulletin*, 1957, *54*, 431–466.

Swensen, C. H., & Sipprelle, C. N. Some relationships among sexual characteristics of human figure drawings. *Journal of Projective Techniques*, 1956, *30*, 224–226.

Tolor, A. Teachers' judgments of the popularity of children from their human figure drawings. *Journal of Clinical Psychology*, 1955, *11*, 158–162.

Vane, J., & Eisen, V. The Goodenough D–A–P test and signs of maladjustment in kindergarten children. In B. I. Murstein (Ed.), *Handbook of projective techniques.* New York: Basic Books, 1965.

Vernier, C. M. *Projective test productions: I. Projective drawings.* New York: Grune & Stratton, 1952.

Zims, P. *Picasso and Portraiture.* New York: The Museum of Modern Art, 1996.

Chapter 13

VALIDITY OF CLINICAL JUDGMENTS BASED ON HUMAN FIGURE DRAWINGS*

ZEV WILLIAM WANDERER†

The literature establishes that clinicians have routinely been making diagnostic judgments based on techniques of equivocal validity. In a study considering clinical as well as experimental specifications for a suitable methodology, it was found that Draw-A-Person experts are capable of identifying mental defectives far beyond chance expectations. Four remaining matched groups (schizophrenics, neurotics, homosexuals, and normals), however, were found not to be identifiable, even after the experts were permitted a second chance to make a correct diagnosis. The expertness of the judges, as predicted from the ranks they were accorded by their peers, was unrelated to their actual performance.

A major responsibility of the psychologist is to insure that the techniques that he uses actually do what they purport to do. As Meehl once put it, "Regardless of one's theory about personality and regardless of one's choice of data, whether Rorschach, MMPI, ... intuition, table, equation, or rational hypotheses developed in a case conference—the honest clinician cannot avoid the question 'Am I doing better than I could do by flipping pennies?' [Meehl, 1954, p. 136]." The assurance of validity is particularly urgent in the area of psychodiagnosis. Clinicians often contend that they do not use their tests in a mechanical, additive way, but that their decisions are ultimately complex judgments. Clinical judgments, however, are not exempt from scientific scrutiny. Hunt con-

*Reprinted with permission: Wanderer, Z., Validity of clinical judgments based on Human Figure Drawings, *J. Consult. & Clinical Psych.* 1969, 33, 143–150.

*Based on the author's dissertation at Teachers College, Columbia University, in partial fulfillment of the requirements for the degree of Doctor of Philosophy. Partially supported by the Behavior Research Institute of California (Grant 69-002).

†Currently with the Center for Behavior Therapy, 415 North Camden Drive, Beverly Hills, California 90210. The author wishes to express appreciation to Edward Joseph Shoben, Jr., who supervised the entire project; to Laurance F. Shaffer and Stanley Lieberfreund, who provided guidance in the report of the research; and to Richard Lindeman and William Frank, who were especially helpful with the statistical aspects of the study. Special thanks are due Karen Machover and Solomon Machover for their long consultations and thoughtful suggestions during the formative stages of the study. Valuable editorial assistance was provided by Aviva Wanderer.

cluded that "we should consider the individual clinician as a clinical instrument, and study and evaluate his performance exactly as we study and evaluate a test [Hunt, 1946, p. 317]."

At a 1958 Society for Projective Techniques symposium, Kenneth Little summarized the situation regarding the validity of projective techniques: "It is somewhat embarrassing to have to say that the published evidence on projective techniques indicates that they have either zero, or at best, very low positive effective validity indices. Even in those studies with the most positive of results, correlations are of an order of magnitude which make predictions for the individual largely a waste of time [Little, 1959, p. 287]."

In 1949, Karen Machover standardized the administration and formalized the interpretation of a figure-drawing test which later became known as the Draw-A-Person (DAP) test. Although she saw *S*'s verbal associations to his drawings as an auxiliary source of personality information, she relied heavily on universal symbolism and other psychoanalytic constructs in the absence of, or in addition to, those associations. The decision to study the DAP as the subject of the current investigation was based on three criteria: its widespread use (Sundberg, 1961), contradictory conclusions reported in reviews of the literature (Jones & Thomas, 1961, pp. 256–258; Lublin & Lublin, 1967; Swensen, 1957, pp. 460–461), and the allegation that "few of Machover's hypotheses have been explicitly tested by definitive studies [Swensen, 1957, p. 460]."

Quest for a Method

A validating use of statistics that makes no assumptions beyond those of the theory of probability is the method of correct matchings (Meehl, 1954, pp. 11–12). Dating back to Vernon's (1936) early graphological experiments, the matching method keeps the criterion constant and turns to individual differences in the dependent variable. In that way, it differs from classical experiments, modeled after those in the physical sciences which systematically vary the independent variable and record changes in the dependent variable. In a matching study which uses judges who base their judgments on test data, the judges are the *S*s, and their judgments are the dependent variable. Judgments should be expected to vary in response to the differential stimuli represented by the productions of discrete criterion groups. Hence, the method is called "differential"

(Andrews, 1948). Tables, prepared by Chapman (1934) and Dudek (1952), provide expected frequencies for such forced-choice matches.

The requirements set forth in the American Psychological Association's (1954) *Technical Recommendations* concerning the report of validity information imply, by analogy, procedures for the proper validation of a test. Consideration of these recommendations along with the findings of relevant studies (e.g., Bolotin, 1960; Chambers & Hamlin, 1957; Dana, 1962; Dawes, 1962; Dennis, 1960; Mogar, 1962; Mosteller & Bush, 1954; Secord, 1952; Wallon, 1959), criticism (e.g., Brown, 1952; Hamlin, 1954; Hammer, 1959; Schneider, 1950; Shneidman, 1959), unpublished manuscripts, and personal communications by Karen Machover and Solomon Machover, provided enriching sources for conceptualizing the method elected here. In sum, the empirical literature suggested that a concurrent validity study, applying the method of correct matchings of global judgments (Cronbach, 1950) to clinically homogeneous groups, would be appropriate. Researchers have cautioned that judges be experts, that samples be relevant, that demographic and sampling variables be controlled, and that the task be clearly defined—not too simple, yet not unmanageably complex.

Hypotheses

1. Diagnostic judgments, made by experts using the DAP, agree, beyond chance expectations, with criterion statuses.

2. Differences in accuracy of DAP judgments vary between clinical groups beyond chance expectations.

3. The judges' diagnostic accuracies are positively related to their reputed expertness, defined by ranks accorded them by their peers.

PROCEDURE

Consultations were held with the Machovers in order to determine which five clinical groups should be most appropriate to a diagnostic investigation of the DAP. Among those suggested were a psychotic, a neurotic, a mental defective, and a homosexual group, in addition to a group of normals. Other recommendations resulted in the decisions that all Ss be American Caucasian adult males residing in the northern United States.

The Criterion Groups

In order to avoid contamination of the criteria by the variable being investigated, *S*s were selected only if they were never given the DAP for diagnostic purposes (except for the mental defectives, who are almost routinely given the DAP in state institutions, but who are certified as mental defectives on the basis of their scores on standardized IQ tests). The *S*s who passed all of the selection criteria were administered the DAP de novo in accord with the instructions and materials detailed in Machover's (1949) monograph.

The sample groups were carefully matched for age, ethnic status, socioeconomic class, marital status, and other relevant variables, except for the mental defectives, whose very condition precluded their being matched for intelligence and education.*

The overall principle in the determination of the external criteria for the group labels was that the five clinical groups represent different life situations, recognized by commonly encountered diagnoses. Thus, the schizophrenics had been so diagnosed and committed to a state hospital for most of their adult lives; the neurotics, on the other hand, lived and worked in the community, but attended an out-patient psychiatric clinic on a regular, weekly basis. The mental defectives achieved IQ scores well into the defective range and had been legally certified and committed to a state school for mental defectives. The homosexuals lived and worked in the community, did not receive any form of psychological treatment, denied that such treatment was ever officially indicated to them, belonged to a national society for homosexuals, and in each instance classified themselves as practicing homosexuals. The normals who were finally selected lived and worked in the community, attended an evening college, denied having been seen for psychological treatment, and obtained "nonpsychiatric" scores on the Cornell Medical Index.†

---

*Tables and appendices detailing this, and other information, are embodied in the longer dissertation upon which this report is based. Microfilm and Xerox copies of the dissertation may be ordered from University Microfilms, Ann Arbor, Michigan, Pub. No. 65-7406.

†Thanks are due the following who provided accessibility to clinical groups: Sherman O. Schachter and the staff at the New Hope Guidance Center, Brooklyn; Norman Kilpatrick and the officers of the Mattachine Society; Sidney Robbins and the staff at Central Islip State Hospital, N.Y.; Issac Wolfson and Thomas McCulloch and the staff at Letchworth Village State School, N.Y.; Manny Sternlicht and his students at the Staten Island Community College.

The Judges

Starting with Karen Machover, reputed experts in the interpretation of the DAP were asked to name and rank at least five other experts whom they considered particularly competent in the diagnostic use of the DAP. Each of the nominees was then asked to do the same, etc., until a pool of over 50 names emerged. The experts were contacted in the order of their ranks, so that the 20 highest ranking cooperating experts were designated the judges for this study.*

Preparation of the Data

Five *S*s were selected from each of the criterion groups. Each *S* drew a person and then a person of the sex opposite to that represented in the first drawing. Each *S* and his pair of drawings were assigned a code from a table of random numbers (Kendall & Smith, 1950). The design called for 100 clinical judgments to be made by a total of 20 judges. Each judge received one pair of drawings from each of five clinical groups. Each pair was thus seen by four different judges. Twenty sets of five DAPs each were prepared for distribution in the following manner: Five envelopes were labeled by clinical groups; four copies of each *S*'s code number were placed in the appropriate envelope; one number was drawn from each of the five envelopes to make up a set until all 20 sets were completed.

The Task

Each of the 20 judges received a package containing five pairs of drawings representing one each of the five diagnostic groups. Included also was an enclosure describing the characteristics of the sample, and a letter defining the task: "Identify each coded pair of drawings as to the clinical group from which you feel it has been drawn. This is done by ranking the probability of each diagnosis for each pair." Attached to each pair of drawings was a "Judgment Form" which instructed the judge,

*The author is grateful to the 20 DAP experts who served as judges: Helen J. Anderson, Lauretta Bender, Fred Brown, Hanna F. Faterson, Bernice M. Gurvich, Emanuel F. Hammer, Molly R. Harrower, Asya L. Kadis, Selma L. Landisberg, Solomon Lieberman, Karen Machover, Solomon Machover, Muriel F. Margolis, Hanna S. Marlens, Frank S. Puzzo, Joseph Richman, Joanna Steinberg, Meta Steiner, Rochelle Wexler, and Mildred Zadek.

Please look at the attached pair of drawings by the same person and decide which of the five groups they most likely represent. Place the number "1" on the line next to that group in the list below, for the diagnostic group that seems most probable. Continue ranking the categories by placing a "2" on the line near the next likely possibility, and so on, so that the category which is least likely to be represented by these drawings will be marked with a "5."

The five categories were listed below the instructions with an adjacent space for the rank numbers. The judges were also asked,

Try to pinpoint in four statements the basis for your decision in each case, e.g., a scoring system, formal elements in the drawings, content, a detail, global impressions, a hunch, or your own unique system of evaluating drawings.

Finally, each judge was asked to complete an "Experience Questionnaire."

Auxiliary Experiment

For expository purposes, the study was replicated but with the substitution of cards with chance-determined "judgments." That is, the code numbers of the Ss were set up on a results tabulation chart similar to the one used for the actual DAP results. The E called out the code number of an S, and an assistant* picked a card out of a box and read the "diagnosis" from the card. In order to simulate the forced-choice restriction of the first choice, the card was not replaced until the next "judge's" turn came. This was done for all 20 "judges," for two (rather than five) diagnostic rankings. These randomly drawn data were then compared with theoretical chance and with judgments by DAP experts in appropriate tables.

RESULTS

Chance Expectations for the Experimental Procedure

In the auxiliary chance-illustration replication, the random drawings produced zero to three "successes" per "judge" out of a possible five, with an average of one. The randomly drawn "successes" were tabulated. The chi-square computed to determine the significance of any difference

---

*Thanks are due Louis Garzetta, who painstakingly kept this procedure random, yet simulated the judges' actual task.

between correct matchings produced by the random drawings and those expected by theoretical chance was .815, which, with *df* 2, is nonsignificant. Successes for each criterion group, by this empirical method for demonstrating the effects of chance, averaged close to the expected 20 percent. Similarly, when accurate matchings on a second run of the random drawings were combined with those obtained on the first random drawings trial, the resulting cumulative "hits" resembled frequencies theoretically expected by chance. Thus, the "successes" averaged two out of a possible five (since there were two chances to be correct), and "successes" for each criterion group averaged 40 percent. The chi-square, computed to determine the significance of any difference between the successes obtained on the random drawings and those expected by chance, was .143, which *df* 2, is nonsignificant. The experimental procedure, stripped of the "experts using DAP" variable, generated results essentially identical with those expected by chance alone.

Successes Achieved by DAP Experts

The average number of successes by DAP experts was twice the number arrived at by the random drawings; the DAP successes for the criterion groups averaged close to 40 percent. The chi-square, computed to determine the significance of the difference between the successes of the DAP experts and those obtained by random drawings, was 40.42, which, *df* 2, is significant beyond the .001 level.

After the first and second correct matchings were combined, a chi-square comparison constructed to show the frequency of randomly drawn correct matches over two trials, revealed, again, that the DAP judges' overall performance differed from that produced by random drawings at a highly significant level.

Chi-squares were computed to determine the significance of the differences between the successes of the DAP experts and those expected by chance. Since the computation of chi-square requires that no cell have an expected frequency of less than five, those cells which had fewer theoretical frequencies were combined (Siegel, 1956, p. 109). The resulting frequencies are listed in Table 13-1. For example, although only five judges would be expected to achieve two or more successes on their first-ranked diagnoses by chance alone, as many as 15 DAP experts scored that many successes. Similarly, although only seven judges would be expected to achieve three or more successes over their first and second choices

Table 13-1.
Significance of the Differences between Judges' Successes and Those Expected by Chance

Number of "hits"	Number of judges		Chi-square
	Theoretical chance	DAP experts	
First choice			25.82*
2 or more[a]	5	15	
1	8	4	
0	7	1	
First and second			22.98*
3 or more[a]	7	17	
2	7	2	
0 or 1[a]	7	1	

Note.—All decimals rounded to nearest integer.
[a]Where individual χ^2 cells yielded expected frequencies less than 5, adjacent cells were combined.
*$p < .01$; $\chi^{2.999} = 13.82$, $df = 2$.

combined (by chance alone), as many as 17 DAP experts scored that many successes. The highly significant chi-squares, when viewed superficially, seem to indicate that the demonstrated ability of the experts to discriminate between the five clinical groups, on the basis of the DAP, was not due to chance. Further analysis of the data reveals, however, that the mental defectives were detected almost perfectly when the judges used up their first ranks, and with 100 percent accuracy when the judges' first two diagnostic opportunities were combined.

Variances Between Judges and Between Clinical Groups

For diagnoses ranked first, one judge out of 20 scored a perfect five "hits" out of five possibilities, and one judge scored no "hits." Analyses of the variances between judges indicates that the differences are probably due to chance.

A wide range of successes by DAP experts for the five clinical groups was revealed. Analyses of the variances between groups indicated that the difference in the susceptibility of the various groups to be identified by means of the DAP is statistically highly significant.

The Contributions of the Mental Defective Group

The highly significant variance between groups raises a question: What is the contribution of the mental defective group to the finding that experts can identify clinical groups by using the DAP alone? This question was answered by dropping the mental defective group from the findings and testing the remaining data for significance. The "Total" columns of the accuracy tables were adjusted to show the distribution of the successes of the DAP experts in identifying only four of the original five clinical groups: the schizophrenics, neurotics, homosexuals, and normals. The nonsignificant chi-squares on Table 13-2 strongly suggest that the initially observed ability of the experts to discriminate between the four clinical groups, on the basis of the DAP, was probably due to the obviousness of the drawings by the mental defectives—especially when the experts had two opportunities to be correct.

Table 13-2.
**Judges' DAP Successes Compared with Chance Successes
after Omitting the Mental Defective Group**

	Number of judges		
Number of "hits"	*Theoretical chance*	*DAP experts*	*Chi-square*
First choice			1.32[a]
2 or more	5.83	7	
1	6.70	8	
0	7.50	5	
First and second			3.42[a]
3 or more	6.42	6	
2	7.40	11	
0 or 1	6.18	3	

[a]*ns:* $\chi^{2.95} = 5.99$, $df = 2$.

Consideration of the Possibility of a Misleading Group

The statistical significance, then, of the original finding that experts can identify clinical groups by using the DAP vanished once the mental defective group was omitted. The fact that the schizophrenic group was misdiagnosed more often than any other group raised a different question: If the schizophrenic group were also omitted from the data, would the vanished significance reappear? The "Total" column of the accuracy table was adjusted to show the distribution of successes of the DAP experts in identifying just three of the original five clinical groups. The resulting nonsignificant chi-square indicated that the observed ability of the experts to discriminate the three clinical groups on the basis of the

DAP (such as the correct identification of 11 out of 20 homosexuals) was still within the bounds of chance expectations. The schizophrenic group, therefore, was not sufficiently misleading to determine the chance-like performance of the experts when the mental defective group was omitted.

Distribution of Incorrect Judgments

A table was constructed to determine whether the misdiagnosed *S*s were misdiagnosed consistently, and how they were identified by the judges. Table 13-3 indicates that the outstanding group was the mental defectives, which had only one misdiagnosis. Incorrect judgments for the rest of the groups were fairly scattered with no significantly consistent pattern.

Table 13-3.
Distribution of Incorrect Judgments

	Frequency of judgments					
Criterion status	*Schizophrenic*	*Neurotic*	*Mentally defective*	*Homosexual*	*Normal*	*False negatives*
Schizophrenic	—	7	0	6	4	85%
Neurotic	5	—	0	3	8	80%
Mentally defective	1	0	—	0	0	5%
Homosexual	6	0	1	—	2	45%
Normal	5	9	0	0	—	70%
False positives	85%	80%	5%	45%	70%	

Other Findings

1. Overall interjudge agreement was less than half as great as it would have been had all the judges agreed about all *S*s. The greatest contribution to interjudge agreement was the mental defective group, about which there was 90 percent agreement.

2. The ranks for expertness that the judges received from their peers (in the early nomination procedure) were juxtaposed with the ranks the judges achieved by virtue of the accuracy of their clinical judgments. The resulting Spearman rank correlation coefficient corrected for ties, was $-.36$, which is nonsignificant ($r_{s95} = .377$).

3. Attempts to analyze the judgmental process (judges' statements in

support of their decisions), including the procedure used by Chambers (1954, pp. 17–18, 23–24, 33–34, 56–58), revealed that stylistic differences between DAP judges were the same as between *S*s for any one judge. No differentiating pattern emerged.

4. Analysis of the "culture" of DAP experts revealed that women outnumbered men by better than two to one. There were five times as many experts who were primarily engaged in clinical work than in teaching and research; about two-thirds of the experts worked in institutional settings, and although 76 percent relied "heavily" on the DAP, only 32 percent regarded it as a "primary tool."

DISCUSSION

Adequacy of the Method

The differential findings—that the judgments were consistently valid for one criterion group and consistently invalid for the remaining groups—imply that the procedure contained no elements which would tend to favor or disfavor the object of the investigation. Comparison of the findings with those of Chambers' (1954) study of the Rorschach, which provided the foundation for our design, suggests that the DAP, not the method, was responsible for our results. As in the current study, Chambers found highly significant overall positive results: Her mental defectives were identified 90 percent of the time, far more frequently than were the four other groups. Omission of the mental defective group, however, hardly affected her findings; the resulting chi-square was 16.3, leaving the positive results unchanged and still significant beyond the .001 level. Thus, application of the same basic design which achieved positive results with the Rorschach in the Chambers' study, achieved negative results with the DAP in our study. The negative results must be attributed to the DAP, and not the experimental design.

Five methodological innovations were added here to the basic correct-matchings design:

1. The *S*s were administered the DAP de novo in order to avoid contamination of the criterion by the predictor.

2. A method was used for determining the relative contributions of individual criterion groups to the total results.

3. By requesting the judges to rank their diagnoses, the judges were

freed from the restriction of having to make an absolute decision on a protocol about which they may have lacked confidence because of what they regarded insufficient or conflicting evidence.

4. A procedure for the identification of expert judges proved successful. The nomination and ranking procedure provided an additional source of information for determining the relationship between the judges' reputations among their peers and their relative actual performances.

5. The definition of criterion groups by life statuses, rather than by psychiatric diagnoses or psychological test results alone, provided an operational method of avoiding the hazards of unreliability or nonfactuality of diagnoses per se.

Why Then Is the DAP Popular?

The studies which report positive findings for the DAP are primarily case studies. There is little doubt that there are instances when individuals produce sensationally revealing drawings. As Swensen (1957, p. 461) pointed out, such cases are more likely to be remembered than are the many which are not revealing. Furthermore, such cases are more likely to be submitted for publication than are the less eloquent ones.

Another conjecture about the cause for the positive regard which so many clinicians have for the DAP was advanced by Shaffer.* Prior to and during the administration of the DAP, interview material and behavioral clues are typically observed by the clinician; upon interpreting the drawings that the client has produced, the clinician may attribute the interview and other extratest knowledge, which he has about S, to the drawings, "seeing" in them what he knew already. "Blind" studies eliminate this hazard.

Little has proposed an explanation for the failure of projective techniques to prove valid: the matter of situation generalization. The test tests the organism, he claimed, not the astronomical number of alternative stimulus situations in which the organism functions and about which the clinician attempts to predict. By means of generalization, it is possible to reduce the number of stimulus categories sharply. "We are able to say that one man's candy is another man's brandy and call both consummatory responses, or oral behavior, etc. This inevitably leads to a loss in precision in the prediction of specific behavior so we find our-

---

*L. F. Shaffer, personal communication, 1958.

selves anticipating alcoholism when obesity in fact occurs [Little, 1959, p. 288]."

Hammer has suggested that it is fallacious to conclude that drawings do not reflect psychopathology simply because associations between drawing signs and criterion groups have not been demonstrated.

> All of these "schizophrenic signs" are relatively infrequent in projective draw- ings of the human figure, but where they do occur, they occur in the drawings of schizophrenics. . . . To test these hypotheses adequately, only instances where the sign does occur should be included. For example, to wait to accumulate twenty subjects' drawings and then compare the incidence of schizophrenia in the subjects who submitted these drawings, would be the only way to assess fairly the validity of the sign. (Hammer, 1959, p. 30)

Essentially, Hammer is simply proposing to ignore false negatives in DAP predictions. A high incidence of true positives would mean that some drawings reflect some blatant characteristics of the Ss who pro- duced them, but one could still wonder about how much confidence could be placed in an instrument which, used alone, would send a large proportion of schizophrenics merrily on their way, since they would be identified as anything but schizophrenics.*

Perhaps the most basic question to investigate is: What causes clinical psychologists to believe in and use instruments which repeatedly fail the test of diagnostic validity? Could the occasional, eloquent drawing pro- vide the clinician with partial reinforcement, producing greater resis- tance to extinction? An experiment investigating Shaffer's† hypothesis that beliefs of psychologists direct their reinforcing acts could shed much light and may prove convincing even to the committed.

REFERENCES

American Psychological Association. *Technical recommendations for psychological tests and diagnostic techniques.* Washington, D.C.: Author, 1954.

Andrews, T. G. *Methods of psychology.* New York: Wiley, 1948.

Bolotin, M. The use of human figure drawings in evaluating children and adoles- cents of special educational and cultural background; an examination of the effectiveness of current diagnostic criteria with the Draw-A-Person Test as applied to Puerto-Rican children and adolescents. *Dissertation Abstracts,* 1960, 20, 4030. (Abstract)

---

*See footnote after references.

†L. F. Shaffer, personal communication, 1959.

Brown, F. House-Tree-Person and human figure drawings. In D. Bower & L. E. Abt (Eds.), *Progress in clinical psychology.* New York: Grune & Stratton, 1952.

Chambers, G. S. *An investigation of the validity of judgments based on "blind" Rorschach records.* (Doctoral dissertation, University of Pittsburg) Ann Arbor, Mich.: University Microfilms, 1954. No. 9964.

Chambers, G. S., & Hamlin, R. M. The validity of judgments based on "blind" Rorschach records. *Journal of Consulting Psychology,* 1957, 21, 105–109.

Chapman, D. W. The statistics of the method of correct matchings. *American Journal of Psychology,* 1934, 46, 287–298.

Cronbach, L. J. Statistical methods for multi-score tests. *Journal of Clinical Psychology,* 1950, 6, 21–26.

Dana, R. H. The validation of projective tests. *Journal of Projective Techniques,* 1962, 26, 182–186.

Dawes, R. M. A note on base rates and psychometric efficiency. *Journal of Consulting Psychology,* 1962, 26, 422–424.

Dennis, W. The human figure drawings of bedouins. *Journal of Social Psychology,* 1960, 52, 209–219.

Dudek, F. J. Determining "chance success" when a specific number of items are sorted into discrete categories. *Journal of Consulting Psychology,* 1952, 16, 251–256.

Hamlin, R. M. The clinician as judge: Implications of a series of studies. *Journal of Consulting Psychology,* 1954, 18, 232–238.

Hammer, E. F. Critique of Swensen's "Empirical evaluations of human figure drawings." *Journal of Projective Techniques,* 1959, 23, 30–32.

Hunt, W. A. The future of diagnostic testing in clinical psychology. *Journal of Clinical Psychology,* 1946, 2, 311–317.

Jones, L. W., & Thomas, C. B. Studies on figure drawings. *Psychiatric Quarterly Supplement,* 1961, 35, 212–261.

Kendall, M. G., & Smith, B. B. Tables of random sampling numbers. In H. Arkin & R. R. Colton (Eds.), *Tables for statisticians.* New York: Barnes & Noble, 1950.

Little, K. B. Problems in the validation of projective techniques. *Journal of Projective Techniques,* 1959, 23, 287–290.

Lublin, I., & Lublin, S. C. The Draw-A-Person Test: A Minimal Validity Investigation. Paper presented at the meeting of the Western Psychological Association, San Francisco, May 1967.

Machover, K. *Personality projection in the drawing of the human figure.* Springfield, IL: Charles C Thomas, 1949.

Meehl, P. E. *Clinical versus statistical prediction.* Minneapolis: University of Minnesota Press, 1954.

Mogar, R. E. Anxiety indices in human figure drawings: A replication and extension. *Journal of Consulting Psychology,* 1962, 26, 108.

Mosteller, F., & Bush, R. R. Selected quantitative techniques. In G. Lindzey (Ed.), *Handbook of social psychology.* Vol. 1. Cambridge, MA: Addison-Wesley, 1954.

Siegel, S. *Nonparametric statistics for the behavioral sciences.* New York: McGraw-Hill, 1956.

Schneider, L. I. Rorschach validation: Some methodological aspects. *Psychological Bulletin*, 1950, 47, 493–508.

Secord, P. F. A note on the problem of homogeneity-heterogeneity on the use of the matching method in personality studies. *Psychological Bulletin*, 1952, 49, 41–42.

Shneidman, E. S. Suggestions for the delineation of validity studies. *Journal of Projective Techniques*, 1959, 23, 259–262.

Sundberg, N. D. The practice of psychological testing in clinical services in the United States. *American Psychologist*, 1961, 16, 79–83.

Swensen, C. H. Empirical evaluations of human figure drawings. *Psychological Bulletin*, 1957, 54, 431–466.

Vernon, P. E. The matching method applied to investigations of personality. *Psychological Bulletin*, 1936, 33, 149–177.

Wallon, E. J. *A study of criteria used to differentiate the human figure drawings of normals, neurotics, and psychotics.* (Doctoral dissertation, Purdue University) Ann Arbor, Mich.: University Microfilms, 1959. No. 59-418.

Editor's Note

The Editor of the *Journal of Personality Assessment* has invited the following discussion by Emanuel Hammer.

Wanderer misses the point. Machover says, for instance, that transparency of the body wall in a Person drawing, allowing the internal organs (stomach, heart, kidney) to show through, is a sign of schizophrenia. Most schizophrenics do not do this, but when it does occur it *is* a sign of schizophrenia. It is like hallucinations. Most schizophrenics do not hallucinate, but most patients who hallucinate (barring those with alcoholic DTs or drug-induced states) are schizophrenics. Thus, Wanderer's citing a study in which most schizophrenics do not draw "transparent" bodies as disproving Machover's hypothesis is clinically naive or else shows a misreading of her book.* Thus, if of 100 schizophrenics, only 14 showed "transparencies," this would not, as Wanderer maintains, constitute negative evidence against the D–A–P. Especially, if, as I have found, of the 14 displaying "transparencies," all proved psychotic. The only authentic research design would be to wait to accumulate 20 D–A–Ps characterized by "transferencies" (or in the other example, patients with hallucinations) and count how many of these are schizophrenic.

And, drawings of a Person by schizophrenics who did not demonstrate "transparency" (or who did not hallucinate) would not, as Wanderer mockingly says, "send them merrily on their way." For there are many other signs of schizophrenia (see Hammer, E., *The House-Tree-Person Clinical Research Manual*, Los Angeles: Western Psychological Services) which may, in the D–A–P (or in the psychiatric interview), pick up the schizophrenic process.

---

*Thus, by quoting me out of context (p. 313), Wanderer makes his that I advocate "ignoring false negatives."

E.F.H.

Chapter 14

DAP: BACK AGAINST THE WALL*

Invited by the Editor of the journal in which it initially appeared to provide a discussion to the foregoing study of Wanderer's "The Validity of Clinical Judgments Based on Human Figure Drawings," the writer, after evaluating research design and statistical treatment, reacts from the vantage point of the clinician.

Methodological and conceptual criticism of Wanderer's study, "Validity of Clinical Judgments Based on Human Figure Drawings," revolves around (*a*) correlation procedures, (*b*) sampling errors, (*c*) arbitrary categorization of data, (*d*) overlap between diagnostic groups employed, (*e*) the insufficiency of fractionated material as projective samples, and, most importantly (*f*) clinical considerations.

H as Wanderer's study cracked open the hard nut of the question of the basic validity of the Draw-A–Person technique?

As a research question runs the gauntlet through evidence and counterevidence, one has to try to make sense of the resulting confusion. Wanderer's study joins those on the side which have failed to demonstrate that psychologists can offer valid diagnoses on the basis of figure drawings (Sherman, 1958a, 1958b; Sipprelle & Swensen, 1956; Swensen, 1957; Whitmyre, 1953). Along with this, several of Machover's (1949) interpretive hypotheses have emerged bearing evidence suggesting their lack of validity (Blum, 1954; Fisher & Fisher, 1950; Grams & Rinder, 1958; Hammer, 1954; Reznikoff & Nicholas, 1958; Ribler, 1957).

Yielding a mixture of results, Hammer and Piotrowski (1953) found (a) a reassuring degree of both reliability and validity in the interpretation of aggression reflected in the House-Tree-Person drawings, and also, (b) that what variation there was among the clinicians' interpreta-

*Appreciative thanks are warmly extended to John N. Buck and Robert L. Wolk for their fruitful comments and suggestions.

tions appear to be secondarily influenced by their own projections and/or degree of sensitivity.*

On the other hand, and in contradistinction to the findings of Wanderer, a number of studies have demonstrated clear-cut differences between the DAPs of "normal" and pathological groups (Anastasi & Foly, 1941; Berrien, 1935; Eigenbode, 1951; Goldworth, 1950; Gunzburg, 1954; Holzberg & Wexler, 1950; Hozier, 1959; Plaut & Grannell, 1955; Reznikoff & Tomblen, 1956; Schmidl-Waehner, 1942; Singer, 1950; Springer, 1941; Wexler & Holzberg, 1952). Steinmann (1952) devised a scoring system which was found by Graham (1955) to correlate .70 with the degree of pathology in psychosis. Hiler and Nesvig (1965) also demonstrated that psychiatric patients could be differentiated from normals on the basis of projective drawings. They validated the characteristics of pathology as reflected in the following qualities: "bizarreness," "distorted aspects," "incompleteness," and "transparency" of drawings. The most valid of the criteria was "bizarreness," which subsumed a drawing looking either "grotesque," "inhuman," "sinister," "sick," "ghoulish," "weird," or "gnome-like." In a cross-validation sample, it was found that 46 percent of the patients and only 2 percent of the control group produced a drawing which, by independent judgment, was "bizarre."

Griffith and Peyman (1965) found that eye and ear emphasis in the DAP was, to a statistically significant degree, associated with ideas of reference. Albee and Hamlin (1950) devised a scale which, while unable to differentiate between schizophrenics and anxiety neurotics, did reliably differentiate between these two groups and a normal one.

Wanderer's study is now added to the negative side of the mixed results which have proliferated over the years. As we evaluate his study, there are, however, several ways in which it appears the hypotheses were handicapped.

No significant correlation is found between the "expertness" of the judges and the validity of their sortings. With all the experts possessing national reputation, however, they quite evidently fall into a tight cluster with little of the spread necessary to allow a statistically meaningful correlation. The proper research design would have been to simply compare "experts" (say with more than twenty years experience) to a control group (say with less than five years experience).

---

*We might view the latter finding as raising the question of the advisability of a personal psychothera-peutic experience for the projective technique interpreter, as it has long been advocated by many for the therapist.

Totally disqualifying one facet of the study, the judges did not even see the same set of five cases. There is, therefore, neither common ground nor any defensible basis for appraising one expert against another in correlating validity and "degree of expertness." Surprisingly, scientific method was abandoned to a situation where one judge may have had a relatively classical set of drawings while another a quite confusing set.

In Table 13-1, "Number of Hits" is put into the categories of "0", "1," or "2 or more." This kind of lumping of the data seems rather arbitrary. Combining all "hits" of 2, 3, 4, and 5 into this last category tends to dilute the data favoring the hypothesis. The judge who attained five out of five correct sortings does thereby not contribute any more weight to the hypothesis than the one who attained only two out of five correct matchings.

Also, the fact that the judges were asked to sort one DAP set into each of five categories did not allow a judge to elect to call two of the cases psychotic when they looked that way to him. Thus, in this instance, when a judge was wrong on his first choice, he was automatically wrong for a 40 percent rather than a 20 percent assessment, i.e., the second case felt to also fall in the category already used up now had to be placed in a different one. Had both drawings been allowed to be classified schizophrenic, it here might have resulted in only a 20 percent error. (Then, of course, the same handicap occurred, now on the next level, when going through the drawings a second time, the judges again had to put only one case in a category.)

Wanderer subtracts the influence of the conspicuous contribution to the validity of the sortings made by the mental defective cases. It is hard to understand why he did not merely rotate each category and use analysis of variance to solve this problem more neatly.

Wanderer quotes the writer, in reference to that rare but striking schizophrenic sign which may appear in a drawing, as saying that the most appropriate way to test its validity statistically would be to compare in what groups it occurs *when* it does occur. Wanderer then criticizes this as a procedure ignoring false negatives. His argument here would be very much like contending that hallucinations or delusions in a psychiatric patient cannot be used as suggestive of a psychotic process since they do not occur in *most* psychotics. Wanderer's misconception of "false negatives" would result in the most striking diagnostic clues being the very ones which "research" demonstrates should be ignored.*

To turn to Wanderer's sample, there is a question of overlap in the five groups (with the limited sample of 20 in each) which tends to contaminate the criteria. Experience in outpatient mental hygiene clinics is that there is a high proportion of borderline and ambulatory schizophrenics in this population. Wanderer doesn't indicate how, or if, he sifted them out of his "neurotic" (mental hygiene clinic) sample. Additionally, we know that intense homosexual conflicts are frequently part of the psychotic, as well as the neurotic, picture; and this would clearly overlap with the DAP's of the homosexual group. In fact, the *overt* homosexual group, having come (at least comparatively) to peace with needs in this direction, may flood their drawings with *less* of the homoerotic than would the neurotic and psychotic groups, patients in whom the problem areas press insistantly forward in their projective responses.

When the comparison is between homosexual and normal groups, Machover et al. (1959) demonstrate statistical significance in the reliability and the validity of DAP differentiation, "blindly" done. The average two-way, total-scale intercorrelation among three graduate-student judges, who each independently scored the protocols, was found to be .83. The efficacy of differentiating male homosexual from nonhomosexual controls was significant at beyond the .001 level of confidence.

As to how many of Wanderer's "homosexual" group may have been neurotic, or psychotic, we don't know. There was no procedure to assay nor rule these out.

The complications of overlapping of groupings may be seen more clearly in the examples that (A) a neurotic depression and (B) a psychotic depression, may look more alike than different in a projective sampling, particularly of just two drawings obtained. The same may be true of (C) a neurotic paranoid integration and (D) a paranoid type of schizophrenic. In fact, on this brief sample, #A, looking more like #B than like its official category-mate #C, and #C looking more like #D than like its experimentally-defined companion #A would mean that the depressive and paranoid dimensions, respectively, would emerge but not be differentially related to whether their presence was of neurotic or psychotic proportions. When such is the case, we could scarcely move toward the conclusion that the drawings here provided nothing diagnostically valid. The same point may be made when the major drawing theme is the pivotal one of strong dependency needs—whether, in line

---

*"Some circumstantial evidence" says Thoreau, "is very strong, as when you find a trout in the milk."

with Wanderer's groups, on the part of (a) a "normal" subject sustained by a marriage to a warm, nurturing, maternal woman; (b) a "neurotic" heavy drinker; (c) a "homosexual" whose preferred erotic activity is performing fellatio; or (d) an institutionalized patient responding to the dependency support provided by the hospital. As Hutt (1968) points out, "Projective tests seem to be especially valuable in assessing covert factors. . . . They are less successful in delineating or predicting overt behavior which is likely to be the end-product of many intervening factors."

Wanderer's study rests on a basic assumption of mutually exclusive pigeonholes for people. His data, however, if viewed from the broad perspective, stand as a banner to the refusal of complex human beings to fit into neat categories (at least on brief segments of behavior).

As far back as 1947, Tomkins suggested that the psychiatric entities "do not, in our opinion, represent homogenious entities even at the level of symptomatology." Schafer (1954), too, speaks of "researchers who naively expect that dumping all patients described as "paranoid" (or "anxious," "schizophrenic," "well-adjusted," etc.) into one group will consistently yield highly instructive (results) . . . and whose conception of test theory and research stops right there" (p. 285). The fact that the schizophrenic group, in Wanderer's study, was misdiagnosed more often than all of the other groups is consistent with the view that there is not a schizophrenic group per se. A proliferating of more varied types is reflected in Beck's (1954) expansion of four to six subtypes of schizophrenia as reflected in the Rorschach. Evelyn Hooker makes the point more broadly in asserting that there is no such entity as *the* homosexual. In describing some of the "worlds" of homosexuals seen in one large city, she reports no common pattern of personality structure, much less dynamics, in homosexuals. Willis (1967) similarly found no similarity among homosexuals other than in their choice of sex object.

The mentally defective group was undoubtedly diagnosed validly because of its clear-cut, lowered intellectual and conceptual qualities. But it may also have been easier to diagnose because mental defectives are a more distinct entity whose members more intimately share a common denominator with less spread and variability. And where each of the other four groups had crossover features with each other, this one group had few or none (at least in one direction, i.e., probably not a single "normal," "neurotic," "psychotic," or "homosexual" was also mentally defective).

Shaffer and Schafer are, I think, both right; Lawrence Shaffer partly so, and Roy Schafer more so. We do, I am sure, tend to read *into* projective material from what we know of the case. But with this providing the frame of reference, we then can read *from* the drawings significantly further. If—as in actual practice (operating neither "blindly" nor employing a mere splinter of the battery)—we know the patient to be in a psychotic depression and we find no affect, depressive or otherwise, in the projective drawings (or elsewhere in the projectives) we may extend from the known into the previously not-known. We can then understand that a state of emotional dehydration is present and here employed as a last-ditch defense against the intolerable despondency and despair. The blandness may involve defensive denial of the inner experience. To follow the thread into the tissue of the understructure, we can then link up surface and subsurface so that it makes sense of the apparent inconsistency. If an individual offers a drawing production seeped in sadism and gore (and his Rorschach and TAT is similarly so) but behaviorally he is mild and meek, do we discard the projective level data as invalid, or do we deduce that this man's surface behavior of meekness is maintained at the price of considerable repression, inner strain, and tension?

In these cases, we can see illustrated the principle that a small projective sample may be insufficient to convey the central diagnostic quality of the patient, but may nevertheless still contribute deeper understanding to the personality picture.

Roy Schafer (1954) vigorously underscores the dangers of item interpretation and emphasizes a reliance instead on themes which extend across many projective products. Similarly, in the writer's *The Clinical Application of Projective Drawings* (Hammer, 1958), may be found, prominently asserted: "In actual clinical practice, the dangers of basing interpretative deductions on isolated bits of data are obvious. In practice, confirmation of interpretative speculations on the basis of one drawing must be checked against not only the other drawings, but the entire projective battery, the case history, the clinical impression gleaned during the interview with the subject and all other available information." An experimental investigation which takes a mere chip of this procedure bears little resemblance to clinical practice and, as a study, has built into it only the slimmest chance of surviving its handicap.

Another basic consideration has always been the subject's perceptions of the purpose of the test and his particular reason for the examination, a highly determining variable coloring the subject's style and responses (Cronbach, 1946; Hutt et al., 1950; Murstein, 1968; Tolor, 1968)—crucial material unavailable in "blind" assessment studies. Imagine, for example, the subject's frame of mind being examined to support an insanity plea in a murder case vs. as a candidate to psychoanalytic school vs. to the police academy.

In accord with the above, Tolor (1968) speaks of the "situational factors (which) can exert great influence on all types of performance, and must be taken into account." Holt (1970) agrees:

> To predict almost any kind of behavior or behavioral outcome, one does better to assess the situation in which the behavior occurs in addition to assessing the actors' personalities.

Tolor then goes on to join Buck (1966) and Machover (1949) in underscoring the importance of the patient's verbal associations to his own drawings, data whose absence in Wanderer's study fractionates the already fractionated material further. As Tolor (1968) advocates,

> Place greater weight on associations produced in response to the drawings and do not depend solely on (the graphic projection). . . . Enlist the patient's assistance in establishing interpretive hypotheses. The mode used by a patient to reconcile disparate performance, to rationalize behavior, and to gain insight represents important data for interpretation.

A projective device, by its nature, has a buckshot quality. Because of its uncertain aim, a projective technique cannot be appraised on the basis of whether or not it invariably focuses upon the same dimension in each subject. Sometimes in the DAP, a diagnostic hint emerges, but sometimes a personality need, sometimes a psychodynamic clue, and sometimes an expressive style of personality. Two drawings of a person do not constitute a system in itself, but only a small facet of an unfolding system of responses maintaining itself in contact with other systems of the patterning.*

Only a minority of the experts employed as judges in Wanderer's study regard the DAP as a "primary tool." No one uses the DAP alone. It was never intended by Machover, nor anyone else, as anything more than a supplement, a graphic adjunct to the verbal techniques. Therefore, Wanderer's statement, " . . . but one could still wonder about how much confidence could be placed in an instrument which, *used alone* (italics supplied) would send a large proportion of schizophrenics merrily on their way, since they would be identified as anything but schizophrenics,"

---

*Sometimes, for example, with one schizophrenic the pathology comes through on one technique and with another on a different technique, and frequently only in the relationship among the techniques. This is, of course, the reason we employ multiple measurements from diverse modalities.

reflects an astonishing failure to understand the role and utility of projective drawings in the battery.

Overall, Wanderer's study demonstrates what we know clinically: that to order and integrate findings from the various sources of data in the testing situation, the clinician cannot rely solely on any small, compartmentalized sampling. A five or ten minute projective yield cannot, alone and when "blindly" interpreted, serve as the basis for a diagnosis.*
Interpreting a personality must be in terms of its inner unity and consistency across some degree of spread; only thereby may we, at times, reveal the man.

Anything less belongs with parlor tricks. It is in line with this that we may view the especially pertinent study of Caligor (1962). He found that paranoid trends could be detected in only 25 percent of a group of paranoid schizophrenics when one drawing of a human figure was employed. He returned to the problem, employing a set of eight such drawings, and found that 85 percent of the cases could be validly detected on the basis of the more extensive drawing projections.

Yet in spite of its defects—statistically, in terms of sampling, experimental design, and clinical sophistication—the impact of Wanderer's study still retains some voice which speaks to the intellect. As scientist-practitioners, we cannot ignore our everyday clinical evidence, nor can we, on the other hand, ignore the things that go on inside the limitations of the tight research design. In a field which is after truth rather than in much possession of it as yet, we must draw our working guidelines simultaneously from the microscopic analysis of bits and pieces of human behavior and also from our broader experience of its totality.

Clinicians may respond in one of three ways. They may ignore studies such as Wanderer's. *But that makes little sense.* They may, on absorbing the encounter with Wanderer's experiment, drop the DAP from the battery. *But that would make little sense, too,* unless they were using the DAP blindly, without the rest of the battery, and merely to establish a diagnostic category. They may, harmonizing the implications of Wanderer's with that of Caligor's study, resonate to the limitations of a two-drawing technique. They may then strengthen the projective drawing assessment

---

*At least if the sample is of drawing products. Can an equally brief sample of Rorschach behavior or of TAT stories (the first two cards of the former, or the first story or two of the latter), or of MMPI answers, or of interview do so?

with an expansion in width and depth.* And that, to this clinician, *makes more sense.*

REFERENCES

Anastasi, Anne, & Foley, J.P., Jr. A survey of literature on artistic behavior in the abnormal: Experimental investigations. *J. Gen. Psychol.,* 1941 23, 187–237.

Beck, S.J. *The Six Schizophrenias.* New York: American Orthopsychiatric Association, 1954.

Berrien, F.K.A. A study of the drawings of abnormal children. *J. Educ. Psychol.,* 1935, 26, 143–150.

Blum, R.H. The validity of the Machover DAP technique. *J. Clin. Psychol.,* 1954, 10, 120–25.

Buck, J.N. *The House-Tree-Person Technique, Revised Manual,* Beverly Hills, CA: Western Psychological Services, 1966.

Caligor, L. The detection of paranoid trends by the 8 Card Re-Drawing Test. *J. Clin. Psychol.,* 1952, 8, 397–401.

Cronbach, L.J. Response sets and test validity. *Educ. Psychol. Meas.,* 1946, 6, 475–494.

Eigenbode, C.R. Effectiveness of the Machover signs and others in differentiating between a normal group and a schizophrenic group by use of the projective drawing test. Unpublished master's thesis. George Washington University, 1951.

Fisher, S., & Fisher, R. Test of certain assumptions regarding figure drawing analysis. *J. Abn. Soc. Psychol.,* 1950, 45, 727–732.

Goldworth, S.A. A comparative study of the drawings of a man and a woman done by normal, neurotic, schizophrenic and brain damaged individuals. Doctoral dissertation. University of Pittsburgh, 1950.

Graham, S. Relation between histamine tolerance, visual autokinesis, Rorschach human movement, and figure drawing. *J. Clin. Psychol.,* 1955, 11, 370–373.

Grams, A., & Rinder, L. Signs of homosexuality in human figure drawings. *J. Consult. Psychol.,* 1958, 22, 394.

Griffith, A. & Peyman, D. Eye-ear emphasis in the DAP Test as indicating ideas of reference. In Murstein, *Handbook of Projective Techniques,* New York: Basic Books, 1965.

Gunzburg, H.C. Scope and limitations of the Goodenough drawing test method in clinical work with mental defective. *J. Clin. Psychol.* 1954, 10, 8–15.

*The writer, for example, does not employ, nor teach, the DAP or the H–T–P but rather an integrated drawing battery including the combined use of these two techniques, the H–T–P–P both achromatic and chromatic (in pencil and then again in crayon), its searching Post-Drawing Interrogation (Buck, 1966), the Draw-A-Person-In-The-Rain modification which attempts to elicit clues to the self-concept under conditions symbolizing environment stress, the Draw-An-Animal approach useful for disclosing the biological side of the bio-social coin, the Eight-Card-Redrawing Test which digs down into the deeper layers of the subject's psychosexual identification, the Unpleasant Concept Test, and with children, the Draw-A-Family procedure.

Hammer, E.F. Relationship between diagnosis of psychosexual pathology and the sex of the first drawn person. *J. Clin. Psychol.*, 1954, 10, 168–170.

Hammer, E.F. *The Clinical Application of Projective Drawings*, Springfield, IL: Charles C Thomas, 1958.

Hiler, E. & Nesvig, D. Evaluation of criteria used by clinicians to infer pathology from figure drawings. *J. Consult. Psychol.*, 1965, 29, 520–429.

Holt, R., Yet another look at clinical and statistical prediction. *Amer. Psych.* 1970, 25, 337–349.

Holzberg, J.D., & Wexler, M. The validity of human form drawings as a measure of personality deviation. *J. Proj. Tech.*, 1950, 14, 343–361.

Hozier, A. On the breakdown of the sense of reality: A study of spatial perception in schizophrenia. *J. Consult. Psychol.*, 1959, 23, 185–194.

Hutt, M.L. Psychopathology, assessment and psychotherapy. In Rabin, A.I. (Ed.), *Projective Technique in Personality Assessment.* New York: Springer, 1968.

Hutt, M.L., Gibby, R.G., Milton, E., & Potthurst, K. The effect of varied experimental "sets" on Rorschach test performance. *J. Proj. Tech.*, 1950, 14, 181–187.

Machover, K. *Personality Projection In the Drawing of the Human Figure.* Springfield, IL: Charles C Thomas, 1949.

Machover, S., Puzzo, F., Machover, K., & Plumeau, F., An objective study of homosexuality in alcoholism. *Quart. J. Studies Alcoholism*, 1959, 20, 528–542.

Plaut, E. & Crannell, C.W. The ability of clinical psychologists to discriminate between drawings by deteriorated schizophrenics and drawings by normal subjects. *Psychol. Rep.*, 1955, 1, 153–158.

Reznikoff, M., & Nicholas, A. An evaluation of human figure drawing indicators of paranoid pathology. *J. Consult. Psychol.*, 1958, 22, 395–397.

Reznikoff, M., & Tomblen, D. The use of human figure drawings in the diagnosis of organic pathology. *J. Consult. Psychol.*, 1956, 20, 467–470.

Ribler, R.I. Diagnostic prediction from emphasis on the eye and the ear in human figure drawings. *J. Consult. Psychol.*, 1957, 21, 223–225.

Schafer, R. *Psychoanalytic Interpretation of Rorschach Testing*, New York: Grune & Stratton, 1954.

Schmidl-Waehner. Formal criteria for the analysis of children's drawings. *Amer. J. Orthopsychiat*, 1942, 17, 95–104.

Sherman, L.J. Sexual differentiation of artistic ability? *J. Clin. Psychol.* 1958a, 14, 170–171.

Sherman, L.J. The influence of artistic quality on judgments of patient and nonpatient status from human figure drawings. *J. Proj. Tech.*, 1958b, 22, 338–340.

Siprelle, C.N., & Swensen, C.H. Relationships of sexual adjustment to certain sexual characteristics of human figure drawings. *J. Consult. Psychol.*, 1956, 20, 197–198.

Singer, R.H. A study of drawings produced by a group of college students and a group of hospitalized schizophrenics. Master's thesis. Pennsylvania State University, 1950.

Springer, N.N. A study of the drawings of maladjusted and adjusted children. *J. Genet. Psychol.*, 1941, 58, 131–138.

Steinmann, K. The validity of projective technique in the determination of relative intensity in psychosis. Unpublished doctoral dissertation. School of Education, New York University, 1952.

Sundberg, N.D. The practice of psychological testing in clinical services in the United States. *American Psychologist,* 1961, 16, 79–83.

Swensen, C.H. Empirical evaluation of human figure drawings. *Psychol. Bull.,* 1957, 57, 431–466.

Tolor, A. The Graphomotor Techniques, *J. Proj. Tech. & Personal. Assess.,* 1968, 32, 222–228.

Tomkins, S.S. *The Thematic Apperception Test.* New York: Grune & Stratton, 1947.

Wanderer, Z.W. Validity of clinical judgments based on Human Figure Drawings. *J. Consult. Clin. Psych.* 1969, 33, 143–150.

Wexler, M., & Holzberg, J.D. A further study of the validity of human form drawings in personality evaluation. *J. Proj. Tech.,* 1952, 16, 249–251.

Whitmyre, J.W. The significance of artistic excellence in the judgment of adjustment inferred from human figure drawings. *J. Consult. Psychol.,* 1953, 17, 421–424.

Willis, S. *Understanding and counseling the male homosexual.* New York: Little Brown, 1967.

Chapter 15

CRITIQUE OF SWENSEN'S "EMPIRICAL EVALUATIONS OF HUMAN FIGURE DRAWINGS"*

In a recent review[6] of research in the field of figure drawings, several fallacies are expressed which invite correction before other research workers fall into the use of the same misconceptions. In the face of so comprehensive and integrated a review of the literature, criticism of Swensen's article is perhaps supererogatory, but three points of clarification must be made.

Swensen[6] reports that Holzberg and Wexler[4] found no significant difference between normals and schizophrenics in drawing naked feet with the toes delineated, in drawing feet with the toe nails indicated, or in a tendency to begin a drawing on one part of the page and then start some place else on the page, turning the page over, or showing other signs of disorganized sequence. Also, no significant differences were found between normals and schizophrenics in the frequency of drawing internal organs which showed through a transparent body wall. Swensen interprets these findings as contraindicating Machover's hypotheses concerning these signs' suggestion of schizophrenic processes in the subject.

The occurrence of naked feet with toe nails delineated, the occurrence of disorganized and bizarre sequence in the order of the various parts of the human figure drawn, and the representation of internal organs almost invariably, in my experience, are associated with schizophrenia. In view of this experience, I cannot help suspecting that the responsibility for the lack of statistical support for these clinical findings lies on the shoulders of the experimental approach rather than on those of the hypotheses: All of these three "schizophrenic signs" are relatively infrequent in projective drawings of the human figure, but where they do occur, they occur in the drawings of schizophrenics. Thus, to test these hypotheses adequately, only instances where the sign does occur should

---

be included. For example, to wait to accumulate twenty such drawings and then compare the incidence of schizophrenia in the subjects who submitted these drawings, would be the only way to assess fairly the validity of the sign. If one had to wait until two hundred drawings were accumulated in order to obtain twenty in which these signs occurred, and then one found that in eighteen of the twenty the subject was actually schizophrenic, this would then constitute an investigation of the meaning of such a sign. However, to investigate a relatively infrequent occurrence by comparing fifty "normals" with fifty schizophrenics and deducing from the respective instance of zero and two frequencies of such signs that there is "no statistically significant difference" between the two groups does violence to the actual clinical use of such signs and to the statistically sophisticated investigation of their meaning.

It is much like hallucinations as a "sign" of schizophrenia. Clinically this is a well-established phenomenon. But if an experimental approach were, parallel to the research design above on the projective drawing hypothesis, to count how many of 100 diagnosed schizophrenics suffered hallucinations and found only 18 percent did so, this would provide rather weak and uncertain statistical support. But if a more clinically sophisticated approach were employed, we would count how many of the 18 hallucinating patients are schizophrenic and might find (experience suggests) 17 of 18 of them are, compared to a control group in which probably none hallucinates. High—very high—statistical support here results. No one maintains that most schizophrenics hallucinate. What we maintain, in the field, is that (barring substance abusers or organics) hallucinating is a manifestation of psychosis. Similarly, most schizophrenics do not draw internal organs in their D–A–Ps, while almost all subjects doing so have reality-testing impairments of psychotic proportions.

(This point, more or less, had also to be made to Wanderer's promulgated misconception, but is equally demanded by Swenson's.)

The second point this writer wishes to make concerns those studies investigating hypotheses which are formulated on a not-too-careful reading of Machover's contribution. Swensen states that Machover reports that the drawing of knee joints suggests a faulty and uncertain sense of body integrity, and occurs chiefly in schizoid and schizophrenic individuals. Swensen then interprets Holzberg and Wexler's[4] finding, that normal women show the knee joint significantly more often than hebephrenic schizophrenic women, as a direct contraindication of Machover's hypothesis.

Actually, a reading of the section of Machover's book in which the meaning of "joints" is discussed (and it is only one paragraph) will find the following sentences: "The schizoid, the frankly schizophrenic individual, and the body narcissist in decline, will lean on joint *emphasis* (italics mine, E.H.) in order to stave off feelings of body disorganization," and "Most drawings that involve joint *emphasis* (again my italics)..." Thus, the flavor of the hypothesis concerns overemphasis upon detailing of joints in the drawings. The mere inclusion of knee joints in the drawings, without overemphasis, is consistent with the better reality contact and assessment of the normal women as compared with the hebephrenic schizophrenic women, and is not research data opposing the hypothesis as clinically employed.

Elsewhere, Swensen points out that "erasures are considered an expression of anxiety" but that Goldworth[2] found that, in general, normals employed more erasures than other groups. Swensen concludes that, "These results appear to contradict Machover."

This type of research reasoning embodies a popular fallacy in which groups of subjects are compared with other groups of subjects, and extremes in each group tend to cancel each other out, thus yielding a more benign Mean for the group. But clinicians find that neurotic and psychotic groups tend to deviate from the norm in either direction. Thus, sick individuals will draw a figure much too large (at the grandiose side of the continuum) or much too small (reflecting direct feelings of inferiority and inadequacy), they will either draw with too light a line (reflecting anxiety, hesitancy and uncertainty) or too heavy a line (reflecting aggression and inner tension); similarly they will erase too much or not erase at all. As with all areas of behavior, it is the deviation in either direction from the Mean which are clinically noteworthy. Group comparisons, then, on any variable tend to obscure the extreme emphasis, in both directions, of that group and to cancel out the noteworthy occurrences.

In regard to the specific hypothesis about erasures, some erasure, with subsequent improvement, is a sign of adaptiveness and flexibility. Overemphasis upon erasure, particularly in the absence of subsequent improvement in the drawing, is the correlate of excessive self-doubt, self-disapproval, and conflicts which result from perfectionistic demands upon one's self. A total absence of erasures, on the other hand, may denote a lack of adaptive flexibility.

In cases such as this, a comparison of Means has no valid meaning. The only research design that is applicable would involve employing a three-point (or five-point) rating scale: (a) overemphasis, (b) "normal" emphasis, and (c) underemphasis and absence. Then the comparison between groups which is appropriate would be in regard to percentages falling in the extreme categories, not with the obscured picture of the Means.

The last point that requires clarification in Swensen's review concerns the basic premise of projective drawings as a reflection of the self. Swensen reports Berman and Laffal's[1] comparison of figure drawings with the body type of the subjects offering the drawings. A Pearson r of .35, significant at the .05 level of confidence, was yielded on the basis of Sheldon's body types. In inspecting Berman and Laffal's data, Swensen points out that "only" 18 of their 39 subjects drew figures that were judged to be of the same body types as the subject's body type, and concludes that for some subjects, the figure drawn represents the subject's own body, but for the majority of subjects, the figure drawn represents something else. Swensen deduces, "Since in clinical work the reliable diagnosis of the clinical case is of paramount importance, this lack of consistent evidence supporting Machover, . . . suggests that the DAP is of doubtful value in clinical work."

Here, Swensen is entangled in a relatively unsophisticated notion of the concept of the self. Some subjects tend to project themselves as they experience themselves to be, while other subjects tend to project themselves as they wish to be. The idealized version of the self is an integral component of the self-concept and is necessary in describing personality. It is not the chaff, to the real self as wheat. In actual clinical context, most drawings are neither one nor the other, but actually represent a fusion of both the realistic perceptions of one's self and the ego-ideal. In addition, the picture is further complicated by the fact that the perceptions of one's self *as one fears one might be* also color the total picture. Since the *self* actually includes what we are, what we wish to be, and what we fear we might sink to, we must expect all three to flood projective drawings and not regard any deviation from perfect correlation on any one of these variables between the drawing and the subject as a contraindication of the basic hypothesis.

The trouble with Swensen's interpretation of the results of Berman and Laffal's study is that he too narrowly defines the self as both experienced by the subject and as projected in his drawing. As the present writer points out elsewhere,[3] a still additional facet that must be reckoned with in the understanding, and investigation of, projective drawings involves a perception of significant figures in one's early developmental years. Thus, the projective drawing interpreter and/or research worker must grapple with the problem of disentangling the influences of four different projections on the drawing page:

For example, a subject who suffers from "castration anxiety" will reveal *the fear of what he may become,* in his drawing. A subject who feels himself to be obese may draw a fat person (*what he feels himself to be*); another subject who suffers from obesity but who has not yet lost the capacity to yearn for, and strive for, an ideal figure will draw a very shapely person (*what he wishes to be*). A child who experiences his father as threatening may, as one subject recently did, draw a male with teeth bared, a dagger in one hand, and scissors in the other, with a generally menacing facial tone and violent look in the eyes (*his perception of others*).

In the face of a complex world, the research worker is obligated to recognize the complexity of the variables he attempts to come to grips with in his investigations, and steer vigorously away from the dangers of atomistic studies, naively conceived, and dogmatically interpreted.

REFERENCES

1. Berman, S., & Laffal, J. Body type and figure drawing. *J. Clin. Psychol.,* 1953, *9,* 368–370.
2. Goldworth, S. A comparative study of drawings of men and women done by normal, neurotic, schizophrenic and brain-damaged individuals. Unpublished Ph.D. thesis, Univer. of Pittsburgh, 1950.
3. Hammer, E. F. *The clinical application of projective drawings.* Springfield, IL: Charles C Thomas, 1958.
4. Holzberg, J. D., & Wexler, M. The validity of human form drawings as a measure of personality deviation. *J. Proj. Tech.,* 1950, *14,* 343–361.
5. Machover, Karen. *Personality projection in the drawing of a human figure.* Springfield, IL: Charles C Thomas, 1949.
6. Swensen, Jr., C. Empirical evaluations of human figure drawings. *Psychol. Bull.,* 1957, *54,* 431–466.

Chapter 16

THE DRAW-A-PERSON-IN-THE-RAIN: ITS RELATION TO DIAGNOSTIC CATEGORY*

J. S. VERINIS, E. F. LICHTENBERG AND L. HENRICH

EXPERIMENT I: PROBLEM

The reviews of Roback[13] and Swensen[14] on the Human Figure Drawing Test indicate that a number of Machover's[11] original contentions are unsupported by research. The need to shift from Machover's specific indicators to more global, comprehensive ratings is made quite clear, and several authors have attempted to move in this direction (i.e., Kahn and Jong[8] and Lewinsohn.[9] The result, in general, has been an increase in the clinical predictability and value of the drawings.

Another way to try to make the drawings more predictive has been to ask the patient to draw an object other than a person,[2,10] to draw the person from another standpoint,[12] or to draw the person in a standardized situation.[3] The present report is concerned with an extension of the person in a standardized situation approach, as Ss were asked to draw a person in the rain.[7]

The rationale is as follows: Two of the factors assessed by many clinicians who are trying to formulate a decision such as whether to hospitalize a patient or what treatment approach might be most appropriate (implicit in these decisions is the formulation of a diagnostic impression) are the amount of stress that the patient is experiencing and the adequacy of his defensive structure to handle this stress without a psychotic decompensation and regression. The rain, it is hypothesized, is equivalent to the subjective stress, and the quantity and intensity of the drawn rain should be indicative of the amount of stress that the S feels he is under. The person's defenses against this stress should be symbolized by his drawn defenses against the rain (i.e., umbrella, raincoat,

*Reprinted with permission, Verinis, J. S., *et al.,* "The Draw-A-Person in the Rain: Its Relationship to Diagnostic Category and Other Personality Indicators," *J. Clinical Psych.,* July '74.

tree) and how well they are protecting the person against the rain.

With regard to the primary diagnostic groups of neurotic reaction, character disorder, and psychotic-borderline of psychotic reaction, the following expectations were generated. The neurotic generally is described as a person under a great deal of stress (i.e., anxiety, guilt), but whose defensive structure is adequate enough to ward off any regression or decompensation into psychosis.[6] The modal neurotic drawing thus is hypothesized to have a great deal of rain and other precipitation present. The person will have some form of defense against the rain, and this will be providing him some protection.

The character disorder usually is pictured as having much of his symptom behavior as egosyntonic rather than ego alien as in the neurotic reactions; consequently, the subjectively experienced stress on him is minimal.[4] The modal character disorder drawing thus is hypothesized to have little or no evidence of rain in the picture but usually accompanied by some rain gear such as an umbrella, raincoat or hat. That is, defenses are present despite feelings of being under minimal or no stress. The defenses are often minimal, also.

The psychotic or borderline psychotic reaction is described as experiencing great amounts of stress so intense that his ability to function is paralyzed. His defensive structure is weak, and he generally is unable to fend off this stress except through regression and decompensation.[1] The modal drawing for this diagnostic group is hypothesized to have, like the neurotic, a great amount of rain and precipitation present and, unlike the neurotic, no adequate protection against the rain. The figure will be drawn totally defenseless or with the semblance of a defense present, but with it apparent that this defense is not protecting the person from the rain (i.e., an umbrella is over the *S,* but the rain is still falling through onto the person).

This paper describes a series of experiments that attempt to validate these formulations. Drawings were collected from a variety of previously diagnosed mental patients, and a blind diagnosis was made solely on the basis of the characteristics described in Table 16-1. If the above formulations are accurate, one would expect the drawing diagnosis to approximate the actual diagnosis on a better than chance level.

Method

The first sample was a randomly selected group of 25 adolescents, aged between 10 and 17, who were seen in the outpatient psychiatry department at Mount Sinai Hospital. Four were female and 8 were African-American. The drawings had been collected by the examining psychologist, and the independent psychiatric diagnosis was taken from the patient's chart. It is not known what effect the psychologist's report had on the psychiatrist's diagnosis or what effect the results of the drawings had on the psychologist's conclusions. Only those adolescents whose diagnosis clearly fit into one of three general categories were included (i.e., patients with adjustment reaction of adolescents were excluded).

The second sample was composed of 42 hospitalized adult patients admitted to Mount Sinai Hospital, a private short-term facility with an average patient stay of 18 days. The drawings were collected under the guise of an activity and were not made available to the psychiatrists when they were formulating their diagnosis. The diagnoses were collected from the patients' charts. The age range was from 19 to 68; 21 of the patients were male, all were white, and the majority were private.

The third sample consisted of 13 female, white, chronic mental patients hospitalized at the Galesburg State Research Hospital for an average of 6.3 years. All had a diagnosis of psychosis. The drawings were collected during a ward meeting by the ward attendant.

The fourth sample was a group of 43 court-referred adolescents incarcerated at the Audy Home, a Chicago juvenile detention center, until their time of trial. The drawings were collected by the psychologist connected with the center and were not available to the court appointed psychiatrist who reached an independent diagnosis. The age range of these patients was 11–17. Twenty-one were female and 22 were African-American.

All the drawings were placed into one of three diagnostic categories (neurotic, character disorder, psychotic-borderline) by each of the three authors. The judges were asked to use only the criteria (amount of rain and adequacy of defenses) described in Table 16-1 to make their classifications. Their subjective reports indicated that this was not difficult to do. Only two of the authors did the classification on the Chicago juvenile detention center sample, as the third author was the psychologist who collected all the data and therefore would have been a biased judge. This

338 *Advances in Projective Drawing Interpretation*

Table 16-1.
Drawing Characteristics Related to Diagnostic Category

Diagnostic Category	Rain	Defenses Against the Rain
Neurotic	Present	Adequate—figure is protected by umbrella, rain clothes, tree, etc.
Character Disorder	Not present or a few isolated drops	Defenses present, often minimal in nature. Occasionally absent.
Psychotic-Borderline Psychotic	Present—often excessive	Totally absent or if present clearly inadequate as protection, as figure is still getting wet.

classification was made independently and without prior knowledge of the patient's diagnosis or the other judge's classification.

Prior knowledge of the population from which the drawings were taken was believed to be a biasing factor for the judges. That is to say, if the judges had a rough idea of the distribution of the different diagnostic groups within each of the patient populations, that this knowledge tended to bias them toward certain diagnostic categories. This factor could inflate the judge's classification accuracy. To control for this bias, base rates were calculated for each population group from which the drawings were taken. This was done by consulting the institution records for the year the data were collected and getting the total of all patients who fell in the three diagnostic categories of interest. The basic rate percentages for the different samples are as follows:

1. Mt. Sinai Adolescent Outpatients: Neurotics 39%, Psychotic-Borderline 10%, Character Disorder 51%
2. Mt. Sinai Adult Inpatients: Neurotic 50%, Psychotic 40%, Character Disorder 10%.
3. Galesburg Chronic Patients: Neurotic 5%, Psychotic 90%, Character Disorder 5%.
4. Audy Home Adolescents: Neurotic 3%, Psychotic 14%, Character Disorder 83%.

These base-rate percentages were applied to the existing samples to determine judge chance accuracy; i.e., how accurate would a judge be when he applied his knowledge of the population base rate without any reference to the drawings? Thus, in the Mt. Sinai Adolescent sample (N = 25), chance accuracy rate would be obtained if a judge randomly guessed Neurotic 9 times, Psychotic-Borderline 3 times and Character Disorder 13 times. These diagnoses were randomly paired with the diagnoses in the sample to yield a chance accuracy rate for that sample. Three by five cards with the diagnoses written on the back were used, and these were drawn blindly and compared to a list of the patients in the sample. When the diagnosis matched, this was judged a correct guess. The number of cards was determined by the sample size, and the percentage of cards with each diagnostic label was determined by the base rate for that population. This was done three times for each sample, and the average of these three rates was the chance accuracy rate for that sample.

Results

Mount Sinai Adolescent Outpatients. Judge 1 *correctly identified 76 percent* (19 out of 25) of the adolescent patients as to diagnostic category on the basis of their drawings alone. Judge 2 correctly identified 71 percent and Judge 3, 68 percent. The range of interjudge agreement was between 84 percent (Judges 1 and 3) and 96 percent (Judges 1 and 2). *By chance, each Judge was expected to be correct 32 percent of the time,* and each did significantly better than chance (Table 16-2) using the proportion difference test.[5]

Table 16-2.
Accuracy of Diagnostic Category Predictions

	Chance	*Judge 1*	*Judge 2*	*Judge 3*
Mt. Sinai Adolescents N = 25	32%	76%*	71%*	68%*
Mt. Sinai Adults N = 42	38%	47% NS	50% NS	47% NS
Galesburg Adults N = 13	84%	85% NS	77% NS	85% NS
Audy Home Adolescents N = 43	43%	67%**	63%**	

**p < .05; *p < .01.

Mount Sinai Adult Inpatients. Judge 1 correctly identified 21 of 42 (47%) of the adult Inpatients, Judge 2, 50 percent and Judge 3, 47 percent. The chance accuracy rate was 38 percent, and none of these classification percentages was significantly better than chance (Table 16-2). The judge agreement ranged from 64 percent (Judges 1 and 3) to 84 percent (Judges 1 and 2).

The diagnosis used in this analysis was the admitting diagnosis formulated by the psychiatric resident within 3 days of the patient's admission to the hospital. The main drawback to the use of this criterion is that it is subject to change, as the resident's first impression is sometimes superficial. The discharge diagnosis then was employed, with the following results: Judge 1: 49 percent, Judge 2: 49 percent, Judge 3: 51 percent. None of these percentages was significantly different from the chance rate either.

Galesburg Chronic Adult Inpatients. Of the 13 patients in this sample, Judge 1 felt that 11 of 13 (85%) met the psychotic-borderline criteria outlined earlier, Judge 2, 77 percent and Judge 3, 85 percent. The chance accuracy percentage was 84 percent, and none of these accuracy percentages was significantly different from chance (Table 16-2). Judge agreement ranged from 92 to 100 percent.

Audy Home Adolescents. Of the 43 patients in this sample, Judge 1 had an accuracy percentage of 67 percent as opposed to 63 percent for Judge 2 (Table 16-2). Both of these were greater than expected by chance (chance percentage = 43%). Judge agreement was 95 percent.

Since IQs were available for all of these patients, it was decided to explore the possibility that the differences in drawings might be related to intellectual conceptual capacity rather than to the nature of their emotional pathology. The 41 percent cases agreed on by both judges were separated into three diagnostic groups on the basis of the judge-given diagnosis. Character disorders had a mean IQ of 93.3 and range of 81 to 135 (N = 10), the psychotic-borderlines had a mean 95.5 and a range of 70 to 110 (N = 10), and the neurotics had a mean 96.0 with a range of 72 to 123 (N = 12). These differences were not significant using a single factor analysis of variance.

A further investigation into the interaction of intellectual level with the judges' diagnostic accuracy was undertaken by dividing the patients into three groups according to intellectual level: high IQ with IQs 111 or higher (N = 4), average IQ with IQs between 90 and 110 (N = 16), and low IQ with IQs below 89 (N = 22). The judges' predictive accuracy for each of these groups was computed simply by tallying the number of correct classifications made with each IQ level and combining the figures for each judge to get one total accuracy percentage. The judges correctly classified the high IQ patients 2 out of 8 times, or 25 percent of the time. With the average IQ patients, the judges were correct 59 percent of the time (19 out of 32). With the low IQ patients, the judges were right 82 percent (36 of 44) of the time. Thus, it appears that the drawings are much more predictive of diagnostic category with low-intellectual-level patients and that the diagnostic accuracy of the technique decreases as the patient's intellectual level rises.

IQs were available on 17 of the Mount Sinai Adolescents, so the same analysis was made in an attempt to check the authenticity of this trend. The predictive accuracies were as follows: 73 percent for the high-IQ patients (N = 5), 88 percent for the average patient (N = 6), and 83 percent for the low-IQ patients (N = 6). These results are considered to support the hypothesis that is being developed.

The interaction of patient race with the judges' diagnostic accuracy also was explored in a *post hoc* analysis of the 21 African-American adolescents. The judges were right 32 times out of the total 42 classifications, or 76 percent of the time. This is substantially above the overall accuracy percent (67% to 63%) for the total Audy Home sample and is suggestive of a greater predictive accuracy with African-American patients. A similar pattern was noted with 8 African-American adolescents from the Mount Sinai sample. The predictive accuracy for these *S*s was 18 correct diagnoses out of the total of 24 classifications, or 75 percent. This result supports the Audy Home trend.

Patient sex also was considered a variable of interest; of the 21 female adolescents, the judge predicted diagnosis accurately 30 out of 42 times for a predictive accuracy of 72 percent. This too is above the overall accuracy percentage for the Audy Home cases, although only slightly. Similar patterns were noted with the four female adolescents from the Mount Sinai sample in that predictive accuracy was 75 percent (or 9 correct diagnoses out of 12) and with the 21 female inpatients from Mount Sinai, the predictive accuracy was 57 percent or 36 correct diagnoses out of a total of 63. Both figures are slightly above the more general accuracy percentages reported for these studies.

EXPERIMENT II: PROBLEM

The results of the first experiment seem clear enough. Judges who use only an adolescent patient's drawing of a person in the rain consistently can predict the patient's broad diagnostic category (neurotic, character-disorder, psychotic-borderline psychotic) at a better than chance rate.

The second experiment is an attempt to investigate characteristics of adolescent patients, other than their psychiatric diagnosis, that might be related to their drawings of a person in the rain.

Method

Drawings were collected from 23 hospitalized adolescent patients (ages 13–17) at the Hawaii State Hospital. The patients' psychologist, who was unaware of the research objective, was asked to rate the patients on two 7-point scales: the amount of stress the patient is currently under (1 = very much to 7 = minimal) and strength of defenses (1 = very strong to 7 = weak). The drawings were rated independently on the same two scales by two of the authors.

Six of the patients were female, and all were racially mixed with various components of whites, Orientals, and Hawaiians.

A second sample of drawings was collected from 79 patients at the Audy Home, a court-related, short-term juvenile detention center in Chicago. These drawings were rated on two 7-point scales—amount of anxiety present (1 = no anxiety present to 7 = extreme anxiety) and strength of defensive structure (1 = weak to 7 = strong). The drawing also was placed into one of three diagnostic categories (Psychotic-Borderline, Neurotic, Character Disorder). The rating was done by two of the authors.

The 79 adolescents in this sample also were asked to complete the Taylor Manifest Anxiety Scale and the Barron Ego Strength Scale. The drawings and tests were administered during classtime in the special school connected with the Audy Home.

The tests were scored by a clerk in the psychiatry department at Mt. Sinai Hospital, while the drawings were rated independently by the authors. The ratings were averaged for comparison with the test scores.

Results

In Sample 1, a correlation[5] was run between the "amount of stress patient is currently under" rating by the patient's psychologist and the average of the "stress" ratings made on the patient's drawings by two of the authors. The result was an r of .93, which reached an extremely high level of statistical significance (p .0005). The correlation between the "strength of patient's defenses" ratings was .55. This was also significant ($p = .005$).

In Sample 2, a multiple correlation was run on the test scores and judge ratings. The significant correlation was a negative one (r .56, p .01), as makes sense, between manifest anxiety and ego strength.

EXPERIMENT III: PROBLEM

In view of the fact that the data were collected on adolescent psychiatric patients, the authors decided to collect drawings of "a person in the rain" from a sample of nonpatient adolescents. These data could be used to place the patient drawings in proper perspective.

Method

Drawings were collected from 139 high school students during class time. None was diagnosed as having any serious emotional or behavior problems. The high schools were from a racially-mixed, lower-middle-class area with relatively intact family structures. Seventy of the students were white, 69 were African-American. There were 88 males and 51 females. The age range was between 14 and 18, mean age 15.8 years. The drawings were placed by two of the authors into the different diagnostic categories with 87 percent accuracy.

Results

Of the drawings, 48.9 percent were placed in the neurotic category (some stress but adequate defenses), while 43.2 percent received a psychotic-borderline diagnosis (much stress and no defenses), and 7.9 percent were labelled character disorder (no stress). The data were analyzed to determine whether "too much stress" and "no defenses drawings" clustered along any sexual or racial lines. In terms of sex, 43.3 percent of the male drawings fell into this category, compared to 43.1 percent of the female drawings. This was not a significant difference.

In terms of race, 16 (34%) of the 46 white males made a psychotic type drawing, as compared to 53 percent of the 42 African-American males. This difference was compared by the chi square for independent samples[6] and yielded a borderline significant Chi ($x^2 = 2.97$, *df* 1, *p* .10). Of the 24 white females, 5 (21%) made a psychotic type drawing, as compared to 39 percent of the African-American females. This difference was significant ($x^2 = 11.3$, *df* 1, *p* .001). The racial difference in type of drawing appears pronounced, especially with females.

In terms of the race of the drawn figure, all the white adolescents drew a white figure. Fifty-three percent of the African-American males and 74 percent of the African-American females drew a white figure. The comparisons between the African-American males and females and their white counterparts were all significant (p .001). An interesting trend was that the 68 percent (13/19) of the African-American males and 80 percent (4/5) of the African-American females who drew an African-American figure made drawings that were classified as much stress-no defense drawings. The suggestion is of more stress and more problems for those African-American adolescents who have made a racial identification with the African-American race.

In terms of the sex of the drawn figure, white male adolescents drew a man 69 percent of the time, a woman 19 percent, and an ambiguous figure 12 percent. The African-American males drew men 91 percent of the time and women 9 percent of the time. A comparison of these differences yielded a chi square of 7.30, which was statistically significant (df 1, p .05).

White females drew a woman 78 percent of the time and a man 12 percent of the time as compared to 33 percent women, 44 percent men, and 23 percent ambiguous for African-American females. This difference also reached significance (x^2 = 8.46, df 1, p .02). The rater agreement on sex of the drawing was 90 percent and on race 95 percent.

SUMMARY

Concerning the heart of this study: the first experiment describes the relationship of a patient's drawing of a person in the rain to his psychiatric diagnosis. Drawings were classified into one of three diagnostic classes by independent judges. The validity criterion was the psychiatrist's independent diagnosis. The results showed that it was possible to predict adolescent patients' diagnostic category.

In the second experiment, one sample of patients was rated on (a) amount of current stress and strength of defenses, and (b) their drawings of a person in the rain by independent judges. The correlations were .93 and .55, respectively.

The third experiment consisted of obtaining a sample from a nonpatient adolescent population for comparison purposes. As expected, the majority of the drawings fell in either the neurotic (49%) or psychotic-borderline (43%) category. Again, as expected, there were no sexual differences in type of drawing, and, not as expected, there was a greater preponderance of psychotic-borderline psychotic drawings from the African-American adolescents.

REFERENCES

1. Bellack, L., & Loeb, L. *The Schizophrenic Syndrome.* New York: Grune & Stratton, 1969.
2. Buck, J. N. The H–T–P Test. *J. Clin. Psychol.,* 1948, *4,* 151–158. T16:02
3. Burns, R. C., & Kaufman, S. *Kinetic Family Drawing.* New York: Brunner-Mazel, 1971.
4. Cleckley, H. *The Mask of Sanity.* St. Louis: Mosby, 1959.
5. Dixon, W., & Massey, F. M. *Introduction to Statistical Analysis.* New York: McGraw-Hill, 1957.
6. Kutash, S. Psychoneuroses. In Wolman, B. *Handbook of Clinical Psychology.* New York: McGraw-Hill, 1965, pp. 948–975.
7. Hammer, E. *The Clinical Application of Projective Drawings.* Springfield, IL: Charles C Thomas, 1958.
8. Kahn, M., & Jong, M. Human figure drawings as predictors of admission to a psychiatric hospital. *J. Proj. Tech.,* 1965, *2,* 319–22.
9. Lewinsohn, P. M. Psychological correlates of overall quality of figure drawings. *J. Consult. Psychol.,* 1965, *29,* 504–12.
10. Loney, J. Clinical aspects of the Loney Draw A Car Test: Enuresis and encopresis. *J. Pers. Assess.,* 1971, *35,* 265–74.
11. Machover, K. *Personality Projection in the Drawing of the Human Figure.* Springfield, IL: Charles C Thomas, 1949.
12. Ponzo, E. An experimental variation of the Draw A Person technique. *J. Proj. Techn.,* 1957, *21,* 278–85.
13. Roback, H. Human figure drawings: Their utility in the clinical psychologist's armamentarium for personality assessment. *Psychol. Bull.,* 1968, *70,* 1–19.
14. Swensen, C. H. Empirical evaluations of human figure drawings, 1957–1966. *Psychol. Bull.,* 1968, *70,* 20–44.

PERSONALITY OF THE CLINICIAN AND THE INTERPRETATION OF PROJECTIVE DRAWINGS

Chapter 17

HOSTILITY AS A FACTOR IN THE CLINICIAN'S PERSONALITY AS IT AFFECTS HIS INTERPRETATION OF PROJECTIVE DRAWINGS (H–T–P)*

EMANUEL F. HAMMER AND ZYGMUND A. PIOTROWSKI

Previous studies in projective techniques have been aimed at obtaining insight into the manner in which personality dynamics, needs, conflicts and phantasies of a subject are revealed by his responses to a projective device. The study of the role of the clinician and the significance of his personality factors in the interpretation of projective techniques have awaited study until the establishment of working tenets in regard to the interaction of the personality of the subject with the projective material. If psychodiagnostic tools are to be sharpened and made more valid, investigation must now be made of the correlation between the interpreter's own needs, conflicts and phantasies and the interpretations he makes from a patient's projective protocols.

A study by Bruner and Goodman (1947) highlighting the connection between needs and perception deserves mention in this regard. It was found that poor subjects overestimated the size of coins more than did rich subjects. This was considered to be a reflection of the greater financial need of the poor children, and was taken to substantiate the hypothesis that needs affect perception and judgment.

The present study was set up to investigate the question of whether or not clinicians' needs, as with the needs of the subjects in the study by Bruner and Goodman above, influence and distort their apperception or 'reading' of a set of projective protocols, namely a series of drawings of House, Tree and Person (HTP).

There has already been some experimentation done on the effect of

*Grateful acknowledgment is made to Mrs. Susan Deri for her interpretation and ranking of the Szondi Profiles and to John N. Buck for his fruitful suggestions and criticisms.

*Adapted with permission: from the *Journal of Projective Techniques,* May, 1952.

the clinicians' personality upon his rating of the overt behavior of subjects by Frenkel-Brunswik (1951). She states that "drive ratings may be influenced by . . . the intensity of the drive in question in the personality of the rater" (p. 390). She found that raters showed a stronger tendency to project when rating children of their sex than when rating children of the opposite sex. Hence, she concludes that "we must acknowledge that there are various subjective factors that seem to influence the perception of others even in clinically trained observers (p. 393).

Does the same hold true for clinically trained projective testers? This question is the aim of the present study. The particular trait (the expression of which represents a need) chosen for study in this experiment was that which is roughly referred to as "hostility" or "aggression." The decision to focus upon this personality area grew out of the writers' experiences which have led them to feel that the two areas in which clinicians tend to differ most in their interpretations are those of hostility and sexuality. The former was investigated in the present study; and the latter is to be investigated in a subsequent study.

PROCEDURE

The freehand drawings of House, Tree and Person had been used in a previous study (Hammer, n.d.,a) as a device to tap the personality of 400 children of elementary school age, ranging from grades one to eight. Of these 400, 148 were African-American children (Hammer, n.d.,c) and 252 white children in gratifyingly representative (from a socioeconomic viewpoint) semiurban, semirural schools.

The H–T–P was employed because it is a quick and easy-to-administer projective technique which seems to be penalized less by group administration than most other projective devices. It was employed also because four of the six clinicians* who served as interpreters had received special training in the H–T–P technique directly under John N. Buck (1948a, 1948b, 1950), its innovator, and the remaining two had received their H–T–P training at Lynchburg State Colony, the institution at which this technique had been developed.

In the present study, these 400 H–T–P's were given to the clinician-judges to be rated independently on a scale of aggression from zero to two. A rating of zero represented no apparent aggression or hostility, a

*Three of the six were experienced staff psychologists while the other three were on an intern level.

rating of one represented mild aggression or hostility, while a rating of two represented severe aggression and hostility. In regard to giving a rating of one or two, the clinicians were instructed to give the former rating if in a psychological report on the subject's H–T–P they would ordinarily mention that there was *mild* aggression or hostility present, and to give a rating of two if they would ordinarily cite *severe* aggression or hostility as present.

Three clinicians served as judges for the drawings of all eight grades of children while three additional clinicians served as judges for the third, fifth, and seventh grades in order to afford the opportunities for a spot check.

Correlations of the judgments of the three principal judges were then computed. All six judges, principal and secondary, were put in rank order according to the degree of hostility they apperceived in the H–T–P's (of the students in the third, fifth and seventh grades) they had rated. This rank order was then compared with the rank order in which the judges were rated for hostility by one of the writers, then Supervisor of Intern Training at the institution at which the study was conducted. The supervisor rated the clinicians on the basis of the degree of overt aggression and hostility manifested by them in their interaction with patients and staff members. The clinicians were placed in rank order of hostility before they judged the drawings and they did not know of the dual end to which their ratings would be put until after their data were handed in and their consent obtained.

The drawings were rated by the six clinicians on the basis of the following qualitative signs for aggression and hostility from the *Guide for Qualitative Research with the H–T–P* (Hammer, n.d.,b):

> The drawing of attic windows which are open implies hostile phantasy which causes the person guilt. It has been observed that subjects who are extremely prone to phantasy in hostile fashion frequently provide themselves with what might be called "safety valves" by drawing open windows in the area symbolizing phantasy thinking, the roof.
>
> Windows drawn without panes, curtains or shutters (hence, like the "keyhole" tree below, another depiction of unrelieved, enclosed, white space) may imply hostility.
>
> A tree which consists of a looping line representing the tree's branch structure (unclosed at its junction with the trunk) and two vertical lines closed or unclosed at the trunk's base (thus resembling a key-hole) is taken to indicate strong hostile impulses.
>
> Two-dimensional branches that are drawn resembling clubs or sharply

pointed branches or leaves, especially with little organization, imply strong hostility.

A mutilated Person, or a degraded Tree or House, it goes without saying, serves to underscore the patient's hostility. The use of degrading details which serve to symbolize feelings of aggressive hostility may include such depiction as an outhouse drawn beside a House that is otherwise a mansion, a large conspicuous garbage can drawn on the front porch, or a dog drawn as urinating against the trunk of the Tree.

Sharply pointed fingers and toes, as well as other similarly treated details are a reflection of aggressive tendencies, as are teeth prominently presented in the drawing of the face.

Sharply squared shoulders in the drawing of the Person connote overdefensive, hostile attitudes.

Well-outlined, but unshaded hair, in the drawing of the Person suggests hostile phantasy concerning sexual matters.

Arms that are drawn folded across the chest suggest attitudes of suspicion and hostility.

The Person carrying weapons such as guns, blackjacks, etc., clearly indicates aggressive and hostile tendencies.

The Person presented in a threatening attitude (example, fist upraised, etc.) bespeaks aggressive hostility.

Drawings made conspicuously too large for the page, without adequate form page space framing them (particularly when they touch or almost touch the page's side margins), tend to indicate a feeling of great frustration produced by a restraining environment, with concomitant feelings of hostility and a desire to react aggressively (either against the environment or the self, or both).

The qualitative points listed above were employed as broad guideposts in an effort to increase, in some measure, the objectivity of the qualitative approach employed in the present study. The greater the number or intensity of signs of hostility and aggression in a set of drawings, the more inclined the clinicians were to go up the continuum from mild to severe in their ratings. Since the dynamic interrelationship of a sign with all other signs available is of prime importance, however, the drawings were viewed as a Gestalt. An attempt was made to take the total constellation into account at all times.

The six clinicians then submitted to six administrations of the Szondi Test each. The Szondi was chosen as a projective technique to tap the degree of hostility and aggression in each of the clinicians because it represented the clinical tool with which these particular clinicians, had as yet, had no experience and little orientation. In regard to the Szondi technique the clinicians were, for the most part, unsophisticated and uninformed. The Szondi profiles of the six clinicians were submitted to Mrs. Susan Deri for her to place the clinicians in rank order in regard to the degree to which, in her opinion, each clinician possessed hostile and aggressive impulses. This rank order was then correlated with the rank order of the clinicians in regard to the degree of aggression and hostility they interpreted in the 400 H–T–P's.

RESULTS

Rank-difference correlations among the ranks of the three judges were .74, .78 and .84 with standard errors of .031, .030, and .014 respectively.

All six clinicians, the three main and the three secondary judges were placed in rank order in regard to the degree of hostility they manifested in interpersonal relationships as judged by the supervisor. A comparison of this rank order with the rank order of the degree of hostility they saw in the H–T–P drawings is presented in Table 17-1.

A rank order correlation of .94 with a standard error of .48 is obtained.

The correlation between the rank order of the clinicians in regard to the degree to which they apperceived aggression and hostility in the H–T–P drawings and the degree to which they revealed aggression and hostility, on the Szondi, as a personality component, is also .94 with a standard error of .48. Table II indicates that a reversal in rank order is found in regard to clinicians C and D.

A similar correlation of .94 with the same standard error of .48 is obtained between the rank order of the clinicians' aggression as judged by the supervisor and as judged by Mrs. Deri's analysis of their Szondi profiles.

As high a correlation was found, then, between the degree of hostility the clinicians "saw" in the H–T–P's and the degree of their own hostility as judged by both their supervisor and Mrs. Deri as exist between the judgments of the supervisor and Mrs. Deri.

DISCUSSION

To turn to the question of the correlation of the judgments made by the three main judges, correlations ranging between .74 and .84 suggest a reasonably high degree of reliability among clinicians rating qualitative factors such as hostility and/or aggression on the basis of the H–T–P. In spite of these reassuringly high correlations, however, it appears that

Table 17-1.
Comparison of Rank Order of the Average Hostility Index* Given the 400 Drawings
by Each of Six Clinicians and the Rank Order of the Degree of Hostility
in Each Clinician as Judged by Their Supervisor.

Clinician-judge	Average Hostility Index Awarded the Drawings	Rank Order** of Hostility Index Awarded the Drawings	Rank Order** of Supervisor's Rating	Difference in Rank Order
A	0.49	1	1	0
B	0.51	2	3	1
C	0.57	3	2	1
D	0.63	4	4	0
E	0.90	5	5	0
F	1.12	6	6	0

*A rating of zero represents no apparent aggression and hostility, one represents mild and two represents severe aggression and hostility.
**In order of increasing hostility.

Table 17-2.
Comparison of Rank Order of the Average Hostility Index* Given the 400 Drawings
by Each of Six Clinicians and the Rank Order of the Degree of Hostility
in Each Clinician as Judged by Their Szondi Profile.

Clinician-judge	Average Hostility Index Awarded the Drawings	Rank Order** of Hostility Index Awarded the Drawings	Rank Order** of Hostility on the basis of Szondi	Difference in Rank Order
A	0.49	1	1	0
B	0.51	2	2	0
C	0.57	3	4	1
D	0.63	4	3	1
E	0.90	5	5	0
F	1.12	6	6	0

*A rating of zero represents no apparent aggression and hostility, one represents mild and two represents severe aggression and hostility.
**In order of increasing hostility.

much subjectivity enters into and distorts the interpretation of these factors on projective drawings.

The supervisor's judgment* of the degree of the clinicians' hostility and aggression as manifested in their interrelationship with patients and staff members was found to correlate to a marked degree with the proneness

---

*The validity of the supervisor's judgments were supported by the correlation with the clinicians' Szondi protocols.

of the clinicians to see hostility in the drawings of other subjects.

This finding may be partially explained by the differences in *sensitivity** on the part of the various clinicians to the particular personality factor aggression. In addition, the differences among the clinicians' interpretations of the projective technique is probably further due to the fact that when interpreting a projective technique clinicians tend to *project†* as well as interpret. This conclusion appears to be supported by (1) the relatively high correlation between the supervisor's ratings of hostility in the clinicians and the degree to which they saw hostility in the 400 H–T–P's they interpreted, (2) the relatively high correlation between the degree of aggression and hostility in each clinician as suggested by his Szondi profile and the degree to which he apperceived aggression and hostility in the projective drawings he interpreted, and (Brink, 1944) the fact that clinician F, for instance, awarded the drawings an average hostility index which approaches the point of being twice the mean hostility index awarded by the other five judges (so marked a deviation, on the part of one trained clinician, from the other five suggests the operation of *projected* hostility, beyond *sensitivity* on his part).

Since all visual perception involves the process of selection, to greater or less degree, it is to be expected that there would be individual differences between clinicians in the extent to which they interpret various personality factors from projective drawings of their subjects. Anyone who has had experience as a supervisor of psychology interns or has worked in a setting with many psychologist-colleagues has been impressed with the shortcomings of the role objective factors play in the interpretation of projective techniques and the degree to which subjective factors color such interpretations. Just as a subject's performance on a projective technique is a function of his personality, his needs, conflicts, desires and past experiences, so too, although to a lesser degree, is the interpretation of a projective protocol influenced by the personality pattern of the interpreter.

Projective interpreting deals with material which is emotional, often-

---

*This term is used as a concept denoting *sensitivity* to the perception of existing situations or stimuli (in accord with the concept of Bellak and Abt that a stimuli that is congruent with a preexisting configuration is more readily perceived than one that is not).

†*Projection* is used to denote the process of attributing one's own feelings, conflicts, etc., to outside stimuli, people or situations. This concept when applied to projective tests is broadened to include not only unacceptable and repressed but also acceptable and conscious tendencies.

times subjective and usually partly unconscious—material which the interpreter finds difficulty in viewing in a wholly objective manner. Projective drawings produce latent as well as manifest, symbolic as well as concrete material, some of which cannot be directly assessed, but must first be perceived and interpreted through the eyes of the interpreter. It is at this point that his own needs may infiltrate and influence his interpretive formulations.

CONCLUSIONS

As the results of the study were obtained from one group of clinicians only, and that group a small one consisting of but six members, the reliability of the results should be tested on other and larger groups. The following tentative conclusions, however, (the further reliability and validity of which can be established only by future and more extensive studies) seem justified:

1. There is a relatively high degree of reliability among clinicians in the present investigation in their ability to judge the degree of aggression and hostility as manifested in a subject's free-hand drawing of a House-Tree-Person.

2. In spite of this high degree of reliability, the clinicians' interpretations appear to have been, in part, determined by their own projections and areas of sensitivity.

3. Content or qualitative analysis of projective technique protocols, notably projective drawings, should therefore be employed with caution until more objective research is available and the subjective aspect of interpretation is controlled or minimized.

4. More extensive studies of the role played by the personality of the clinician in interpreting projective techniques should be undertaken with larger groups of clinicians and in investigation of other projective techniques such as the Rorschach and TAT.

REFERENCES

Bender, L. 1937. Art and Therapy in the Mental Disturbances of Children. *Journal of Nervous and Mental Diseases, 86,* 249–263.

Bruner, J., & Goodman, C. 1947. Value and Need as Organizing Factors in Perception. *Journal of Abnormal and Social Psychology, 42,* 33–44.

Brink, M. 1944. The Mental Hygiene Value of Children's Art Work. *American Journal of Orthopsychiatry, 14,* 136–146.

Buck, J. N. 1948a. The H–T–P. *Journal of Clinical Psychology, 4,* 151–159.

Buck, J. N. 1948b. The H–T–P Technique, a Qualitative and Quantitative Scoring Manual. Monograph Supplement, *Journal of Clinical Psychology, 5,* 1–120.

Buck, J. N. 1950. Administration and Interpretation of the H–T–P Test, mimeographed copy, VA Hospital, Richmond, Va., 1–87.

Fleming, J. 1940. Observations on the Use of Finger-Painting in the Treatment of Adult Patients with Personality Disorders. *Character and Personality, 8,* 301–310.

Frenkel-Brunswik, E. 1951. Personality Theory and Perception. In R. R. Blake and G. V. Ramsey (Eds.), *Perception, An Approach to Personality,* New York: Ronald Press. Pp. 356–419.

Hammer, E. F. n.d.,a. Frustration-Aggression Hypothesis Extended to Socio-Racial Areas: Comparison of Negro and White Children's H–T–P's. Paper pending publication.

Hammer, E. F. n.d.,b. Guide for Qualitative Research with the H–T–P. *Journal of General Psychology* (In Press).

Hammer, E. F. n.d.,c. Comparison of Intellectual Functioning Level of Negro Children and Adolescents on Two Intelligence Tests, One an Emergency Scale. *Journal of Genetic Psychology* (In Press).

Levy, J. 1934. The Use of Art Techniques in Treatment of Children's Behavior Problems. *Journal of Psychoaesthetics, 39,* 258–260.

Naumburg, M. 1947. Studies of the Free Art Expression of Behavior Problem Children and Adolescents as a Means of Diagnosis and Therapy. *Nervous and Mental Disease Monograph, 71,* 225.

Piotrowski, Z. A. 1950. A Rorschach Compendium-Revised and Enlarged. *Psychiatric Quarterly, 24,* 543–396.

Precker, J. A. 1950. Painting and Drawing in Personality Assessment. *Journal of Projective Techniques, 14,* 262–286.

Schmidl-Waehner, T. 1942. Formal Criteria for the Analysis of Children's Drawings. *American Journal of Orthopsychiatry, 12,* 95–104.

Waehner, T. S. 1946. Interpretations of Spontaneous Drawings and Paintings. *Genetic Psychology Monograph, 33,* 70.

Wolff, W. 1946. *The Personality of the Pre-School Child,* New York: Grune and Stratton.

Chapter 18

PERSONALITY FACTORS IN THE ACCURATE INTERPRETATION OF PROJECTIVE TESTS

TODD BURLEY AND LEONARD HANDLER

This is a particularly *pivotal* chapter. In it we find the answer to the question posed by the current state of projective drawings buffeted by the clash between the mixed data of research studies, on the one side, versus the surviving confidence generated by clinical study after clinical study, on the other side. The authors of this chapter surge through the door opened by Hammer and Piotrowski in the preceding chapter, to add confirming data and a basic broadening of its implications. The two chapters join together to salvage the heuristic state of projective drawings, its promise and its substance, from going down under the broadsides from some of the research psychologists.

The psychoanalytically enriched and creative flow of the discussion of the creative process at the end of the Discussion section is an added dividend which the reader should find deeply illuminative.

Overall, reacting to this study, it becomes apparent that Burley and Handler are among those psychologists who combine advanced clinical skills with imaginative research thinking to stand out as investigators who know, innovatively, what they are doing.

ABSTRACT

This study investigated the relationship between accurate Draw-A–Person Test interpretation and the variables of empathy, intuition and cognitive flexibility. Undergraduate and graduate subjects rated as good or poor DAP interpreters were tested with the Hogan Empathy Scale, The Intuition portion of the Myers-Briggs Type Indicator, and the Remote Associates Test (RAT) as a test of cognitive flexibility and creativity. Good interpreters scored significantly higher on empathy, intuition, and creativity. These differences were not due to differences in intelligence. A relationship was described between the variables of empathy, intuition, and cognitive flexibility (creativity) on the one hand, and adaptive regression in the service of the ego, on the other hand, to explain the process involved in good interpretation.

Interpretive approaches to projective tests range from those which emphasize various quantified cognitive factors, normative data, and specific test "signs" (thinking approaches) to those which emphasize the clinician's phenomenological experience of the data, and related affective or visceral associations ("feeling" approaches). However, traditional research on the Draw-A–Person Test (DAP) has been focused primarily upon the drawing itself, placing a great deal of emphasis on specific objective drawing characteristics and signs (Scribner & Handler, 1987). Some psychologists have even discarded the DAP as a valid assessment instrument, citing as their reasons research which emphasizes the confounding variable of artistic ability and studies which are negative or equivocal concerning many objective DAP signs (Swensen, 1957, 1968). However, others continue to use the technique with good results. Thus, for example, Hammer (1968) states, "In the hands of some students, projective drawings are an exquisitely sensitive tool, and in the hands of others, those employing a wooden, stilted approach, they are like disconnected phones" (p. 385).

Many mental health professionals recognize the symbolic content of the art which they view in countless museums around the world and they continue to speculate freely about the personalities of the various artists whose works they view and admire. They also have few qualms about relying upon subjective skills in their psychotherapy work. Yet, they are often reluctant to take the same intuitive, subjective approach in the interpretation of various projective tests, especially the DAP. Instead, they search endlessly for a more objective, quantified method.

Rather than continue to focus on objective signs, we decided to begin a series of studies to investigate various personality factors of test interpreters who demonstrate special skill in *qualitative* interpretation, compared with those who are especially poor in this type of interpretive process. This is not a new idea; Hunt (1946) recommended that "we should consider the individual clinician as a clinical instrument, and study and evaluate his performance exactly as we study a test" (p. 317). This approach would lead us to examine the validity of the "clinician as interpreter" and would steer us clear of the vexing question of whether figure drawings per se are valid. Thus, for example, a number of researchers have indicated that there are significant individual differences among examiners in the accuracy of projective test interpretation (Fancher, 1966, 1967; Gordon, 1966, 1967; Hammer & Piotrowski, 1953; Mintz, 1959; Prybil, Hunt & Wallace, 1968). Recent research (Tharinger & Stark, 1990) indicates the superiority of a qualitative, intuitive, holistic approach, compared with a more objective sign approach, to differentiate mood disordered and anxious children from normal control subjects, using the DAP or the Kinetic Family Drawing Technique.

A number of researchers have found that subjects with little or no experience in the interpretation of projective tests can judge figure drawings with the accuracy of experienced clinicians (Albee & Hamlin, 1950; Handler, 1985; Levenberg, 1975; Schmidt & McGowan, 1959; Scribner & Handler, 1987; Simms, 1951). Schmidt and McGowan (1959) concluded that facility with figure drawing analysis is at least in part related to an affective rather than a cognitive orientation, while Hammer and Piotrowski (1953), opening up the whole area of the personality of the clinician, found a very high correlation between degree of hostility in the clinician and the clinician's proneness to detect hostility in figure drawings.

Scribner and Handler (1987) compared "good" and "poor" under-graduate DAP interpreters on the Leary Interpersonal System, a multilevel, interpersonal circomplex personality assessment method. They found that good interpretive skill was significantly related to an affiliative approach and poor interpretive skill was associated with a disaffiliative approach. This association was even stronger when unconscious personality levels were tapped. Seventy-three percent of the subjects who were good interpreters saw themselves as responsible and cooperative in relationships with others, whereas, 85 percent of subjects who were poor interpreters saw themselves as dominant and competitive in their relationships with others. Their approach to life emphasized power, dominance, order, and precision. Scribner and Handler concluded that the ability to "read" human figure drawings in an intuitive, impressionistic manner was consistent with an affiliative rather than with a disaffiliative orientation (Scribner & Handler 1987), but noted that an affiliative interpersonal orientation is necessary but not sufficient to be a good interpreter.

The present study is an attempt to explore several additional related variables which, it is hypothesized, are related to accurate DAP interpretation utilizing an experiential approach: intuition, empathy, and cognitive flexibility (as one type of creativity) and to hopefully shed some light on the *process* involved in intuitive interpretation. Therefore, it was hypothesized that those subjects who were more accurate in a qualitative approach to the interpretation of the DAP would be more empathic, more intuitive and more cognitively flexible (creative) compared with those subjects who were poor in DAP interpretation. Empathy and intuition were chosen as variables because they are considered by many to be an integral part of our assessment and psychotherapy endeavors.

METHOD

The subjects came from two sources: the first group of 64 subjects were undergraduate volunteers from an introductory psychology class; the second group consisted of an entire second year graduate class in clinical psychology. Each of the graduate students had completed a sequence of courses and practica which dealt with projective techniques, including the DAP.

The subjects were shown three pairs of DAP protocols (a male and a female drawing in each pair), each pair generated by a different patient and each pair accompanied by a separate list of forced choice interpretations. There were 14 forced choice items for each of two patients and 15 items for the third patient. The forced-choice items were constructed by the first author and were based on long-term therapeutic contact with the patients. The correct answers for each question were validated by obvious and clear-cut behavioral and clinical observations of the therapist. These were the same stimuli and forced choice interpretations which were employed in three previous studies (Handler & Finley, 1994; Scribner & Handler, 1987; and Scribner, 1989).

The undergraduate subjects were told that drawings such as those they had before them were used by clinicians to understand what people were like. They were further instructed to look carefully at each pair of drawings and then to try and understand the person who drew them. They were then asked to rate the patient who drew each pair of drawings, using the forced choice questionnaires. The subjects were asked to check one of each pair of statements which was more descriptive of the patient whose drawings they were studying. For example, one pair of forced choice items was: (a) Has difficulty containing her emotions vs. (b) Is apparently quite capable of appearing cool. No information was given concerning the patients other than their age, sex and race. The instructions for the graduate group were essentially the same, except that the initial introductory statement above, concerning the use of figure drawings "to understand people" was omitted, because it was deemed unnecessary for this trained graduate group. The total number of interpretive errors was then tabulated for each subject.

Nineteen graduate subjects (out of an entire class of 22) completed all the tasks involved in the study. The graduate subject whose error score was the median score (10) was discarded, thereby forming two groups of nine subjects. The graduate subjects with scores above the median became the Graduate Good group (GG) and those subjects with scores below the median became the Graduate Poor group (GP). The twelve most accurate and the twelve least accurate undergraduates were chosen as the Undergraduate Good (UG) and the Undergraduate Poor (UP) groups, respectively. Only 24 subjects out of the total of 64 were chosen in order to approximate the number of subjects in the graduate group, allowing for probable attrition. One of the subjects in the UG group failed to complete later portions of the study. Consequently, one subject from the UP group was chosen randomly and removed, thus equalizing the sample. This procedure resulted in an extreme groups design, compared with the procedure used for the small graduate group, in which the good and poor groups were formed by a median split.

Each subject was then given the Remote Associates Test (RAT) (Mednick & Mednick, 1967) as a measure of creativity and cognitive flexibility; the Myers-Briggs Type Indicator, (MBTI) (Myers, 1962) to provide a measure of intuition; the Hogan Empathy Scale (HES) as a measure of empathy (Hogan, 1969); and the California Psychological Inventory (CPI) (Gough, 1975) to measure "Psychological Mindedness," Flexibility, and "Intellectual Efficiency."

The first two CPI subscales, Psychological Mindedness and Flexibility, were used because of face validity; their titles seemed to describe variables which were similar to those tapped by the RAT, and the MBTI. The Intellectual Efficiency Scale (IE) was used to determine whether the groups differed in intellectual ability. The IE Scale has significantly differentiated Mensa members from normative samples (Southern & Plant, 1968) and high achievers from low achievers in a college sample (Flaherty & Reutzel, 1965). In addition, the IE scale correlates significantly with the Slossen Intelligence Scale (.52); the Shipley Institute of Living Scale (.39) (Martin, Blair, Sodowski & Wheeler, 1981); the Teiman Concept Mastery Intelligence Test (.58); the Miller Analogies Test (.44); the Kuhlmann-Anderson Intelligence Test (.50); and .41 with military staff ratings of officers' intellectual competence (.41) (Gough, 1975).

The Remote Associates Test (RAT) (Mednick & Mednick, 1967) is a 30-item test of creative thinking, defined as cognitive flexibility, in which the subject is presented with three seemingly unrelated words and is asked to find a fourth word which is related to all three. For example, the subject is presented with the words "cookies," "sixteen," and "heart." The correct answer is "sweet." The score is the number of items correctly answered. Several of the items allow for two correct answers. The subject is asked "to form associative elements into new combinations by providing mediating connective links" (Mednick & Mednick, 1967, p. 1). This test was chosen over other creativity measures because it is said to be a test of *convergent* rather than divergent thinking. That is, the task requirement of the RAT closely resembles the task of putting together a number of detailed observations of the drawing in order to come up with an integrated interpretive understanding of the patient who drew it. Normative findings indicate that the means for various college undergraduate groups range from 13 to 19; graduate school means from one sample were 20.

Mednick and Halpern (1962) obtained a correlation of .70 between RAT scores of architecture students and advisors' ratings of their design creativity, but a low correlation of these advisors' ratings with the students' grade point averages. In addition, M. Mednick (1963) found a highly significant correlation between RAT scores of psychology graduate students and the research creativity ratings of these students by their advisors. Again, the RAT scores were not correlated with grade point average.

Mednick and Mednick (1967) report that out of 82 research proposals which won contracts, 75 percent had been written by scientists scoring above the group's RAT median, and that similar results were found for a group of scientists in a chemical firm. RAT scores were also found to be related to quality and originality of anagrams constructed from a stimulus word (Higgins, 1966).

The validity of the RAT as a measure of creativity has been emphasized in a number of additional studies (e.g., Bal, 1988; Brown & Rogers, 1991; Forbach & Evans, 1981; Higgins & Dolby, 1967; Isen, Daubman & Nowicki, 1987; Katz & Pestell, 1989; Koberg & Hood, 1991; Martindale, 1972; Mendelsohn, 1976; Mendelsohn & Lindholm, 1972; Smith & Blankenship, 1991).

The Hogan Empathy Scale (HES) is a 64 item pencil and paper test which is said to measure sensitivity to subtle nuances in interpersonal behavior. Test-retest reliabilities ranged from .84 to .92 (Black & Phillips, 1982; Greif & Hogan, 1973). Validity is reported as excellent (Chlopan, McCain, Carbonell, & Hagen, 1985). The HES correlated between .42 and .58 with social acuity in various groups (Greif & Hogan, 1973). The scale significantly differentiated normals from subjects known for low empathy (Kurtines, Weiss, Hogan & Athanasiou, 1972; Kurtines & Hogan, 1972). In addition, Christiansen (1977) found a significant correlation between scores on the HES and both peer and faculty ratings of empathy among a group of occupational therapy students. Significant negative correlations were reported between scores on the HES and personality traits known to interfere with empathy (anxiety, obsessiveness, depression) in medical students (Kupfer, Drew, Curtis & Rubinstein, 1978). A number of additional recent studies have demonstrated the validity of the Hogan Empathy Scale (Cesare, Tannenbaum, & Dalessio, 1990; Friesen & Wright, 1985; Pecukonis, 1990; Riggio, Tucker & Coffaro, 1989; Wise & Cramer, 1988).

The Myers-Briggs Type Indicator (MBTI) is a very widely used pencil and paper inventory based upon Jung's theory of psychological types. The MBTI yields either a type category score, or continuous scores for each of the four scales tapped by the test (sensation-intuition, introversion-extraversion, thinking-feeling, and judging-perceiving). The Sensing-Intuition (SN) scale is designed to reflect a person's preference between two opposite ways of perceiving. This reflects reliance on gaining awareness of the world through the five senses, while the intuition function reflects meanings, relationships, ideas, and associations that are derived indirectly from unconscious processes. To obtain individual scores for each scale, the difference between the two numerical scores which compose each bipolar index is calculated and 100 is added to that difference score (Myers, 1962). This procedure was used in the present study.

Test-retest reliabilities of the MBTI are typically quite high. Reliabilities ranged from .69 to .87 (Carlyn, 1977; Webb, 1964) with reliabilities of the Intuition scale ranging from .75 to .87.

Validity studies have been very positive; many researchers have reported excellent construct validity as well as predictive-validity in a variety of clinical and counseling situations (Bushe & Gibbs, 1990; Carlson, 1980, 1985; Carlyn, 1977; Harmon, Armsworth, Hwang & Vincent, 1991; Matta & Kern, 1991; Patz, 1992; Roush & Atwater, 1992; Tan & Lo, 1991; Tennyson, Jennison, & Vaziri, 1991; Thompson & Borrello, 1986a & 1986b;). Continuous scores are reported to be quite stable over time (Carskadon, 1977; Levy, Murphy & Carlson, 1972; Tzeng, Ware, & Bharadwaj, 1991; Tzeng, Ware, & Chen, 1989).

Validity for the Intuition scale is good as well. For example, sensers (as opposed to intuiters) are attracted to practical vocations (Stricker & Ross, 1964), place a high value on authority and work, tend to be rated by faculty as pragmatic and as willing to take direction, and as people who "like to proceed orderly toward well-defined goals" (Carlyn, 1977, p. 469). On the other hand, intuiters are said to have considerable tolerance for complexity, to spend more time on non-required reading, and to prefer teachers who give open-ended instructions and allow them to use their own initiative. They express a strong need for autonomy, have a positive attitude toward change, and are more likely to be rated by faculty as imaginative, compared with the sensing types (Carlyn, 1977). MacKinnon (1966) found that over 90 percent of the creative writers, architects, research scientists, and mathematicians studied at The Institute for Personality Assessment and Research were intuitive types. Support for the validity of continuous unipolar ratings of the Intuition scale are reported by Comrey (1983), Mendelson (1965), and Tzeng, Ware & Chen (1989).

RESULTS

The errors made for the undergraduate group ranged from 5 to 36, out of 43 possible errors, while the corresponding number of errors for the graduate group ranged from 4 to 14. The median error score for the undergraduates was 19, while the median for the graduate students was 10. The range of error scores for the UG group was 5–13, while the range of errors for the UP group was 24–36. The corresponding error range for the GG group was 4–9 and for the GP group the range was 11–14. The mean scores for the UG and UP groups on the Remote Associates Test were 17.36 and 12.91, respectively ($t = 3.120, p = .0009$, one tailed). The corresponding means for the GG and GP groups were 24.00 and 21.11, respectively ($t = 1.468, p = .08$, one tailed). The mean scores for the UG and UP groups on the HES were 41.09 and 36.00, respectively ($t = 2.395, p = .01$, one tailed). The corresponding mean scores for the GG and GP groups was 43.11 and 39.55, respectively ($t = 1.750, p = .05$, one tailed). The mean scores for the UG and UP groups on the Intuition Scale were 115.737 and 91.737, respectively ($t = 1.954, p = .03$, one tailed). The corresponding mean scores for the GG and GP groups were 129.44 and 110.33, respectively ($t = 2.365, p = .02$, one tailed). These results indicate significant differences for all three measures, for both the undergraduate and the graduate groups. In all cases the good groups scored higher on all three measures.

The mean scores for the Intellectual Efficiency (IE) Scale of the CPI for the UG and UP groups were 39.45 and 38.45, respectively (t = .5171, ns). Mean scores for the GG and GP groups were 41.00 and 41.67, respectively (t = .3050, ns). Thus, it appears that the significant differences found with the other three variables is not a function of group differences in intellectual efficiency. There was a marginally significant difference on the Psychological Mindedness Scale of the CPI for the UG and UP groups (means = 11.6 and 10.3, respectively, t = 1.325; p = .10), but no significant difference for the GG and GP groups (means = 14.7 and 14.0 respectively, t = 0.570, ns). There were no significant group differences for Flexibility (UG and UP means = 13.2 and 12.4, respectively; t = 0.400, ns; GG and GP means = 15.3 and 14.9, respectively; t = 0.260, ns).

The results of the Remote Associates Test, the Hogan Empathy Scale and Myers-Briggs Type Indicator measures all support the hypothesis that there is a significant difference between the "good" and "poor" DAP interpreters in the areas of cognitive flexibility, empathy, and intuition. The graduate and undergraduate subjects who were good interpreters scored significantly higher in cognitive flexibility (creativity), empathy, and intuition.

The range of scores for the undergraduates on the Hogan Empathy Scale was 30–50, and for the graduates, 32–50. In an attempt to maximize the number of correct group placements an arbitrary cutting point of 37 was established for the undergraduates. Nine of the 11 good test interpreters were correctly identified (82% while only 6 of the 11 poor interpreters were correctly identified (55%). Using an arbitrary cutting score of 40 for the graduates, 8 of the 9 (89%) good interpreters were correctly identified, while only 5 of the 9 poor interpreters were correctly identified (56%).

On the Myers-Briggs the range of scores for the undergraduate group was 57 to 151, and 85–147 for the graduates. Using an arbitrary cutting score of 102 for the undergraduates to maximize correct group selections, 8 of the 11 good interpreters were correctly predicted (73%) but only 5 of the 11 poor interpreters were correctly predicted (45%) (see Table 18-1). Using a cutting point of 115 for the graduate group, 8 of the 9 good test interpreters were correctly identified (89%) while 7 of the 9 poor test interpreters were correctly identified (78%).

Table 18-1.
Percentage of Correct Predictions for Good and Poor Interpreters for All Three Measures

Group	Hogan Empathy Scale	Myers-Briggs	Remote Associates Test
Undergraduate Good	82	73	82
Undergraduate Poor	55	45	82
Graduate Good	89	89	78
Graduate Poor	56	78	78
Mean	70.50	71.25	80.00

On the Remote Associates Test, the range of scores for the undergraduates was 5 to 20, while the range for the graduate students was 14–27. If an arbitrary cutting point of 13 is used for the undergraduates, 9 of the 11 good interpreters are correctly identified (82%) and 9 of the 11 poor interpreters are correctly identified (82%). If a cutting score of 25 is used for the graduate group, 7 of the 9 good interpreters are correctly identified (78%), and 7 of the 9 poor interpreters were correctly predicted (78%).

The findings indicate that if such arbitrary cutting points are used, it is easier to predict membership in the group of good interpreters compared with prediction of membership in the group of poor interpreters. Percents of correct prediction ranged from 73–89 for the good interpreter groups (mean of 82% across all three measures) and 45–82 for the poor interpreter groups (mean of 61% across all three measures). Predictions were somewhat more accurate for the graduate groups compared with the undergraduates [a range of 56–89% correct prediction for the former (mean of 78%) compared with a range of 45–82 percent correct prediction for the latter (mean of 70%)]. The findings indicate that the Remote Associates Test score predicts group membership best for both the good and the poor interpreters, and for both the undergraduate and the graduate groups.

If the criterion of *simultaneous* correct placement on any two or on all three of the tests is used, with the same cutting points used above, the results are as follows: for the GG group, 9 out of 9 subjects (100%) were correctly predicted, but only 6 of the 9 GP subjects (67%) met the criterion. For the UG group, 9 out of 11 subjects met the criterion (82%) and for the UP group, 8 out of 11 (73%) met the criterion. This procedure increases correct group placement somewhat compared with individual test results: from 73 to 89 percent for the good interpreters for individual measures, to 81 to 100 percent for the criterion of two or more simultaneous correct placements. Corresponding numbers for the poor interpreters are 45–82 for individual measures, compared with 67–73 percent when the criterion of simultaneous correct placement on two or more tests is used. However, for the poor groups, the Remote Associates Test by itself predicts group membership most accurately (78–82% correct placement). It is important to note that these cutting points must be cross-validated on other samples before they are of much value.

DISCUSSION

It appears from the data reported that there are indeed significant differences in ability to interpret the DAP within groups of trained and untrained examiners. Four of the poorer interpreters among the trained graduate students made interpretive errors 33 percent of the time. However, a few of the more accurate interpreters made errors only nine percent of the time. Although one of the undergraduates almost equalled this performance, the remainder of the UG group made significantly more errors than the GG group. The median for the GG group was 10, while the median for the undergraduates was 19. The error range for the undergraduates was quite large, from a low of 10 percent to a high of 84 percent.

There are several reasons which may account for the more restricted range of errors for the graduate students, and for the more robust findings with the undergraduates. First, the graduate students were a more homogeneous and highly selected group, comprising about 5 to 10 percent of applicants to the clinical training program. Second, the selection procedure for the two groups differed; with the undergraduate groups we took the eleven most extreme subjects to form each group, but we split the graduate group at the median because the total group was smaller. In addition, training should (at least theoretically) bring about greater accuracy on the part of the test interpreter. However, the important point is that even after training, fairly large differences in the number of errors were still observed.

The fact that there are still significant differences in interpretive ability in the carefully selected, carefully trained graduate group suggests that more systematic attention needs to be given to the variables of intuition, empathy and creativity in training graduate students to use a qualitative approach to assessment. The finding that there are significant individual differences in interpretive ability even after training also has important implications for research concerning the validity of projective test data where "trained" psychologists are used as raters. These results suggest the need to assess, standardize and control for the interpretive proficiency of the raters who are used as subjects in studies where qualitative evaluations are to be made. Authors who design studies to investigate the validity of clinical instruments would do well to report data regarding the accuracy rates of these raters, just as they might report validity coefficients of tests. Perhaps each rater could have a predetermined accuracy average, much like a baseball player has a batting average. Thus, for example, Layton (1983) found that while six out of seven psychologists were able to place drawings in the correct reference group with a high degree of accuracy, the seventh rater did not do so significantly better than chance. Significant psychologist differences in interpretive ability were also reported in a family drawing validity study by Howitt (1984).

The findings of the present study, along with those reported by Scribner and Handler (1987) and by Scribner (1989), can be integrated to form a picture of the good qualitative DAP interpreter and to illuminate the process of accurate interpretation, utilizing a qualitative approach. The good qualitative interpreter is an open, empathic person whose thinking is flexible, a person whose openness to the drawings (and through them, to the artist) is evident as intuitiveness. Empathy involves such attributes as being perceptive to a wide range of cues, having insight into one's own motives, and the ability to accurately evaluate the motives of others. Utilizing this approach to the interpretation of drawings requires a certain amount of affective "tuning in" to one's own feelings and to the feelings of others. Thus Handler's (1985) directions to the would-be DAP interpreter include the suggestion that the interpreter "become intimately involved with the drawing"* (p. 188). *Good DAP interpreters must be able*

---

*This is parallel to Hammer's (1996) suggestion that the DAP interpreter place his/her body *in the body stance of the drawn figure,* and also to imitate its facial expression, and thus feel kinesthetically, as well as visually, *being* the drawn Person, and behind it the drawer—what the individual looks like, feels like, from the inside.

As an exercise, the reader is invited to turn back to Chapter 3 and put him/herself into the body experience of Figure 7: Strained eyes tensely peering out of the eye sockets, head similarly strained and tilted off its upright posture by bulging neck muscles, the whole figure reflects this intense tightness as it pulls up on its toes. At the same time, there is the counterpull of taut control: the shoulders pull in and down as the wrists tug toward expressing a feeling of being manacled, bound into constraining incapacity to move.

All in all, impulses and controls pit their force against each other. This position, we can now sense in our own muscles, is too discomforting to long be sustained before over-extended controls part and impulses *to allow themselves to become the person drawn.* This suggestion involves the creative "loss of distance" emphasized by Kris as "adaptive regression in the service of the ego" (Kris, 1952). If the clinician can experience what it is like to be the person drawn, then he/she will be able to understand the artist. Thus, Kris states, "We started out as part of the world which the author created; we end as co-creators: we identify ourselves with the artist" (Kris, 1952, p. 56). In this regard, recent findings (Scribner, 1989; Scribner & Handler, 1993) indicate that poor intuitive DAP interpreters emphasized their need to control activities and experiences, whereas the good intuitive interpreters expressed a willingness and ability to relinquish control of what they experienced and simply allowed themselves to experience fully and openly, relaxing their stance toward reality in order to permit ego regression to occur.

Using a qualitative approach, the good interpreter would be ready and willing to engage fully in order to transcend mechanistic patterns of thought. This sounds similar to the concept of psychoanalytic listening developed by Kohut (1959, 1977) as well as by other analysts. Although this process is in part similar to the concept of "adaptive regression in the service of the ego" described by Kris (1952), it goes beyond the emphasis of the dynamic aspects of regression and the primitive, immature content of thoughts and feelings. What is added here is openness in turning toward the object and the ability to approach it with freshness, spontaneity, and interest (Schachtel, 1984). Introspection and self reflection in the regressive process is probably not enough to achieve valid interpretation. What is needed, in addition, is the ability to become again reconnected, with cognitively reorganized creative understanding.

Several studies support the theorized relationship between good DAP interpretation and both creativity and adaptive regression in the service of the ego. Murray and Russ (1981) report a significant positive correlation between adaptive regression and the scores on the Remote Associates Test in college students. In addition, Domino (1976) and Martindale (1972) report a similar significant correlation between the Remote Associates Test and the degree of creativity expressed in dreams. Domino found more primary process thinking in the dream reports of creative subjects compared with matched controls. For example, the creative subjects demonstrated significantly more condensation and symbolism in their dreams.

---

erupt through. The subject, resultantly, is desperate and terrified and under extreme pressure to not explode into acting-out.   (E.F.H.)

Murray and Russ' data emphasize that both primary process and secondary process thinking are involved in adaptive regression, the former to provide access to creative material and the latter to evaluate the primary process data. Thus, the picture of the effective qualitative interpretive process may be described as one in which the clinician regresses in the service of the ego, experiences through regression and empathy the personality of the artist, and then cognitively reorganizes this knowledge in a creative and meaningful manner.

Russ (1993) emphasizes the similarities between primary process thinking and creativity. Russ and others (see Suler, 1980) emphasize that the concept of regression to an *earlier* mode of thinking is not a necessary one, but rather that the major issue is the ability to achieve access to the primary process content. Russ states, "Creative individuals may be more able to tap into the primary process and utilize the process in adaptive ways" (p. 20). Thus, the finding of this study that the good interpreters were more cognitively flexible, suggests that they may be more capable of tapping into primary process thinking. Russ (1993) quotes Martindale who states, "Because primary process cognition is associative, it makes the discovery of new combinations of mental elements more likely" (p. 216).

It is important to emphasize that this study, which concerns the validation of the *clinician using the DAP* rather than the focus upon the drawing itself, is considered by us as an important way station in the process of discovering the crucial variables involved in effective interpretation of all the projective tests we utilize in our assessment procedures. In this regard, our results support the view of Bruno Klopfer, who emphasized the importance of an intuitive approach to the Rorschach and believed that it could be demystified and communicated effectively (Klopfer, 1956). We feel certain that the process described here for the DAP will eventually be discovered to be the same or to be quite similar to the process required for other projective tests, and for interview data as well, thus joining even more the processes of assessment and psychotherapy, as part and parcel of each other.

REFERENCES

Albee, G. & Hamlin, R. (1950). An investigation of the reliability and validity judgments inferred from drawings. *Journal of Clinical Psychology, 5,* 389–392.

Bal, S. (1988). Creativity, cognitive style and academic achievement amongst university students. *Psychological Studies, 33(1),* 10–13.

Black, H. & Phillips, S. (1982). An intervention program for the development of empathy in student teachers. *The Journal of Psychology, 112,* 159–168.

Brown, J., & Rogers, R. (1991). Self-serving attributions: The role of physiological arousal. *Personality & Social Psychology Bulletin, 17(5),* 501–506.

Bushe, G., & Gibbs, B. (1990). Predicting organization development consulting competence from the Myers-Briggs Type Indicator and stage of ego development. *Journal of Applied Behavioral Science, 26(3),* 337–357.

Carlson, J. (1985). Recent assessments of the Myers-Briggs type indicator. *Journal of Personality Assessment, 49,* 356–365.

Carlson, R. (1980). Studies of Jungian typology: II. Representations of the personal world. *Journal of Personality and Social Psychology, 38,* 559–576.

Carlyn, M. (1977). An assessment of the Myers-Briggs Type Indicator. *Journal of Personality Assessment, 41,* 461.

Carskadon, T. (1977). Test re-test reliabilities of continuous scores on the Myers-Briggs Type Indicator. *Psychological Reports, 41,* 1011–1012.

Cesare, S., Tannenbaum, R., & Dalessio, A. (1990). Interviewers' decisions related to applicant handicap type and rater empathy. *Human Performance, 3(3),* 157–171.

Chlopan, B., McCain, M., Carbonell, J., & Hagen, R. (1985). Empathy: Review of available measures. *Journal of Personality and Social Psychology, 48(3),* 635–653.

Christiansen, C. (1977). Measuring empathy in occupational therapy students. *The American Journal of Occupational Therapy, 31,* 19–22.

Comrey, A. (1983). An evaluation of the Myers-Briggs Type Indicator. *Academic Psychology Bulletin, 5,* 115–129.

Domino, G. (1967). Primary process thinking in dream reports as related to creative achievement. *Journal of Consulting and Clinical Psychology, 44,* 929–932.

Fancher, R. (1966). Explicit personality theories and accuracy in person perception. *Journal of Personality, 34,* 252–261.

Fancher, R. (1967). Accuracy versus validity in person perception. *Journal of Consulting Psychology, 31,* 264–269.

Flaherty, M. & Reutzel, E. (1965). Personality traits of high and low achievers in college. *Journal of Educational Research, 58,* 409–411.

Forbach, G. & Evans, R. (1981). The Remote Associates Test as a predictor of productivity in brainstorming groups. *Applied Psychological Measurement, 5,* 333–339.

Friesen, W., & Wright, P. (1985). The validity of the Carlson Psychological Survey with adolescents. *Journal of Personality Assessment, 49(4),* 422–426.

Gordon, C. (1966). Some effects of information, situation, and personality on decision-making in a clinical setting. *Journal of Consulting Psychology, 30,* 219–224.

Gordon, C. (1967). Some effects of clinician and patient personality on decision-making in a clinical setting. *Journal of Consulting Psychology, 31,* 477–480.

Gough, H. (1975). *Manual for the California Psychological Inventory.* Palo Alto: Consulting Psychologists Press.

Greif, E. & Hogan, R. (1973). The theory and measurement of empathy. *Journal of Counseling Psychology, 20,* 280–284.

Hammer, E. (1968). Projective drawings. In A. Rabin (Ed.), *Projective techniques in personality assessment* (pp. 366–393). New York: Springer.

Hammer, E. (1996). Personal Communication.

Hammer, E. & Piotrowski, Z. (1953). Hostility as a factor in the clinician's personality as it affects his interpretation of projective drawings (H–T–P). *Journal of Projective Techniques, 17,* 210–216.

Handler, L. (1985). The clinical use of the Draw-A–Person Test (DAP). In C. Newmark (Ed.), *Major psychological assessment instruments,* (pp. 165–216). Boston: Allyn & Bacon.

Handler, L., & Finley, J. (1994). Convergent and divergent thinking and the interpretation of figure drawings. Unpublished manuscript.

Harmon, M., Armsworth, M., Hwang, C., & Vincent, K. (1991). Gender and ordinal position in children of alcoholics and non-alcoholics. *TACD Journal, 19(2),* 35–42.

Higgins, J. (1966). A further study of correlates of the Remote Associates Test of creativity. *Psychology, 3,* 18–20.

Higgins, J. & Dolby, L. (1967). Creativity and mediated association: A construct validation study of the RAT. *Educational and Psychological Measurement, 27,* 1011–1014.

Hogan, R. (1969). Development of an Empathy Scale. *Journal of Clinical Psychology, 33,* 307–316.

Howitt, P. (1984). Kinetic Family Drawings and clinical judgment: an evaluation of judges' ability to differentiate between K–F–Ds of abusing, control, and concerned parents. Doctoral Dissertation, University of Windsor, Canada.

Hunt, W. (1946). The future of diagnostic testing in clinical psychology. *Journal of Clinical Psychology, 2,* 311–317.

Isen, A., Daubman, K., & Nowicki, G. (1987). Positive affect facilitates creative problem solving. *Journal of Personality & Social Psychology, 52(6),* 1122–1131.

Katz, & Pestell (1989). Attentional processes and the finding of remote associates. *Personality and Individual Differences, 10(10),* 1017–1025.

Klopfer, B. (1956) (Ed.). *Developments in the Rorschach Technique, Vol. II, Fields of Application.* New York: Harcourt, Brace & World.

Koberg, C., & Hood, J. (1991). Cultures and creativity within hierarchical organizations. *Journal of Business & Psychology, 6(2),* 265–271.

Kohut, H. (1959). Introspection, empathy and psychoanalysis. *American Psychoanalytic Association Journal, 26,* 21–47.

Kohut, H. (1977). *The restoration of self.* New York: International Universities Press.

Kris, E. (1952). *Psychoanalytic explorations in art.* New York: International Universities Press.

Kupfer, D., Drew, F., Curtis, E., & Rubinstein, D. (1978). Personality style and empathy in medical students. *Journal of Medical Education, 53,* 507–509.

Kurtines, W. & Hogan, R. (1972). Sources of conformity in unsocialized college students. *Journal of Abnormal Psychology, 80,* 49–51.

Kurtines, W., Weiss, D., Hogan, R., and Athanasiou, R. (1972). Socio-psychological determinants of drug use. Unpublished manuscript, Johns Hopkins University.

Layton, M. (1983). Special features in the Kinetic Family Drawings of children. Doctoral Dissertation, Temple University.

Levenberg, S. (1975). Professional training, psychodiagnostic skill, and Kinetic Family Drawings. *Journal of Personality Assessment, 39*, 389–393.

Levy, N., Murphy, C., & Carlson, R. (1972). Personality types among Negro college students. *Educational and Psychological Measurements, 31*, 641–653.

MacKinnon, D. (1966). The nature and nurture of creative talent. In D. Byrne & M. Hamilton (Eds.), *Personality research*. Englewood Cliffs, N.J.: Prentice-Hall.

Martin, J., Blair, G., Sodowski, C., & Wheeler, K. (1981). Intercorrelations among The Slosson Intelligence Test, The Shipley-Institute of Living Scale, and The Intellectual Efficiency Scale of The California Psychological Inventory. *Educational and Psychological Measurement, 41*, 595–598.

Martindale, C. (1972). Anxiety, intelligence, and access to primitive modes of thought in high and low scorers on The Remote Associates Test (1972). *Perceptual and Motor Skills, 35*, 375–381.

Matta, K., & Kern, G. (1991). Interactive videodisc instruction: The influence of personality on learning. *International Journal of Man-Machine Studies, 35(4)*, 541–552.

Mednick, M. (1963). Research creativity in psychology graduate students. *Journal of Consulting Psychology, 27*, 265–266.

Mednick, S., & Halpern, S. (1962). Ease of concept attainment as a function of associative rank. *Journal of Experimental Psychology, 6*, 628–630.

Mednick, S., & Mednick, M. (1967). *Examiner's Manual: Remote Associates Test.* Boston: Houghton Mifflin Co.

Mendelsohn, G. (1976). Associative and attentional processes in creative performance. *Journal of Personality, 44*, 341–369.

Mendelsohn, G., & Lindholm, E. (1972). Individual differences and the role of attention in the use of cues in verbal problem solving. *Journal of Personality, 40*, 226–241.

Mendelson, G. (1965). Review of the Myers-Briggs Type Indicator. In O. K. Buros (Ed.), *The sixth mental measurements yearbook*. Highland Park, N.J.: The Gryphon Press.

Mintz, E. (1959). Relationships between diagnostic errors and personal anxieties of psychologists. Unpublished doctoral dissertation, New York University (Dissertation Abstracts 1959, No. 3370).

Murray, J., & Russ, S. (1981). Adaptive regression and types of cognitive flexibility. *Journal of Personality Assessment, 45*, 59–65.

Myers, I. (1962). *Manual: The Myers-Briggs Type Indicator.* Palo Alto: Consulting Psychologists Press.

Patz, A. (1992). Personality bias in total enterprise simulations. *Simulation & Gaming, 23(1)*, 45–76.

Pecukonis, E. (1990). A cognitive/affective empathy training program as a function of ego development in aggressive adolescent females. *Adolescence, 25(97)*, 59–76.

Prybil, M., Hunt, W., & Wallace, R. (1968). Some learning variables in Clinical judgment. *Journal of Clinical Psychology, 24*, 32–36.

Riggio, R., Tucker, J., & Coffaro, D. (1989). Social skills and empathy. *Personality & Individual Differences, 10(1),* 93–99.

Roush, P., & Atwater, L. (1992). Using the MBTI to understand transformational leadership and self-perception accuracy. *Military Psychology, 4(1),* 17–34.

Russ, S. (1993). *Affect and creativity.* Hillsdale, NJ: L. Erlbaum Associates.

Schachtel, E. (1984/1959). Metamorphosis: on the development of affect, perception, attention, and memory. New York: Da Capo Press.

Schmidt, L., & McGowan, J. (1959). The differentiation of human figure drawings. *Journal of Consulting Psychology, 23,* 129–133.

Scribner, C. (1989). Interpreting the Interpreter: Case Studies of Ten Intuitive DAP Interpreters. Doctoral Dissertation, University of Tennessee.

Scribner, C., & Handler, L. (1987). The Interpreter's Personality in Draw-A–Person Interpretation: A Study of Interpersonal Style. *Journal of Personality Assessment, 51,* 112–122.

Simms, N. (1951). An analysis of human figure drawings for orthopedic and nonorthopedic children. Unpublished M.A. thesis, University of Nebraska, Lincoln.

Smith, S., & Blankenship, S. (1991). Incubation and the persistence of fixation in problem solving. *American Journal of Psychology, 104(1),* 61–87.

Southern, M., & Plant, W. (1968). Personality characteristics of very bright adults. *Journal of Social Psychology, 75,* 119–126.

Stricker, L., & Ross, J. (1964). Some correlates of a Jungian personality inventory. *Psychological Reports, 14,* 623–643.

Suler, J. (1980). Primary process thinking and creativity. *Psychological Bulletin, 88(1),* 144–165.

Swensen, C. (1957). Empirical evaluations of human figure drawings. *Psychological Bulletin, 54,* 431–466.

Swensen, C. (1968). Empirical evaluations of human figure drawings. *Psychological Bulletin, 70,* 20–44.

Tan, B., & Lo, T. (1991). The impact of interface customization on the effect of cognitive style on information system success. *Behaviour & Information Technology, 10(4),* 297–310.

Tennyson, T., Jennison, J., & Vaziri, N. (1991). Dialysis staff attitudes toward providing end-stage care. *Loss, Grief & Care, 5(1-2),* 151–160.

Tharinger, D., & Stark, K. (1990). A qualitative version quantitative approach to evaluating the Draw-A-Person and Kinetic Family Drawing: A study of mood and anxiety-disorder children. *Psychological Assessment: 2(4),* 365–375.

Thompson, B., & Borrello, G. (1986a). Second order factor structure of the MBTI: a construct validity assessment. *Measurement and Evaluation in Counseling and Development, 18,* 148–153.

Thompson, B., & Borrello, G. (1986b). Construct validity of the Myers-Briggs Type Indicator. *Educational and Psychological Measurement, 46,* 745–752.

Tzeng, O., Ware, R., & Bharadwaj, N. (1991). Comparison between continuous bipolar and unipolar ratings of the Myers-Briggs Type Indicator. *Educational & Psychological Measurement, 51(3),* 681–690.

Tzeng, O., Ware, R., & Chen, J. (1989). Measurement and utility of continuous unipolar ratings for the Myers-Briggs Type Indicator. *Journal of Personality Assessment, 53,* 727–738.

Webb, S. (1964). An analysis of the scoring system of the Myers-Briggs Type Indicator. *Educational and Psychological Measurement, 24,* 765–781.

Wise, P., & Cramer, S. (1988). Correlates of empathy and cognitive style in early adolescence. *Psychological Reports, 63(1),* 179–192.

Editor's Comment

This is, as I said in the introduction, an important chapter. And one particular way it is important is as a beacon of illumination of the lasting and vexing problem of mixed research results, continually positive and negative, regarding the validity of projective drawings.

The essence, the profundity, here is that projective drawing interpretation is revealing itself to be more of an Art than a Science. The data by Burley and Handler suggest that approximately—very approximately—half of the psychologists are adept at this art, and about half are not. This may prove to explain the phenomenon that has plagued the field, that about the same proportion of research studies has long been emerging, about half favoring and about half failing to demonstrate the validity of drawings as a reflector of the person drawing. The research findings may be more dependent on the psychologist's personality than on the drawings, per se.

E.F.H.

CASE STUDIES

Chapter 19

CASE STUDIES: INTRODUCTION

We who practice projective techniques extensively, like the more casual practitioner, cannot escape its mixed experimental history, but the former can outwit it (outwit in what the dictionary calls the archaic sense, meaning not to outsmart but to surpass in wisdom).

Experiments come and go, but the seasoned clinician knows deeply within—as he has learned from case after case after case—that it simply cannot be but that what a person draws is in certain ways himself, of himself and more truly himself than even he knows. Leonardo da Vinci early recognized this when he complained of the long years of study even the gifted students, who came to him to apprentice, had to practice before they stopped projecting of themselves into the subjects they sculpted or drew or painted. More contemporaneously we have the observations, quoted at the opening chapter of this book, of John Steinbeck: a "man's writing *is* himself" and of Samuel Butler, who stated more broadly that "Every man's work, whether it be literature or music or pictures... or anything else, is always a portrait of himself."

When it comes to turning to the experiments versus drawing upon the creative artists for their respective truths, I, for one (joining with Freud), choose the artist hands down. Confirming this, and extending John Steinbeck's and Samuel Butler's insight into the drawing arena, we have the genius of the graphic arts, Paul Gauguin, who wrote in his journal that every painting is a key to the personality of the artist. In his *The Writings of a Savage* (edited by Daniel Guerin, 1991), we find Gauguin has reflected quite brilliantly that:

> For anyone *who knows how to look* [italics added], a work of art is a mirror that reflects the artist's mood. When I see a portrait by Velazquez or Rembrandt, I scarcely see the features of the face he painted, whereas I have an intimate impression of the inner portrait of the painter himself. Velazquez is essentially royal. Rembrandt, the magician, is essentially a prophet.

381

Here Paul Gauguin intuitively senses that which the experimental evidence is uncovering, that global analysis is more valid than is item analysis.

Gauguin goes on:

> ... one should be able to recognize the king even if he was naked in a throng of bathers.

Similarly, regarding the artist, one should be able to sense him and his qualities even though he is to be discerned only behind his painting.

To convey the process which brings the painter into his very painting we are reminded of Courbet (Guerin, 1991) who, when a woman asked what he was thinking of before a landscape he was painting, gave this illuminatingly profound reply: "I am not thinking, Madam. I am moved."

Picasso (Rose, 1996), sensing the projective process (upon which the H–T–P and D–A–F, in turn, rest) in his painting and drawing, appreciated, "My fingers tell me what I feel."

Thus, a number of intuitive (arguably, great) painters and writers have discerned *the style is the man.* And the awareness of a single genius often proves worth ten research studies (particularly of the poor methodology of many of them).

It was Gordon Alport who memorably appraised, "A major challenge before our field is to prove what we simply *know* to be true."

REFERENCES

Guerin, D., *The Writings of a Savage.* Northvale, N.J.: Jason Aronson, 1991.
Rose, C., *Picasso: Painting and Portraiture,* Charlie Rose Show, Channel 13, 1:30–2:30 p.m., Sept. 9, 1996.

Chapter 20

CASE S.G.: ORGANIC BRAIN DAMAGE
AND CHRONIC ALCOHOLISM*

JOHN N. BUCK

John N. Buck, the father and further developer of the House-Tree-Person, was the Chief Psychologist at Lynchburg State Colony, Virginia, which thereby became the "home" of the H–T–P where other workers (including myself) early joined in the task—more than the task, in the adventure. Those were exciting times.

John Buck casts a long shadow into not only graphomotor techniques but, more broadly, into clinical psychology. Buck saw more keenly than others, and keenly understood what he saw.

His masterliness is demonstrated in the case below where he discerns and grapples with that most difficult of our diagnostic challenges, uncovering the presence of organic brain damage from among the manifold and varied syndromes (see Chapter 2).

HISTORY

This 40-year-old, white, unmarried male is the fourth of seven children; the others are said to be "normal." A native Virginian, he had entered the hospital for the second time prior to administration of this H–T–P. Between his two colonizations, he had twice received treatment for alcoholism at the Western State Hospital. His environment, both socially and economically, was superior. However, his overindulgent and protective mother thwarted all the efforts of his father to prepare S. G. for an adequate adult role.

He graduated from high school in the usual period of time and attended the University of Virginia for several semesters. He never has, even remotely, been self-supporting. He says, "I was born a gentleman—only a fool would work."

Since he was 6 years of age, when presumably he had an encephalitis,

*Adapted with permission. Hammer, E., Case 'C,' in Buck, J., *The House-Tree-Person Technique: Revised Manual*, 198–219, Western Psychological Services, 1984.

he has become progressively more and more asocial. He reacted violently to the death of his mother 16 years ago, and after he had threatened to kill his father, he was institutionalized.

In recent years he has been consistently alcoholic outside of an institution. Organic deterioration seems to have taken place.

See drawn House and Tree.

Figure 20-1. **House.**

Figure 20-2. **Tree.**

Figure 20-3. **Person.**

QUALITATIVE ANALYSIS

I. Details

House: (1) The windows lack panes [indicative of hostility and possible oral and/or anal eroticism, P2].* (2) The door and the steps were the last items drawn [S. G. determines the terms on which he will make contact, P1].

Tree: (1) There is a deeply shaded area on top of the left lower branch [on being questioned, he said that this symbolized the death of his mother, P2].

Person: (1) The mouth and the arms were the last items drawn [the hostility-expressing modes were suppressed until last, P1]. The Person is a "stick man" [the S aggresses against the examiner and mankind in general, P2].

II. Proportion

House: The door and the windows are too small relative to the wall in which they appear [inaccessibility and lack of interest in others, P2].

Tree: The Tree is small in comparison to the page's size [this symbolizes his feeling of inadequacy, P2].

Person: The malproportion throughout the Person is general, obvious, and great [savage caricaturing of a fellowman, and through him, of people in general, P3].

III. Perspective

General: The disorganization of the spatial relationship of the details illustrates the "segmentalism" of detail presentation which is almost never found in the absence of an organic disturbance. Therefore, for example, for the *House:* (1) the door placed far above the steps; (2) the door placed slightly above the windows; (3) the roof which is said to be *covering* the door is shown *below* the door; (4) the chimney suspended above the roof, P3; for the *Tree:* branches which are never attached to the trunk, and not always attached to each other, P3; for the *Person:* arms which are not attached to the trunk, P3.

The House and the Tree are in the upper left corner of the page [regression of concept and basic insecurity, P2]—one suspects that the Person would have been placed there, too, but for the fact that the Person,

---

*To conserve space, the probable degree of deviation is indicated by the letter P and a number, P1 representing mild pathology, on to P3 suggesting marked pathology.

as it does with many psychopaths, produced a hostile aggressive reaction which engendered a different (central) type of placement, P1.

Line Quality

General: Poor motor control and excessive force were exhibited in each of three wholes [evidence suggestive of the presence of organic damage, P2].

VI. Criticality

General: The marked diminution of the critical faculty is pathognomonic of organic disturbance, since S. G. obviously is not psychotic, [P3].

VII. Attitude

General: He expressed freely and frankly his wholehearted distaste for the entire task [as stated elsewhere, "work" is abhorrent to him, P2].

IX. Comments

A. Drawing Phase
House: The few comments that he made while he was drawing indicated a recognition of his inadequacy, with some feeling of frustration at his inability to perform better [organic impotence, P2].

Person: While he was drawing the Person, he launched into a lengthy, irrelevant, but well worded account of his trip to the New York World's Fair [the marked disparity between the concept quality of his verbal comments and his drawings, favoring the verbal, suggests the presence of a major organic component, P2].

B. Post-Drawing
House: Mr. G's comments revealed an inferior grasp of reality [intellectual deterioration, P2].

Tree: (1) He described his Tree as a delicate Tree needing much personal care and attention [he feels that he deserves kind and painstaking care by others; that a parasitic existence is his right, P2]. (2) In answer to T7, and in justification of his statement that the Tree looked more like a woman than a man, he said, "The hair on top of the head or along under the arms and other places" [from one of his prior intelligence level and cultural background such a statement strongly suggests intellectual deterioration and psychosexual confusion, P2]. (3) The weather about the Tree was said to be bitter cold; a wind of gale proportions was blowing and probably would damage the Tree [the environment is cold, hostile, oppressive, P2]. (4) While he was being questioned in the P–D–I, he wrote *Elberta* under his Tree [he has a compulsive need to structure the situation, P2].

General: His P–D–I was seasoned with many spontaneous, irrelevant, and lengthy comments [The S constantly attempted to impress the examiner with his wide range of information, P2].

C. Associations

House: Mr. G's House reminded him, among other things, of his many drinking bouts [by degrading himself he expressed aggression toward his family, P2].

Person: His Person made him think, among other things, of a friend whom he had once fought and whose eyes he said he had blackened, after which it was easier to distinguish the friend from the friend's twin brother [S. G. wishes to convince someone outside his family that he is physically dangerous. In actuality he has had to be protected from the other patients, P2].

X. Concepts

House: This is a small tenant house on his father's farm, a house to which he has gone many times to sober up [again he debases his family by self-degradation, P2].

Tree: This is a peach tree, despite the fact that his father has nearly 10,000 apple trees [a subtle expression of his freely verbalized feeling that he is not of the common herd, P1]. This also points up his confused psychosexuality, for the peach tree usually is regarded as definitely feminine [P2].

Person: The Person is a friend in delirium tremens, shouting for beer, while Mr. G. stands out of sight, also waiting for beer [the implication is that Mr. G. drinks like a gentleman. This also represents aggression against a man who is not in a hospital as Mr. G. is, P2].

SUMMARY

Quantitative: At the time when S. G. attained I. Q. scores on the H–T–P in the high imbecile-low moron range, he still scored a Wechsler-Bellevue I. Q. of 94 [the Performance I. Q. was 66]. This disparity, since S. G. is not psychotic, strongly indicates that organic deterioration has taken place. The almost uniform depression of the scores for the disparate wholes and for Perspective, Proportion, and Details, respectively, also indicates a well-advanced mental deterioration of an organic nature.

Qualitative: S. G.'s H–T–P reveals the presence of the following characteristics which are typically found in the drawings of Ss with organic mental deterioration: (1) disorganization for all three wholes [the proportional and positional relationship of the details is badly distorted]; (2) very inferior criticality; (3) poor motor control; (4) the classical, small, tortuous, one-dimensional Tree; (5) strong feelings of violence and destructiveness; (6) poor reality grasp.

In addition there are seen: (1) sexual maladjustment; (2) strongly hostile feelings toward persons whom he holds in ill-concealed contempt [the free and frank verbal expression of which has frequently caused him difficulty]; (3) inability to form lasting, responsible, sharing, affectional relationships; (4) hostility towards his family, so strong, that he is willing to degrade himself if in so doing he can also degrade his relatives; (5) ideas of persecution; (6) delusions of grandeur.

Impression: Psychopathic personality [post-infectional] with asocial trends; organic intellectual deterioration [chronic alcoholism].

Chapter 21

AN ARTIST IN MID-LIFE CRISIS

YVONNE L. ZAHIR

Do we have here one more case of mid-life crisis? Do we here have another middle-aged person suffering the condition of balding, of slowing down, of having to switch his athletic activity to less taxing ones, of his joints going, of loss of sexual prowess and of physical attractiveness, of the appearance of a potbelly, of an evaporation of available years to yet achieve one's goals defining "success," and, more dreadfully, of mortality—of one's death or of abandonment via one's mate's demise just around the corner?

The writer of this case is up to something more, and nimbly descends to deeper strata as its subject stumbles along the trajectory of his life which along the way goes into tailspins, tailspins that lead him to undo his priesthood and frantically lead to a pursuit of sexuality across two orientations, heterosexuality and homosexuality, and finally finds the latter veering toward pedophilia.

This case study is part of a study on midlife issues, of two female and two male artists in midlife who were asked to participate in the House-Tree-Person projective test. I was interested in seeing if this technique might reveal meaningful material typical of midlife issues.

The following case is of one of the male subjects, one whom I found to be a most interesting and revealing individual.

"Midlife crisis," a familiar phrase today, is the focal point of the life of my client, Leon. A fifty-seven-year-old, Leon spent his young adult years preparing to become a priest. He feels he came "late" into midlife and its crisis. After serving twelve years as a priest, he left the ministry, married and became the father of two daughters. He explains that, because of his years as a priest, he was late entering what he considered the "normal way of life."

Leon, whose mother gave birth to him when she was in her late forties, is the youngest boy in an Irish family, with his older brothers, two, ten, and twelve years older than he.

Both parents are now deceased; their marriage ended in divorce after twenty-five years. Throughout his early childhood, Leon wished for, but did not have, a close relationship with his father, who the boy felt showed favoritism to his twelve-year-older brother.

This brother, a "clown" or "rebel" in the family, was the one with whom he felt closest. Furthermore, this same sibling, a known "troublemaker," was the one Leon wanted to imitate. The subject expressed that his parents were constantly busy with the other boys, noting that to be last-born was to be relegated to become somewhat unnoticed.

Though not overly devout, Leon's family attended church regularly. While growing up, Leon felt he always wanted to be a priest, and he chose to enter the seminary directly upon his graduation from high school. His studies led to ordination and twelve years in service as a priest. His subsequent decision to leave the active ministry came with his marriage to a former nun, a woman who served in a nearby convent. Leon claimed the marriage was a happy one, and two daughters were born of the union. But the marriage then terminated in divorce after ten years.

Leon's interest in other women led to his having some extramarital affairs at least two years prior to the divorce. He next fell in love with a very "passionate" woman, immediately following his divorce, and he then invited her to live with him and his younger daughter. This relationship, satisfactory to Leon, began to "cool" about two years later; he discovered that his partner had fallen in love with another woman. She soon left Leon to be with her.

Following this shocking discovery, Leon then spent the next two years dating several women, and finding another partner, he entered into a serious relationship with her. After it proved to be enduring, he invited her to move into his home and to live with him and the younger daughter. The daughter objected to this arrangement; she had liked the previous woman who had lived with them. She found this new woman to be less "warm" and resented her being there. The next two years were stormy ones in which Leon attempted to balance his need for this woman and still have the affection of his youngest child who was now a twelve-year-old.

When I met Leon and asked him to volunteer to be a part of the present study on midlife issues, he was most interested in finding a way to resolve these conflicts in his relationships.

He agreed to a two-hour session in which he would produce eight drawings, the achromatic H–T–P–P drawings, using a number two lead pencil, followed by the chromatic H–T–P–P drawings, using a box of eight standard crayons.

I believed that his drawings would reveal his present difficulties, and that by his becoming more conscious of his thoughts around the issues brought forth in the art produced, he might become motivated to pursue a more active "reaching out" for therapy and a deeper understanding of his personality.

In the first set of drawings (done in pencil), we see a House which is on stilts, built on a sloping hill and with large glass windows which look out to an ocean (Fig. 21-1).

Figure 21-1. **House.**

Leon describes this drawing as a house which is built on a platform and stilts, so there could be as close a connection to water as possible. In his description, he pointed out the large chimney at the roof edge as leading down into the house and ending in a conversation pit in the living room. He stated that this would be the kind of house where he could go to achieve serenity and peace.

As an investigator using this projective to lend information about the "self," I was curious about how open this individual would be, to sharing information about himself. One would look at the possible ways to enter the house to have a sense of how open the client might be. There is here no visible door to serve as an entrance. The stairs which led to the edge of the house looked uneven and not easily negotiated. I began to have a sense early on that this person would not be very open to sharing information about himself.

Figure 21-2. **Tree.**

The large glass windows can be seen as a way to look in to see the interior, yet the solid glass is a barrier to the physical entry of an individual. Thus exhibitionism, but not accessibility, is suggested.

In the second drawing produced (Fig. 21-2), we see a Tree in full foliage. There is a shortened trunk, the root system is exposed somewhat and there is a small animal drawn near the left root. There is no ground line drawn as well as no grass shown. In taking the image of the drawn Tree as an image of the self, we wonder where the grounding is in this person's life?

When asked to now "draw a person," Leon draws a standing, nude female. In drawing the nude figure, Leon reworked the drawing a couple of times, "to get it right." He seemed to have the most difficulty with the legs which he erased several times in an attempt to get them in proportion. Although he is an accomplished artist, the legs were quite a "problem" for him, again suggesting the problem he experiences with his psychological footing.

I was impressed when viewing this figure, with the rather strange look coming from the eyes. I could not determine if she was looking outward or looking down. There is a rather tentative smile on the face. Her hair is short and the figure looks a bit masculine. There is no ground line for her to stand upon (Fig. 21-3).

The fourth drawing produced was of a standing, nude male (Fig. 21-4). The drawing was reworked two or three times. Leon seemed to have great difficulty producing this image. This figure is depicted with closed eyes. There is a smile on the face. There are many lines drawn depicting the shoulder area. The arms are drawn rather rigidly at his sides. The left arm is shorter than the right and appears to have only two digits depicting fingers in this hand. The right arm appears longer with a hand that has more fingers on it.

The legs were originally drawn quite long and then erased but not erased completely. Subsequently both legs were shortened. Again, one notes the absence of a ground line: there is nothing for the figure to stand on. Yet at the same time the legs resemble a sturdy tree trunk, adding compensatory grounding.

As we move rapidly into the chromatic portion of this projective, I asked Leon to draw a House using the crayons. The House was very similar to the first House drawn. In this drawing, however, the House is seemingly cut in half. Only a portion of the House is seen and the stairs which previously led to it are now missing. The House remains on stilts with very large picture windows and a balcony present once more. In the very large roof area the chimney is now somewhat shorter, and does not extend very far beyond the roof line (Fig. 21-5).

The ocean is drawn both beneath the House and along the edge of the

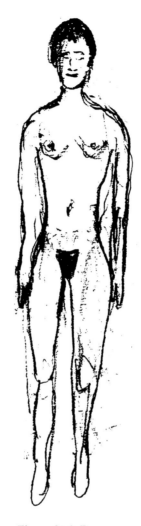

Figure 21-3. **Person.**

drawing as well. Although one can see similarities, a difference is that the water now appears to be more active beneath the House.

Hammer's chapter on the achromatic-chromatic comparison (Chapter 4) presents his discovery that the drawings in crayon bring the client into early childhood associations and allow for a deeper, underlying, basic and more regressed state: a picture of the impulses beneath the defenses is thus more apparent in the crayon expression. The active motion of water beneath the chromatic drawing of the House could indicate a movement into the unconscious (represented by water) as becoming more activated.

Figure 21-4. **Person.**

As we move to the chromatic Tree, we see a tree in full foliage, and compared to the achromatic, with roots more fully exposed. A tiny animal appears to be running away from the Tree. Leon described this animal as being a rabbit. It appears that the use of crayon has the effect of more activating the psychological material produced (Fig. 21-6).

As we turn now to the third chromatic drawing (Fig. 21-7), we see a

Figure 21-5. **House.**

nude female drawn in red. She is strikingly off balance in almost violent motion, depicted by the spirals of color which encircle her legs and the even larger swirling lines encircling her head and shoulders. Her hair is flying wildly away from her head. Her face has a grimacing and angry quality to it. The arms are flung about in the air.

The female torso looks rather realistic with well-formed breasts, yet the hip line is disjointed and the pubic area appears to have a form which resembles a penis.

As Leon produced this drawing, he nervously asked if other artists who were part of my study had also drawn nudes? I answered that their

Figure 21-6. **Tree.**

artwork was private, yet reassured him that I believed that most artists did draw nude figures as part of their work.

We moved next to the last of the chromatic drawings. Leon drew a nude male in shades of reddish-purple, with purple being the predominate shade (Fig. 21-8). This figure also appeared to be in quite a lot of motion, with the arms drawn in swirling action.

The figure has a smile on his face while his eyes look downward.

In discussing the questions and answers in the Post Drawing Inquiry we are particularly interested in the client's possible areas of conflict which could benefit from counseling.

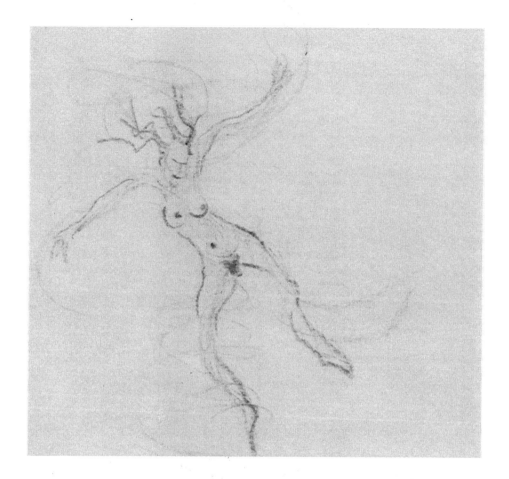

Figure 21-7. **Person.**

In asking if he would like to own the House drawn in achromatic media, he responded that he would like to own it. When asked why, he responded, "to have control of it and feel it was my own."

Where in this man's life does he have the deep need for control? When asked what the House reminded him of, he replied, "Freedom, security, beauty and strength." I would wonder what it is that holds him back from the freedom he desires to have?

Because this House was drawn precariously on stilts with much contact with water, I would be cautious about any type of aggressive therapy

Figure 21-8. **Person.**

with this individual. With the House as a representative of the self, already standing in water (the symbol of the unconscious), would too much stirring of the water, that is of unconscious content, cause this house to topple, or if not, to undermine the support, the mere "stilts" that is in place?

Moving into the inquiry questions regarding his Tree drawings, Leon repeatedly describes the Tree as being big and strong. (He states, "its a big, strong oak.") Where in his life does Leon desire more strength? It was of special interest to note that Leon did not even realize that he had drawn an animal in both drawings until he reached the questions regarding the chromatic responses. He described the rabbit for the first time when asked where the Tree was actually located? He replied, "In a forest. There is a rabbit down below . . . playing." His element of surprise led me to believe that if the rabbit could represent an instinctual side of himself, that it was at first unnoticed until he moved into the use of crayons and also gave his response to that chromatic (impulsive?) energy.

In the achromatic responses to the first figure drawn I was surprised to hear Leon identify the female figure as being "probably . . . sort of me."

What was more puzzling was the fact that although this was a nude figure standing rather rigidly, faced forward and without much expression, Leon responded to the question, "What does this person make you think of?" with the reply "movement, grace and harmony." It felt to this examiner that he was not truly in touch with the material.

This type of response would indicate a certain amount of tension and denial around his perception of females and/or the female qualities felt within himself.

In his responses to the second achromatic figure drawn (male) he was more realistic when he described the male as standing "at ease."

What was perhaps most dramatic and impressed me most was the lack of recognition of the mood of the female in the chromatic expression. When asked "What mood is he/she in?" Leon responded that the mood was, "Loved, ectasy, joyful." One would wonder at why this man could not see the grimacing face and wildly flying hair? When I consulted with other clinicians familiar with drawings and their interpretation, there was indeed a consensus that the figure hardly represented a look that seemed "joyful."

My impression was growing that Leon perhaps had some very strong conflictual feelings surrounding his sexual identity. I followed an intuitive hunch and formed a question for him to consider around his comfort with his maleness and the indications of conflict around the female aspect. I asked questions of the time he had spent in the service of his priestly duties. What were some of the contacts and the experiences he had with other men and/or women? He most readily expressed his experiences of "cheating" on Mother Church by having affairs with women while a priest.

He unexpectedly then revealed that he had also recognized in himself a very strong attraction to young boys whom he coached on a sports team. His face flushed at this disclosure and he asked me if I considered him to be "bad" to have such feelings?

The experience of working closely with psychic content in the exploration of his projective drawings had evolved into a sense of trust which expressed itself in this very intimate, and painful, disclosure. I assured him that I did not think of him as being "bad" and in fact that I felt that he was strong enough to reveal feelings that could serve him well if used to explore in depth within a counseling setting.

I referred Leon to a sensitive psychiatrist whom I knew had experience with drawing interpretation, in the event that this and/or art therapy proved an avenue which was comfortable for Leon to continue working with.

One can imagine the amount of strong energy that was needed for this individual to "control" the impulses that he experienced. He now made a career choice to not work around young boys who might provide a continued source of homosexual pedophilia stimulation for him.

This experience of coming into contact with the profound impact that art can have, particularly in the exploration of meaningful psychological content at various stages in the journey of life, has been for me, a deep and very meaningful teaching, as well as growth, experience.

It is my wish to follow the growth and development that Leon may find on his journey of self-discovery.

Initially, in the H–T–P, we are struck with the exceedingly rare presentation of a House up on stilts. With the subject building a home life, first on abandoning his priesthood and marrying a nun, the break-up of the marriage, a second marriage, his second wife leaving him for a lesbian relationship, and finally his homosexual attraction to boys, it is not at all surprising that he projects his House as on stilts and as made mostly of glass: as resting on a flimsy, shaky, uncertain, and vulnerable foundation.

In this compelling case study of a professional artist at midlife, we, at the same time, find confirming demonstration of the relatively newly uncovered and, as it turns out, a now central hypothesis in projective drawings: that the achromatic ones spring from and express more of the defensive layers, and the chromatic drawings, in contrast, dig deeper and under these defenses to express the impulses beneath, i.e., what is defended against. There is overlap to be sure. And this differentiation is only relatively so. But it remains the most exciting of all the recent developments not only in projective drawings but more broadly in all projective techniques. Thus, in this innovated extension of our tools downward into the lower levels of personality, a hierarchal portrait of the subject is derived — and a more refined instrument for diagnostic and prognostic assessment has been forged (see Chapter 4).

In the present case, we see this most clearly and in highly dramatic form. But first, as we move from the pencil female to the pencil self-sex Person, we note that whereas the other-sex Person is given fully human legs, the subject's own-sex Person is given excessively sturdier and the more exaggeratedly durable underpinnings that look somewhat like a tree trunk—connoting outsized, well-rooted and compensatory stable footing. The subject had begun by giving this male Person elongated legs reminiscent of the stilt-like underpinnings to the House, but then his defenses appear and they predominate: he erases, shortens and thickens the male's legs to the tree-trunk-like base. These mobilized defenses and their resultant stability are consistent with this same quality to the priest component (sturdiness, steadiness) of his past life. Then when given crayons, both of his chromatic Persons fairly explode, from under his defenses, with rampant impulses taking off. In his real life, these may well have been the impulses of his affairs and more currently of his emerging homosexual pedophilic yearnings. In these chromatic drawings, his impulses, we see, are experienced as uncontrollable, as unstable, as chaotic, as unleashed and as off-balancing. They also, particularly the female drawn, have a phantasmagoric quality. (It brings, to my mind, the furiously, hallucinogenic-like, unsettling dream scene in *Fiddler on the Roof*). This scary, apparition-like aspect of the subject's impulses demonstrate the panic which may be mounting as he faces, we may well guess, his sexual promptings toward young boys.

At the same time, this has prognostic relevance, in that it suggests a need, and motivation, for psychotherapeutic assistance. This man inhabits a complex and unbearable reality and squirms to manage it as best he can.

Our subject, then, is a man who, more than most, has two contrasting and pronounced sides to his nature. And the two components of the projective drawings, the achromatic and chromatic, respectively, reflect this—the priest in him and its inherent controls, on the one hand, and on the other, the hedonist thrust breaking out, or, as it were, the liberated Id escaping the control-invested alliance of Superego and Ego.

We are reminded of Michael Ryan (1995), the poet visited by agonizing perversions, who in his *Secret Life: An Autobiography*, perhaps the most open, sensitive and revealing account I have read on the subject, sheds a more penetrating light on this pleasuring, yet tortured, human condition. "Every sex addict has his own thing," he writes, "the thing he likes the most, although 'like' is hardly the word for the inexorable pull I felt and sought and still sometimes feel but, with God's help, one day at a time do not act on."

Our subject in the current case study, like Ryan, is blocked in by his sense of self-loathing and his constructive ethic of personal accountability. Our subject, like Ryan and also as with Vincent Van Gogh, has his art as a means of providing himself with the internal mooring with which to impose order on his mucked-up feelings, to order on canvas (whether through formal or informal balance) the sense of disorder within.*

Finding himself now in an acutely conflicted, unbearable process, torn between his rampant impulses (reflected in his chromatic drawn Persons) and

---

*With Van Gogh, his art served to stave off his advancing psychosis until, finally, he lost this struggle.

his dug-in controls (reflected in his achromatic male), seeking to ease out of the tensions as best he can, our case may be on the verge, as stated above, of a real readiness to accept assistance and therapy — in order to establish his controls more surely over his clamoring impulses and to aid him in his questing for inner peace.

E.F.H.

REFERENCE

Ryan, M., *Secret Life: An Autobiography,* New York: Pantheon Books, 1995.

Chapter 22

TWO CASES INVOLVING SEXUAL ABUSE

CORINNE E. FRANTZ

This chapter draws upon two cases in which sexual enactment occurred in the form of incest. The first involves a projective drawing battery obtained from both a father and his daughter. In the course of the daughter's evaluation through the medium of the drawings, the relating of the occurrence of a previous incestuous relationship between the daughter and her younger brother was shared with the examiner. The parents had been made aware of its occurrence prior to this evaluation; however, denial of the experience on the part of the mother and father continued to exist. The added possibility of repressed incestuous fantasy or experience between the daughter and father is hinted at in the coordinance between the father's male drawing and the daughter's Most Unpleasant Concept.

The second case involves a dramatic series of drawings made by a woman who experienced, years later, her recollection of incest with her father. At the time she made the drawings, she was undergoing psychotherapy within a hospital setting.

These two cases offer a fascinating glimpse into the powerful role projective drawings can play in revealing aspects of the individual's inner experience and psychodynamics and, at the same time, give us clues about the experience of incest survivors.

CASE I

Father

The father is a 50-year-old man who was originally referred for a neuropsychological evaluation to help clarify the cognitive sequela to a minor cerebral vascular accident he had recently suffered. His symptoms resolved into a right visual field defect with decreased reading ability although comprehension of what he read was intact. Visual-spatial organization skills were intact and there was no difficulty noted in his drawing ability. He was administered a battery of projective drawings to help clarify the nature of his psychological adaptation to the changes in his cognitive functioning.

Figure 22-1.

On the surface, his achromatic drawing of a House appears very conventional with a few noteworthy exceptions. On the one hand, the chimney has attention called to it by the detail of its rim, while on the other hand it appears insufficient in size for the overall proportions of the House, and is not quite attached to the roof. There is an attempt to compensate for feelings of masculine inadequacy by drawing attention to his phallic-ness. The elongated nature of the chimney becomes even more apparent on the chromatic drawing of the House. The superficial conventionality of his self presentation is in contrast to the presence of a small, very dark square which was drawn almost as an afterthought in the upper left hand corner of the roof. During the inquiry he described the House as, "A fairly good-sized house. It has a complete second floor. Despite the fact that it's like a center-hall colonial, it's very airy with lots of light." He explained the small dark square as being, "A vent pipe. You have it over your johns." This is a most unusual detail to have added and suggests that his wish to portray a wholesome, pleasant appearance is in danger of being contaminated by an experience of himself as psychologically living close to a sewer. The conflicted need to both deny and reveal the presence of unacceptable impulses emerges. This interpretation is strengthened by the prominence the sewer vent acquires in the chromatic drawing.

Figure 22-2.

A struggle with feelings of depression surrounding his experience of family life is indicated by the contrasting heavy darkness of the sewer vent and the presence of yellow light emanating from the three windows on the right side of the chromatic House. The yellow light emanating from the three windows attempts to counterbalance the darkness of the sewer vent, once again suggesting an attempt to portray a cheery, outward appearance, once again not successful. The emptiness of the ground floor windows and the lack of a pathway leading up to the door of the achromatic House suggest that there is no genuine availability for contact with others. This is an individual who is essentially closed off. Despite an attractive, eye-catching pathway to the chromatic House, there is no doorknob by which to gain access through the door once one gets there.

Serious conflicts over sexuality are conveyed by his drawings of a man. His achromatic drawing of a man conveys a self experience of being

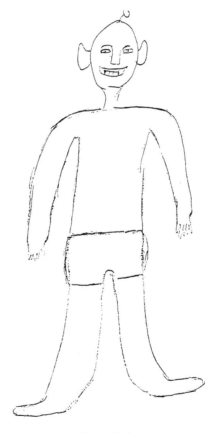

Figure 22-3.

ridiculous and a buffoon on the one hand, and inhuman on the other hand, an eerie, alien being. The treatment of the hand and fingers expresses acute feelings of inadequacy and a sense of hampered mastery.

The oversized ears, at the same time, suggest an underlying paranoid experience in his relationship with others. The infantile sense of masculine impotence is conveyed by the single hair curling out of the top of his head and is compensated for by the very phallic-looking feet and the display of himself in a bathing suit.

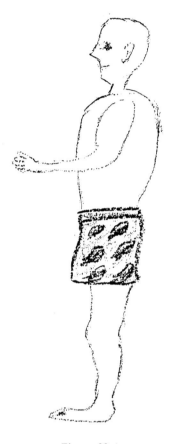

Figure 22-4.

On the chromatic male, the use of the color red to delineate the swimming trunks calls attention to the genital region. On inquiry, the subject says, "I don't know if they are fish [on the trunks] or whatever," possibly another phallic, or even sperm, symbol. The overly large chest suggests once again a need to portray himself as more masculine and virile than he actually feels. A touch of red is added to the ear and to the foot (the latter representing a toenail) to give emphasis to the paranoid and phallic statements, respectively, of the achromatic male drawing.

Once again, the foot takes on a strong phallic quality—It actually looks snake-like.

In summary, this is a protocol of a man who is struggling with feelings of depression by unsuccessfully trying to deny or discount their presence. What emerges from beneath the surface is an experience of himself as impotent, buffoon-like, and alien, verging toward feelings of depersonalization. Despite his efforts to present a well-adjusted facade, he struggles with the threat of being overwhelmed by unacceptable impulses, particularly of a sexual nature.

Daughter

In the process of sharing the results of his evaluation with him, the father indicated to the examiner that his 15-year-old daughter was a source of great difficulty at home. She was physically assaultive to his wife and had run away from home on more than one occasion. At the father's request, his daughter was seen for a separate evaluation to help offer appropriate treatment recommendations. As part of a full projective battery, the following drawings were obtained.

The House is portrayed in a purely two-dimensional view which conveys a lack of depth also within the personality. At the same time, it is highly embellished with bushes and curtains at the window, suggesting someone who calls attention to herself and tries to impress by her surface appearance but who lacks an experience of underlying dimension in her sense of who she is. The superficial 'prettifying' of the drawing suggests an hysterical personality integration. The apparent accessibility for contact with others, which she is likely to convey in her initial interactions gives way to a highly conflicted stance which is seen in her chromatic drawing of the House. Her availability for meaningful interaction with others is actually only a superficial come on. In fact, contact with others is highly conflictual as symbolized by the bold red door barricaded behind a thick and high picket fence which blocks and will allow no approach.

Both the achromatic and chromatic Trees contain phallic imagery. The former is seen in the clear division of the upper trunk into three main branches, suggestive of male genitalia as uncovered in investigations of sexual symbolism (1). The latter suggests phallic identification in its aggressive, upwardly thrusting stance.

The superficial presentation of the achromatic female is one of

Figure 22-5.

innocence. However, one notices an off-the-shoulders déclote. The superficial self-presentation of innocence belies a deeper experience of herself as a seductress. This is further reinforced by the lack of innocence of her chromatic female.

Her drawing of a Person in the Rain depicts a woman not only in rain but in the middle of a heavy downpour. What immediately catches one's attention is the heavy black line down her center shaped suggestive of the female genital opening.

Her drawing of the Most Unpleasant Thing she can think of has fascinating parallels with her father's self portrayal. Namely, she depicts an eerie, inhuman being. There is also a strong paranoid element in her experience. On inquiry, she describes, "It's something I saw a long, long time ago ... about the age of 13 ... in my room. It's like someone who works with the devil. There's a whole story that goes with it. I had borrowed a tape from a friend. I had on one song. I was lying in my bed. I wasn't asleep. It came at the foot of my bed. There was a black door behind it with carvings and a doorknob, and a redish kind of white light going through the doorknob. There was something on its chest: it had more red. It stood there for one second. I lay there without any thoughts

Figure 22-6.

in my head. I blocked everything out: the thought of this and of going somewhere at all. And it disappeared. It went back kind of through the door but the door didn't open. When it was there, I didn't hear or see anything. But when it went away, the song was right where it had left off." [E: Did you have any feelings about it?] "I had no feelings while it was there. But after it left and even now, it scares me. It's a really wierd feeling. A lot of tension inside." She denied any drug use at the time of this experience. The quality of it is reminiscent of a screen memory.

What is striking about her drawing is the threatening, eerie quality of her experience. The figure has the appearance of a man wearing an animal mask with horns for ears. The feet and hands, however, are missing. The affective tone of the drawing closely parallels the affective tone of her father's achromatic drawing of a man. In the daughter's drawing, the being has a tail but the tail loses all of it's substance. It is only barely and vaguely alluded to, is especially wide and is displaced. All of these features suggest it to be symbolic of an anxiety-ridden and

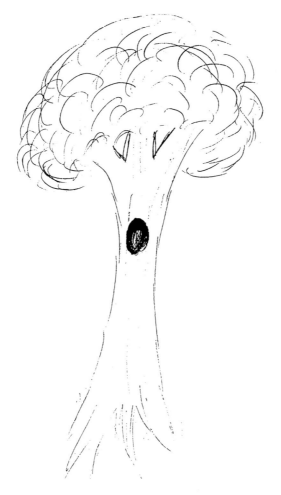

Figure 22-7.

conflict-laden sexualized experience. It raises the hypothesis that a sexual approach was made to her, and that incest with her brother may have represented similar feelings toward her father.

CASE II

The series of drawings made by the woman in this case* were done at different points in time during an inpatient hospital stay. They were

*This case came to my attention through a supervisee, Dr. Sandra Burns, whom I wish to thank for sharing the clinical material.

Figure 22-8.

drawn at the time that she had began to remember experiences of sexual abuse by her father when she was much younger. At the time of her recollection, she was in her early fifties. She had an earlier history of alcohol abuse in her twenties and a serious suicide attempt.

The first drawing depicts a woman absorbed in her work within a confined space, around which circulates a sense of overwhelming threat. The image suggests that she has found a haven of immersion in her artistic work, but the feeling tone is that the power of assault may be capable of breaking through what appears to be a glass enclosure. Both the dragon and the snake are pressed against the boundaries of the enclosure. The drawing is replete with phallic images which assault and attack. The use of dissociation is portrayed by the self-contained enclosure in which the woman sits, while the use of repression is suggested by the seeming obliviousness of the woman doing her work, as well as by the sharp demarcation of the light rays from the ceiling lamp which

Figure 22-9.

appear to both illuminate and protect the woman in the center. The overwhelmingly threatening tone of the drawing and the defense of mere glass, however, convey how vulnerable she feels are her efforts at protection.

The rest of the drawings eloquently convey a relentless experience of victimization. The picture which she labels as "Intimate Family" portrays that she experienced her mother as colluding in and being an enabler in the sexual abuse by her father. In essence, the mother figure offers the young child to the sexually aggressing man. The mother's eyes are closed or looking down, suggesting her electing not to see what is happening. The child is made to dutifully comply, to 'jump through hoops' as it were. The patient's depiction of the mother is consistent across the pictures. In each case, her experience of the mother is of "not seeing" and of reacting automatically. In addition, the mother's hands which hold the bicycle look limp, impaired, and crippled, while the

Figure 22-10.

mother's hands which hold the tray, with only a few morsels of food on it, do not have an effective grip. Her experience of her mother is of someone who is inadequate and useless, as perfunctorily offering empty mothering, choosing a bicycle as the gift for the one-legged child and bringing or serving an empty dish to the drastically emaciated and starving youngster.

In contrast to her depiction of the mother figure, the man is given overwhelming, brutalizing and phallic power. In the drawing of an "Intimate Family", his penis is drawn as a gun, which magnifies it's threatening and damaging significance. The men attacking the woman crouched against the wall have not only phallus-symbolizing spears, but one of them carries an axe in an assaultive stance.

The subject's sense of severe damage and mutilation is conveyed by the girl's missing leg in one picture and her emaciated, starving frame in another. Her terribly damaged sense of self and self-esteem is, once

Figure 22-11.

again, poignantly portrayed by her dropping the letters of her name into the fire.

While these drawings vividly capture this woman's excruciating experience of victimization and abuse, her drawings simultaneously convey the adaptation of masochism, identification with the aggressor and consequent self-victimization. It is she who drops the letters of her own name into the fire and, in the last drawing, rips out her own breasts from her chest. Time and time again in her drawings she accentuates the threatening experience of the penis by drawing instead a gun, spears, adding axes, etc. In other words, she dramatizes her experience as if to call screaming attention to the fact that she has suffered terribly. She actively presents

Figure 22-12.

herself *as a victim*. In the fourth drawing, to the men with spears and axe attacking the crouched naked person, she adds a wall and makes the wall excessively high, calling attention to how cornered, helpless and attacked she feels. Her drawings reiterate an extended shriek of protest!

In the last drawing which appears to be a self-representation, all of these elements are captured and, furthermore, the victimization and damaged self-esteem are interwoven into an experience of masochism and self-display. She rips her own breasts out of her chest, holding one of them aggressively like a ball. She does to herself what she experienced was done to her. The foot is trampling her down into a frying pan as tears fall from her eye, but at the same time the foot is worn like a hat. The frying pan's handle is positioned to look like a huge protruding penis extended from her own body, suggesting that a part of her may yearn for and demonstrate an aggressive penis of her own. The latter wish may be because she experiences the possession of power as the perogative of the aggressive, assaultive male. The combination of acquiring a huge, metal-

Figure 22-13.

lic penis and removing her own breasts serve to make her the aggressive male and not the suffering, helpless, victimized female.

SUMMARY

These two cases illustrate the range of clinical material one may encounter in the H–T–P evaluation of individuals who have been the victims of incest. The first case is more subtle and possibly more typical of what a clinician may see when an individual initially presents for treatment of a behavior disorder which is unconsciously linked to the damaging effects of sexual abuse. The daughter evidenced considerable acting-out behavior including promiscuity, physical altercations with her mother, and attempts to leave home. Feelings regarding her victimization of herself through her promiscuity were dissociated. At the time of of the evaluation, she had yet to form any links between her self-victimization and her experience of sexual victimization within the family.

The second case vividly illustrates the experience of sexual victimiza-

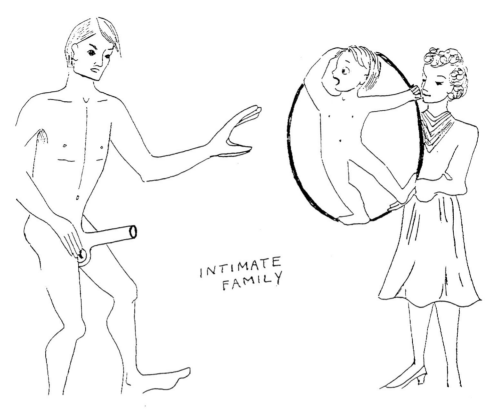

INTIMATE
FAMILY

Figure 22-14.

tion with conscious awareness. The drawings are an eloquent cry of protest and expose the various facets of self-victimization. The drawings provide valuable insight into those aspects of the self-victimization of which the individual is not fully aware.

REFERENCES

1. Hammer, E.F.: An investigation of sexual symbolism—a study of H–T–P's of eugenically sterilized subjects. *J. Proj. Tech.,* 17:401–413, 1953.

In the projective drawings of Corinne Frantz's case of a father and daughter, we note the compelling interlock between the psychodynamics of family members which drawings might uncover. As interpreters, what tugs at our imagination is the intriguing congruence between the father's projective image of himself (in his pencil drawing of the male Person) and his daughter's Unpleasant Concept drawing. It is as if she took his drawing of himself and elaborated

Figure 22-15.

it further, meaningfully making it more sexualized and more frightening, thereby suggesting it is the advancing phallic father she is perceiving and fighting off.

The fascinating phenomenon we witness is of the meeting of one unconscious with another when they are on the same wavelength—in this case the incestual one. The daughter picks up her sensing of her father's image of himself and elaborates it further, both phobically and in the Devilish direction—expressed (a) in her earlier hallucinatory-like experience and (b) currently in her Unpleasant Concept drawing.

To turn now to the chapter's last case, we see how richly—how meaningfully—deeply—poignantly—personally—movingly—communicatively—with what immediacy—projective drawings can convey a subject's *experience.* And in addition to these simply human elements, there are in this case, as in most cases, the uncovering of professional considerations of the related psychodynamics, defense mechanisms, specific traumas, both weaknesses and strengths, and as touched upon below, diagnosis and prognosis.

In this case's drawings both the trauma and the defenses, as Dr. Frantz

Figure 22-16.

alludes to, are particularly central: an identifying with the aggressor, a putting herself out of harm's way by donning her enemy's cloak as it were. Thus, she renounced her femininity in the service of a powerful, brutalizing, sadistic, exploitative, phallic identity.

At the same time, in the orchestration of her personality, we hear the counterpoint (to her adopted sadism), notes of her deeper masochism—which the patient feels are drawn from the strings of the female components within her. The foot she draws pressing down, oppressing down, on her head, more than all else expresses this. Dr. Frantz sensitively reads the drawing projection as the foot being worn as a hat. (With less creative thinking the patient could have drawn a whole foot extending from the top of the page rather than figure out a way to rip it off and hug the head.) A woman's hat is a feminine adornment, and in this drawing the patient embellishes herself with it as a sufferer. Masochism always has an element of display, of advertisement, even of dramatizing: in this case, of one's neediness and deprivation (the drawing of the emaciated, starving child), of injury and crippling impairment (the drawing of the child with one missing leg), of exploitation (the drawing of the father-figure with pistol-penis advancing on the girl in the hoop held by the

Figure 22-17.

mother), of threat (most of the drawings of phallic attack)—all in all, weaving an identity out of her victimization. The drawings all exude an implacable cadence of doom . . . of doom and of betrayal.

As to the *diagnosis:* With the vivid outpouring—a virtual torrent—of agonized material, the main diagnostic question is one of how sick is this woman? In spite of the depth of the pain and the acuteness of the damage within, this woman has maintained personality integration and operant, intact, effective, unshattered secondary process thinking. Her adaptation stays within neurotic and characterological bounds. Her creative art expressions are rational, communicative and uncontaminated by primary process thinking or by deeper (schizophrenic) pathology. Her Ego maintains control and in the projection in the drawings, representational meanings come about with unscattered and conscious intention.

Hence, the *prognosis,* in spite, perhaps even because of, the patient's intense distress, is favorable. This is a noticeably resilient woman. And she has not lost her capacity to hold on. Nor her strength; nor her determination to protest— and to fight back.

E.F.H.

Figure 22-18.

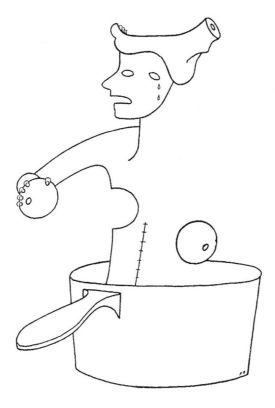

Figure 22-19.

Chapter 23

A "BLIND" CASE ANALYSIS:
A MAN IN THE CLOTHES OF A CLOWN IN THE
CLOTHES OF A MAN*

EMANUEL F. HAMMER

With a Postscript by John N. Buck

The following case was seen in response to a challenge made over the telephone by a rather skeptical psychiatrist-colleague, who had been treating a 37-year-old man and wished to obtain a psychological evaluation. But he wanted the evaluation done "blindly", as he put it, so that he could be sure that the results came solely from the psychological examination and were in no way the result of constituted inferences made from data otherwise known about the patient. By "blind" analysis the psychiatrist meant that he did not want the writer to know anything about the patient or his symptoms other than what came through the projective examination. He had no objection to the writer's conducting the projective-technique-restricted examination, however.

The psychiatrist was putting projective techniques to the test, to determine whether or not anything of importance could be learned about a person from the way in which he drew a House, a Tree, and a Person, composed stories related to pictures, and interpreted ink-blots.

The writer explained to the psychiatrist that the soundest and most effective use of projective technique evaluation is not one in which the procedure is attempted blindly. However, the psychiatrist remained firm. And a challenge is a challenge.

When the man, Mr. C., appeared for the psychological examination, he was well-dressed and had an air of assurance and poise. He was

*Appreciative thanks are extended to Drs. Joy Roy and Robert Wolk for their helpful comments and editorial suggestions.

*Reprinted with permission: Buck, J., *The House-Tree-Person Technique: Revised Manual,* 296–304, Western Psychol. Services, 1984. Case by E. Hammer.

pleasant and cooperative, and readily participated in the psychological examination.

H–T–P PROJECTIVE DRAWINGS

The writer ordinarily follows up the achromatic H–T–P with a supplementary drawing of another Person, of the sex *opposite* to that of the first Person drawn. Thus one House, one Tree, and *two* Persons (one of each sex) are elicited. Then the pencil and the finished drawings are taken away. The patient is given new sheets of paper and a set of crayons and one House, one Tree, and two Persons (one of each sex) again are obtained.

In this case, however, the patient had already given a relatively full and extensive Rorschach and T–A–T; time was running out, and "C" had to catch a train. So after "C" had completed the achromatic House, Tree and a Person of each sex, no P–D–I was attempted, and the chromatic drawing phase was abbreviated to merely a Tree and one Person.

"C's" first drawing, that of a House, was drawn in a slow, meticulous manner. Compared to his other drawings, the House is small, constricted, and set way back from the viewer. Feelings of inadequacy, inferiority, constriction, and withdrawal in the home situation, past and present, are suggested.

The wide and conspicuous driveway implies a need to present himself as interested in social and interpersonal contacts, in relatedness to others. But since the driveway does not reach the House and is U-shaped rather than merely leading *to* the House, it conveys the impression that this man's emotional accessibility is more apparent than real. The roadway leads people past him, rather than to him. We may then *hypothesize,* but not yet *deduce,* that a seemingly cordial and friendly exterior is used to conceal an underlying detachment and a need for retreat from others. In keeping with the merely token acceptance of the fact that society expects him to be reasonably accessible, the windows on the ground floor are placed well above the usual level in relation to the door, and all the windows have the shades half-lowered.

His drawings of Trees, both achromatic and chromatic, emphasize the bark, a finding frequent in people hypochondriacally oriented with feelings of physical disjointedness and inadequacy.

Both the chromatic Tree and the achromatic Male Person have the top of the drawing sliced away, as it were. Thus, the suggestion is offered that

Figure 23-1.

"C" attempts to deny that phantasy area, presumably because of the unacceptable content of his phantasy and the guilt it produces.

The first male drawing attempts to give an impression of virility and masculine prowess: The crew-cut hair, the bullneck, and the broadened shoulders. However, these are belied by the anxiety—indicating difficulty that "C" experienced with the crotch area, the flaccid droop of the toes, and the apparently withered hands. As in his drawing of the House with his withdrawal tendencies tucked away behind a superficially cordial front, reaction-formation again is used, this time combined with compensation in an effort to conceal his feelings of sexual impotency behind a characterological parade of masculinity, i.e. exaggerated maleness.

Following this unsuccessful attempt to present a virile front convincingly, "C's" next drawing is of a provocatively-posed, nude female. His attempt to present the female as sexually exciting also does not quite succeed. She has a cold, doll-like, immobile, uninviting expression made only superficially attractive with dabs of rouge and the absence of clothing. The body lacks feminine shape and grace with no hip curve or waist

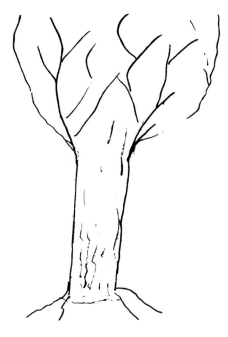

Figure 23-2.

delineation. The breasts appear shapeless, crooked, and devoid of youth and appeal, at least in Western culture.

Despite the profuse hair at the vaginal area, erotic emphasis actually is shifted to the legs. This is consistent with "C's" many eroticized Rorschach responses involving legs (and is discussed more fully later under the Rorschach section of this report).

Following the attempt to draw a sexualized woman, "C's" next drawing of a Person (chromatic) is a male clown. Here "C" portrays graphically his major need to play a role which will amuse and disarm rather than antagonize. Thus, he attempts to indicate the harmlessness of his drives. On top of that, following his transgression of contemplating a female in raw sexual terms, he draws a skirt on the male clown and then places a cross-hatching of lines across the pelvic area as if to protect the genitals. Hence, two defensive maneuvers are used by "C" to protect himself against genital damage: (1) harmless lack of assertion, and (2) effeminacy.

In terms of the former, the prison-like garb of the pencil male Person reflects feelings of guilt and concern with punishment. At the same time, there is another element in the jacket as well: it has fully four buttons, but nowhere is there an indication that he can get out of his jacket, i.e.,

Figure 23-3.

shed defenses and be more open, get down to more basic exchange (whether *social* as suggested by the *U*-shaped driveway going past rather than to the House, or *sexual* as the later drawings suggest).

The arms of the chromatic Person are attached to the trunk well below the shoulder level: by the time "C" drew this last whole, he may have felt fatigued and quite probably overwhelmed by the associations aroused by all the projective material that had preceded it, and by the male role and, as the displaced arms suggest, inadequacy in carrying it off.

In addition, a depressed and resigned quality comes through beneath the clown paint, *i.e.*, shows through his unsuccessful attempts to use the reaction formations of cheerfulness, gaiety and carefreeness:

Following "C's" stream of associations through his three Persons, we find that a particularly virile facade and an ambivalently-perceived sex object produce massive fear within him and result in his presenting himself as an innocuous, passive, and female-like character.

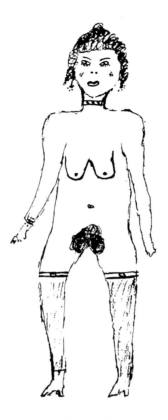

Figure 23-4.

EXCERPTS FROM RORSCHACH SECTION OF REPORT

As both confirmation and elaboration of the H–T–P picture, the following excerpts from the Rorschach section of the report are of interest:

> The patient's intrinsic definition of the Rorschach situation was in compulsively-toned competitive terms.
>
> This led to fully twelve responses on the first Rorschach card, where the average is closer to four or five. Thus, the subject attempted to compete with previous subjects or with an imaginary standard by trying to show that his imagination, his astuteness of observation, or his diligence was inexhaustible.
>
> His resigned submissiveness has its deepest roots in a fear of assuming the active male role. One of the patient's Rorschach responses offers a parallel to the H–T–P drawing sequence from virile male to clown. To Card VIII the patient projects, "Here's a bull; no, it's a a rat, it's a rat, or it might be a hyena." On the positive side, we see that the patient can project an image of virility, a bull, but this rapidly gives way (with increasing conviction) to a symbol which

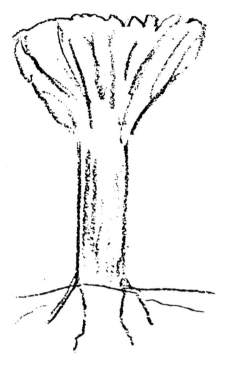

Figure 23-5.

retreats to stealth rather than assertion (the rat), and ends up with the hyena which is, in spite of its wily and insidious qualities, in some ways an animal-equivalent of his drawn clown. In addition, the hyena may connote the feeling that the patient may take over only the leavings that more assertive competitors no longer want.

A similar sequence occurs on another Rorschach card. First, the patient sees "Moose standing up with horns," but then offers as his next response, "A big tree without any branches." He doesn't dare be masculinely assertive for long and retreats into a "castrated" position out of fear of terrible damage ("Rips in a piece of material," "Wounds, raw skin," and "Poodles with bloody paws.") He then ends up not knowing which way to turn (*i.e.* "A dog with two heads running either way"). The quantitative Rorschach picture (high *W,* reduced *M* and *FM*) suggests reduced buoyancy and vitality as personality assets, consistent with the above qualitative indications.

On still another card, the patient once more dares be assertive for only a little time, retreating rapidly to a position in which he gives up his masculine prerogatives. The response, "Animal, light and fast with long legs," is immediately followed with the projection, "Body of a chicken, without the wings."

The patient's entire performance on Card V deserves mention in this regard. He opens with the response, "Woman's legs, in old-fashioned days,"

Figure 23-6.

(we are reminded of the eroticized leg treatment on the drawn female, with the perception of them in an old-fashioned setting being consistent with the Oedipal indications on the T–A–T). His next two responses, "Mouth of a big bird of prey," and "Mouth of a crocodile"—both "ready to bite"—reveal his massive fear of bodily damage as retribution for his tabooed sexual interest. He then retreats for security into a safe and innocent response, "A butterfly." He has the capacity to experience security, however, for he then comes out of this response with a return to the percept, "Legs." Although to some degree culturally-endorsed, the patient's *continual* shift of erotic focus to the legs may be linked with his "castration" anxiety by the formulation that seeing a person without a penis is too anxiety-producing as an example that he might lose his own. Thus, by focusing on the legs as a symbol of a penis in a woman, he attempts to shut out his fear and permit himself sexual arousal. His fetishistic leanings thus serve as a defense against his "castration" anxiety.

In an attempt to avoid the threat of "castration" the patient has given up both the use of his penis and his masculine assertiveness. The implications of this unconsciously-motivated switch to femininity are far-reaching. He probably could not usurp any of the father's strength through the normal identification process. He could not pattern his ego-ideal along male lines. And finally, he probably could not adequately engage in heterosexual activity.

FOLLOW-UP

After receiving the report, the psychiatrist called the writer to tell him something about the patient. It turned out that the patient had been married for six years but had never had intercourse. Impotency problems were at the core of his reasons for seeking psychiatric treatment. Along with this, he had frequent masturbatory fantasies of half-undressed women in which his attention was focussed upon their legs and high heels.

The psychiatrist knew little about the etiological or developmental influences in this case, since he had had only the initial interview with "C". The psychiatrist's impression, however, was consistent with the title of this chapter: that "C" was a man who hid under the protective disguise of a clown over which, on a secondary level, he then placed the superficial varnish of being a virile, impressive male.

Thus, who is this man? He is a man buried under many layers. One gets the sense of layer upon layer. His basic self is an individual who, in turn, hides in cloaks of absurdity and damage (the deeper, chromatic expression), and that, in turn, is more superficially tucked away behind exaggerated masculine posturing (the relatively more surface achromatic drawing).

The core of his terror has something to do with instinctual, mostly sexual, drives.

POSTSCRIPT TO CASE C
BY JOHN N. BUCK

General Comments

This case is of major interest for several reasons: (1) Dr. Hammer offers a masterly illustration of content analysis; (2) it demonstrates how the H–T–P and the Rorschach frequently corroborate and complement one another; (3) it shows that rich diagnostic and prognostic material may be derived from an H–T–P protocol even though no historical material is available (there is no P–D–I) and the chromatic House is missing.

Specific Comments

Details: "C" identified the small hatched rectangle attached to the right side of the House, (from the point of view of the observer) as a woodshed. Ss from whom intimate interpersonal relationships present almost insoluble problems frequently degrade their Houses in this or in similar ways.

The vine-like lines implying the presence of bark on the chromatic Tree are sometimes seen in the drawings of Ss plagued by obsessive drives which they feel are obvious to others.

The relatively sturdy Tree trunks imply that "C" does not believe that his adjustment problems are due to innate flaws.

Proportion: The branch structure of each Tree is inadequate in size when compared to the trunk: "C's" satisfaction-seeking resources are limited and produce frustration and tension.

The contrast in size between the shoulders and the hands and feet of the achromatic Person is striking and pathetic. "C" feels painfully inadequate in his attempts to make satisfying psycho-social relationships.

The huge chromatic Person strikingly points up "C's" feelings of frustration and ineptness: his unsatisfied needs and drives seem to balloon within him. The reversed leg taper drawn by one of "C's" intelligence reveals the degree to which his emotions inhibit his functions as a man.

Perspective: The House is a facade only, serving as a prim, precise mask to cloak his feelings of inadequacy in the home.

The hands and feet of the achromatic Person create the impression that "C's" approach to psycho-social relationships is on a diffident, tiptoe basis and not warm and sharing.

Color: The chromatic Tree was produced with brown crayon only: this is not an unconventional use of color or a denial of reality. The Person first was outlined in black: then, suddenly, "C" went color wild, using no less than five additional colors for his clown (purple, red, orange, green, and yellow). Yet the brighter colors were used only as after-thoughts and as ornamentation. One cannot say that this is unconventional usage, since no standards for color use have been or could well be established for a clown's garb.

Neither can one say that "C's" use of color shows a loss of adequate reality testing. It does suggest, however, and strongly, that basically "C" is reserved and colorless, much as he would give almost anything to be a more dynamic and popular person.

Concepts: A comment concerning "C's" drawing of the female Person: psychosexually immature male Ss who cannot establish "normal" hetero-sexual relationships frequently draw females in a manner which degrades them; perhaps this is the "sour grapes" system of devaluing something which one cannot possess and/or enjoy.

"C's" Trees are of the type which is often identified as a strong but feminine figure: such Trees often are produced with Houses similar to "C's" by Ss who have identified strongly with their mothers; by Ss whose psychosexual development is inadequate. In the absence of the P–D–I, one can only assume that "C's" Trees were seen by him as feminine and powerful, but this assumption seems sound and affords a strong second-ary confirmation of the validity of Dr. Hammer's content analysis of the drawn Persons.

In considering the chromatic Person, one should bear in mind that as a clown "C" would occupy a position of some prominence. Those watching him would regard his blunders and posturing with amused tolerance at the worst. He would have the close attention of a group with whom he need not attempt to make close, sharing relationships.

Conclusion

To assign a specific diagnostic category (which seems unnecessary in view of the wealth of dynamic material elicited), one might say "C" has a deep-seated character neurosis of long duration, which probably will not incapacitate him, but will handicap him rather severly and subject him to much frustration and dissatisfaction. The Prognosis does not seem too promising. Apparently only prolonged, intensive psychotherapy would offer much hope of improvement.

AUTHOR INDEX

SUBJECT INDEX

A

Achromatic drawing, 12 (*see also* Chromatic
    drawing)
    achromatic to chromatic distance, 120–24
    achromatic to chromatic series, 70–72,
        73–76, 126–27
Acting-out, x, 45–76
    aggressive behaviors, 45–76, 351–52
    assessment of potentials, 46–49
        integration of behavioral picture with
            projective drawing data, 50–60
        multiple determinism, 51
        psychomotor versus verbal modality,
            46–51
        tapping into personality via psycho-
            motor, 46–47
    prediction of acting out, x, 45–77
        chromatic drawings, 69–75
        detailing, 65–66
        direct acting-out on paper, 51–60
        dissociation, 67–69
        placement of horizontal axis, 67
        pressure of pencil on paper, 65
        sequential emergence of drives, 63–65
        size of images, 60–63
        stroke length, 65
        symmetry, 66
    projective testing and overt behavior,
        79–85, 321
        prognostication of overt acting-out
            behavior, 79–85, 321
Adolescents and projective drawing, 211–13
    characteristics of drawings, 211–12
    analysis of H–T–P components, 215
Affectively toned associations, 295
Aggression, 45–76, 351–52
Alan, case study of, 263–87
Alcoholism

projective drawings detailing distorted
    body image and hostility, 291–92
Alloplactic, 6
Ambivalence, 4
Anthropomorphism, 21–25, 28, 104
Anxiety as depicted by shading, 293
Australian aborigine male rite of passage
    depiction, 293
Autoplastic, 6

B

Body image
    height of person drawn, 292
    height of person decreased, athleticism
        portrayed increased, 292
    higher self-esteem, happier mood drawn,
        292
    lower self-esteem, dysphoric mood
        projected, 292
    self-esteem revealed in relational
        drawings, 5
Body language, 6

C

California Psychological Inventory, 363
Case studies and illustrations
    Alan, child with self-doubt, 263–87
    blind case analysis using H–T–P and
        Rorschach, 429–39
    castration anxiety, 80–84, 429–39
    child in cloak of Indian warrior, 114–15
    chromatic series, adult, 73–76, 90–92
    chromatic series, children
        core emptiness, 222–24, 224–29
        inadequacy and antagonism, 230–34
    Don Juanism, 115–18
    exhibitionist, male, 104–6, 106–9

447